Deliver Us from Evil

An Uneasy Frontier in Christian Mission

Edited by

A. Scott Moreau, Tokunboh Adeyemo,
David G. Burnett, Bryant L. Myers and Hwa Yung

LAUSANNE COMMITTEE
FOR WORLD EVANGELIZATION

World Vision Publications
800 West Chestnut Avenue
Monrovia, California 91016-3198 USA

Association of Evangelicals in Africa

Printed in the United States of America.

10 09 08 07 06 05 04 03 02   5 4 3 2 1

MARC books are published by World Vision International, 800 West Chestnut Avenue, Monrovia, California 91016–3198, U.S.A.

Library of Congress Cataloging-in-Publication Data

Deliver us from evil : an uneasy frontier in Christian mission / edited
by A. Scott Moreau ... [et al.].
    p. cm.
"MARC books"—T.p. verso.
A collection of papers and case studies presented at the "Deliver Us
from Evil" Consultation held in Aug. 2000 in Nairobi, Kenya.
Includes bibliographical references (p.   ).
    ISBN 1-887983-39-2
    1. Spiritual warfare—Congresses. 2. Demonology—Congresses. 3.
Spiritual warfare—Developing countries—Congresses. 4.
Demonology—Developing countries—Congresses. I. Moreau, A. Scott,
1955- II. Consultation on "Deliver Us from Evil" (2000 : Nairobi, Kenya)

    BT975 .D45 2002
    235'.4—dc21
                                        2002006251

Permissions:
    "The Domination System and God's Domination-Free Order" (Table 16-
1) is excerpted from ENGAGING THE POWERS: DISCERNMENT AND RE-
SISTANCE IN A WORLD OF DOMINATION by Walter Wink, copyright ©
1992 Augsburg Fortress. Used by permission.
    Table 18-1 is excerpted from Norman Allison, "Make Sure You're Get-
ting Through," *Evangelical Missions Quarterly* 20 (1984): 167–68. Used by
permission.

Editor in Chief: Edna Valdez. Senior editor: Rebecca Russell. Copyediting
and typesetting: Joan Weber Laflamme/jml ediset. Cover design: Karen Newe.
Cover photo: Cathedral image by Corbis, background image by AbleStock.

 This book is printed on acid-free recycled paper.

Contents

Preface

In the 1993 Intercessory Working Group meeting in London apprehensions over developments in spiritual warfare had reached such levels that a full day of the meeting was devoted to discussion. A statement was developed expressing the concerns and issues to be addressed (see Appendix).

Several involved in that meeting felt that further work needed to be done. Over the next few years an informal group of people who shared a concern about contemporary trends in spiritual warfare and a conviction that the Lausanne Committee for World Evangelization (LCWE) was in a position to offer guidance discussed the possibility of organising a consultation to address the issues. Eventually, under the direction of the Theology and Strategy Working Group of Lausanne, a planning committee was formally brought together to organise the proposed consultation. The planning committee members included representatives from Africa, Asia, Europe and the United States. Over the following years planning committee members engaged in regular teleconferences. In August of 1998 they met together in Oslo, Norway, for three days of planning. There they put together the administrative preparations necessary for the consultation and articulated their concerns which made the consultation necessary. The reasons for the consultation given below come from the documents that were developed in Oslo and sent to all who were invited to participate.

Reasons for the consultation

There are several reasons for giving priority to this consultation theme.

First, there has been a heightened interest in this subject in evangelical circles in the last decade or so. This, however, was preceded by trends that built up this interest. In the secular world there has been growing disillusionment with a purely rational approach to life. Many mainline denominations that traditionally were closely linked to the rational (or even secular) approach to life have experienced recent declines. At the same time, Pentecostal and charismatic churches, characterised by greater openness to new spiritual experiences, have grown greatly.

Further, Christians have had more contact with Islam, Hinduism, Buddhism and Shamanism as a result of large-scale immigration to the West. In effect, the West has been invaded by occult ideas and practices from the East since the 1960s.

At the same time, Christians in the non-Western world have in their own ways been wrestling with some of these issues for a much longer period. Yet because of the lack of serious theological groundwork on the subject, there is also much confusion on the topic within the non-Western churches.

As a result, there are fuzzy borders and a variety of interpretations and practices on issues like prayer in spiritual warfare, possession, demonisation, and territorial spirits. Among these newer practices and emphases, questions as to what is biblical, what is extra-biblical, and what is non-biblical or even non-Christian have been raised.

There have been changes in belief and practice in evangelical circles fostered by a flood of books, courses and seminars, which have disseminated a new vocabulary with prominence given to demons, spirits and supernatural beings of different kinds.

In response to these issues churches have tended to fall into one of five categories. First are those that dismiss the idea of the spirit world with disdain. Second are those who are just not aware of the world of the spirit to any degree and have not, therefore, developed any related disciplines. Next are those who are aware of the world of the spirit, pray, believe in the supernatural and have absorbed and gone along more or less with current changes of practice but have many questions and some discomfort and frustration about it all. Fourth are those who have accepted the views of their leaders or examined it for themselves and unquestioningly adopt the newest teachings and practices associated with spiritual warfare. Finally are those who always have had what they considered to be biblical views and prayer disciplines related to the spirit world and who dismiss the new approaches as unbiblical and therefore unacceptable.

The net effect is divisiveness among evangelicals at a time when there is a greater need than ever for the church to develop an understanding of and use all the armour of God. This is especially important in view of the extensive efforts being made to reach unreached peoples and enter countries where there is almost no Christian presence and the vigorous counterattacks of the powers of darkness on many who are in frontier evangelistic situations. Additionally, there is a need to combat the effects on the church of secularisation and the experience-centred cultures of post-modernism in the West.

Some of these trends raise serious issues for world evangelisation. Christian ethics is undermined when human responsibility is set aside by a reductionistic approach that inappropriately attributes all setbacks or difficult circumstances to demonic activity. Questions of the proper contextualisation of the gospel in a culture may be missed because the answer is seen to be limited to doing some type of appropriate spiritual warfare. In addition, the nature of the authority of Scripture is called in question by the willingness to consider ideas and follow practices that are admittedly extra-biblical. Finally, the unity or even the ability of believers to co-operate can be seriously undermined.

Procedure for the consultation

The resulting Lausanne consultation on spiritual conflict, entitled "Deliver Us from Evil" (DUFE) was convened August 16–22, 2000. In choosing the participants the planning committee sought representation from a broad spectrum of theological views. It was our hope that any new insights gained would be communicated to people of different strands of spirituality through their own networks. The speakers included academic theologians and missiologists as well as practitioners engaged in ministry. The committee, recognising that spiritual warfare practices and issues tend to be more overtly expressed in non-Western contexts, sought a venue in a non-Western setting. Thus the consultation was held in Nairobi, Kenya, and the Association of Evangelicals in Africa (AEA) served as host and co-sponsor.

Twelve plenary papers and 10 case studies from a broad variety of geographic orientations and perspectives were presented at the consultation. In addition, a biblical reflection started each day. Most of the plenary papers and case studies were made available in advance of the consultation by means of the World Wide Web (www.lausanne.org/dufe/) and e-mail. Thus, participants were expected to have read all papers prior to the presentations, giving the presenters freedom to summarise their papers and move beyond them, engaging in discussion over the issues raised. As a result, a significant portion of our time together was given to discussion to ensure that all voices were heard.

Writers were encouraged to utilise, and where appropriate, express biblical frameworks in their presentations. They were also asked to keep in mind the issues of the role of prayer and worldview as well as the objectives of the consultation and to integrate thinking from them where possible in their papers.

It was anticipated that one of the more important contributions of the consultation would be a statement to go to the churches. Towards that end an editorial committee was appointed and met daily to assimilate the presentations and discussion into a working draft of the consultation statement. A large block of time on the last day was given over to plenary discussion and amendment of the draft statement into its final form, which was formally accepted by all consultation participants.

Contents of this volume

Because it sets the stage for the discussion to follow, we start the compendium with the official statement issued by the DUFE Consultation participants. The intention of the statement is to provide common ground on which all believers may stand as well as elucidate areas of controversy and tension remaining in spiritual conflict.

The papers from the consultation, which form the bulk of the content, are split into three sections: (1) reflections on theology and the history of the church; (2) reflections from the front lines; and (3) reflections on contemporary issues. It should be noted that after the actual consultation many of the authors revised their papers based on feedback received at the consultation. All were then edited to fit style and space constraints for this volume. Since the authors come from a variety of theological perspectives, at times they present conflicting views. The editors felt it important that this should not be resolved through editorial changes. Thus the papers here reflect accurately the reality of the tensions and discussion at the consultation.

The first section, "Reflections on theology and the history of the church," is the foundation for our discussion. Hwa Yung, from Malaysia, orients us to spiritual conflict issues from the perspective of systematic theology. Ricardo Barbosa de Sousa, a missionary in Brazil, reflects on Job as a biblical example providing important insights. Christopher Thomas, Church of God Theological Seminary professor, explores the demonic, healing, and deliverance within the frame of the New Testament, especially the Gospels. Tokunboh Adeyemo, general secretary of AEA and co-host of the consultation, reflects on the weapons of warfare presented in the New Testament Epistles. Finally, Europeans Oskar Skarsaune and Tormod Englesviken offer a significant survey of spiritual warfare perspectives through the lens of church history.

In the second section, "Reflections from the front lines," eight case studies provide contemporary examples of the struggles people face around the world to live Christ-centred lives in the midst of spiritual battles. The reflections come from Ethiopia, Brazil, North America, Europe, East Asia, India and Africa. They give a rich backdrop illustrating issues and struggles common to believers around the world. They also illustrate the role culture and theology play in approaches taken to dealing with the manifestations of evil found in local settings.

The third section, "Reflections on contemporary issues," generated more intense discussion than any other at the consultation. Charles Kraft of Fuller School of World Mission starts the section in his exploration of contemporary trends in spiritual conflict. Jerry Mungadze, Zimbabwean clinical psychologist, follows with an insightful reflection on the interrelationship of psychological and biblical perspectives, giving particular attention to dissociative identity disorder. Knud Jørgensen, European mission foundation director and co-host of the consultation, follows this with a passionate discussion on spiritual conflict in political and economic arenas. Indian evangelical leader Juliet Thomas offers insights on worship in relation to spiritual conflict. David G. Burnett, of All Nations Christian College, surveys folk religions and their relationship to spiritual warfare, and Scott Moreau of Wheaton College offers his perspective on the recent innovations concerning territorial spirits. Marguerite Kraft of Biola University focuses on issues of contextualisation in spiritual warfare, and Charles Kraft closes this section with a broad discussion of issues related to spiritual power.

We conclude with an appendix and a bibliography. Because of its significance for the planning for the Nairobi consultation, the Appendix is the 1993 statement on spiritual warfare from the Intercession Working Group (IWG) of the LCWE meeting in London.

Finally, the bibliography includes all the resources cited throughout the text as a basis for further reflection and study.

– A. Scott Moreau, General Editor

Contributors

Tokunboh Adeyemo (Kenya) has written a number of books, including *Salvation in African Tradition* (1978), *The Making of a Servant of God* (1994) and *Is Africa Cursed?* (1997). Since 1978, he has served as the General Secretary of the Association of Evangelicals in Africa (AEA). He has been Chairman of the International Council of the World Evangelical Fellowship since 1980.

Ricardo Barbosa de Sousa (Brazil) has been a pastor of the Planalto Presbyterian Church in Brasilia, Brazil, for 20 years. He is also a member of the board of Latin America Theological Fraternity and author of books and articles.

David G. Burnett (United Kingdom) is Academic Dean at All Nations Christian College, UK, where he teaches social anthropology, sociology of religion and folk religions. He was a missionary in India and also has considerable experience in Africa. He has written several books on worldview, traditional religion and Eastern religions.

Tormod Engelsviken (Norway) is Professor of Missiology at the Norwegian Lutheran School of Theology in Oslo. He was a missionary to Ethiopia and has been a member of the Lausanne Theology and Strategy Working Group. He has written several books and articles on topics related to mission, ecumenism and the Pentecostal/charismatic movements, including a book on possession and expulsion of evil spirits.

V. Ezekia Francis (India) is the Founder-President of Berachah Prophetic Ministries. His main focus is training and equipping leaders for spiritual conflict and various types of prayer related to spiritual conflict. He has authored several books on the theme of the return of Christ.

Amsalu Tadesse Geleta (Ethiopia) has served as a teacher and Dean of Studies at Nekemte Christian Education College. He earned his master of philosophy degree from Norwegian Lutheran School of Theology-Spring 2000. He is a preacher, teacher and author of articles and the book *Dekemezmurinet.*

Neuza Itioka (Brazil) is a Brazilian-born Japanese who has served in Brazil with OC International since 1985. She teaches extensively on spiritual conflict and intercession, training pastors and leaders in deliverance and inner healing.

Knud Jørgensen (Norway) was born in Denmark, where he was trained in journalism and theology. He served with Radio Voice of the Gospel in Ethiopia and with the Lutheran World Federation in Geneva. Since 1981 he has worked with various agencies in Norway and is presently Director of the mission foundation Areopagos.

Charles H. Kraft (United States) has taught in the School of World Mission at Fuller Seminary since 1969 as Professor of Anthropology and Intercultural Communication. Prior to this, he was a missionary in Nigeria and taught African languages at Michigan State and UCLA. He has authored over 20 books and numerous articles.

Marguerite Kraft (United States) is Professor of Intercultural Studies at Biola University. She has lectured in the Philippines, Kenya, Thailand, Nigeria, Papua New Guinea and New Zealand. She is the author of *Understanding Spiritual Power: A Forgotten Dimension of Cross-cultural Mission and Ministry* (Orbis Books, 1995).

Ole Skjerbæk Madsen (Denmark) graduated in theology from the University of Copenhagen in 1975. He is the author of publications on Coptic liturgy, practical theology, charismatic renewal and the encounter between Christianity and the new religious movements. After 24 years of parish ministry in the Lutheran Church, he has served as Project Manager for Areopagos since January 2000.

A. Scott Moreau (United States) is Associate Professor and Chair of the Missions and Intercultural Studies Department at Wheaton College as well as editor of *Evangelical Missions Quarterly*. Prior to teaching at Wheaton, he served a decade in Africa with Campus Crusade for Christ. He has written and edited numerous books and articles, including the *Evangelical Dictionary of World Missions* (Baker Books, 2000).

Bryant L. Myers (United States) is the Group Vice President for International Program Strategy at World Vision International. He is responsible for the strategic development of World Vision's ministries of transformational development, emergency relief, advocacy, church relations and Christian witness.

Jerry Mungadze (United States) is Founder and Director of Mungadze Association, which operates a specialty unit that treats Dissociative Identity Disorders. He received advanced training in counseling, psychology, Bible and theology. He lectures and consults internationally on issues related to dissociative disorders, traumatology, and cult and occult problems.

Oskar Skarsaune (Norway) was a Research Fellow in Church History from 1973 to 1978, earned the doctor of theology degree in 1982, and has been Professor of Church History at the Norwegian Lutheran School of Theology, Oslo, since 1980. He served as guest professor at Caspari Center for Biblical and Jewish Studies, Jerusalem, 1983, and at The Lutheran Theological Seminary, Hong Kong, 1990–91.

John Christopher Thomas (United States) is Professor of New Testament at the Church of God Theological Seminary in Cleveland, Tennessee. He has published widely in the area of New Testament and is an elected member of Studiorum Novi Testamenti Societas. He has served as an Associate Pastor of the Woodward Avenue Church of God in Athens, Tennessee, since 1981.

Juliet Thomas (India) serves under Operation Mobilization, India as Director of Arpana Women's Ministries. She has also been member of Lausanne Committee since 1984 and has served as Chair of the Lausanne Intercession Working Group (1990 to 1999). She served on the Board of World Vision India from 1988 until she stepped down as Chair in 2000.

Yusufu Turaki (Nigeria) has been Professor of Theology and Social Ethics at the Jos ECWA Theological Seminary (JETS), Jos, Nigeria, since 1980. He is also involved with church administration, leadership at various levels and theological education and research and writings in theology and social ethics. He is currently the Education Consultant of the Evangelical Church of West Africa and the Regional Director of International Bible Society Nigeria.

Hwa Yung (Malaysia) is a Methodist minister from Malaysia. He has studied in Australia, Britain and the United States. He is the Director of the Centre for the Study of Christianity in Asia, a newly established mission research centre at Trinity Theological College, Singapore.

Deliver Us from Evil
Consultation Statement

Introduction

Spiritual conflict is an emerging, yet uneasy, frontier in taking the whole gospel to the whole world. Enthusiasm and concern rest side by side. Trying to come to grips with the many complex issues, thirty practitioners, missiologists, pastors and theologians gathered in Nairobi, Kenya from 16 to 22 August, 2000. Together, we discussed issues of spiritual conflict in the "Consultation on Deliver Us from Evil," convened by the Lausanne Committee for World Evangelization and the Association of Evangelicals in Africa. The consultation objective was to seek a biblical and comprehensive understanding of 1) who the enemy is; 2) how he is working; and 3) how we can fight him in order to be most effective in the evangelisation of all peoples.

Our group included practitioners of deliverance and prayer ministries from Latin America, Africa, Asia, Europe, Australia, and the United States; pastors and evangelical leaders from Africa and North America; an executive of a relief and development agency; an African psychologist working in North America; theologians from Asia, Europe, and North America; missionaries working in Africa and Latin America; mission executives from Europe and North America; and missiological educators from North America and Europe. Among us were Presbyterians, Pentecostals, Methodists, Anglicans, Lutherans, Baptists and members of the Evangelical Church of West Africa, Church of South India, Berachah Prophetic Church, Evangelical Covenant Church, Brethren Church, Christian and Missionary Alliance and Bible Church (United States).

We noted with interest that most of the consultation participants from Western societies had come to recognise the realities of the unseen or spiritual realm as a result of their cross-cultural experience. Those from the Two Thirds World frequently reported their experiences with Western missionaries, who were unaware of these spiritual realities, and were thus unable to minister to the spiritual realities that Two Thirds World people experience on a day-to-day basis.

As we have met in Nairobi, we have learned from the insights of sisters and brothers from East Africa and the East African revival. We particularly affirm how our East African sisters and brothers lift up Jesus and his crucifixion in the face of spiritual conflict. We realise afresh that the only way to break the power of Satan in everyday life, in society and in culture is by walking in the light so that Satan may not bind us in the darkness.

As we pray the prayer "Deliver us from evil" we pray to be delivered from personal sin, natural evils, evil spirits and powers, and evil in society.

Origins

Our point of departure includes the Lausanne Covenant, the Manila Manifesto, and the 1993 LCWE Statement on Spiritual Warfare, all of which state the reality of our engagement in spiritual conflict:

> We believe that we are engaged in constant spiritual warfare with the principalities and powers of evil, who are seeking to overthrow the church and frustrate its task of world evangelisation. (Lausanne Covenant, 1974)

> We affirm that spiritual warfare demands spiritual weapons, and that we must both preach the Word in the power of the Spirit and pray constantly that we may enter into Christ's victory over the principalities and powers of evil. (Manila Manifesto, 1989)

> We agreed that evangelisation is to bring people from darkness to light and from the power of Satan to God (Acts 26:18). This involves an inescapable element of spiritual warfare. (Lausanne Statement on Spiritual Warfare, 1993)

The Consultation and participants recognise the relevance of spiritual conflict to world evangelisation. We are not trying to side with any particular view, but to expand evangelical thinking in an emerging area that has controversy. This statement indicates areas of common agreement, areas of unresolved tensions, warnings and points to areas needing further study and exploration. Our intention is to encourage churches of all traditions to use this statement to stimulate forthright discussion, serious reflection and practical ministry on spiritual conflict to the glory of God.

Common Ground

THEOLOGICAL AFFIRMATIONS

We affirm the biblical witness that humans were created in the image of God to live in communion with the Lord, in fellowship with other humans and as stewards of God's creation. The relation between God and humankind was broken through the mysterious entry of evil into God's creation. Since the Fall, evil has influenced all aspects of the created world and human existence. It is God's plan to redeem and restore God's fallen creation. God's redemptive purpose is being revealed and realised in the history of salvation, and fully in the gospel of the incarnation, death, resurrection, ascension, and return of God's son, Jesus Christ. We are called to participate in God's mission of fighting evil and the Evil One in order to restore what was destroyed as a result of the Fall. We live in a world with tension between the kingdom that has already come in Christ and the continuing realities of evil. God's mission will be completed when Christ returns, the kingdom of God comes into power, and evil is destroyed and eliminated forever.

1. Calling people to faith in Christ, inviting them to be delivered from the domain of darkness into the kingdom of God, is the missionary mandate for all Christians. We affirm a holistic understanding of evangelisation that finds its source in our relation with Christ and his call to us to become intimate with him in the fellowship of believers. The Holy Spirit empowers us for world evangelisation through the interrelated ministries of word (proclamation), deed (social service and action) and sign (miracles, power encounters), all of which take place in the context of spiritual conflict.
2. Satan is a real, personal, spiritual and created being. Satan tempted Jesus in the wilderness, sought to destroy him, and yet in light of the resurrection morning found himself defeated. Satan continues to actively oppose God's mission and the work of God's Church.[1]
3. The powers and principalities are ontologically real beings. They cannot be reduced to mere social or psychological structures.[2]

4. Satan works by taking what God has created for human well-being, and perverts it toward his purposes, which are to destroy and devalue life by enslaving individuals, families, local communities and whole societies. Satan contextualises his efforts differently in various societies and cultures.

5. Satan uses deception in an attempt to redirect human allegiances to anyone or anything other than God. In addition to the personal level, Satan does this with regard to all institutionalised forms of religious or ideological allegiance, including the church.

6. Satan and "the rulers, authorities, the powers of this dark world, the spiritual forces of evil in the heavenly realms" are at work through:[3]

   a) Deceiving and distorting;
   b) Tempting to sin;
   c) Afflicting the body, emotions, mind and will;
   d) Taking control of a person;
   e) Disordering of nature;
   f) Distorting the roles of social, economic and political structures;
   g) Scapegoating as a means of legitimising violence;
   h) Promoting self-interest, injustice, oppression and abuse;
   i) The realm of the occult;
   j) False religions; and
   k) All forms of opposition to God's work of salvation and the mission of the church.

7. A primary purpose of the life and ministry of Jesus was to expose, confront and defeat Satan and destroy his works.

   a) Christ has decisively defeated Satan at the Cross and through the resurrection.
   b) Jesus confronted Satan through prayer, righteousness, obedience and setting the captives free.
   c) In the ways Jesus ministered to people, he mounted an enormous challenge to the institutions and structures of the world.
   d) Christians share in Christ's victory and are given the authority of Christ to stand against the attacks of Satan in the victory we have in Christ.[4]

   The model for spiritual authority is Jesus and his obedience and submission to God on the Cross.

8. While we acknowledge that God is sovereignly in control of creation, the biblical evidence indicates a variety of causes of

illness and calamity: God, Satan, human choices or trauma and a disordered universe are all cited. We understand that we may not know with certainty the exact cause of any particular illness or calamity.

9. The elements of a worldview that is Christian, within our respective cultural contexts, must include:

   a) God is the creator and sustainer of all that exists, both seen and unseen. This creation includes humans and spiritual beings as moral creatures.

   b) People were made in the image of God, in which the aspects of the human person are inseparably connected. Body, soul, emotions and mind cannot be separated.

   c) God remains sovereign over all creation in history, and nothing happens outside God's ultimate control. Thus, the world cannot be conceived of as a closed universe governed merely by naturalistic scientific laws. Neither can it be considered a dualistic system in which Satan is understood to be equal to God.

   d) Because we reject a dualistic worldview, [we believe] the blessings of God and the ministrations of the angelic host, the consequences of sin and the assaults of Satan and demons cannot be isolated solely to a spiritual realm.

   e) Any teaching on spiritual conflict that leads us to fear the Devil to such an extent that we lose our confidence in Christ's victory over him and in God's sovereign power to protect us must be rejected.

   f) All matters concerning spiritual conflict must be viewed first and foremost in terms of our relation with and faith in God, and not simply in terms of techniques that we must master.

   g) The return of Christ and the ultimate consummation of his victory over Satan gives us confidence today in dealing with spiritual struggles and a lens through which we are to interpret the events in the world today.

10. The person and work of the Holy Spirit are central in spiritual conflict:[5]

   a) The empowering of the Holy Spirit, the exercise of spiritual gifts and prayer are prerequisites for engaging in spiritual conflict.

   b) The exercise of spiritual gifts must be accompanied by the fruit of the spirit.

   c) The work of the Spirit and the Word must be held together.

SPIRITUAL CONFLICT IN PRACTICE

1. We listened to reports on the history of the church's dealings with Satan and the demonic and noted:
   a) There are striking similarities between what happened in the history of the ancient church and what is happening in demonic encounters and deliverance today.
   b) Deliverance from satanic and demonic powers and influence in the ancient church was used as proof of the resurrection and the truth of the claims of Christ by the church fathers.
   c) Preparation for baptism included the renunciation of the Devil, the demonic and prior religious allegiances from the life of the convert, as well as repentance. This practice continues in some churches to this day.
   d) The unwillingness or inability of the contemporary Western church to believe in the reality of the spiritual realm and engage in spiritual conflict arose out of a defective Enlightenment-influenced worldview, and is not representative of the total history of the church in relation to spiritual conflict nor has it been characteristic of Christianity in the Two Thirds World in contemporary history.
   e) Every Christian has access to the authority of Christ and demons recognise Christ's power when exercised by Christians.
   f) The history of evangelism is replete with examples in which the response to the gospel was accompanied by power encounters, but power encounters in and of themselves are never a guarantee of a positive response.
   g) Church history also points to a link between idolatry and the demonic.
2. Working for positive strongholds for God through a "gentle invasion" that overcomes evil with good and wins people by love is as important as breaking down satanic strongholds. Thus, we affirm the importance and primacy of the local church and its life of faith.
3. Worship is spiritual conflict. It is not aggressive, spectacular spiritual conflict; not a strategy nor a means to an end; but involves mind, body and spirit responding with all that we are to all that God is.
4. Spiritual conflict is risky and often costly. While there are victories, there is often a backlash from the Evil One in various forms of attack such as illness and persecution. Nonetheless, we do

not shrink from spiritual conflict, since to avoid it is costly to the kingdom of God.

5. The ministry of spiritual conflict is grounded in the transformative power of relationships, not techniques or methods.

6. The point of departure for spiritual conflict is our relationship with Jesus and listening to the Holy Spirit.

7. We affirm the complexity of the human person. We need to distinguish the psychological from the spiritual when it comes to ministry and counselling. Deliverance ministries and psychological counsellors often fail to recognise this distinction. Failure to do so can do harm.

8. Holiness is central to the Christian response to evil:
   a) In the exercise of spiritual authority, those who do not give adequate attention to character and holiness truncate the whole biblical picture of spiritual growth and sanctification.
   b) To practice spiritual conflict without adequate attention to personal holiness is to invite disaster.
   c) The pursuit of holiness applies not only to the individual, but to the family, the local church and the larger community of faith.
   d) While holiness includes personal piety, it applies to social relations as well.

9. Engaging the Evil One is not the work for heroic individuals. Those engaged in this ministry must seek the support of a group of intercessors.

10. Following up on individuals who have experienced freedom through spiritual conflict must be an inseparable part of the ministry. The local church must be encouraged to incorporate people into the Christian community and to disciple them; not to arrange for this is sin.

11. We were saddened by stories of people, emboldened by self-assured certainty and money, who come from outside, overwhelm local Christians and carry out hit-and-run ministries of spiritual conflict that (1) presume superior knowledge of the local reality; (2) treat local Christians as inferior or unaware, (3) claim credit for things that local Christians have been praying and working toward for years and (4) leave uneven results and sometimes pain, alienation and even persecution of the local church, while claiming great victory.

12. Spiritual conflict involves more than one enemy; it must engage the flesh, the Devil and the world:

a) We view with alarm social evils such as injustice, poverty, ethnocentrism, racism, genocide, violence, environmental abuse, wars, as well as the violence, pornography and occult in the media.

b) These social evils are encouraged or supported by human institutions in which the principalities and powers work against God and God's intention for humankind.

c) The task of the church in combating the principalities and powers in the socio-political context is to unmask their idolatrous pretensions, to identify their dehumanising values and actions and to work for the release of their victims. This work involves spiritual, political and social actions.

13. We fail to find biblical warrant for constructing elaborate hierarchies of the spirit world.

Warnings

1. We urge caution and sensitivity in the use of language when it comes to spiritual conflict. While biblical, the term *spiritual warfare* is offensive to non-Christians and carries connotations that seem contradictory coming from those who serve a Lord who died on a cross. Additionally, there is a large range of meanings attached to various spiritual conflict terms such as healing, deliverance, power encounters, possession, demonisation, powers and so on. Also, new terms are constantly being coined (eg, Strategic Level Spiritual Warfare, deep-level healing, etc....).

2. We call for watchfulness to avoid any syncretism with non-Christian religious beliefs and practices, such as traditional religions or new religious movements. We also affirm that new believers are reasonable when they expect the gospel to meet their needs for spiritual power.

3. We call for discernment concerning magical uses of Christian terms and caution practitioners to avoid making spiritual conflict into Christian magic. Any suggestion that a particular technique or method in spiritual conflict ministry ensures success is a magical, sub-Christian understanding of God's workings.

4. We encourage extreme care and the discernment of the community to ensure that the exercise of spiritual authority not become spiritual abuse. Any expression of spiritual power or authority must be done in compassion and love.

5. We cry out for a mantle of humility and gracefulness on the part of cross-cultural workers, who having recently discovered the reality of the spirit realm, go to other parts of the world where people have known and lived with the local realities of the spirit world and the struggle with the demonic for centuries.

6. Because spiritual conflict is expressed in different ways in different societies, we strongly caution against taking ideas, methods or strategies developed in one society and using them uncritically in another.

7. Because we must resist the temptation to adopt the Devil's tactics as our own, we warn practitioners to take care that their methods in spiritual conflict are based on the work of Christ on the cross:

   a) Submitting to God through his substitutionary death on the cross, Christ deprived Satan of his claim to power;

   b) Christ's willingness to sacrifice himself, in contrast to fighting back, is a model for spiritual conflict; and

   c) When we separate the Cross from spiritual conflict, we create a climate of triumphalism.

8. We call for actions that ensure that our approaches and explanations of spiritual conflict do not tie new converts to the very fears from which Christ died to free them. Being free in Christ means being free from fear of the demonic.

9. We warn against an overemphasis on spirits that blame demons for the actions of people. Demons can only work through people – and people can actively choose to co-operate. Spirits are not the *only* source of resistance to the gospel.

10. We warn against confusing correlations or coincidence with causation in reporting apparent victories as well as the uncritical use of undocumented accounts to establish the validity of cosmic warfare.

11. We warn against using eschatology as an excuse not to fight against all forms of evil in the present.

Areas of Tension

1. In the early church, demonic encounters were most often seen where the church encountered non-Christians. The history of evangelisation frequently links power encounters with the evangelisation of non-Christian people. The biblical text reveals that while it is possible that a demonic spirit may afflict a believer physically,[6] there is no direct evidence that demons need

to be cast out of believers. On the other hand, we also heard the testimony of brothers and sisters from every continent to the contrary. This raises the question of how we are to understand the effect of the demonic in the lives of Christians. We were unable to resolve this tension in our consultation, but believe the following are helpful to note:

a) We are aware that in many cases, new Christians today have not gone through processes of renunciation of pre-Christian allegiances, processes that have been normative in the pre-Enlightenment Church. Some Christians may have lost their faith; there are others who call themselves Christians, but are only Christians in a nominal sense. Some claim that these might be reasons that Christians might appear to be susceptible to the demonic.

b) We affirm that being in Christ means the Christian belongs to Christ and that our nature is transformed. However, just as with sin and our need to deal with sin in our body, mind, emotions and will, we wonder if the demonic, while no longer able to claim ownership of Christians, may not continue to afflict them in body, mind, emotions and will unless dealt with.

2. While it is possible that Satan manifests himself more strongly in certain places than in others, and that some spirits seem to be tied to certain locations, we agreed there seems to be little biblical warrant for a number of the teachings and practices associated with some forms of spiritual conflict which focus on territorial spirits. We experienced tension over whether there is biblical warrant for prayer warfare against territorial spirits as a valid tool for evangelisation. We agreed, however, on the invalidity of the claim that prayer warfare against territorial spirits is *the* only key to effective evangelisation.

3. Tension exists concerning the extent to which we can learn and verify things from the spiritual realm from experiences not immediately verifiable from Scripture, in contrast to limiting our understanding of the spiritual realm from Scripture alone. Some have maintained that experience is crucial to understanding spiritual conflict; this is a point to be explored in ongoing dialogue.

4. We are not agreed as to whether or how the truths about spiritual realities and spiritual conflict methodologies can be verified empirically. Some engage in active experimentation in spiritual

conflict ministry as a means of developing generalities concerning spiritual conflict, while others are not convinced of the validity of this way of learning.

Frontiers That Need Continued Exploration

1. While affirming the Lausanne position on the Bible, there is an urgent need for a hermeneutic that:
   a) Allows culture and experience to play a role in the formulation of our understanding and theology of spiritual conflict. The basis and test of such a theology is Scripture, as faithfully interpreted by the Spirit-guided hermeneutical community of the global church.
   b) Allows an examination of issues that arise in Christian experience not directly addressed in Scripture.
   c) Accepts the fact that the Holy Spirit has surprised the church by acting in ways not explicitly taught in Scriptures (Acts 10 and 15) and may be doing so again.
2. There is an urgent need to incorporate the study of spiritual conflict into theological curricula in schools and training centres around the world.
3. There is an urgent need to develop criteria and methods that allow us to evaluate ministry experience in a verifiable way.
4. The emerging understanding of the complexity of the human person needs significant exploration and examination. Specifically, we call for:
   a) A sustained dialogue between those engaged in deliverance ministries and those in the medical and psychological professions;
   b) Urgent sharing worldwide with deliverance practitioners of the current state of knowledge of Dissociative Identity Disorder (DID, formerly called Multiple Personality Disorder);
   c) A diagnostic approach that allows practitioners to discern the difference between DID "personalities" and spiritual entities; and
   d) A dialogue between theologians and the medical and psychological professions that develops a holistic understanding of the human person, inseparably relating body, mind, emotions and spirit as they function individually and relationally.

5. We call for a more interdisciplinary approach to the description of spiritual conflict, drawing on the insights of relevant disciplines.

6. We call on the churches to develop an understanding of sanctification that addresses all of the human person: our spiritual, emotional, mental and physical selves. Such a holistic understanding of sanctification will include the development of spiritual disciplines, inner healing and deliverance. All need to become tools supporting the sanctification of Christians through the Word by the Holy Spirit.[7]

7. There is a need to explore the role in spiritual conflict of the practices of Baptism, Holy Communion, confession of sin and absolution, footwashing and anointing with oil.

8. We would like to see a serious examination of the deception and the seductive power of advertising in terms of its role in fostering envy, consumerism and false gods.

We praise God, that while we represented various theological, cultural and church traditions and positions on spiritual conflict, we have been blessed and inspired by learning from each other. This encourages us to believe that it is possible to develop an understanding of spiritual conflict and its practice within the Christian community, so that in time it becomes part of the everyday life of the church. We invite the church to join us in continued study and in the incorporation of appropriate ministries of spiritual conflict into the life of the church. We particularly call on the churches in the West to listen more carefully to the churches in the Two Thirds World and join them in a serious rediscovery of the reality of evil.

Notes

[1] Job 1–2; Zech 3:1; 1 Chron 21:1; Matt 4:1–11; Matt 12:23; Luke 8:12; Luke 22:3; John 12:31; 13:2; 16:11; Col 2:15–22.

[2] Mark 3:22; 1 Cor 2:6–8; 15:24–26; Col 2:15; Eph 1:21; 3:10; 6:10–18.

[3] 2 Cor 2:11; 1 Thess 3:5; 1 Tim 2:14; Rev 12:10; Matt 8:16; Matt 9:32; Mark 5:1–20; Mark 9:17; Luke 8:30; Job 2:7; Matt 9:32–33; 12:22–23; 15:22–28; Job 1:16–19.

[4] John 12:31; 16:11, 33; Col 2:15; Heb 2:14; 1 John 3:8; Rev 5:5; Eph 6:10–18; James 4:7; Luke 9:1; Matt 28:18; cf Matt 12:28; Eph 6:11, 13.

[5] Gal 5:21–22; 1 Cor 13:4–7; Eph 6:17.

[6] Luke 4:38–39; 13:10–13; 2 Cor 12:7–9.

[7] John 15:3; 17:17.

Deliver Us from Evil

I.

Reflections on theology
and the history of the church

1

A systematic theology that recognises the demonic

Hwa Yung

Up until recently, under the pressure of modernity, most theological writers have either ignored the demonic or reinterpreted it in some demythologised, impersonal and structural sense. Few have wrestled seriously with the understanding of the demonic as personal malevolent spiritual beings. But the rise of the Pentecostal-charismatic renewal on the one hand and the New Age movement on the other, both in the West, together with the increasing growth of non-Western Christianity, have forced the church to wrestle much more with a badly neglected area of theological reflection. Michael Green's excellent study *I Believe in Satan's Downfall*[1] may be said to have marked the new trend.

The reason why so little serious study has been done on the demonic in the past is that modernity's worldview, shaped largely by the Western Enlightenment, is highly anti-supernaturalistic. Thus among those in the West who are strongly influenced by this, the demonic is often systematically denied. Even so, this is not universally the case in Western culture. Beneath the surface level of modern Western societies, there have always been varying degrees of superstitions, dependence on astrology, occult practices and spiritism. Partly due to the growing influence of non-Western religions and culture, these practices increasingly have become much more open and popular, especially within the New Age movement.

Given the increasing recognition of the importance of the subject, how are we to approach the formulation of a more comprehensive biblical-based demonology? The question indeed is not whether it should be from above, that is, starting from the Bible, or below, that is, beginning with empirical evidence. As in all of theology, our understanding of God is derived from revelation and further clarified and explicated through our experiences. Three issues are involved here. First, we must examine the problem of how contrasting worldviews shape our understanding of the demonic. Second, we need a more careful study of Scripture that allows us to transcend the biases of our own limited worldviews. That will give us a clearer understanding of what the Bible teaches about the demonic. Third, we need to draw together the vast experiences of Christians throughout history and from different cultures, and carefully analyse these in light of Scripture. Much that has been written in recent years on spiritual warfare has an anecdotal character. It comprises a vast body of empirical data that is potentially extremely helpful and therefore should not be jettisoned by those who have difficulties with some of these writings. How they are to be interpreted is a moot point. Careful attention to these issues will help us in formulating a systematic theology that takes the demonic seriously.

Worldviews

Our interpretation of Scripture and our theology are shaped largely by our worldview. What is a worldview?

DEFINING WORLDVIEW

Charles H. Kraft defines a worldview as

the culturally structured assumptions, values, and commitments underlying a people's perception of REALITY. Worldview is the major influence on how we perceive REALITY. In terms of its worldview assumptions, values, and commitments, a society structures such things as what its people are to believe, how they are to picture reality, and how and what they are to analyze. People interpret and react on this basis reflexively without thinking.[2]

Thus, a worldview contains assumptions, values and commitments which give order and meaning to life and death and shape our understanding of reality. Because it is so crucial to a person, any threat to it will be unconsciously resisted. As Paul G. Hiebert, another missionary anthropologist, says:

The worldview incorporates assumptions about . . . the "givens" of reality. Challenges to these assumptions threaten the very foundations of their world. People resist such challenges with deep emotion, for such questions threaten to destroy their understanding of reality.[3]

For example, Western theology has been largely controlled by a dualistic worldview. Such a worldview has a two-tier account of reality: the upper spiritual realm which deals with belief in God, the sacred and "other-worldly" matters, and the lower physical realm which concerns the natural world governed by scientific and mechanistic laws. Because the two realms are distinct, with little or no interaction, there is little or no place to fit any beliefs in the supernatural, the miraculous, and angels or demons within such a worldview.

In contrast, non-Western cultures generally tend to have holistic worldviews in which the world is perceived as an organic whole. There is no sharp demarcation between the spiritual and physical realms. Rather, they closely interact with and interpenetrate each other, and each can only be fully understood in relation to the other. Belief in the supernatural and miraculous and in angelic and demonic beings fits comfortably within such worldviews.

Because many Western missionaries or Western-trained pastors (including those from the non-Western world) approach non-Western cultures with a dualistic mind-set, their preaching of the gospel often fails to address crucial questions posed by non-Western cultures with respect to the supernatural and miraculous. As we shall see, this results in some very serious consequences for non-Western recipients of the gospel. However, before discussing these, we will first examine in greater detail the differences between dualistic and holistic worldviews.

CONTRASTING DUALISTIC AND HOLISTIC WORLDVIEWS

The emergence of a dualistic worldview in the Western world with its strongly mechanistic overtones can be traced to the impact of the Enlightenment and, at a deeper level, to the Greek dualism that underlies much of Western thought. Various authors, including David Bosch in *Transforming Mission*,[4] have studied the impact of Enlightenment thought. The empiricist trend initiated by Copernicus, Bacon, Hume and others, combined with the Rationalism introduced by Descartes, produced a climate in which autonomous reason became the final criterion for truth. Reason replaced faith and revelation as the point of departure. This led to a radical anthropocentrism that increasingly had little room for God.[5] The rise of modern science and the subject-object distinction by which Enlightenment thought operated led increasingly to the objectification of nature. This in turn paved the way for the introduction of direct causality as the means for understanding reality. The result was a mechanistic view of a closed universe which supposedly could be fully explained once all the scientific laws were discovered.[6] This meant that in principle all problems were solvable,[7] and that there was no place for the miraculous and supernatural.[8]

At a deeper level, the early incorporation of the Platonic body-soul distinction into Christian theology had laid the foundation of a pervasive dualism within Western thought.[9] Indeed, the Chinese theologian Carver Yu, in a sustained argument, *Being and Relation*, asserted that the roots of Western dualism can be traced even further back to the pre-Socratic Greeks.[10] The adoption of their understanding of reality as "reality-in-itself," uncontaminated by anything other than itself, led to the view that reality is made up of discrete self-subsistent things, with dynamic interaction and interpenetration of being categorically excluded in principle.[11] This view, filtered through the philosophies of the Enlightenment, has further led to the concept of a closed mechanistic universe.[12] In sum, this perception of the unrelatedness of the world gave rise to the dualistic model of reality in the Western mind, with all its implications, in contrast to a holistic, biblical one.[13]

Given this background, we can easily understand Paul Hiebert's description of the modern Western mind as having a two-tier view of reality.[14] The dualistic view of reality sees the world in terms of soul and body, spirit and matter, and sacred and secular. Further, if Yu is correct, these dichotomies effectively split the world into two separate, almost iron-clad and unrelated parts, which Hiebert speaks of as the upper and lower realms of high religion and science respectively.[15] The former deals with spiritual and other-worldly matters, with beliefs in God and inner religious experience; the latter deals with this-worldly and secular matters which are governed by scientific laws within a mechanistic and closed universe. But there is no real interpenetration and interaction between the two tiers! Within such a worldview there is simply no place in which to fit the miraculous dimension, answers to prayer, the ministration of angels, the work of a personal devil and demonic powers, and related ideas.

This naturalistic and dualistic worldview contrasts sharply with the supernaturalistic and more holistic worldviews that are found in many non-Western cultures. In Hiebert's analysis, most non-Westerners have a three-tier view of reality, wherein the world is perceived as an organic whole.[16] Like the modern Western view of reality, it has an upper realm of high religion and a lower realm of science. But these are not iron-clad categories. The physical world, which corresponds with the realm of science or folk science, is not merely controlled mechanistically by impersonal forces and laws. Hiebert argues that many tribal religionists, for example, "see the world as alive. Not only humans, but also animals, plants, and even rocks, sand and water are thought to have personalities, wills and life forces. Theirs is a relational, not deterministic, world."[17] Further, as well as the upper religious realm which deals with theological ideas and other-worldly matters, there is a middle tier in the non-Western worldview. Hiebert calls this the realm of folk and low religion which deals with local gods and goddess, ancestors, spirits, demons, astrology, charms, and so on. These are not merely other-worldly powers but relate directly to life in the physical world. But most important, unlike the modern Western two-tier worldview wherein the upper and lower realms are almost totally unrelated, the typical non-Western worldview is three-tier and perceived as an integrated and interrelated organic whole.

Although there may be some variation in details, the above is now generally accepted as an accurate analysis of the difference between the modern Western and non-Western worldviews.[18] Hiebert's analysis is based on a folk Hindu worldview, which combines elements from both animism and Hinduism.[19] Analysis from other animistic societies, for example, the Philippines,[20] bears out the same pattern. Even in the West, underneath the surface level of the general secularization of society, among the less well educated or those who delve into the occult world of witchcraft, astrology and the like, a similar type of worldview exists.[21] A number of important elements are common to all these perceptions of reality. They are all holistic worldviews in which spirit and matter and the sacred and the secular are seen as parts of an organic whole. The universe is an open one in which each part interpenetrates and interconnects with every other. Within such a world, God and deities, angels and ancestral spirits, the Devil and demons, astrology, charms, miracles and other supernatural or occult practices, as well as all empirical realities in the physical world interact together as a daily reality of life.

Hiebert draws attention to two important consequences when the dualistic worldview of the Western missionary encounters the three-tier worldview of many non-Western people. First, because the average Western missionary's worldview does not have the middle tier, the missionary has no answers for the questions posed by the non-Western hearer of the gospel from this realm of his or her worldview. Yet, for many, if not most, non-Christians in the non-Western world, the questions posed from the middle tier are probably the most important for their daily existence. After all, it is the realm wherein the gods, spirits, ancestors, stars and so forth directly affect their daily lives, careers and families, their fortunes or their fate. Hiebert refers to this as "the flaw of the excluded middle" in the Westerner's worldview,[22] and it is this that has often prevented the gospel from penetrating the non-Western mind and heart. Hiebert's analysis finds abundant support from the fact that where the gospel today is making most headway in the Two-thirds World, it almost invariably takes a Pentecostal-charismatic form[23] which takes seriously the issues posed by the middle tier!

Second, if a person with the three-tier worldview is converted without the questions posed by the middle tier being adequately answered by the gospel, the tendency is for the new Christian to return to the diviner or witch doctor for answers to such questions.[24] This is indeed a common phenomenon in non-Western Christianity. In Malaysia, for example, often Christians from Chinese, Indian and indigenous backgrounds are known to visit temple priests, witch doctors *(bomohs)* or astrologers in times of sicknesses, for answers to personal and family problems, to choose an "auspicious" day for weddings and the like. In his study *Melanesians and Missionaries*, Darrell Whiteman argues that the failure to address the middle tier of the Melanesians' worldview resulted in a conversion to a Western cultural Christianity rather than a properly indigenous Christianity.[25] This inevitably led to a "split-level" Christianity, wherein the rational belief level of the indigenous convert was Christianised but the subrational level of consciousness remained decidedly pagan.

Given the above, does it therefore mean that we must set aside the modern Western worldview in favour of some non-Western or pre-modern version of a supernaturalistic worldview? The danger of doing so is that we may end up slipping back into a tribal animistic worldview or adopting that of the New Age or of post-modernity, all of which are equally unchristian.[26] Is there then a Christian or a biblical worldview?

ELEMENTS OF A BIBLICAL WORLDVIEW

It has been pointed out that there cannot be only one single Christian worldview because every worldview is distinguished by different surface-level cultural characteristics.[27] Moreover, there are clear advantages in Christians from different cultures possessing different

Christian worldviews. This prevents any one culture from making its own interpretation of Scripture normative and thereby provides the necessary checks and balances against any cultural distortion of the message of Scripture. This in turn allows for the universal body of Christ to read Scripture more comprehensively, rather than selectively.

Nevertheless, Christians coming from different cultures must share some basic similarities in their respective worldviews because of their common faith. What are some elements which would mark out a worldview as being distinctively Christian or biblical, and which would also allow us to take the demonic dimension seriously? The following is a suggested list:

- *God is the creator of all that exists, both seen and unseen. The unseen world of spiritual realities is as real as the world of empirical science. The fundamental distinction in this worldview is rooted in the ontological difference between God the creator and creation, and not in a dualism of spirit and matter.* Therefore the world as God created it is an integrated whole, wherein the spiritual and the material interpenetrate and interact with each other.
- *God in his wisdom created animals, which are non-moral creatures, and humans and spiritual beings, who are moral creatures. Among the spiritual beings, it would appear that there are good angels, who are faithful and obedient to God, and evil angels, like Satan and his minions, who have revolted against God's authority.* Similarly, humanity has also rebelled against God. Thus much of the world, both in the seen and unseen realms, which God created is in a state of rebellion against its creator.
- *God nevertheless remains sovereign over all creation in history, and nothing happens outside God's perfect will.* Thus, whilst the world may be in a state of rebellion, and Satan and his minions continue to try to defy God's authority, *there does not exist a metaphysical dualism in which good and evil are equal powers in this world.*
- *The world is not a closed universe governed merely by naturalistic scientific laws. Rather, it must be seen as an open universe in which both the natural laws of science and supernatural laws, many of which we do not yet fully comprehend, intersect and operate together in a complex manner.* In such a universe the so-called supernaturalistic phenomena such as answers to

prayer, miracles, angelic protection, demonisations, exorcisms, the power of charms and talismans, spiritual gifts and the release of the Holy Spirit's power, and so forth, should be view as natural, as was the case in the New Testament.[28]

- God created humans and the world good, but through the Fall sin entered the world. The biblical account (Gen. 3) asserts that sin is not merely a spiritual matter. It has psychological (3:7–10), social (3:11f., 16) and ecological (3:17–19) consequences. This again points to a holistic worldview which sees the world as an integrated whole. This holistic emphasis is also found in other parts of Scripture. For example, the effect of the blessings and curses in the Old Testament covenant are not merely spiritual but sociopolitical and ecological as well (Deut. 28). Sin and rebellion against God led not just to spiritual estrangement from God, but also to the self-destruction of the nation of Israel (Isa. 1:2–9; Hos. 4:2f.). Salvation is not merely spiritual, but the reversal of the result of the Fall involves the redemption of the whole world as well as the "sons of God" (Rom. 8:19–21). *Within such a worldview, neither the blessings of a good God and the ministration of the angelic host, nor the consequences of sin and the assaults of Satan and demons can be restricted to the spiritual realm. They will necessarily affect human life in the material realm as well. Diseases, natural disasters, famines and droughts, accidents, socio-political disorders, economic oppressions and the like could be either the consequences of divine judgement, satanic assaults, human sinfulness or some combination of these factors.*

- In the face of the reality of evil and the assault of demonic powers, the Christian's confidence is founded on the sovereignty of God over all creation. It is further reinforced by the certainty of our salvation in Christ through the Cross, which is also the means by which Christ has defeated Satan decisively. Thus whilst we must be watchful (1 Pet. 5:8), the Christian does not need to fear the Devil and his demons. *Any teaching on spiritual warfare which leads us to fear the Devil to such an extent that we lose our confidence in Christ's victory over him and in God's sovereign power to protect us must be rejected outright because it has gone beyond appropriate biblical limits.*

- Unlike animism and magic in which the spirits can be controlled and manipulated if we know the right techniques, Christians depend entirely in such matters on their relationship with a sovereign and saviour God. They commune with God through prayer and stand by faith on Christ's victory. *In other words, the Christian worldview sees all matters concerning spiritual warfare first and foremost in terms of our relationship with and faith in God, not in terms of techniques which we must master.* This does not mean that we do not need to learn how to do exorcism and the like, but rather it is a reminder that techniques are quite secondary without a proper relationship with God and a life of holiness and prayer (Acts 19:14–16).

- *The Christian hope of our final and total victory in Christ over all evil is founded on the resurrection of Christ and the assurance of his Second Coming.*

Elements of a biblical demonology

The second major question that needs to be addressed is what are the elements that constitutes a proper understanding of demonic powers which apply across space and time. The first issue within this question, then, is what is normative and what is culturally conditioned?

Are the Bible's teachings on the demonic normative or culturally conditioned?

We have already noted that the modern Western worldview tends to reject the demonic. Walter Wink clearly expresses this:

We moderns cannot bring ourselves by any feat of will or imagination to believe in the real existence of these mythological entities that traditionally have been lumped under the general category "principalities and powers." . . . It is as impossible for most of us to believe in the real existence of demonic or angelic powers as it is to believe in dragons, or elves, or a flat world.[29]

This denial of belief is of course not limited to demonic powers. From D. F. Strauss to R. Bultmann and on to the more recent "Myth-of-God-Incarnate" and "Jesus Seminar" schools, modern humanity has found it difficult to believe in many of the traditional beliefs of Christianity. Like Bultmann, many assert that such beliefs must be demythologised in order to get to what lies behind the "myths."

Many modern scholars have therefore repeatedly attempted to demythologise or at least reinterpret the biblical material on the demonic, especially "principalities and powers," in different ways. They have been variously viewed in terms of existential categories such as sin, law, flesh and death, or socio-political structures that dehumanise, such as racism, economic oppression, and sexism, or as the inner spiritual dimensions of such structures or institutions of power.[30]

But increasingly it is recognised that this approach is deeply flawed. To begin with, many scholars have found the word *myth* ambiguous and slippery. The word is used for a whole range of varied concepts, from a flat, three-tiered earth to the Incarnation and Resurrection. Often it is used with the assumption that since the former is clearly false the latter must also be, without asking whether there may indeed be other evidence for their truthfulness. Further, it is based on the Enlightenment assumption that modern humanity always knows better than the ancients. The collapse of the modern worldview has clearly belied this claim.[31]

More specifically, Clinton Arnold has noted that Bultmann and others have tried to demythologise the New Testament teaching on the demonic on the grounds that it belongs to the mythology of Jewish apocalyptic with its emphasis on a cataclysmic end of history. But Arnold argues that language about the demonic does not belong exclusively to Jewish apocalyptic literature but rather to all the prevailing worldviews of Paul's time, whether Jewish or Gentile:

> While it is true that Paul shares many ideas with Jewish apocalyptic, including the notion of evil spirits wreaking evil throughout the earth, Jewish apocalyptic was not the only view of the world during Paul's time that attributed evil to the work of hostile spirits. . . . The Gentiles to whom Paul preached also believed in personal evil forces who influenced humanity on many levels. . . . Regardless of the particular world view . . . both Jews and Gentiles could understand what Paul had to say on the topic of evil spirits. The concept of evil spirits was something agreed upon by all in the first century.[32]

To sum up, one cannot simply dismiss the demonic as a cultural hangover from New Testament times. It may be conceded that Jewish apocalyptic language and the specific terms for demons in the Bible are often culturally conditioned. But whether demons are real or not must be judged on the basis of the evidence available. On this, both biblical revelation and the sum total of empirical evidence from all over the world point to the ontological reality of such beings.

MAJOR ELEMENTS IN A BIBLICAL DEMONOLOGY

If the Bible's teaching on the demonic cannot simply be demythologised, what are its major constituent elements?

Satan or the Devil is a real personal spiritual being

The first point to be made is that Satan is real. The name *satan* in Hebrew means "adversary" or "opponent." It appears as such in a neutral sense in the Old Testament in a number of passages (e.g., Num. 22:22, 32; 1 Sam. 29:4). But in three passages in the Old Testament (Job 1 and 2; Zech. 3:1f.; 1 Chron. 21:1) it refers to a heavenly supernatural being. Although not a major figure in these passages, nevertheless "a developing understanding of Satan can be traced through the three passages, as the word *Satan* progresses from being a common noun describing a function to being a proper noun, and as his opposition to God and association with evil come to clearer expression."[33] Further, while it is difficult to be sure of what was originally believed about him, "all the texts betray an awareness of Satan's fundamental opposition to God and humanity."[34] Nevertheless, Satan remains subordinated to God.

In the New Testament, Satan's character as the primary enemy of God and humanity becomes clear. He is referred to as Satan *(satanas)* or the Devil *(ho diabolos).* He is one who tempts Jesus in the wilderness (Matt. 4:1–11; par.), seeks to oppose his mission (Luke 8:12; Matt. 12:23) and destroy him (Luke 22:3; John 13:2), but who in turn will be defeated instead (John 16:11). Other details concerning him are also found in the New Testament.

However, as to the origins of Satan and other demonic spirits, the Bible provides no answer. Many scholars have speculated about Isaiah 14 and Ezekiel 28 being allusions to the fall of Satan. But the actual intention of these and other passages remains uncertain.[35] It would therefore be wise not to be dogmatic. What is almost certain is that Satan and his minions are angelic beings created by God who subsequently rebelled against God.

Principalities and powers

The Bible not only teaches the existence of Satan but also the reality of demons. There are numerous references to fallen angels, demons and evil spirits in the Old Testament. To begin with, there are some rather ambiguous references to "sons of God" (Gen. 6:1–4), "gods" (Ps. 82), "powers in the heavens above" (Isa. 24:21f.) and the "princes of Persia . . . and of Greece" (Dan. 10:13, 20), all of which can be and have been interpreted to refer to fallen angels.

There are also more specific references to demons (Deut. 32:17; Ps. 106:37f.) and evil spirits (Judg. 9:23; 1 Sam. 16:14ff., 23; 18:10; 19:9; 1 Kings 22:19–23).[36] There are numerous accounts of encounters of Jesus and the apostles with demonic powers in both the Gospels and Acts.[37] To this we must add the New Testament teaching on what Paul often refers to as the "principalities and powers," which have been the focus of much discussion in recent years.

Paul's vocabulary on the powers reflected the language of demonology in the Judaism of his day. But nonetheless, the language was not exclusive to Judaism. Much of it was shared with the surrounding pagan culture. Arnold asserts:

> While "principalities" (archai) and "authorities" (exousiai) seem to be uniquely Jewish expressions for the unseen realm, many of the other words he used were also used by Gentiles to refer to the world of spirits and invisible powers. Words like "powers" (dynameis), "dominions" (kyriotetes), "thrones" (thronoi), "angels" (angeloi), "world rulers" (kosmokratores), "demons" (daimonia), "elemental spirits" (stoicheia) and "rulers" (archontes) were known and used by pagans, as evidenced in their magical and astrological texts.[38]

Further, we have noted earlier that some scholars have attempted to demythologise these powers and principalities by interpreting them as sinful and oppressive existential, socio-political or institutional structures. It may be true that the principalities and powers must be taken into consideration in discussions of sin in social structures and human institutions. Nonetheless, the evidence points clearly to the fact that Paul perceives them as personal, malevolent, spiritual beings and not merely as impersonal and sinful structures and institutions.

Finally, against the background of some recent writings on spiritual warfare, it is important to note what Paul does not teach. Arnold has noted that Paul is silent on at least five areas: *an explanation of the angelic rebellion and fall, the names of the angelic powers, the order within the angelic hierarchy, the activities of certain demons and how they are thwarted, and the territories ruled by evil spirits.*[39] Other biblical writers are similarly silent on these topics. Therefore, the proper Christian approach is to avoid going beyond what Scripture teaches (cf. Deut. 29:29).

The manner in which Satan and his demons work in the world

While the Bible is largely silent on some issues, at the same time it has quite a lot to say about how Satan and his minions work. And unlike the various versions of secularised views that have emerged through the Enlightenment, Satan and his minions do not restrict their work to the spiritual realm alone. Within a holistic worldview their influence is recognised at every level of human existence.[40] The following is a summary listing.

Sin and temptation. While the Bible does not teach that sin is caused only by Satan and his minions, it nevertheless emphasises that they are opposed to God's work in every way. They therefore not only entice us through temptations of all kinds but also fully exploit our human propensity to sin through the weakness of our flesh and our enslavement to it, apart from the power of the Holy Spirit. In extreme cases, as with demonised persons, we find Satan taking over their personalities and forcing them into sinful acts against their wills.

Demonisation. There are a number of clear incidents involving demonised persons in the Gospels and the Acts. The deliverance of such persons through the authority of Jesus Christ has been repeatedly replicated down the ages. This ministry of deliverance continues today, especially where the gospel regularly encounters those who come from a background of non-Christian religious practices, occult involvement or addictions to sins of all kinds.

Illnesses. Many Christians are not in the habit of thinking of illnesses as having demonic origins. Even so, the Gospels contain a number of clear references to this: the woman who was bound by a spirit of infirmity for 18 years and described by Jesus as one "whom Satan has bound" (Luke 13:16); the mute man who spoke after the demon was exorcised by Jesus (Matt. 9:32). Epilepsy (Luke 9:42), muteness and blindness were attributed to demonic spirits (Mark 9:25). Even in cases where there are no specific references to demonic powers, there may be hints that such are involved. The clearest example is the healing of Peter's mother-in-law (Luke 4:39), where Luke reports that Jesus "rebuked" the fever. The same word is used by Luke in an exorcism narrative (Luke 4:35, 41). Again, this has been the experience of many who have been involved in the ministry of healing.

Disruption of nature. Demonic powers also worked through the natural elements. The clearest example of this in the Bible comes from Jesus' stilling the storm, with words literally meaning "Be muzzled" or connoting "Be silenced" (Mark 4:39). Another example comes from the practice of some form of black magic, linked with human sacrifice by the king of Moab (2 Kings 3:27). The result was that the "fury against Israel was great," which very likely referred to a gross disordering of the natural elements which prevented the Israelites from securing the victory against Moab. Such occult influences on nature are commonly known in cultures where non-Christian religions and occult practices flourish.[41]

Disorder in society and the state. Arnold argues that the powers influence society and state first and foremost through the individuals therein, and secondly, through the Pauline concepts of "world" *(kosmos)* and "this age" *(aion).*[42] The latter would correspond closely to our present-day understanding of structural evil. Similarly, G. B. Caird argues in his comments on Ephesians 6:10–12 that "the real enemies are the spiritual forces that stand behind all institutions of government and control the lives of men and nations."[43]

The realm of the occult and astrology. This is the realm where sometimes humans have been given to think that they are in position to manipulate the powers of darkness for their own advantage. Often they discover too late who the real masters are![44] In fact, in mediumistic practices in East Asia, those involved often have little choice in the matter because they are simply "possessed" and co-opted by the spirits to do their bidding.

Non-Christian religions and cults. While it has to be firmly stated that most religions contains some things that are high and noble, in practice they are often linked in different ways to occult practices. For example, priests in Buddhist and Hindu temples and Muslim Sufis leaders are often involved in such practices. Similar examples are found in the Bible.[45]

Opposition to God's work of salvation and the mission of the church. This is so commonly described in the New Testament that there is little need for any elaboration.

Given the above reality, how does the Christian respond to the powers of darkness? The Bible's answer is clear: Christ has decisively defeated Satan at the Cross. To this we will now turn.

Christus Victor *and the defeat of Satan*

Earlier we noted that the Bible does not postulate an absolute dualism of God and Satan as two equals. Rather, God as creator and

Lord of history remains sovereign over all creation, including Satan, who is no more than a rebellious creature. Moreover, the New Testament clearly teaches that Jesus' coming has inaugurated the coming of the kingdom of God in power. In Jesus' own words, "But if I drive out demons by the Spirit of God, then the kingdom of God has come upon you" (Matt. 12:28). Thus the "strong man" who claims to hold this world in his power is now bound (12:29). This binding of the strong man is, of course, inseparable from the victory of Christ over Satan through the Cross.

Evangelical theology has tended to interpret the cross through the penal substitution model, and rightly so. However, often it is unconsciously assumed that this model exhausts the meaning of the Cross. Penal substitution may indeed be the basic model for understanding the cross, but it needs to be supplemented by other models as well.[46] In particular, in relation to dealing with demonic powers, the *Christus Victor* model, which stresses Christ's victory over sin, Satan and death, is crucial.

The New Testament sometimes depicts humanity as being under the power of Satan (Matt. 4:8f.; 2 Cor. 4:4). But through the Cross, Christ has dealt Satan a fatal blow and thereby given us victory over him. This thought is especially developed in John's Gospel (12:31; 16:11, 33). The rest of the New Testament takes this up (Col. 2:15; Heb. 2:14; 1 John 3:8; Rev. 5:5) and develops further the thought that we share in Christ's victory (Eph. 6:10–18; James 4:7).

These elements in the New Testament form the basis of the *Christus Victor* model, which has been popularised in the twentieth century through the writing of the Swedish scholar Gustav Aulen in his book by that name.[47] He defines this view, which he also calls the classic view, "as a Divine conflict and victory; Christ – *Christus Victor* – fights against and triumphs over the evil powers of the world, the 'tyrants' under which mankind is in bondage and suffering, and in Him God reconciles the world to Himself."[48] Through the Cross all forces hostile to humanity, whether sin and death, the Devil and his hosts, the demonic structures in the world and occult forces, all forms of oppressions and existential alienation, and the like, are overcome and defeated. Christians are thereby set free and share in Christ's triumph over them.

This theory was very prominent in the writings of the patristic Fathers.[49] For example, Irenaeus saw humans as having sold themselves to the Devil through sin, and the work of Christ as primarily a victory over the powers which hold us in bondage, namely, sin, death and the Devil.[50] Thus Irenaeus writes:

For Adam had become the devil's possession, and the devil held him under his power, by having wrongfully practiced deceit upon him, and by the offer of immortality made him subject to death. . . . Wherefore he who had taken man captive was himself taken captive by God, and man who had been taken captive was set free from the bondage of condemnation.[51]

Other patristic writers sometimes spoke of Christ dying as a ransom paid to the Devil or, less often, to God. Later writers, like Luther in his exposition, also drew attention to this view as one side of his teaching on the Cross.[52]

Clearly this view draws attention to an important aspect of the New Testament interpretation of the death of Christ. That it has been often neglected in evangelical thought in the twentieth century is due to the latter's preoccupation with penal substitution. Yet the victory of Christ logically flows out of his substitutionary atonement on the Cross. Because the penalty for sin has been paid and judgement averted, sin, Satan and death no longer have any hold over redeemed humanity. Christians are therefore now in position to appropriate the authority of Christ (Luke 9:1; Matt. 28:18; cf. Matt. 12:28f.) and to stand on the victory that we have in him (Eph. 6:11, 13).

The war continues until Christ's return

Nevertheless, God in his sovereignty has not yet completely destroyed Satan and his host. They remain extremely dangerous and potent. The Christian is called to be always on guard. But Satan does not have unlimited powers. One image that has been used is that he is like a fierce Alsatian on leash. He may growl and bare his fangs with utmost ferocity, but he cannot hurt us unless we are careless enough to get too near. This is an imperfect analogy, but it illustrates the limits of Satan's power.

Paul further reminds us that the war is still on (Eph. 6:10–18). It is sometimes argued that Paul is speaking only of the Christian being on the defensive and not the offensive. But this is a moot point. Both the imagery used in the Bible and the realities of Christian mission speak of offence as well as defence. For example, Ephesians 6:10–18 speaks of standing our ground three times (vv. 11, 13), thus implying defence. But one can hardly speak of "the sword of the Spirit, which is the word of God" (v. 17) as a merely defensive weapon! Or again, there is no way that we can interpret Jesus' various commissions to his disciples (Luke 9:1f.; Matt. 28:18–20) in purely defensive terms.

Given that the above constitute the key elements in a biblical demonology, does it therefore mean that all teachings that fall under the term *spiritual warfare* are thereby validated? It does not necessarily follow. While it must be said that the recent flood of writings on spiritual warfare has certainly provided a corrective to the gross neglect of this subject within the church in the modern period, many things said remain highly speculative and questionable.

For example, in his critique of some present-day writings on spiritual warfare, *Territorial Spirits and World Evangelization*? Chuck Lowe argues that they manifest two serious defects.[53] The first is that much of these teachings suffer from a tendentious use of Scriptures. Lowe faults the approach of Peter Wagner and others, sometimes called "Strategic-level Spiritual Warfare" (SLSW),[54] in its use of Scripture on the grounds that it is "a pre-existing practice in search of justification. It finds what it is looking for, or creates what it needs."[55] In a series of detailed chapters, Lowe demonstrates that this tendentiousness applies not only to the reading of Scripture by Wagner and others but also to their use of history and empirical data.

Second, Lowe suggests that SLSW reflects evangelicalism's domestication by the forces of modernity. It tends to give too much emphasis to technique with "its application of mechanistic methods to all of life."[56] He goes on to state that "the rise of technique is a form of secularization. Theoretical rationalization denies the existence of God through naturalistic science or rationalistic philosophy. Functional rationalization manages his power through the application of technique. Either way, the end result is the same: God becomes redundant."[57] Lowe argues that in seeking to increase efficiency through the application of the management techniques of the factory floor to church life and pastoral action, evangelicalism has been unwittingly undermined by modernity's mechanistic mindset. The same applies to SLSW. "If God can be managed, so can Satan: SLSW is born."[58] Thus the most serious critique of this approach may actually be Wagner's own claim that SLSW is a form of "spiritual technology for completing the Great Commission in our generation."[59] Such an emphasis on technique and technology reflects a mechanistic worldview that is clearly at odds with that of biblical Christianity.

The thrust of biblical teaching on how the war against Satan and his host can be won is far removed from the technique-centred approach of SLSW. Take, for example, Revelation 12:11, which was written in the context of intense persecution and, one may surmise, ferocious satanic attack. Yet the writer does not anywhere speak of techniques which will ensure victory. Rather Christians are called to overcome the powers of darkness by standing on the victory won by "the blood of the Lamb," through the faithful "word of their testimony," and by learning not to "love their lives so much as to shrink from death." Taken together with Ephesians 6:10–18, these two passages appear to sum up the overall thrust of New Testament teaching, which focuses our attention on standing firm on Christ's victory, faithful witness even in face of martyrdom, and diligent trusting prayer.

Issues that require further study

We have looked at the question of worldviews and also the basic elements that should constitute a biblical demonology. We will now finally turn to some issues that need further studies in our attempt to build a systematic theology that takes the demonic seriously.

TERRITORIAL SPIRITS

One of the more controversial topics raised in recent discussions on spiritual warfare is the concept of territorial spirits; that is, the idea that some demons have been assigned specific territories to rule over. This is in fact one of the key components on the SLSW approach. Lowe rejects this and argues that "the Bible does not portray demons as geographically specific."[60] But there are reasons to think that Lowe has overstated his case in the attempt to demolish some of the fundamental tenets of SLSW. Basing their analyses on references to "sons of God" (Deut. 32:8, as found in the Septuagint and the Dead Sea Scrolls), "gods . . . sons of the Most High" (Ps. 82:6), "the prince of Persia . . . the prince of Greece" (Dan. 10:13, 20), and other related passages, both Arnold[61] and Page[62] have argued in support of the idea of territorial spirits.

On the basis of existing evidence to date, it would appear that Page's approach best represents the overall position of scriptural teaching. He affirms that the Bible teaches the existence and activity of territorial spirits. But, he argues, this

> does not constitute grounds for thinking that Christians can or should attempt to identify them and the areas they control. The presence and influence of the princes were disclosed to Daniel, but not because he sought to discover their identity or functions. Nor is there any evidence that Daniel prayed for their defeat. Proponents of spiritual mapping run the risk of indulging in the sort of speculation that Scripture consistently avoids

and of falling into an unhealthy subjectivism. Moreover, there is the ever present danger of exaggerating the role of territorial spirits in such a way that the biblical teaching on divine sovereignty is compromised.[63]

All these point to the need for further study before we can come to a clearer consensus.

DOES SATAN HAVE DOMINION OVER THE WORLD?

A second issue that needs consensus concerns Satan's claim that he has authority over "all the kingdoms of the earth *(oikoumene)*" (Luke 4:6). He further claims that "all their authority and splendor . . . has been given to me, and I can give it to anyone I want to." Does he indeed have such authority? And, if he does, how was it given to him?

On the first question, Sydney Page argues that Satan is merely lying.[64] After all, he is "a liar and the father of lies" (John 8:44). Moreover, if it is true that Satan has authority over the world, surely that contradicts the belief in God's sovereignty over the world.

But in response to Page, two things may be said. First, Satan's claim to have authority over "all the kingdoms of the earth" is reinforced by the references to him as "the prince of this world *(kosmos)*" (John 12:31; 14:30; 16:11) by Jesus, and as the "god of this age *(aion)*" (2 Cor. 4:4) and "the prince of the power of the air" (Eph. 2:2[65]) by Paul. It would be strange that Jesus and Paul would use such language if indeed Satan is lying.

Further, it is clear that the Bible uses the term *world* in at least two ways: first, the world which God created; and second, human society in rebellion against God. It would appear that in the references above made by Jesus and Paul, the "world" or "age" is used in the second sense. In that sense Satan is indeed "the ruler of this world." Satan may be exaggerating his powers in making the claim that he has authority over all "the kingdoms of the earth," because God remains sovereign over God's creation. Nevertheless, it appears that he does rule over a limited sphere, that of the "world" of humankind in rebellion against God, with its pride and arrogance, disordered priorities and false values, disobedient hearts and evil sociopolitical structures. And in this he is not lying!

It would appear that humankind through the Fall gave Satan authority over our lives and our communities. This would sound terribly glib, except for the fact that Paul reminds us that it was because "sin entered the world through one man, and death through sin, and

in this way death came to all men, because all men sinned," and
that "the result of one trespass was condemnation for all men" (Rom.
5:12, 18). And further, it was this that has led to our enslavement to
sin (Rom. 7:7–25). It must be admitted that nowhere does the Bible
explicitly teach that it was our sin that gave Satan authority over us
and the "world." But Christian theology has always linked the tyr-
anny of sin, death and Satan over human life together. Thus, it would
appear right to conclude that it is indeed human sin that gave Satan
authority over us.

This would also tie in with what we said earlier about the Cross.
Penal substitution is the basic model for the Atonement. But it must
be complemented by the *Christus Victor* model. The latter flows from
the former. Penal substitution frees us from sin and its condemnation. Once that has been dealt with, we are freed from bondage to
sin, death and Satan; we can now share in Christ's victory through
his death over all three. Thus the logic flows as follows: it was our sin
which gave the Devil authority over our lives in the first place; but
once Christ has dealt with that, we can have victory over the Devil!

What is meant by "flesh" or "sinful nature"?

A third area that also needs re-examination is how we are to understand the "flesh" *(sarx)* or "sinful nature." The word *sarx* carries
different meanings, one of which refers to the sinful principle opera-
tive in humanity. It is often translated "flesh" (Rom. 8:3, RSV) or
"sinful nature" (NIV). However, much of the discussion on *sarx* consciously or unconsciously perceives it as some static metaphysical
reality, in line with the Greek understanding of *physis* or "nature,"
although the word is never used in connection with the idea of the
sinful principle in humanity. This is reflected in the language that is
used for sin or sinful nature: "a total corruption of man's being," "sin
which defiles every part of man's nature," original sin being defined
as "inherited sin," and that "a person is not a sinner because he sins,
he sins because he is a sinner." Consequently, in our theological
understanding we think of the "flesh" or "sinful nature" as something metaphysical in humanity, in the same way that we think of
human nature as something metaphysical. According to this view,
sanctification would require some metaphysical change taking place
in the depth of our being, even though it is never so stated. The role
that we assign to Satan is hardly more than that of a tempter!

It appears that the New Testament conceives of the "flesh" in much
more dynamic terms. When Paul, for example, speaks of the "mind

of the flesh" (Rom. 8:5f.), he juxtaposes it with the "mind of the Spirit." The latter is not some metaphysical part of redeemed humanity, but rather some aspect of our being in which the Spirit is dynamically at work. Should not therefore the "mind of the flesh" similarly be conceived of as something in which evil is dynamically at work instead of merely as some static metaphysical part of fallen humanity? Could it be that such an understanding would be truer to New Testament teaching? H. Seebass, in his exposition of Paul's understanding of the "flesh" in Colossians 2:18, asserts that "'the mind of the flesh . . . is preoccupied with angelic powers to whom as *sarx* man seems to be in subjection."[66] Similarly, in Ephesians 2:2f. Paul pursues a related thought: "In its desires the flesh is open to the powers and influences of this world, which themselves are not flesh and blood."[67]

The above, together with other descriptions of him in the Bible, clearly means that Satan is certainly more than just a tempter in relation to sin. He actively seeks to influence us. He instigates us to rebellion. He blinds us with lies. He instills fear to prevent us from being faithful, and he offers pleasures to draw us from obedience. He desires to mould our thinking with values that are opposed to God. Often, he goes even beyond these to constrain us to sin and do evil, this being most clearly seen in the lives of the demonised. *Taken together, does this not suggest the possibility that, as much as the Spirit is dynamically at work in the "mind of the Spirit," the Devil is dynamically at work in the "mind of flesh"* (Rom. 8:5f.)?

If such is the case, this raises the intriguing possibility that we may need to rethink our language about sin and sinful nature and how to link these much more with spiritual and demonic bondage in our lives. Although we may not have to jettison traditional conceptions *in toto*, we need to expand our ideas of how Satan keeps us in bondage and how sanctification occurs. We may need to think of life in terms of two spheres, one in which Satan is at work to hold us in bondage to sin and death, and the other in which God is redemptively at work to effect freedom from sin and death. Before our conversion, we are primarily in the satanic sphere and under his bondage. After conversion and as we grow in holiness, we are moved gradually and increasingly into the sphere of divine operation. Such a conception of sin and grace will need more careful stating. But it will explain some things in a clearer manner, such as how we are to understand the grip of sin in our lives even after conversion. Space, however, prohibits a fuller discussion here.

THE PROBLEM OF EVIL

Systematic theological discussions on the problem of evil also have tended to ignore the demonic dimension as an active source of evil and suffering. The focus is usually placed on resolving the tension between the goodness of God and God's sovereignty over creation. Bringing in the demonic does not fully resolve the tension, but it can contribute significantly to mitigating the force of the objection that God often appears powerless in the face of evil and suffering. A proper understanding of spiritual warfare informs us that the forces of darkness may be countered and indeed be defeated through prayer. This means, for example, that natural disasters can be averted, sickness healed, and so forth. Thus, while we may not have complete victory over evil until the return of Christ, we can nevertheless know substantial victory over many of its manifestations here and now. Arguments along such lines will provide us with a far stronger theodicy.

Notes

[1] Michael Green, *I Believe in Satan's Downfall* (Grand Rapids, Mich.: Eerdmans, 1981).

[2] Charles H. Kraft, *Christianity with Power: Your Worldview and Your Experience of the Supernatural* (Ann Arbor, Mich.: Servant Books, 1989), 20.

[3] Paul G. Hiebert, *Anthropological Reflections on Missiological Issues* (Grand Rapids, Mich.: Baker, 1994), 38.

[4] David Bosch, *Transforming Mission: Paradigm Shifts in Theology of Mission* (Maryknoll, N.Y.: Orbis Books, 1991), 262–345.

[5] Ibid., 269.

[6] Ibid., 265.

[7] Ibid., 266.

[8] Ibid., 273.

[9] Brian J. Walsh and J. Richard Middleton, *The Transforming Vision: Shaping a Christian World View* (Downers Grove, Ill.: InterVarsity Press, 1994), 107–16.

[10] Carver Yu, *Being and Relation: A Theological Critique of Western Dualism and Individualism* (Edinburgh: Scottish Academic Press, 1987).

[11] Ibid., 64–114.

[12] Ibid., 77f.

[13] Ibid., 147–235.

[14] Hiebert, *Anthropological Reflections*, 189–201.

[15] Ibid., 199. Hiebert speaks here of the two realms of high religion and science. Elsewhere he also speaks of the Western worldview as being sharply dichotomised "between the *supernatural* and the *natural*. The former has to do with other worldly concerns, such as God, Satan, heaven, hell, sin,

salvation, prayer and miracles. Nature – the world of matter, space, and time – was increasingly seen as an autonomous realm operating according to natural laws that could be understood by scientists and used to solve human problems on this earth" (219). In Hiebert's conception the first two realms of the high religion and science correspond to the supernatural and natural realms, although that is sometimes not clear in his writings.

[16] Ibid., 193–98.

[17] Ibid., 196.

[18] See, e.g., Kraft, *Christianity with Power*, 195–205.

[19] Compare also Rabindranath R. Maharaj, *Death of a Guru* (London: Hodder, 1974).

[20] Rodney L. Henry, *Filipino Spirit World* (Manila: OMF, 1986), 17–35.

[21] See, e.g., Doreen Irvine, *From Witchcraft to Christ* (Eastbourne: Kingsway, 1994).

[22] Hiebert, *Anthropological Reflections*, 189–201.

[23] It should be pointed out that much of indigenous non-Western Christianity invariably takes on a Pentecostal-charismatic form. But this is not necessarily because its members trace their beginnings to the Pentecostal-charismatic movements in the West. Rather, often non-Western Christians have simply found that the Bible's teachings on the miraculous are similar to their pre-Christian experiences of the same. The power now comes from the true God they have come to know.

[24] Paul G. Hiebert, *Anthropological Insights* (Grand Rapids, Mich.: Baker, 1985), 222–24; Hiebert, *Anthropological Reflections*, 198.

[25] Darrell Whiteman, *Melanesians and Missionaries* (Pasadena, Calif.: William Carey Library, 1983), 436–39.

[26] Indeed, this problem has been noted by Hiebert (see *Anthropological Reflections*, 224–28).

[27] Charles H. Kraft, *Anthropology for Christian Witness* (Maryknoll, N.Y.: Orbis Books, 1996), 67f.

[28] The very restrictive and almost deistic view of the world as a closed universe arose out of the limited scientific understanding of the nature of the universe in the eighteenth and nineteenth centuries. In contrast, the idea of an open universe is fully consonant with the latest findings of theoretical physics. The "undoubted unpredictabilities" provided for by both quantum theory and chaos theory "would have to be interpreted . . . as signals of an underlying ontological openness" (John Polkinghorne, *Science and Theology: An Introduction* [London: SPCK, 1998], 89). Further, in contrast to the four dimensions of space-time that we are so used to, the latest theories of the universe postulate that there are up to eleven dimensions in the universe (Steven Weinberg, "A Unified Physics by 2050?" *Scientific American* 281:6 [December 1999]: 36–43). It would be appropriate to ask whether any of these dimensions relate to "spiritual" rather than "physical" realities.

[29] Walter Wink, *Naming the Powers: The Language of Power in the New Testament* (Philadelphia: Fortress Press, 1984), 4.

[30] Clinton E. Arnold, *Powers of Darkness: Principalities and Powers in Paul's Letters* (Downers Grove, Ill.: InterVarsity Press, 1992), 169–76. It

should be noted that some scholars have applied the phrase "principalities and powers" to sociological structures of various sorts in a neutral sense, although that is not the position adopted here.

[31] See further, I. Howard Marshall, "Myth," in New Dictionary of Theology, ed. Sinclair B. Ferguson and David F. Wright (Leicester: Inter-Varsity Press, 1988).

[32] Arnold, Powers of Darkness, 171.

[33] Sydney H. T. Page, Powers of Evil: A Biblical Study of Satan and Demons (Grand Rapids, Mich.: Baker, 1995), 37.

[34] Ibid.

[35] Green, I Believe in Satan's Downfall, 33–42; Page, Powers of Evil, 37–42.

[36] Page, Powers of Evil, 43–86.

[37] Ibid., 137–265.

[38] Arnold, Powers of Darkness, 91. A full list of the terms used by Paul on Satan and demonic powers is given in Arnold, Powers of Darkness, 218. On the background and use of these terms in magic and astrology in Jewish and Gentile literature, see Clinton E. Arnold, Ephesians: Power and Magic: The Concept of Power in Ephesians in Light of Its Historical Setting, Society for New Testament Studies Monograph 63 (Cambridge: Cambridge University Press, 1989), 51–69.

[39] Arnold, Powers of Darkness, pp, 98f.

[40] See Green, I Believe in Satan's Downfall, esp. 58–194; and Arnold, Powers of Darkness, 183–209.

[41] See, e.g., George Otis, The Twilight Labyrinth: Why Does Spiritual Darkness Linger Where It Does? (Grand Rapids, Mich.: Chosen Books, 1997), 136–50. In Southeast Asia, for example, it is common practice to employ bomohs (witch doctors in Indonesia and Malaysia) or temple priests to ensure that good weather prevails at times of important official functions and important sport tournaments.

[42] Arnold, Powers of Darkness, 202–5.

[43] G. B. Caird, Paul's Letters from Prison – Ephesians, Philippians, Colossians, Philemon (Oxford: Oxford University Press, 1976), 91.

[44] Green, I Believe in Satan's Downfall, 112–47.

[45] Ibid., 148–94.

[46] J. I. Packer, "What Did the Cross Achieve? The Logic of Penal Substitution." Tyndale Bulletin 25 (1974), 19–25.

[47] Gustav Aulen, Christus Victor: An Historical Study of the Three Main Types of the Idea of the Atonement (London: SPCK, 1970).

[48] Ibid., 4.

[49] Ibid., 16–60.

[50] Ibid., 22–28.

[51] Irenaeus, Against Heresies, III, 23.1, quoted in Aulen, Christus Victor, 19–20.

[52] Paul Althaus, The Theology of Martin Luther (Philadelphia: Fortress, 1966), 208–11.

[53] Chuck Lowe, Territorial Spirits and World Evangelization? (Sevenoaks, Kent: Mentor/OMF, 1998).

[54] It should be pointed out that scholars differ in their assessment of Wagner's overall approach, with some viewing it much more positively than the position adopted here. Further, whilst I agree with much of Lowe's critique of Wagner's teaching on SLSW, this does not necessarily mean that I reject other aspects of Wagner's approach. Indeed, his work has rightly challenged many parts of the Western church to rethink its understanding of the demonic.

[55] Lowe, *Territorial Spirits*, 145.

[56] Ibid., 147.

[57] Ibid., 148.

[58] Ibid.

[59] Quoted in Ibid., 149; see also ibid., 147–51.

[60] Ibid., 29.

[61] Arnold, *Powers of Darkness*, 62–64.

[62] Page, *Powers of Evil*, 43–65.

[63] Ibid., 65.

[64] Ibid., 98.

[65] See Arnold, *Powers of Darkness*, 196f.

[66] H. Seebass "Flesh," in *The New International Dictionary of New Testament Theology*, ed. Colin Brown (Exeter: Paternoster, 1975), 1:676.

[67] Ibid.

2

Spiritual warfare and Job's dilemma

RICARDO BARBOSA DE SOUSA

Satan is a liar and the father of lies. That is how Jesus defined him. Since he is a liar and the father of lies, it is not hard to conclude that he is the ultimate source of all human alienation. Spiritual warfare is the great battle that the church of Christ, the "pillar and foundation of the truth" (1 Tim. 3:15, NIV), must undertake in the arduous task of freeing people from the bondage of lies and all alienations.

The church's mission, as defined by Jesus in his Nazareth sermon, is to announce the redeeming truth of the gospel, proclaim liberty to all those entrapped by every form of lie and deceit, help restore sight to the blind, and set free the oppressed. This mission has always involved a great spiritual conflict, an everlasting battle against Satan's alienating lies.

This is a vast theme, and any attempt to reduce it to speculative abstractions could lead us into other forms of alienation. I will approach the subject from biblical and pastoral perspectives and chose Job as an exemplar of spiritual conflict. Job's story is one of a spiritual struggle that begins with a wager between God and Satan. Satan questions the real motivations behind Job's spiritual integrity. He cannot believe that anyone will worship and serve God unselfishly, out of love and devotion, without expecting anything in return. But God believes the contrary to be the case.

The wager centres on spiritual experience in its deepest and most personal sense. It arouses a response in the affections and the depth of each individual and enables each to reflect on theology, social structures and human relationships.

The aim of this wager is not to compare forces and see who is more powerful, which is what normally happens when we are talking about war. God never intended to prove his power, as if his glory were at stake. We will see that the whole purpose of this great spiritual drama is to transform us and lead us to a better understanding of God's ways.

It is in this context that I intend to reflect on Job's spiritual conflict. I will be focusing on the way he faced the problems, the changes it brought to his life, his theology and his relationship with God and those around him.

The battle scene

The first two chapters of the Book of Job set the scene and define the characters in this conflict. On the one hand we have God, portrayed as sovereign Lord over all that happens on earth and in heaven. Job sees God as Creator, Judge and Sustainer of all creation. Walter Wink affirmed "in primitive Israel there really was no place for Satan in people's faith." God was the only Lord and everything that happened, for good or for evil, was attributed to God.[1] In the Old Testament, God is always the ultimate source of all that happened in heaven and on earth. He takes full responsibility over both good and evil. That is why the prophet Isaiah, speaking in the Lord's name, said that Cyrus would fulfil his role in the divine purpose of redeeming Israel, despite the fact that he neither knew nor feared God. God takes responsibility for Cyrus's actions when he describes Cyrus's role and concludes by saying, "I form the light and create the darkness; I bring prosperity and create disaster; I, the Lord, do all these things" (Isa. 45:7, NIV). This is an important concept that Job uses in dealing with spiritual conflict.

On the other hand, we have Satan himself, who comes before the Lord together with the "sons of God." He is presented to us as an accuser, and this expression is later used in the New Testament to define his role. He questions Job's real motives for being so righteous and faithful. These suspicions raise doubts about God's word and, consequently, the relationship between God and humankind. Satan does not have any power of his own and cannot act independently of God. Before bringing upon Job the misfortunes that would turn his life into a wretched existence, Satan suggests that God afflict Job and watch him blaspheme. On hearing this proposal, which acknowledges God's sovereignty over human life, God says to Satan, "Very well, then, everything that he has is in your hands" (Job 1:12). God takes upon himself Satan's actions when he says, "You [Satan] persuaded me to let you attack him [Job] for no reason at all" (Job 2:3b). Satan also recognises this when he says to God, "But stretch out your hand and strike his flesh and bones, and he will surely curse you to your face" (Job 2:5). Although evil was suggested and executed by Satan (God is not responsible for its origin or its continuation), Satan acknowledges that ultimately it was God's hand that caused Job's afflictions. Thus Satan is not an autonomous being.

Then we have Job, whom Satan views with mistrust, but who is considered by God to be a righteous, honourable, and God-fearing man who avoids evil. The target of Satan's accusations is Job in his relationship with God. He does not question what God says about his servant Job. His scepticism centres on the motives and secret intentions of Job's piety. These suspicions do not only undermine Job's intentions, they also threaten God's covenant with his people. Satan believes no one worships and serves God without expecting something in return. Underneath his righteousness and integrity, Job conceals his real motives: he expects some kind of reward from God. Satan doubts that anyone will love God without expecting some retribution. If Satan's suspicions are confirmed, he can justify his own fall. Job's spiritual conflict takes place in the arena of relational and affective bonds and not in the arena of power.

Satan's strategy

As we have just seen, the story is about a wager. On the one hand, God reaffirms Job's integrity and awe of God. On the other, Satan questions the motivations behind this relationship and proposes a wager. God trusts in the power of love, in the relationship based on affection. This is the power that God will use against Satan's challenge. This power is in itself quite fragile, for its strength lies in captivating the heart and obtaining a response that is personal, loving and devoted. From Job's perspective, spiritual warfare is not a struggle between two opposing forces, each striving to prove itself to be stronger than the other. Rather, it is a conflict between God, who loves freely and unconditionally, and the accuser, who does everything within his means to prove that such love is impossible. What is at stake in this wager between God and Satan is Job's relationship with his Lord.

In a similar scene, that of the temptation in the desert, we have the same issue at stake. When Satan approaches Jesus to tempt him, his first question is, *"If you are the Son of God,* tell these stones to turn into bread" [italics added]. The issue is not whether Jesus could turn stones into bread or jump off the Temple and order the angels to save him. The issue is about what he had heard at the Jordan River, "This is my beloved Son, with him I am well pleased." Satan is not concerned with Jesus' ability to turn stones into bread or to put on a show that demonstrates his power over cosmic forces. Satan wants to raise suspicions, undermine and eventually destroy the unique relationship the Son has with the Father. He is a liar and the father of lies. He introduces a false reality in order to destroy the only true reality. He presents a false reality of power in order to destroy the true reality of the Father's eternal love for his Son.

During Jesus' whole life and mission, his spiritual struggle was to preserve the love, affection and obedience he has for his Father. In his last breath, following the shame and humiliation of the Calvary, he once more declared his love for his Father by saying, "Father, into your hands I commit my spirit." It was this relationship of love and affection – of obedience and submission – that defeated sin and brought about the triumph of the Cross. The Cross is the triumph of love over power.

The risks of dualism

To seek power is always a diabolic choice. That is why both Job and Jesus refuse the ever-so-common and popular path of dualism that considers the world to be divided between two great powers or two mighty forces, each striving for domination over people and history. A book on spiritual warfare was recently published in Brazil. It defines this conflict in the following terms, "In the world there are two opposing kingdoms, two forces that clash in a struggle to control the eternal destiny of all human beings, two powers in confrontation: the power of darkness and the power of light."[2] As the editor sees it, the world is literally divided between two great forces, one good and one evil. We urgently need to choose which side we are on, put on our spiritual armour and head off to defend our Lord Jesus' threatened kingdom. Neither Job nor Jesus sees the world in this manner. The great apocalyptic proclamation is that the Lord reigns.

Soon after having been violently afflicted by the catastrophes brought on by Satan, Job did not say, "The Lord gave me blessings and Satan took them from me. So now I shall bind the enemy and demand back what was taken from me." On the contrary, his words reveal that, although Satan had been the author of all the misfortunes that befell him and his family, he continued putting God at the centre of all that happened. He said, "The Lord gave and the Lord has taken away, blessed be the name of the Lord." When we embrace dualism, spiritual warfare becomes a fight for power, a test to prove who is stronger and more powerful. We enter the arena created by Satan himself and end up using his weapons in the fight. We opt for power and control, and fall into the great trap that Satan has prepared for us. Jesus, when tempted, never used his power to prove himself to Satan or even to the world. One of the thieves crucified with Jesus challenged him, "Aren't you the Christ? Save yourself and us!" Yet Jesus did not feel the need to show off his power to prove that he was truly the Christ. His power and identity had already been proclaimed by the Voice at the Jordan River.

One of the dangers in spiritual warfare is that we may be led into using the same weapons Satan uses, the weapons of power. The world is not divided between two forces. That is why C. S. Lewis says that there is no such thing as a spiritual war, but rather an internal rebellion that is under control. The power that obtained victory over sin and Satan is the power of love, of incarnation, of abandonment, and of self-giving. These are our weapons in this war.

As seen in Job's story, Satan wants to prove that no one loves God selflessly, that no one seeks and serves God simply because God is God, that Job's integrity and righteousness were nothing more than a means of obtaining things from God, and that people only truly love themselves and not God. In this conflict it is important to realise that God's weapons are not the same as Satan's. While Satan resorts to violence, destruction, suffering and pain, thus showing off his powerful arsenal, God uses the covenant made in his name. While Satan destroys, God builds. And while Satan tries to alienate, God reaffirms his eternal, liberating truths.

The dualistic understanding of spiritual warfare that has spread throughout the evangelical church in Brazil and in Latin America has led to other predictable consequences, such as the dissemination of the theology of prosperity and the striving for political power. Both derive from the same spiritual vision that rejects the Cross as the major symbol of Christ's victory. Instead, what matters is the power that will place us among those who control the world. It is a perception that puts Christians in an arena created by Satan, where he himself hands out the weapons. In this struggle for power, which-ever form it may take, Satan will always be the winner.

God has other weapons. God's love transforms our lives and our souls, and frees us from the ambitions of power. It makes us more humble and obedient towards God and his word. We become more committed to God's kingdom and justice, and are filled with love for God, our neighbours and ourselves.

The changes in Job

As we have seen, Job's drama is the result of a wager between God and Satan to test the secret motives that made Job righteous and honest. God trusts in a response based on unselfish love, while Satan expects to see a demand for retribution, as an expression of selfishness. The suffering brought upon Job was designed to reveal which would be his response.

His friends appear on the scene and soon make it clear that their theology only reinforces Satan's argument. For them, it is all quite simple: God blesses the just and punishes the sinner. Therefore, if Job is suffering, it is because he has sinned. Hence, he should acknowledge his sin and confess, in order to get back what was taken from him. In other words, Job should seek God not for God's sake, but for his own sake. But God was the basis of his faith and the object of his love. If he had sought God selfishly, Satan would have won the wager. Job had initially believed in this retribution theology but later rejected the idea and reaffirmed his innocence. He considered himself innocent not because he was not a sinner, but because he could not find in his life a sin that would justify such enormous suffering. In his spiritual battle he has to choose one of three options:

1. Acknowledge that his friends are right and that God is just. This would lead him to deny his innocence and seek God for God's own sake.
2. Acknowledge that his friends are right and that he is innocent. This would lead him to reject God and conclude that God was unjust when God burdened him with such great suffering.
3. Acknowledge that he is innocent and that God is just. This would lead him to reject his friends' retribution theology.

Job chooses the third alternative and this leads him to experience a deep transformation in his manner of speaking about God. He creates what Gustavo Gutiérrez calls the "prophetic language and the contemplative language."

The prophetic language emerges when Job realises that there are other innocent people like him in the world, others oppressed by those who thirst for power. He begins to speak to the poor and suffering using a language that reveals his understanding of the pain of the innocent. The contemplative language arises from the revelation of God as a free and sovereign Lord, whose acts and justice are not determined by humankind but by God's gracious love. When Job recognises God's greatness and majesty, he lowers his head and exclaims that now he sees the Lord with his own eyes.

The reason for the spiritual battle in Job's life was not to determine his capacity for overcoming hardships, nor was it designed to show that God's power is greater than Satan's. Its purpose was to make Job surrender his heart, change his theology (since he used to believe the same things as his friends) and experience God in a way that changed his manner of speaking about God.

Satan's defeat was not measured by power, but by the surrender to God's free and unconditional love. I believe Peter also underwent the same kind of spiritual struggle when the Lord himself called him and said, "Simon, Simon, Satan has asked to sift you as wheat. But I have prayed for you, Simon, that your faith may not fail. And when you have turned back to me, strengthen your brothers" (Luke 22:31–32). When Satan asked to sift Peter, Jesus' response was not the one we often hear in our classical spiritual battles, "You are bound!" On the contrary, Jesus simply said he would pray for Peter, so his faith would not falter. Peter needed sifting. He was too impulsive, and his arrogance and ambition were placing God's kingdom at risk. His weapons of war needed to be neutralised so he could humbly confess his love for the Lord. All Jesus wanted was a declaration of love, not the arrogance of power. Peter was also transformed by the power of God's love and experienced a new language with which to speak of God.

Spiritual warfare and God's silence

The spiritual conflict experienced by Job, Jesus and Peter has one common element: God's silence. It seems to me that in all these cases God allowed Satan to do what Jesus had mentioned to Peter: God let Satan sift them. God's silence is not a mark of indifference but of prayer and intercession. The final response to this silence is the affirmation that, despite the pain inflicted by Satan, our hearts belong eternally to God. Asserting our love for Jesus is the final response to every spiritual battle. We are not involved in a struggle for power. We are not out to show who is more powerful and dominates the universe. Jesus overcame that temptation in the desert and demonstrated his love through the Cross and the Resurrection. God is not interested in showing off his authority or sovereignty. He is in fact the absolute and sovereign Lord, and that was never disputed. He would not share his glory with anyone, not even Satan. The purpose of spiritual warfare is to reveal which side our hearts are on.

Since this is the purpose of the test, God remains silent, waiting for our reply. In certain biblical situations where Satan inflicts pain in order to unmask our most hidden motives, we find God waiting silently for our answer. This is what happened with Job, Peter and Jesus himself. In the role of "accuser," Satan has an important part to play in God's eternal plan: he exposes our masks and hypocrisies, and our alienation and illusions caused by Satan's own lies. That is why Job throughout his spiritual conflict never turned to Satan, but only to God. He sought only the truth that is God himself. God is his counsel and justifier. He is the One who defends his cause and who will grant him salvation and redemption.

Conclusion

The perception of spiritual warfare as a struggle for power and control over people, the world and history has led the evangelical church into using the same weapons as Satan. The church has lost sight of the true and deeper meaning of spiritual warfare, which is to transform us, our ideas and values, as well as those theologies that try to make God fit into evil's power schemes. Our calling is to go up to Calvary, to suffer all the implications of love and service, and to resist all the onslaughts of evil in its attempt to sidetrack us from the path to Jerusalem. Spiritual victory is the result of unselfish and unconditional love for God and his kingdom. As long as we are righteous in our motives and desires, as long as we keep to the path of discipleship and the Cross, as long as we are obedient and devoted to the Lord and his word, we will remain on the side of the One who is and will always be the winner.

Notes

[1] Walter Wink, *Unmasking the Powers: The Invisible Forces that Determine Human Existence* (Philadelphia: Fortress Press, 1986), 11.

[2] Opal Reddin, ed. *Confronto de Poderes* (São Paulo: VIDA, 1996), in English, *Power Encounter: A Pentecostal Perspective* (Springfield, Mo.: Central Bible College Press, 1989). This is a collection of texts from the Pentecostal perspective; the quotation is found on the book's back cover.

3

Spiritual conflict in illness and affliction

JOHN CHRISTOPHER THOMAS

The task of laying a biblical foundation for a theological discussion of spiritual warfare is an extremely difficult one. On the one hand, a comprehensive examination of the many relevant biblical texts would require much more time than can be allotted to this dimension of the issue at a consultation of this nature. On the other hand, such an examination might generate an interpretation of the biblical text that is less than holistic owing to the fact that this issue, as any other, is only one dimension of the biblical witness and undue attention to it might give a false impression of its significance. Thus, I shall attempt to offer one slice of the larger whole as a means of gaining leverage on this challenging issue.

The aspect of this topic on which I shall focus is the origins of illness in New Testament thought. Such an approach is especially suited for this consultation in that often discussions about spiritual warfare focus on the issues of infirmity and healing. By focusing on origins of illness, a better understanding of spiritual warfare may be attained as the role of the Devil and demons in afflicting individuals is seen alongside other origins of illness, thereby preserving the tension of the biblical text itself on this topic.

Much of this presentation is a slightly revised version of J. C. Thomas, "The Devil, Disease and Deliverance: Origins of Illness in New Testament Thought," *Journal of Pentecostal Theology Supplement Series* 13 (Sheffield: Sheffield Academic Press, 1998), 296–319.

In a previous investigation I sought to discover New Testament thinking and attitudes about origins of illness by examining the various New Testament writings on their own terms.[1] That study attempted to allow the different New Testament voices to be heard in all their variety and diversity before putting them into dialogue with one another. In the first portion of this presentation I shall share my thoughts on how the various voices might be placed into dialogue with one another in order to push towards the possible construction of a New Testament theology of the Devil, disease and deliverance.

Origins of illness in New Testament thought

An examination of relevant texts reveals that the New Testament identifies three primary causes of illness and/or infirmities: God, the Devil and/or demons, and what might most appropriately be called natural (or neutral) causes.

GOD AS SOURCE OF INFIRMITY AND/OR DEATH

One of the points on which there is a great deal of agreement in the New Testament materials is that God is often attributed a role in the origins of illness. In fact, God is described as the direct or indirect source of infirmity by the majority of New Testament writers (James, Paul, John, Luke) who deal with the origins of illness, the lone exceptions being Mark and Matthew. Generally speaking, the New Testament writers show little of the reluctance many modern students of the New Testament exhibit in assigning to God an active role in the affliction of individuals with disease and/or death. God's involvement in the origins of illness is not presented in a monolithic fashion but as multifaceted. Specifically, infirmity and/or death can be used by God as a pedagogical device, an instrument of punishment, a source of sanctification, a means of spreading the Gospel or an instrument of salvation. Each of these dimensions is explored briefly.

Infirmity and death as pedagogical device

On more than one occasion and by more than one writer, God is described as sending an illness or death in an attempt to teach those identified as part of the Christian community that sin must not be tolerated but dealt with in an appropriate manner. On such occasions the affliction appears as God's way of calling the believers' attention to their sin. In these situations it is clear that a causal relationship exists between sin and affliction. However, unlike later theological reflection on the subject, there is no suggestion in these texts that the affliction is inherent in the sin. Rather, it is either implied or stated explicitly that the affliction comes directly from God as a result of the sin. For both James and Paul, in cases where God is the origin of an affliction the purpose is to draw the attention of the individual or community to the sin in question and the need for repentance. While James (5) does not indicate the precise nature of the sin which results in illness, other writers disclose the reason for the affliction. Paul makes clear in 1 Corinthians 11 that abuses at the Lord's table have resulted not only in illness but even death. Luke's description of Zechariah's mute condition (Luke 1) is attributed to the unbelief he exhibits in response to the divine promise spoken by the angel Gabriel. Each passage implies that discernment on the part of the individuals and/or the community involved would result in avoidance of such culpable behaviour.

Consequently, had such discernment taken place these afflictions would not have occurred in the first place. In James 5, removal of such afflictions is assured by the combination of confession and intercessory prayer. The communal dimension is evident in at least the Jacobian and Pauline texts.

On one occasion an affliction sent by God plays some role in the salvation of an individual. In the well-known story of Saul's conversion, the encounter with the risen Christ leaves Saul blind, evidenced by the fact that the former persecutor of the church must now be led by the hand in order to find his way (Acts 9:8–9). While it could be argued that the blind condition was simply a byproduct of the brilliance of the Christophany, it would be odd indeed for the reader not to see the hand of God actively at work in this event. The blindness serves to provide Saul with a sufficiently solitary experience in which the significance of his encounter with Jesus might be adequately pondered. In that sense it might be appropriate to describe this affliction as a pedagogical tool by which Saul is brought to faith.

Infirmity and death as punishment

Closely related to the idea of affliction as pedagogical device is that of affliction as punishment by God. In cases where illness or death are the result of divine punishment, they are said to have resulted in relation to a variety of reasons. John (5:14) indicates that the infirmity of the man at the pool of Bethesda is the result of sin and that the continuation of sin might result in a worse physical calamity. While Jesus' warning about "something worse" might serve a pedagogical function, there is no suggestion that the previous infirmity played such a role. On this occasion the nature of the man's sin is not disclosed. The Book of Acts tells of three deaths attributed to the hand of God. The first two deaths are the result of attempts to counterfeit the work of the Holy Spirit within the early Christian community (Acts 5:1–11). Such punishment is all the more significant because it comes to those within the believing community, Ananias and Sapphira. In this passage the only pedagogical value comes through the fear in the community and beyond – fear evoked from knowledge of their deaths. God's hand of judgement is certain.

Opposition to the gospel also can result in divine punishment. Both Herod (Acts 12:19b-23), who is killed by the Angel of the Lord, and Elymas the magician (Acts 13:6–12) are smitten by God. In the case of Herod, the affliction primarily functions as a punitive act, while Elymas's blindness may carry with it the hope of salvation for the magician, as Paul's own blindness serves as a catalyst in his move towards faith in Jesus. It may be significant that most of the examples of God's punitive acts occur in the Book of Acts.

Affliction and the spread of the gospel

God is presented not only as one who sends affliction as a teaching or punitive device, but also as one who can use affliction to further the spread of the gospel. Two New Testament texts present God as using infirmity in precisely this manner. Both the blind man in John (9) and Paul, who suffers from a weakness in the flesh in Galatians (4), experience infirmity in order that God might accomplish his purpose through the revelation of his message. With the blind man the reader is told that this condition exists in order that the works of God might be revealed. Such a statement is a response to the disciples' question about the origin of the man's condition and at the same time a sign that such an action on God's behalf is not viewed as something distasteful by John. Clearly this statement conveys the sense that God may send (or use) affliction to suit his purpose, in this case the manifestation of his works, in order to generate the faith that leads to eternal life. In similar fashion, Paul's illness described in Galatians (4) results in the preaching of the gospel to the Galatians. This illness, which could have proven to be a stumbling block or obstacle to the Galatians, turns out to be the very occasion for them to hear the message of salvation about Jesus Christ. The implication is that God's hand can be seen even in this illness, for it serves his ultimate purpose.

Affliction and sanctification

A final category of affliction attributed to God concerns Paul's thorn in the flesh (2 Cor. 7–10). If the thorn is understood to be a physical ailment rather than a reference to Paul's opponents, it becomes a clear reference to God's use of affliction to work his purpose in the life of his servant. Specifically, Paul explains that the thorn, which comes from a messenger of Satan, is for his ultimate good. Despite Paul's petitions for it to be removed, the thorn is an instrument of sanctification in Paul's life; it is designed to keep Paul from being conceited, owing to the greatness of the revelations disclosed to him. In this case, then, an infirmity, even one which has Satanic connections, can be sent by God and used by him to accomplish his desire in his messenger.

Conclusion

Far from being viewed simply as a source of healing, God, in the view of many New Testament writers, can be depicted as the origin of infirmity or death. When he is described in such a way there always seem to be specific reasons for his actions. Thus, God is seen to be sovereign, one who may act in ways that will achieve his will, a God who is to be approached with (a holy) fear. Such evidence suggests that the New Testament writers did not always attribute infirmity to Satan but worked with a more dialectical worldview, a world where God could also afflict. Such an understanding suggests that God is not only able to use suffering indirectly to accomplish his purposes, but he can also take a direct role in this activity.

THE DEVIL AND/OR DEMONS AS SOURCE OF INFIRMITY

It comes as little surprise that several New Testament writers attribute infirmity to the Devil and/or his demons. What is somewhat unexpected is that not all writers make such attributions, and some writers who make this attribution offer fewer examples than one might be led to expect. While there is a certain amount of diversity in views on the role of the Devil and demons in the sending of affliction, one might attempt to put the evidence together in the following manner.

The nature of the evidence

The attribution of infirmity to the Devil or demons is primarily confined to three New Testament documents: Matthew, Luke and Acts. Neither James nor John gives any hint that the Devil or demons have a role to play in the infliction of infirmity. In Paul, where there appears to be one attribution, the thorn in the flesh, it is perhaps not insignificant that, despite the close connection between the thorn and the messenger of Satan, God is identified as the ultimate origin of the thorn. The only other attribution of an infirmity to a demon, outside Matthew and Luke-Acts, is found in Mark 9, where a demon-possessed boy is afflicted by a "dumb" spirit which, among other things, seeks to kill him. While this text is similar to some of those found in the other synoptic Gospels, it is at least noteworthy that Mark does not make such a connection clear in other places where its synoptic counterparts do.

The relationship of demon possession to infirmity

There are numerous accounts in the New Testament of demon possession as a malady. The victims of demon possession are described as being dominated by the demon or unclean spirit to the extent that they lose the ability to control or perform normal bodily functions. At times, the convulsions and other body or motor responses prove to be so violent and uncontrollable that they place both the victims and those near them in danger of physical harm.

In contrast to claims made both at the scholarly and popular levels, the New Testament writers generally make a clear distinction between demon possession and illness. For example, Mark is very careful to keep the lines of demarcation between the categories distinct, with Mark 9 being the only occasion where demon possession and infirmity converge. This cautious approach, along with the attribution of several infirmities to God and the fact that many accounts of healing in the Synoptics give no hint as to the origin of the infirmity (let alone attribute the illness to a demon), suggests that for the New Testament writers there was no simple equation between infirmity and the demonic. To make such a dubious equation the starting point for an explanation of the origins of illness in the New Testament errs methodologically by not paying sufficient attention to the New Testament documents themselves.

In addition to the numerous cases of demon possession in which infirmity does not play a role, there are a number of occasions in the Synoptics and Acts in which infirmities of various kinds are attributed to demon possession. These maladies include deafness, muteness, blindness and epilepsy. It may not be insignificant that some of these very same infirmities also appear in contexts with no connection to demonic activity. While not all demon possession is directly related to infirmity, there is a connection at several places in Matthew and Luke in particular. In these accounts it is evident that there would be no infirmity if not for the demon possession. On occasions such as these, the remedy for the malady is exorcism. In this regard it should be observed that Mark 9 suggests the existence of different classes of demons, some of whom are more difficult to exorcise than others.

Although careful to distinguish between demon possession and illness, Matthew seems to regard certain forms of demon possession as a category of illness, in that he lists demon possession alongside epilepsy and paralysis as major infirmities which Jesus healed (Matt. 4:24). As such, Matthew occasionally uses healing language where one might expect the vocabulary of exorcism. Luke blurs the lines of demarcation further, not only failing to distinguish between demon possession and infirmity but also leaving the reader unable to be as certain about the origins of illness as do other New Testament writers. However, it is interesting that in Acts, while the lines continue to be occasionally blurred in summary statements, there is not a single concrete example of an illness being directly attributed to demonic activity.

However the evidence is read, there can be little disagreement about the fact that the Synoptics and Acts regard a number of infirmities as being the direct result of demon possession.

Demonic affliction distinct from demon possession

In addition to the attribution of infirmity to demon possession there are also two or three occasions where an infirmity is attributed to demonic activity without any suggestion that the afflicted person is under the (complete) control of the unclean spirit or is regarded as demon possessed. These specific cases include Paul's thorn in the flesh, which is identified with a messenger from Satan; Luke's account of Simon's mother-in-law; and the woman with a spirit of infirmity. In each of these accounts the individual sufferer is afflicted by a spirit but the signs of demon possession are absent. In fact, aside from the affliction, there is nothing in the texts to suggest that the reader is to view the sufferer in anything but a positive light. Thus the reader is led to the conclusion that there is a category of demonically inflicted infirmity separate from demon possession proper. Individuals who suffer in this way are not described as being in need of exorcism (or deliverance) as much as healing, which would involve the removal of the cause of the affliction.

In the case of the woman with a spirit of infirmity, Jesus simply pronounces her well, laying his hands upon her, and she immediately straightens up (Luke 13:10–16). When encountering Simon's mother-in-law (Luke 4:38–39), he rebukes the fever and it leaves. If the fever is to be viewed as demonically induced (as appears likely), it is significant that Jesus does not engage the demon in conversation, as he had done in the previous pericope, but simply rebukes it. That the remedy in cases such as these is not as clear cut as in those of demon possession is demonstrated by the case of Paul, whose petitions for the thorn's removal are met with a revelation that the thorn is there to stay. The messenger of Satan will continue his work, for in this messenger God is himself working on Paul's behalf. Thus, it appears that the New Testament knows of a category of demonic activity separate from demon possession in which individuals who appear to be in a positive relationship with God suffer infirmity.

Attack by sinister forces

A final observation should be offered before concluding this section. There is some evidence within the New Testament that sinister forces could attack a messenger of God in an attempt to thwart the preaching of the gospel. The place in the Acts narrative which describes Paul's snakebite on Malta (28:1–6) suggests that the reader of Acts would see more than coincidence in this event, especially given the previous promises by Jesus about the protection and authority of his followers who encounter all manner of opposition (Luke 10:17–20). Despite this attack, God's messenger is preserved from harm in order to complete the mission to which he is called.

INFIRMITY AND NATURAL CAUSES

A number of infirmities in the New Testament might best be described as owing their origin to neutral or natural causes. This observation is based on several facts. First, the vast majority of New Testament references to infirmities do not give any indication as to the origin of the particular malady in question. Such references occur in every New Testament writing that contains reference to an infirmity. While it is theoretically possible to attribute all these infirmities to the Devil, or a world estranged from God, or the effects of sin in the world, and so forth, the texts themselves do not explicitly offer support for such a view. Second, on more than one occasion it is explicitly stated that sin is not the cause of certain infirmities (cf. esp. John 9 and James 5). James 5 leaves open the prospect of the origin of illnesses which are not the result of sin. Third, in two Lukan texts (13:1–3, 4–5) Jesus makes clear that calamities are not necessarily a gauge of one's spirituality. Fourth, in discussing Paul's co-workers who are ill (Phil. 2:25–30; 1 Tim. 5:23; 2 Tim. 4:20), the Pauline literature never suggests that there is anything sinister behind their condition. This attitude suggests that Paul regards such illness in a somewhat neutral fashion. Therefore, it is fair to say that certain, if not the majority, of infirmities are treated by New Testament writers as neutral in terms of origin.

Responses to illness

Given the various origins of and purposes for infirmity in the New Testament, it comes as no surprise that responses to illness take a variety of forms. However, here too one finds a significant amount of overlap in the responses to infirmity as recounted in the New Testament writings.

Prayer

One of the more common responses to infirmity in the New Testament is prayer. Not only does the evidence of James 5 indicate that prayer plays an integral role in the healing of the sick, but Paul's practice in 2 Corinthians 12 also indicates that prayer may have been his own habit in the face of infirmity. In fact, the evidence from this latter passage suggests that it may have been Paul's habit to continue in prayer about a specific infirmity until either healing occurred or he "heard from God" (as Paul says that he did) that the malady is not to be removed but is to serve a purpose in keeping with the divine will. It may not be going too far to suspect that prayer had a place in the ministry of those with the gifts of healings and perhaps accompanied the practice of the laying on of hands. Mark 9 indicates (as does much of the Marcan narrative) that prayer plays a crucial role in the casting out of demons, as the disciples are there told that "this kind of demon" comes out only by prayer. The idea of prayer in the face of infirmity is also found in Luke-Acts. Thus, it is fair to say that part of the New Testament response to infirmity ordinarily includes some form of prayer.

Discernment

Given the diverse origins of infirmity and the fact that the same malady may be attributed to as many as three separate causes respectively on different occasions in the New Testament, it is clear that discernment plays a crucial role in the process of responding to infirmity. This point may be illustrated by the two attested categories: (1) infirmity that results from sin, and (2) infirmity that results from demon possession.

In cases of sin as the cause of an illness several things are said. First, James 5 seems to assume that when sin is the cause of an illness, such a sin would be readily known to the individual sufferer. This same assumption appears to be present in John 5:14, where Jesus warns the man recently made whole to "stop sinning lest something worse come upon you." Additionally, at least one text reveals the role of the community in the discernment of sin. Paul's admonition to the Corinthians with regard to the illness and death in the community (1 Cor. 11) shows that members of the community should be active in discerning the reason for the presence of such in the church. If they had discerned (judged) themselves, the Corinthians would not have come under the judgement of the Lord as they had. Finally, several texts testify to the fact that a vital role in the discernment process is played by leaders in the community. Of course, one of the primary examples of such discernment is the role played by Jesus. He is not only able to detect when the presence of sin is behind an infirmity (John 5:14), but he is also able to discern when this is not the case (John 9:3; Luke 13:1–5). In addition to Paul's ability in this regard, mentioned earlier, Peter also detects (through the Holy Spirit) the presence of sin among those in the community when he prophesies judgement upon Ananias and Sapphira in Acts 5. From the reader's vantage point, another leader – the narrator of Luke's Gospel – displays the ability to discern the presence of sin in the account of Zechariah's unbelief and resulting punishment.

In the discernment of demonic activity standing behind an infirmity, the New Testament discloses two primary categories. First, demon possession seems to be readily identifiable by most anyone close to the individual so afflicted. This observation is based on the comments made by the father of the demon-possessed boy in Mark 9, the mother of the demon-possessed girl in Matthew 15, and the actions of those who bring to Jesus demon-possessed individuals who suffer infirmities owing to the presence of demons (cf. esp. Matt. 9:32; 12:23). Second, in addition to discernment of this more general nature, the New Testament also testifies to the ability to discern the presence of demonic activity behind an infirmity which might not otherwise be known. Such appears to be the case with Paul's knowledge of the satanic nature of his thorn, as well as Jesus' disclosure about Satan's role (through a spirit of infirmity) in the affliction of a woman who for eighteen years had not been able to stand up straight (Luke 13:11, 16). To these examples might be added the narrators who often inform the readers as to which infirmities are from demonic sources and which are from other sources.

These examples indicate that discernment is extraordinarily important in the New Testament responses to infirmity.

CONFESSION AND INTERCESSION

When sin stands behind an infirmity in the New Testament, one of the responses called for is confession. Although implied in other texts, this response is made explicit in James 5. In this text, when it is determined that sin is the cause of an illness, those individuals are called upon to confess their sin. This confession is to be made to one another (other members of the community) for the express purpose of intercession. The implication of this admonition is that such confession is to result in forgiveness and healing. In fact, it is probably fair to say that when sin is viewed as the cause of an illness, confession would normally be thought to end in healing.

It is significant that confession does not stand alone in James 5 but is to be accompanied by intercession. Intercessory prayer is described as efficacious and has roots deep in New Testament spirituality, which is filled with admonitions that presuppose mutual accountability among believers as a given in the early Christian worldview.

EXORCISM

When an infirmity is the result of demon possession, the only response found in the New Testament texts is exorcism. It is perhaps significant that the exorcisms cited in this presentation are performed only upon those "outside" the believing community.[2] There is no account of an exorcism within the church itself. The picture of Paul that emerges from the letters which bear his name and from the Book of Acts illustrates this point. In the letters Paul never makes reference to exorcism, while in Acts exorcisms are attributed to him. While it is possible to explain this situation as simply the difference in Luke's Paul and the Paul of the Pauline literature, it may also be that the context determines the content. That is to say, perhaps there is no mention of exorcism in the letters because there is no evidence that exorcisms occurred inside the believing community, while Luke's account of Paul focuses on Paul's missionary activity outside the believing community, where exorcisms are said to have taken place. This observation may be supplemented by the fact that there is no mention of exorcisms in the New Testament outside the Synoptics and Acts. Such evidence might suggest that in New Testament thought exorcism occurred solely in a missionary or evangelistic context.

The nearest New Testament analogies to the occurrence of an exorcism inside the community of faith are found in that category of infirmity caused by demons but distinct from demon possession

proper. In these few cases it is true that the affliction is attributed to
Satan or a demon, but there are significant differences as well. Only
in the story of Simon's mother-in-law is there anything remotely
resembling an exorcism, and there the resemblance is simply the
rebuke of the fever and its departure. In the case of the woman in
Luke 13, the condition (aside from its description as a spirit of infirmity – a binding by Satan) and healing (the laying on of hands – no
speech directed to the spirit) resemble what is seen in other non-
demonic infirmities and cures. With Paul's thorn, it is extraordinary
that if exorcism were needed to expel this messenger of Satan, God's
response is that Paul can live with the condition. As with the other
two texts, this passage bears little resemblance to demon possession and none to exorcism. Thus, even with this additional category
of infirmities inflicted by Satan and/or his demons, the New Testament evidence for the presence of exorcisms within the believing
community is very slim if not nonexistent.

As for the methods of exorcism,[3] it would seem that prayer, at
least before the event, is essential. The disciples experience failure
at just this point (Mark 9). In the New Testament accounts of exorcism there is little if any physical contact between the deliverer (Jesus,
the Twelve, Philip, or Paul) and the possessed. Aside from the possibility that the laying on of hands occasionally accompanied exorcism (in Luke's Gospel alone), a point that is not altogether clear,
the closest one comes to such is the account of contact with pieces
of cloth that had touched Paul's body being used to effect healings
and exorcisms (Acts 19). Instead of physical contact the New Testament texts depict a conversation, at most, between the deliverer
and the demon or unclean spirit. Ordinarily such conversations include the cry of the demon, in which there is an acknowledgement
of Jesus' true identity (and authority). On one occasion, Jesus asks
an evil spirit to reveal its name (Mark 5:9), but ordinarily Jesus simply silences the demons, refusing to let them speak, and drives them
out with a word. On most every occasion, the effect is immediate.[4]
Judging from Matthew 12:43–45 and Luke 11:24–26, those delivered from demons are expected to follow up their exorcism with
acceptance of the Gospel in order to ensure that the expelled demons will not return, for such a return would result in a condition
worse than the former state.

MEDICINE

In addition to the responses just described, there is one indication
in the New Testament texts that medicine might also be viewed as

an appropriate response to an infirmity in certain situations. This comment is based on 1 Timothy 5:23, where Timothy is admonished to take a little wine for his stomach's sake on account of his frequent illness (1 Tim. 5:23). The context, which is concerned with Timothy's health, makes clear that the wine is here being prescribed as a medicinal aid. Thus, while perhaps representing only a small strand in New Testament thought, the use of medicine as a response to infirmity cannot be ignored altogether.

Implications for theology and ministry

In the first part of this presentation on the biblical text I proposed one way in which the various writings of the New Testament might be drawn upon in the construction of a New Testament theology on this topic in order to gain some leverage on the larger question of spiritual warfare. In this portion of the presentation I seek to extend the study by offering a set of reflections on the implications of the previous section for theology and ministry. My goal is twofold. First, it is my hope that these reflections will make clearer the way in which this more limited study on origins of illness helps in the understanding of spiritual warfare. Second, it is my hope that these reflections will be received as an invitation to dialogue about this most important topic across a variety of theological disciplines.

THE ROLE OF PRAYER

Earlier it was suggested that prayer, one might even say fervent prayer, is always an appropriate response to infirmity. This observation is based upon the admonition of James 5, which gives explicit directives to the church when there are those in the community who are ill. It is further supported by Paul's apparent practice when faced with the thorn in the flesh and the example of Jesus and others within the narratives of the Gospels and Acts. It appears that such prayer should, in most cases, precede any other action, with the possible exception of anointing with oil.[5] The fact that the cause or origin of a specific infirmity may be unknown should result in no hesitancy about whether or not fervent prayer is appropriate. On the basis of a variety of New Testament texts such prayer, whether offered by a leader, one who possesses the gifts of healings, a group of elders, or other members of the community, should be offered with the full expectation that the infirm person will receive healing. While it is clear that not all are healed in all cases cited in the New Testament literature, it is difficult to ignore the impression that emerges from reading the texts themselves that in the vast majority of cases the writers (and readers with them) exhibit an extraordinary expectancy with regard to healing.

Although the majority of New Testament cases suggests that healings were immediate, there is some evidence to suggest that one is to keep praying for healing until one hears from God. Such an idea may appeal for support to Mark 8:22–26, where Jesus twice lays hands upon a blind man before the man receives complete healing. Additional support for this suggestion may be found in Paul's own approach when faced with the thorn in the flesh. The fact that Paul prayed not once but three times for its removal may imply that the apostle would have kept on praying if he had not heard from God as to its "permanent" nature. Thus, rather than becoming overly discouraged or embarrassed in those cases where the sick are not healed, it appears that individual and community alike are on good grounds to continue in prayer for healing.

THE ROLE OF DISCERNMENT

The suggestion that one should continue in prayer until the infirmity is removed or one hears from God leads rather naturally to the next major implication of this study. Although it is always appropriate to respond to any infirmity with prayer, it is also clear that discernment plays a crucial role in the ministry of healing especially as it relates to the Devil, disease and deliverance. Not only do the New Testament documents indicate that discernment is a part of many situations described, but they also imply that the readers of these documents are to have a place for discernment as an ongoing part of their community life. How might such evidence inform theology and ministry?

Discernment is a topic which is very difficult to define, as it at first glance seems to be an almost entirely intuitive process. Yet, it is possible to gain some understanding of the process by identifying the things discerned in the New Testament and those who are shown discerning them. In order to accomplish this goal, attention is given to the dynamics of the discerning process as it relates to the origins of illness.

The discernment of sin

As noted above, sin is depicted in several New Testament documents as an origin of illness. Several significant factors emerge from an examination of those contexts. On each occasion (James 5; 1 Cor. 11; and John 5), there is the clear assumption expressed that the individual who suffers an infirmity owing to sin would know of the presence of sin and its nature. Despite the fact that someone else (a leader of some sort) indicates a knowledge of the presence of sin, none of these texts suggests that the sufferer would be unaware of the sin or surprised by such an identification. Rather, the individual who bears the infirmity would appear to know full well the nature of the sin and, consequently, would play a crucial role in the discernment process. Thus, the admonitions of James to confess, of Paul to examine, and of Jesus to stop sinning reveal that the first step in discerning the origin of an illness on the part of a believer is an examination of self to discern whether sin may be the origin of a particular infirmity.

Another part of this discernment process is played by leaders in the community. Often in contexts where sin is identified as the origin of an infirmity, the presence of sin is known or alluded to by an individual portrayed as in an authoritative position. In the case of James, the author merely mentions the possibility that sin may lie behind some illness, while Paul, Jesus and Peter (Acts 5) appear to know of sin's presence by the revelatory work of Holy Spirit and/ or the supernatural knowledge of Jesus. While the role of leadership in the discernment process is important, it should not be forgotten that in the New Testament, the discernment by leaders tends to confirm that which should already be known by the individual sufferer.

The community itself also plays a role in the discernment process as it relates to sin. Here there appear to be two primary functions. The community offers the context for the discerning judgement for which Paul calls, and the community provides an appropriate context for confession of sin and the resulting intercession. Thus, the community provides the support and balance necessary for the process of discernment.

The discernment of divine chastisement

Closely related to the discernment of sin is the discernment of the hand of God in affliction, for in the vast majority of New Testament cases there is a clear connection between sin as origin of illness and God as the one who afflicts. If sin as the origin of an infirmity can be discerned by the individual believer, then it follows that the presence of the hand of God in infirmity can also be discerned in those cases. In addition to what has been said about the discernment of sin generally, a few other observations might be offered.

First, on those occasions in the New Testament where an infirmity is deemed to be the result of sin, the implication is that God stands behind the affliction(s). Interestingly enough, sin does not appear to function as an autonomous force as an origin of illness. Rather, in those cases reference is made in an explicit or implicit way to God and/or his agents. Second, often divine affliction is accompanied by a revelation of its origin. This revelation may come through an angelic visitation, prophetically spoken words, words from Jesus or a Christophanic message from the risen Christ. Third, on occasion the divine origin of an affliction is discerned only after sufficient time has passed to allow for an assessment of the results of the infirmity for the gospel's sake, as in the case of Paul's preaching to the Galatians on account of a weakness in the flesh and the case of the blind man in John 9. In addition, the purpose of Paul's thorn is discerned by means of a divine word from the risen Christ only after a period of prayerful intercession.

The discernment of the demonic

The discernment of a demonic origin of infirmity is also described in the New Testament documents. For our purposes, two aspects of the discernment process are most significant. First, it is clear that on certain occasions the discernment of a demonic presence in an infirmity is based primarily upon observation of the person afflicted. For example, when the father of the demon-possessed boy comes to the disciples and then Jesus for help, it is the father who informs Jesus of the boy's condition. From the text it is apparent that the father's assessment is based upon the convulsions which endanger the boy's life. Other similar diagnoses of the demonic origin of certain illness in the New Testament are probably best viewed as in line with the case of this father. However, it is also clear that the same kind of infirmity could be attributed to the demonic on one occasion, God on another occasion, and treated in a rather neutral fashion on still another occasion. Thus, while the observation of various phenomena may be a part of the discernment process with regard to the demonic, it is certainly not the whole process.

The second aspect of the discernment process with regard to the demonic includes what might be called an intuitive dimension. This dimension has special reference to those immediate diagnoses on the part of Jesus and others where an infirmity is attributed without delay to the demonic. Such discernment is the result of a special or supernatural knowledge which appears to be attributable to the Holy Spirit's activity. This ability, as with the ability to discern sin as an origin of illness, is primarily confined to those who are regarded as leaders in a given community. Perhaps the Pauline "gift of discernment" is the means by which the discernment of demonic afflictions is possible (1 Cor. 12:10). If so, then others in the community would be able to operate in this fashion, while the need for this gift among leaders would be especially crucial.

Conclusion

The role of discernment in the healing ministry of the church is crucial and should work to supplement the prayer of the believing community. Although there may be occasions where the Holy Spirit instantaneously reveals the origin and/or purpose of a given infirmity, ordinarily it appears that the process of discernment may take some time to operate. The New Testament picture suggests that discernment requires a communal context, the involvement of the individual sufferer (except perhaps in the case of certain infirmities brought on by demon possession), as well as the leaders of the believing community. There is also a role for other believers to play a part in this process, particularly those with the gift of discernment.

THE ROLE OF CONFESSION

When an infirmity is the result of sin in the life of a believer, the appropriate response is confession. Such confession is to be made to the believing community in order that intercession might be made on behalf of the one who has sinned. It appears that in some New Testament communities public confession was practised. The fact that there is no place for such confession in many contemporary churches is more an indication of the church's superficiality and fragmentation than it is a sign of the early church's naiveté or lack of sophistication. Part of the problem with appropriating such a practice today is that in some parts of the world churches are no longer communities but rather collections of individuals. It would appear that the church has paid the price for failing to provide an opportunity for confession as a regular and ongoing part of the community's worship. Confession on the New Testament order where community does not exist would, no doubt, prove to be foolhardy. Therefore, the challenge facing us is not to give up forever on this vital dimension of community life, but rather to work for the construction of communities where believers are loved and nurtured in a familial fashion. Perhaps a first step in the reappropriation of regular confession (in places where it is no longer practised) would be to make a place for the practice of foot-washing, given its prominent emphasis on forgiveness and the community's involvement in the act.[6]

THE ROLE OF EXORCISM, DELIVERANCE AND SANCTIFICATION

Given the current preoccupation with exorcism and deliverance in some circles, it is especially important to make clear any implications of this study for this dimension of theology and ministry. The following observations are tentatively offered.

First, in the light of the fact that in the New Testament only a small percentage (perhaps 10 per cent) of infirmities are attributed to the demonic, it would seem wise to avoid the temptation of assuming that in most cases an infirmity is caused by Satan and/or demons. Such a realization and in some cases adjustment in thinking could serve to bring a degree of moderation through biblical critique to an area that has been and continues to be sorely abused. As the New Testament texts are not guilty of indiscriminate attributions of infirmities to the demonic, ministers of healing would seem obliged to show a similar restraint and caution in the attribution of origins of illness.

Second, the fact that in the New Testament there is no evidence that exorcisms took place within the church but rather seem to have occurred outside the church in evangelistic contexts suggests that the current specialization in exorcisms by some in the church is misdirected at the least. This statement should not be taken to mean that exorcisms have no place in the church at all but rather to point out that the current practice of many is at odds to some extent with the Scriptures, texts which most practitioners treat as authoritative guides in their theology and ministry.

Third, even though the New Testament gives some evidence that believers may suffer from infirmities in which Satan or demons are involved, these texts give no evidence that believers may be demon possessed or oppressed to an extent where the sufferers lose control of their faculties. Speaking to this issue is complicated by the ambiguity which surrounds the meaning of the word *Christian* in many contexts today. If one wishes to include within the category of believer so-called nominal Christians or those who may no longer consider themselves to be believers but are part of traditions which still regard them as Christian, owing to a previous profession of faith or baptism, then perhaps one can argue for the domination of such "Christians" by demons. However, such modern ways of defining the term *Christian* do not take seriously enough the lines of demarcation which the New Testament draws between believers and unbelievers. Thus, while the New Testament makes clear the reality of the demonic, and perhaps few participants at this consultation would wish to dispute this reality, there is precious little evidence in the

New Testament to support many of the claims that come from some of those in the "deliverance ministry." In point of fact, the very New Testament texts that might be appealed to as support for the view that it is theoretically possible for Christians to suffer an infirmity brought by a demon do not even hint that such believers are in need of exorcism but either treat the removal of the infirmity as an "ordinary" healing or indicate that the infirmity is to remain, in accordance with the divine will.

Fourth, numbers of believers have long had an appreciation for the fact that the Christian journey includes a struggle against the flesh. In fact, it has not been uncommon for phrases like "the Devil has a hold" on a particular individual to describe the extent of the struggle. However, even where such language has been employed there has been little or no suggestion that the person was possessed by the Devil or a demon. Rather, these battles were understood in the context of the pursuit of holiness of life. Perhaps one way forward is for theologians and practitioners to give consideration to the (re)appropriation of the doctrine and practice of sanctification. Such a (re)appropriation might accomplish at least two things: (1) It would provide an opportunity for serious self-examination which acknowledges the reality of the struggle against the Devil, sin and flesh but in a way that is much more at home with the biblical texts. (2) It would facilitate an appropriate use of exorcism language by restricting its usage to those occasions on which demon possession is clearly present.

Fifth, it appears that part of the confusion over exorcism and deliverance has resulted from an uncritical application of exorcism language to describe the spiritual and scriptural experience of sanctification. Since exorcism (often called deliverance) has become for many *the* paradigm for dealing with any number of spiritual problems, it is not surprising that similar expected phenomena have accompanied times of "deliverance." If sanctification again finds a place in the vocabulary and life of the church's spirituality, perhaps those in the tradition may find a way past this current controversial impasse.

THE ROLE OF DOCTORS

It might not be unwise to conclude the second section of this presentation with a final observation about the implications of this study for the use of medicine and doctors. Given the fact that in the Pastorals the medicinal use of wine can be prescribed for Timothy's stomach problems, a total rejection of the use of doctors appears to outdistance the New Testament teaching and thus may do much to harm rather than help.

Spiritual warfare and world evangelisation

In this section we address the issue of spiritual warfare and world evangelisation more directly by offering a set of observations that are based upon the biblical text generally and by making explicit additional implications of the more narrowly focused study in the preceding sections.

First, it should be observed from the outset that the text of the New Testament is very clear about the fact that signs, miracles and wonders are very much a part of the church's proclamation of the gospel. Evidence for this assessment is found in all the Gospels, Acts, the Pauline literature (Rom. 15:18–19; 2 Cor. 12:12; Gal. 3:5; 1 Thess. 1:5), Hebrews (2:4; 6:5), and the Apocalypse. Many of these texts reveal that such miraculous events do not simply accompany or confirm the proclamation of the gospel but are themselves a proclamation of the gospel. Thus, while there may be room for disagreement on the issue of spiritual warfare, it would appear that those committed to the task of world evangelisation must have an appreciation of and place for signs, wonders and miracles as part of gospel proclamation if their evangelistic work is to be in keeping with the text of the New Testament as a whole.

Second, there is indeed a very strong emphasis in certain New Testament books upon the kingdom of God. The Gospels are consistent in affirming both that the kingdom is present and yet has a future dimension. One of the ways in which the kingdom is shown to be present is in the exorcisms which Jesus performs (Matt. 12:28; Luke 11:20). When his followers, the Seventy[-Two], return from their ministry mission, which includes the exorcism of demons, Jesus states that he saw Satan falling (Luke 10:18). Thus, part of the proclamation of the gospel involves conflict between God and his emissaries and the Devil and his forces. It is also significant that it is not uncommon for the New Testament generally to use language that underscores the ongoing conflict between God and Satan. Thus, it is not inappropriate to describe the Christian life as one engaged in spiritual warfare. Yet, it is also clear that this conflict is no dualistic struggle between two equal powers but between an all-powerful God and less powerful forces in rebellion against him.

Third, as observed previously when it comes to identifying the origins of illness, the New Testament is not monolithic in its attribution.

Despite the fact that Jesus and the disciples are engaged in a struggle with the Devil and demons, one cannot always assume that the Devil stands behind a given infirmity. Sometimes it appears that God is at work through an infirmity, while most of the time illness is regarded as neutral with regard to origins. Thus, simplistic equations that always see a relationship between illness and the Devil obfuscate the issue by ruling out of hand God's role and purposes in some illness while at the same time demonising infirmities that the New Testament might treat in a neutral fashion. It is possible that preoccupation with a spiritual warfare paradigm might result in a similar obfuscation of God's role and purposes in evangelising the nations. It seems clear from Scripture that the Devil and demons oppose the mission of the church, and this is a reality that should never be ignored or underestimated. Yet, it is, at the same time, apparent from the biblical text that God may cause providential delays in world evangelisation to accomplish his purposes. Is it possible that the church could be misinterpreting providential delays or struggles in world evangelisation owing to a preoccupation with a spiritual warfare orientation that might not fit every situation? In other words, is it possible that we are sometimes not hearing the voice of God in a given situation because we have predetermined the way in which God must work or the nature of "opposition"?

Fourth, as was seen in the first sections of this presentation, there is some degree of diversity of thought in the New Testament about Satan's role in illness and infirmity. While Luke-Acts and Matthew (to a certain extent) make clear that the Devil and demons are responsible for a number of infirmities and, consequently, the proper response in most instances involves exorcism, other New Testament writers never attribute an illness to the Devil or a demon. This suggests that there was some diversity of thought and practice on this issue amongst early Christians. In this vein, it might not be insignificant that the kingdom of God paradigm, which is dominant in certain New Testament books, is nearly completely absent in others. For example, if one allows the Fourth Gospel to speak on its own terms, the essential message of Jesus is not understood in terms of the in-breaking of the kingdom of God but rather belief in the Son of God which results in eternal life. In fact, the only person in the Fourth Gospel who is ever accused of having a demon is Jesus – an accusation made by "the Jews" and some of the crowd (John 7:20; 8:48, 52; 10:20). Exorcisms and power encounters of that sort find no place in John's narrative. Thus, the mission of the church in this Gospel is not understood in quite the same way as it is in the

Synoptics. The closest one comes to such an understanding in the Johannine literature is the statement in 1 John 3:8 that "for this reason was the Son of God manifest, in order that he might destroy the works of the devil." But a close reading of the text reveals that in this verse "the works of the devil" are equated with sin. None of this is intended to suggest that there is no cosmic struggle within the Fourth Gospel, only to point out that there is some degree of diversity amongst the New Testament Gospel writers on how the work of God is to be made manifest. One of the implications of such diversity of thought in the New Testament for the mission of the church might be that an evangelistic strategy which focuses solely on a "kingdom of God" paradigm may be a less than holistic biblical approach to the mission of the church.

Fifth, it should be abundantly clear that discernment is essential and extraordinarily important in determining whether an illness has its origin in God, the Devil, or neutral causes and in discerning the ongoing activity of the Holy Spirit in leading the church in its missionary work. The Book of Acts is full of examples of how God, through his Spirit, is integrally involved in the mission of the church (e.g., see Acts 1:8; 4:8; 5:32; 8:29, 39–40; 9:32; 10:19; 11:12; 13:1– 4, 9; 15:28; 16:6–7; 18:9; 19:21 (?); 20:22–23; 21:4, 11; 28:25). From this evidence it would appear that part of the church's missionary task is to pay careful attention to what the Spirit is and is not saying with regard to the expansion of the kingdom. This observation is not intended to create doubt in the mind of the reader as to the importance of and need for evangelism, but rather to underscore the need for an absolute reliance upon the Holy Spirit not only to empower the mission but also to direct it. Oddly enough, an overemphasis upon a spiritual warfare paradigm for evangelism might result in less of a reliance upon the Spirit's role by having room for only one aspect of the Spirit's ministry: the power encounter. It should also be noted that prayer is clearly essential in order for the church to accomplish its mission in the power of the Spirit. When in doubt as to how one should pray, it would always be appropriate to pray that the Lord of the harvest send labourers into the harvest.

Sixth, with regard to the issue of territorial spirits, the Old Testament text can speak of spirits and/or angels in several ways. Reference is sometimes made to spirits who happen to be located in certain geographical areas but who do not appear to have control over their places of abode. Specific mention is made of "goat-demons" (Lev. 17:7; Isa. 13:21; 34:14), Lilith (Isa. 34:14), and (less certainly) Azaliel (Isa. 34:14; Lev. 16:8, 10, 26). Second, in the minds of the

Arameans, the gods were tied to specific geographical locations (1 Kings 20:23). Third, in some texts the gods are identified with certain lands and nations (2 Kings 18:33, 35). A couple of Old Testament texts even identify the gods with demons (Deut. 32:8–17; LXX Ps. 96:5). Fourth, certain Old Testament texts describe angels which are connected to specific nations (Dan. 10:13, 20–21). Interestingly enough, there are no hints that believers are to concern themselves with such spirits, as the believer's role (in this case Daniel) is largely defined as that of observer of how God accomplishes his purpose on the broad screen of history. What is perhaps as significant is that there is no evidence in the New Testament that a concern about territorial spirits ever figured into the missionary strategy of the early Christians. In fact, even when it is clear that Satan has hindered Paul from coming to Thessalonica (1 Thess. 2:18), he does not engage in or advocate coming against Satan by means of "spiritual warfare." Thus, while it is possible that Satan manifests himself more strongly in certain places than in others, there seems to be little biblical warrant for a number of the practices associated with some forms of spiritual warfare which focus on territorial spirits.[7]

Seventh, a final observation is offered about the question of demonic influence upon believers. On the one hand, despite the many arguments to the contrary there appears to be no direct biblical evidence that Christians can be possessed or controlled by a demon. The most reasoned apology for such a reading of the New Testament in the end fails to convince owing in part to the fact that in nearly every case the "Christian" in question appears to be one who has left the faith.[8] On the other hand, it is clear that there is at least some precedent for the affliction of a believer by a demon, though here the evidence is skewed by the fact that in the case of Paul's thorn God is involved and he does not remove it even when Paul petitions for its removal. The role of the Devil and/or demons in temptation, deception, persecution and accusation of the believer is documented within the New Testament.

In this presentation I have sought to examine and reflect upon the biblical text particularly as it relates to the issue of spiritual warfare. While listening to the biblical text is a very important part of the theological task, it should be noted that there is more to the theological task than (simply) listening to text. As the hermeneutical method found in Acts 15 reveals,[9] the early church not only had a place for the text in their interpretive activity, but also had a very real appreciation for the activity of the Holy Spirit, as well as an appreciation for the role the believing community plays in the interpretive process. My prayer is that the Lord would allow to exist amongst the delegates of this consultation the kind of atmosphere which would allow for a dynamic interplay among the biblical text, the activity of the Holy Spirit and the experience of the believing community. I commit myself to this interpretive process.

Notes

¹ For this attempt, see Thomas, *The Devil, Disease and Deliverance.*

² By "believing community" I mean those whom the early Christians themselves would have viewed as being in a right relationship with God.

³ On this topic see especially. G. Twelftree, *Jesus the Exorcist* (Peabody, Mass.: Hendrickson, 1993), 143–56.

⁴ The account of the Gerasene demoniac in Mark 5:1–20 is one example of an exorcism that does not seem to be successful on the first attempt.

⁵ The practice of anointing with oil was apparently instituted by Jesus (Mark 6:13), practiced by the church (James 5:14), and tied through healing to the Atonement (Matt. 8:17).

⁶ See J. C. Thomas, "Footwashing in John 13 and the Johannine Community," *Journal for the Study of the New Testament Supplement Series* 61 (Sheffield: Sheffield Academic Press, 1991).

⁷ See especially the helpful thoughts of R. D. Israel, "Territorial Spirits? Old Testament Texts, Traditions and Theology," working paper presented to the Biblical Studies Special Interest Group of the Society for Pentecostal Studies in Chicago, Illinois, 1994, and those of C. E. Arnold, *Three Crucial Questions About Spiritual Warfare* (Grand Rapids, Mich.: Baker, 1997), 143–98.

⁸ For such a reading, see the capable work of Arnold, *Three Crucial Questions About Spiritual Warfare,* 93–97. Perhaps the best case can be made for such an interpretation on the basis of Ephesians 4:26–27, which speaks of giving no foothold to the devil. But even here, one appears to be rather far from demon possession.

⁹ For my thoughts on this, see J. C. Thomas, "Women, Pentecostals and the Bible: An Experiment in Pentecostal Hermeneutics," *Journal of Pentecostal Theology* 5 (1994), 41–56.

4 _____

Our weapons of warfare

TOKUNBOH ADEYEMO

The Christian life is a life of warfare. From the time we accept God's invitation, "Come to Me, all you who labour and are heavy laden," to the time God withdraws us from the battlefront by way of death (the rapture), we are engaged in a serious warfare against three enemies: (1) Satan and his demons (Eph. 6:12); (2) systems that are ungodly, called the "world" (1 John 2:15–17); and (3) self, that is, the old Adamic nature (Gal. 5:17).

The unfortunate thing, however, is that not many Christians realise this fact. Consequently, the majority live as civilians and complain at every test that comes their way which is intended or allowed by God to train them. Many easily fall victim to the enemies because of this ignorance.

The apostle Paul would not have Timothy, his son in the Lord, ignorant of this fact:

> You therefore, my son, be strong in the grace that is in Christ Jesus. You therefore must endure hardship as a good soldier of Jesus Christ. No one engaged in warfare entangles himself with the affairs of this life, that he may please Him who enlisted him as a soldier. (2 Tim. 2:1, 3–4)

On one account in the battle against his own self, Paul wrote, "But I discipline my body and bring it into subjection, lest, when I have preached to others, I, myself, should become disqualified" (1 Cor. 9:27). At the end of his life he could write "I have fought the good fight, I have finished the race, I have kept the faith" (2 Tim. 4:7).

Weapons used in battle, of course, depend upon the nature of the warfare. Weapons used in a village conflict cannot be compared with those used during the world wars. The Bible leaves us in no doubt as to the nature of our warfare and what our weapons should be, as seen in passages such as Ephesians 6:10–18, 2 Corinthians 10:3–6, and Zechariah 4:1–7. The message of these passages can be summarized as follows: the Christian's warfare is spiritual *and* the Christian's weapons are spiritual.

God's weapons

In actual fact it is inaccurate to speak of "our weapons," except in the sense of our moral obligation, because the weapons belong to God. Note that in Ephesians 6:11 and 13, they are described as "the whole armour of God." We are only told to put them on, not to manufacture them. In 2 Corinthians 10:4 they are said to be "mighty in God" or "divinely powerful." In Zechariah 4:6, it is expressly stated that it is not by might or power, but "by my Spirit."

Though the enemies of God are numerous and their tactics and their strategies vary, God's weapon is singular: my Spirit! Do not miss the point: the battle does not belong to you; it belongs to the Lord. And God's weapon for fighting the battle is his Spirit. It does not matter who the enemy is – whether Satan himself, ungodly systems, or the old Adamic nature, God's weapon is his Spirit.

The Greek word translated as "weapons" is the word *hoplon*. Originally, *hoplon* was any tool or instrument used for preparing another thing. In the plural it came to be used for weapons of warfare. Literally, it is used only once in the New Testament in this way (that is, as actual weapons; John 18:3). Elsewhere, *hoplon* is used as a figure of speech for the members of the body as instruments for either righteousness or unrighteousness (Rom. 6:13), the armour of light (Rom. 13:12), the armour of righteousness (2 Cor. 6:7) and the weapons of Christian warfare (2 Cor. 10:4).

In these instances we observe that God's weapons, which believers are told to put on, are singular in form but plural in function. Herein we see God's wisdom.

God's wisdom

Rather than developing different kinds of weapons for different kinds of assaults and combat, and each succeeding generation of weapons being more sophisticated than the one that preceded it,

God who is all-wise brought forth only one weapon adaptable to all weather, all seasons, all ages and all times. Equally, since God's wisdom is foolishness to the world, the way God's weapon functions looks ludicrous to humanity. Moses used a rod to work miracles in Egypt and part the Red Sea (Exod. 4:2, 20; 14:21) as well as defeat the Amalekites (Exod. 17:8–18). Joshua used trumpets and marching to tear down Jericho's walls (Josh. 6:1–22); David a sling to defeat the heavily armed Goliath (1 Sam. 17:45–51). Samson used the jawbone of a donkey to slay 1,000 Philistines (Judg. 15:14–16).

What do all these say? God works in mysterious ways his wonders to perform. Paul puts it this way:

God has chosen the foolish things of the world to put to shame the wise, and God has chosen the weak things of the world to put to shame the things which are mighty; and the base things of the world and the things which are despised God has chosen, and the things which are not, to bring to nothing the things that are, that no flesh should glory in his presence. (1 Cor. 1:27–29)

For this reason the hymn writer penned:

> Stand up! Stand up for Jesus!
> Stand in his strength alone;
> The arm of flesh will fail you
> Ye dare not trust your own.

This is the secret: standing in *his* strength alone! But does that mean that we do nothing? Not at all. It is our responsibility to put on the whole armour, our responsibility to stand.

Believer's weakness (responsibility)

Paul wrote, "But we have this treasure in earthen vessels, that the excellence of the power may be of God and not of us" (2 Cor. 4:7). Our human responsibility is fivefold: (1) have faith in God and in his word (2 Chron. 20:20; 1 Tim. 1:18–19; 1 John 5:4–5), not doubt (James 1:5–6) or division (Luke 11:17); (2) stand positioned all the time, putting on God's whole armour (Exod. 14:13–14; Eph. 6:10–17) rather than living with unconfessed sin (Ps. 6:18; 1 John 1:8–10); (3) watch and pray always (Luke 18:1; Eph. 6:18) rather than sleeping (Matt. 13:25; 26:40–45); (4) be Spirit-filled (Eph. 5:18), not yielding to the flesh (Gal. 5:16); and (5) obey God (John 2:5; Luke 6:46); don't disobey (1 Sam. 15:22–23).

Conclusion

God's weapon of warfare has been tested over the centuries and has never failed. Your case (and mine) cannot be an exception. If the weapon seems not to be working for you, check the list of your fivefold responsibility. All we bring to God is weakness. But it is in our weakness that his strength is perfected (2 Cor. 12:9).

Believers have a competitive advantage over the enemy. Our weapons are made by God, not by human beings. And God resides in us, teaching our fingers to do battle and our hands to make war. Rejoice, therefore, as you go into the battlefield bearing in mind "that greater is he who is in you than the one who is in the world" (1 John 4:4).

5

Possession and exorcism in the history of the church

OSKAR SKARSAUNE AND TORMOD ENGELSVIKEN[1]

It seems natural for a modern reader to consider possession as a category of disease and to regard the exorcism narratives of the New Testament as referring to a form of mental illness. The authors of this chapter suggest that in the history of Christianity from the early period until modern times Christian writers did not primarily approach possession and exorcism in this way but interpreted it in a different and more comprehensive frame of reference. This will be argued by looking at the church in antiquity, the Middle Ages, the Reformation and post-Reformation periods. Finally, these observations will be applied to some of the New Testament texts.

Ancient church texts

In A.D. 197 Tertullian wrote his *Apologeticum*,[2] which is a commentary on two accusations that are directed against Christians: (1) "You do not worship the gods"; and (2) "You do not offer sacrifices for the emperors."[3] The first half of the book (chaps. 10–27) is a comment on the first accusation, and the answer is short and pointed: "We do not worship your gods, because we know that there are no such beings" ("Deos vestros colere desinimus, ex quo illos non esse cognoscimus," Apol. 10, 2).[4] Tertullian then starts with the critique of Greek mythology, which had been used by the Jewish and Christian apologetic tradition. Tertullian intentionally moves towards a climax in chapters 23–27 with a critique against polytheism. By saying, "Your gods do not exist" he does not mean that the Greco-Roman gods are mere projection of the human mind. They relate to real powers that do exist, but they are not what they purport to be. They are not gods, but demons. "And we affirm indeed the existence of certain spiritual essences; nor is their name unfamiliar. The philosophers acknowledge there are demons" (*Apol.* 22, 1).[5] The activity of demons consists in deceiving human beings, tricking them into worshipping the demons as gods. In this way they lead people away from the true God.

Tertullian gives this bold assertion, which probably sounded provocative to the original readers.

> But thus far we have been dealing only in words; we now proceed to a proof of facts, in which we shall show that under different names (god and demon) you have real identity. Let a person be brought before your tribunals, who is plainly under demoniacal possession *(daemone agi)*. The wicked spirit, bidden to speak by a follower of Christ, will as readily make the truthful confession that he is a demon, as elsewhere he has falsely asserted that he is a god. Or, if you will, let there be produced one of the god-possessed *(de deo pati)*, as they are supposed, . . . if they would not confess, in their fear of lying to a Christian, that they were demons, then and there shed the blood of the most impudent follower of Christ. . . . The truth is . . . that neither themselves nor any others have claims to deity, you may see at once who is really God, and whether that is He and He alone whom we Christians own; as also whether you are to believe in Him, and worship Him, after the manner of our Christian faith and discipline. But at once they (the demons) will say, Who is this Christ? . . . Is he not rather up in the heavens, thence about to come again? . . . All the authority and power we have over them is from our naming the name of Christ, and recalling to their memory the woes with which God threatens them at the hands of Christ as Judge, and which they expect one day to overtake them. Fearing Christ in God, and God in Christ, they become subject to the servants of God and Christ. So at our touch and breathing, overwhelmed by the thought and realization of those judgment fires, they leave at our command the bodies they have entered. . . . It has not been an unusual thing, accordingly, for those testimonies of your deities to

convert men to Christianity (*"haec testimonia deorum vestrorum Christianos facere consuerunt";* Apol. 23, 4–18).[6]

This text contains several points that are consistent with other literature of the ancient church.

Justin Martyr (ca. A.D. 160):

For we do continually beseech God by Jesus Christ to preserve us from the demons which are hostile to the worship of God, and whom we of old time served. . . . For we call Him Helper and Redeemer, the power of whose name even the demons do fear; and at this day, when they are exorcised in the name of Jesus Christ, crucified under Pontius Pilate, governor of Judaea, they are overcome. And thus it is manifest to all, that His Father has given Him so great power by virtue of which demons are subdued to His name, and to the dispensation of His suffering (*Dialogue,* 30, 3).[7]

Justin Martyr also wrote:

He [Christ] said, "I give unto you power to tread on serpents, and on scorpions . . . and on all the might of the enemy." And now we, who believe on our Lord Jesus, who was crucified under Pontius Pilate, when we exorcise all demons and evil spirits, have them subjected to us (*Dialogue* 76, 6).[8]

In *Dialogue* 85, 1–3 Justin refers to the exorcisms as the very evidence of the fact that Jesus has risen from the dead and now sits at the right hand of the Father:

For every demon, when exorcised in the name of this very Son of God – who is the Firstborn of every creature, who became man by the Virgin, who suffered and was crucified under Pontius Pilate . . . who died, who rose from the dead, and ascended into heaven – is overcome and subdued. But though you exorcise any demon in the name of any of those who were amongst you – either kings, or righteous men, or prophets, or patriarchs – it will not be subject to you. But if any of you exorcise it in (the name of) the God of Abraham, and the God of Isaac, and the God of Jacob, it will perhaps be subject to you. Now assuredly, your exorcists, I have said, make use of craft when they exorcise, even as the Gentiles do, and employ fumigations and incantations.[9]

Theophilus of Antioch (ca. A.D. 180) wrote that the Greek poets were inspired by demons.

This is clearly evidenced by the fact that even today demons are exorcised from possessed in the name of the true God, and then the deceiving spirits confess themselves that they are the demons who once worked in the poets (*Ad Autolycum* II, 8).[10]

Origen (ca. A.D. 235):

[The critic of Christianity, Celsus (ca. A.D. 175)] "asserts that it is by the names of certain demons, and by the use of incantations, that the Christians appear to be possessed of power." [Origen continues] Hinting, I suppose, at the practices of those who expel evil spirits by incantations. And here he manifestly appears to malign the gospel. For it is not by incantations that Christians seem to prevail (over evil spirits), but by the name of Jesus, accompanied by the announcement of the narratives which relate to him; for the repetition of these has frequently been the means of driving demons out of men, especially when those who repeated them did so in a sound and genuinely believing spirit. Such power, indeed, does the name of Jesus possess over evil spirits, that there have been instances where it was effectual, when it was pronounced even by bad men" (*Contra Celsum* I, 6).[11]

If then the Pythian priestess is beside herself when she prophesies, what spirit must that be which fills her mind and clouds her judgment with darkness, unless it be of the same order with those demons which many Christians cast out of persons possessed with them? And this, we may observe, they do without the use of any curious magic, or incantations, but merely by prayer and simple adjurations which the plainest person can use. Because for the most part it is unlettered persons who perform this work: thus making manifest the grace which is in the word of Christ, and the despicable weakness of demons, which, in order to be overcome and driven out of the bodies and souls of men, do not require the power and wisdom of those who are mighty in argument, and most learned in matters of faith (*Contra Celsum,* VII, 4).[12]

Origen considered that pagans were only able to perform exorcisms by the use of magic and incantations. In contrast, every Christian appears to be able to perform exorcisms simply by calling upon the name of Jesus. In another place Origen emphasises a different aspect of exorcism, namely, that it proves the reality of the Resurrection: "How could a phantom drive out demons or otherwise perform things of great importance?"

Athanasius writes (ca. A.D. 320) that exorcisms prove the reality of the Resurrection:

And how does it happen, if he is not risen, but is dead, that he expels the false gods who by the unbelievers are said to live, and the demons whom they worship, and persecute and destroy them? For where Christ is mentioned, and faith in him, all idolatry is eradicated, all demonic deceit is revealed, and no demon even tolerates that the name is mentioned, but hurries to flee, as it hears it mentioned. This is not the work of a dead man, but a living and first and foremost God. (*De incarnatione verbi,* 32).[13]

It is clear that if Christ were dead, then he would not expel the demons . . . for the demons would not obey one who is dead. But when they obviously are chased away at the use of his name, then it should be clear that he is not dead, especially because the demons see the things that are not visible for humans – should know it if Christ is dead. Then they would simply deny him obedience. But now the demons see exactly what the ungodly do not believe; that he is God, and therefore they flee and fall down for him and say that which they also said when he was in the body, "We know who you are, you the Holy One of God" (*De incarnatione verbi,* 32).[14]

These texts reveal common themes that occur throughout the teaching of the ancient church. The first theme is that the gods of the Gentiles are considered to be demons. The roots of this concept lie in the Old Testament, where the existence of the gods of the Gentiles are not denied. In Psalm 96:5, for example, the gods of the peoples are referred to as '*ĕlilim.* This word often stands in a synonymous parallelism with the word "idol," but also to *shedim,* "demons" (Deut. 32:17; Ps. 106:37), and *se'irim,* "evil spirits" (Lev. 17:7; 2 Chron. 11:15; Isa. 13:21; 32:14). In Deuteronomy 32:17 it is said of apostate Israel: "They sacrificed to demons who were not God, to gods whom they have not known."

Both in the Old Testament and in later Judaism there are *two* approaches in the polemic against pagan cult. There is a "rational" polemic against the images: It is ridiculous to pray to dead things which cannot even take care of themselves, and which are made by humans (cf. Jer. 10:3–5; Isa. 44:12–20; the apocryphal book Solomon's Wisdom, 13:10–19). There is also a polemic to the effect that the Gentiles actually relate to real powers in their cult, but these powers are demonic. "For all the gods of the peoples are demons"(Ps. 96:5). This text is frequently quoted by Justin Martyr, and afterwards by various church fathers. The apostle Paul also seems to assume this thought in 1 Corinthians 10, where he warns the Christians against participating in meals sacrificed to idols. "What do I mean then? That a thing sacrificed to idols is anything, or that an idol is anything? No, but I say that the things which the Gentiles sacrifice, they sacrifice to demons, and not to God; and I do not want you to become sharers in demons" (1 Cor. 10:19–20, supposedly an allusion to Deut. 32:17).

The second theme is the notion that when people worship demons they risk being possessed by them. We would argue that possession is a phenomenon of paganism, which has connection with pagan worship. Possession is not considered to occur among baptised Christian people. The argument for this view can be seen by considering both the practice of baptismal exorcism and the understanding of possession among Christians.

In the church order written by Hippolytus (ca. A.D. 210) mention is made of a possible series of exorcisms during the time immediately prior to baptism. Hippolytus writes, "If anybody has a demon, then let him not hear the Word from the teacher before he has been cleansed" (*Apostolic Tradition* 16, 8). He further writes:

From the day that they (who are to be baptised) are elected, let there be laying on of hands with exorcism every day. When the day of baptism approaches, let the bishop perform exorcism on each one of them, so that he may be certain that the baptised is clean. But if there is anybody who is not clean, he should be set aside because he did not hear the instruction with faith. For the alien spirit remained with him (*Apostolic Tradition,* 20,3).[15]

Hippolytus considers pre-baptismal exorcism almost as a diagnostic tool to reveal and heal possible possession in those seeking baptism. There also seems to be an element to the ritual that prevents future possession in that prayers of exorcism often command the spirits to stay away from the person.

The importance of exorcism before baptism is undoubtedly connected with the understanding of baptism as a "seal," or "protective wall" against possession. It is imperative that the enemy is outside the city at the time the wall is built. If the enemy is inside the city, the wall will be of no use. The demon should not be allowed to slip under the seal of baptism or it would be more difficult to drive it out afterwards. This is seen in the Gnostic material in Clement of Alexandria, *Excerpta ex Theodoto.*

All unbaptised people are also considered possible "dwellings" for unclean spirits. In the Epistle of Barnabas (ca. A.D. 130) it is stated:

> Before we believed in God the habitation of our heart was corrupt and weak, like a temple really built with hands, because it was full of idolatry, and was the house of demons through doing things which were contrary to God. But . . . we became new, being created again from the beginning; wherefore God truly dwells in us (*Barnabas* 16, 7f.).[16]

Concerning the question of possession among baptised Christians, the ancient church unequivocally placed possession in the area of paganism. Where Christ rules, the demons flee. However, is it possible for Christians to nevertheless be possessed? We argue that they may, but only if they actively seek the demons' power. Tertullian tells about a Christian woman who went to the theatre, where people slaughtered and maimed one another as entertainment for the masses, and she came back possessed. "In the casting out the unclean creature was upbraided with having dared to attack a believer, he firmly replied, 'And in truth I did it most righteously, for I found her in my domain'"(*De spectaculis,* 26).[17]

In the literature aimed at Christians, exorcism is very seldom mentioned, and usually only with reference to baptism and allied exorcisms. Exorcism occurs primarily at the border between church and paganism and is primarily a missionary phenomenon. There exorcism is a *sign event* that with evidence for all demonstrates that Christ has conquered Satan and all his army. It is obvious that Christian exorcism made a deep impression on people in antiquity, both

Christians and non-Christians. Tertullian wrote: "It has not been an unusual thing for these testimonies of your deities to convert men to Christianity."[18] Exorcism demonstrated to people that the name of Jesus had power over even the strongest demon, and it was 100 per cent efficient. Several testimonies, both from Christian and pagan authors, confirm that Christians were recognised as exorcists. Celsus, a critic of Christianity, spoke of their *power* over the demons, and both Origen and Tertullian said that the pagans used to fetch a Christian when they wanted help with a possessed person. People in antiquity were also struck by the fact that *all* Christians exorcised demons, and they did it without the usual complicated incantations but with a simple command in the name of Jesus. In contrast, in the ancient magical papyri different names of gods are heaped one on top of the other. Even the Old Testament names of God and the name of Jesus are sometimes included in syncretistic magical formulas as an indirect testimony about the fame of Jewish and Christian exorcism. It appears as if in some parts the practice of the church had not steered completely free from a magical misunderstanding of Christian exorcism. We find, however, little of this magical understanding among the leading theologians of the church.

It looks as if the ancient church placed more emphasis on exorcism than on miraculous healings. The reason for this is not difficult to grasp because Christians were not alone in doing and experiencing miracles. Demons might also perform miracles. In exorcism the demon was directly confronted with Christ in a "power encounter." The demons were forced to proclaim the lordship of Jesus Christ. This is the reason for the great significance ascribed to exorcism in the missionary literature of the ancient church.

The Middle Ages

The church during the Middle Ages reveals both a continuity and discontinuity with the understanding of the early church.

The major tradition from the ancient church was to consider the gods of the pagans as demons masquerading as gods. Theologically, however, the Devil and the demons were considered as "middle beings" *(Zwischenwesen)* between God and human beings. They were created but did not have a physical body. The Devil was seen as having been created before humans as one of the angels, but he fell due to the sin of pride. This fall happened before the fall of humans. It was also assumed that it was possible for humans to have contact both with angels and fallen angels (the Devil and demons).

The biblical basis for some of these ideas was weak. Isaiah 14:12–14 was understood as referring to the primordial fall of Lucifer, even though it does not refer to him at all. Genesis 6:1–4 was the basis for much speculation about the ability of demons to procreate sexually through humans, either by taking on the form of a male *(incubus)* or female *(succubus)*. Neither view can be biblically substantiated.

Especially through the writings of Augustine[19] the understanding of the ancient church was communicated to the theologians of the Middle Ages. The demons are considered similar to God in their immortality and like humans in that they are created. They are different from humans in that they are not capable of doing good, and so are qualitatively inferior. In the large works of medieval theologians the doctrine of angels and demons is always dealt with under the doctrine of creation.[20]

During the Middle Ages, however, many instances of popular religion drawn from non-Christian sources influenced ordinary people's views of Satan and the demons. Pagan notions of spiritual subterranean beings and others were often mixed with the biblical concepts. The result was often a perversion of the biblical message. Grotesque images of the Devil with horns and hoofs, which do not originate in Christianity, dominated the popular fantasy. These images have been preserved with remarkable strength up until our own time and have been used, consciously or unconsciously, as a recent excuse to discard the existence of the Devil as a myth. One reason why the church in the West today has great difficulties in communicating the biblical understanding is the fact that people understand the Christian doctrine and practice on the basis of non-Christian ideas.

Compared to the ancient church, the numbers of exorcisms and their significance seem to have diminished in the Middle Ages, at least according to our sources. One reason may be that after Constantine more and more people were baptised and the number of unbaptised pagans was reduced.

However, the encounter with paganism in newly converted peoples such as the Germanic tribes once again raised the question of the power encounter between Christ and pagan gods. In a famous historical saga written by the Icelandic medieval historian Snorre Sturlason,[21] the Norwegian Christian King Olav (later Saint Olav!) meets a leader of the pre-Christian pagan cult Dale-Gudbrand, who says about Olav:

> He will offer us a different faith than the one we had before, and break all our gods to pieces, and he says that he has a different

god who is much greater and more powerful. It is a wonder that the earth does not break open under him when he dares speak thus, and that our gods allow him to walk. But I think that when we carry Tor (the Norse god of thunder) out of the "hov" (the temple) that is with us; he who stands here in the farm and always has helped us, so that he can see Olav and his men, then Olav's god will melt, and he himself and his men, so that they will become nothing.[22]

King Olav's answer is similar to that of an ancient apologist:

You frighten us with your god, who is blind and deaf and neither can save himself nor others, and who cannot move an inch without somebody carrying him. But now I believe that it is not long before something bad happens to him. Look up, and see toward the East, where our god comes with a great light!

One of Olav's men then struck the idol so that it fell down, and "mice as big as cats, and lizards and snakes" ran out of it. The peasants who had opposed Olav were so frightened that they ran away, but later Dale-Gudbrand returned and drew the only possible conclusion: "We have suffered great damage to our god. But since he was unable to help us, we will now believe in the god that you believe in – and then all of them received the Christian faith."

King Olav follows here the missionary pattern of Boniface, the apostle of the Germans, who almost three hundred years earlier had done a similar thing when he chopped down a holy oak in Geismar.[23] It is not a miracle as such that takes place here, since the destruction of the tree and the idol takes place through the use of human physical force, but the point is that the fear that the pagans have for their gods and sacred objects is removed in the confrontation with the Christians and their God. Their "gods" are revealed to have no positive power whatsoever but rather are tied to the evil forces (mice, snakes). Christ is seen as superior to the former gods.

The same sources also talk about a kind of "exorcistic cleansing of the land:"

At the time of Olav Tryggvason [another Norwegian Christian king] there were two good friends in Iceland whose names were Torhall and Siduhall. One morning before they rose Torhall lay laughing by himself. His friend asked him why he laughed. Torhall answered that he saw many tombs stand open and the *landvetter* [spiritual beings in Norse mythology and in popular religion] preparing to leave; they had their day of departure today. Where Christianity advances, it becomes difficult for the evil powers to stay, so they are forced to leave.[24]

This fight between Christ and the evil forces of paganism is also often reflected in the Nordic fairy tales, where the evil forces, often symbolised by trolls and other beings, are driven away by the Lord's prayer or the cross or cannot stand the smell of "the blood of a Christian man."

It is often assumed that the encounter with paganism in the newly converted tribes also led to a change in the popular Christian view of demonic influence. A new element is the thought of a close connection, almost an identification of humans and demons. It is important to note, however, that the official church rejected this view. These thoughts would, however, towards the end of the Middle Ages in the fifteenth century and the pre-Enlightenment era in Europe, develop into the witch hysteria that led to the execution of tens of thousands of supposed witches.[25]

The witch-hunt is often held against the church (both Catholic and Protestant) as an almost inevitable result of the church's doctrine of the Devil and demons. Several studies have been done of this very sad incident in European history. Some facts should, however, be brought forward in order to correct some aspects of the common picture.[26]

Contrary to popular opinion, Skarsaune has shown four perspectives of the period. First, the witch-hunt in Europe did not belong in the Middle Ages but to the Renaissance and the post-Reformation (or pre-Enlightenment) period. The main period in Europe was between 1580 and 1680. Before and after this one-hundred-year period there were few witch processes. During most of the Middle Ages the official doctrine of the church with its leadership and leading theologians considered belief in witches and witchcraft as superstition. This view again became dominant at the beginning of the eighteenth century and the witch-hunt stopped as quickly as it had begun.

Second, the typical witch was not a beautiful young woman. Most were old women, and about one-fifth were men.

Third, the court cases were not initiated by the church but were held before secular courts. The charges against the witches most often came from the local community, not from the ecclesiastical authorities. The process often related to marginalised peoples in marginal areas (the mountain areas in the Alps, Pyrenees and Norway), and not in the central areas (Rome or the other cities of Europe). Priests often played little or no part in these cases but were sometimes drawn upon as "spiritual experts."

Fourth, the Inquisition in Spain played a surprising role in that it was the investigations of the inquisitor that brought an end to the witch-hunt in Spain! He revealed that it was founded on superstition and that the charges were false.

The reasons for the witch-hunt have been discussed by many. There may be many social, economic and psychological reasons, but the church also has a responsibility because it accepted a "witch doctrine" that made secular courts take the accusations seriously. The understanding of witchcraft was a combination of different ideas, and many were non-Christian. These include the concepts of magic and a covenant with the Devil. The theological justification was expressed in the infamous literary work *Malleus Maleficarum (Witch Hammer)* from 1487.

One reason for the appearance of witch-hunts just before the breakthrough of the Enlightenment may have been a profound worldview change. During this period belief in and fear of evil powers persisted in popular religion while at the same time faith in God's supernatural power to protect against these powers faded. In any case, there is no Christian justification for violent persecution of "witches," and there is also no necessary connection between a biblical understanding of the Devil and demons and this hysteria that gripped some areas of Europe during this time. Any church participation in this persecution must be deeply deplored.

Luther and the Reformers

The Reformation did not significantly alter the worldview of the Middle Ages. In several of Luther's works there are references to Satan and demons, but there is a more biblical orientation.[27]

Humans are in their sinfulness subject to powers of corruption, which are the flesh, the world and the Devil. They are often mentioned together, for they are allies in their efforts to lead people to damnation. Satan, who is the prince of this world, does his work through human sinful nature. He seduces and tempts humans and keeps them in bondage to sin. Luther emphasises that evil is not only a power which has caught humanity but is an effect of a personal evil will. This evil will is the origin of sin, and it catches the will of individual people as well as of the whole of humanity.

Luther's radical view of Satan is based in his own experience of the terrible reality of Satan. "By the grace of God I have come to know a lot about Satan," Luther says.[28] He sees Satan at work in disasters, disease, spiritual struggle *(Anfechtungen)*, suffering and death. He is the great adversary of God and Christ. Satan is behind persecution of Christians. He perverts the Word of God and the gospel. His seduction leads to heresies.

The fight between God and Satan runs through all of history, and in this fight it is not possible to be neutral. In this respect humans have no free will. They are either in the power of Satan or the power of God. In a famous picture he describes how a human being is like an animal on which either God or the Devil rides. The riders fight between themselves for control of the animal. It is God who through Jesus Christ rescues people out of the power of the Devil. The main weapon in this struggle is the gospel, the Word of God.

However, there is no absolute dualism. Satan can only operate within the limits set by God's omnipotence. At last Christ will return and destroy Satan. Until then, Satan has to serve God's purpose for the world. Satan is also seen as an instrument of the law and the wrath of God (as in the Old Testament). Strangely, Luther may call the Devil "God's devil," because he is completely subject to God's power. Satan therefore has a double role; he is God's enemy at the same time as he is God's instrument. Satan tempts people to fall away from God, but God uses this to test people's faith in order to strengthen it.

Luther also holds on to the reality of the demons. He thought that one could and should drive the evil spirits out of the possessed by prayer. He was, however, critical of the Roman Catholic methods and especially the use of blessed water and other holy objects.[29] Thus it was not the practice in itself but the magical elements that he reacted against. Luther's famous hymn "A Mighty Fortress" is a testimony to his realistic conception of Satan and the evil spirits as well as to his triumphant sense of victory in Christ.

One case of possession from the time of the Reformation is that reported by Johannes Bugenhagen. In a letter to the theologians in Wittenberg, among them Luther, he describes his meeting with a possessed girl in Lübeck. The detailed description of this case corresponds wholly with other cases of possession known in history. Luther himself refers to the letter from Bugenhagen and accepts the possession as a fact.[30]

Although the Lutheran confessions do not mention possession and exorcism, they express in many places the biblical and traditional view of the Devil and the ways to guard against him. The Word of God, the name of God,[31] and prayer[32] drive him away. It is of special interest to note that Luther understands the Lord's Prayer, and especially the prayer "Deliver us from evil," as directed against the Devil as well as to God.

As infant baptism became common in the church, the pre-baptismal exorcism became part of the ritual for infant baptism. This ritual was kept, for example, in the Danish-Norwegian Lutheran church for many years after the Reformation. The words used were "Depart [literally: Go out] you evil spirit, and give room for the Holy Spirit." It was removed in 1783 after some controversy accompanying rationalism in theology. A renunciation of the Devil and all his works was retained, however, in the liturgy and is still used today.

In 1547 Bishop Peder Palladius held a lecture for pastors, in which he gave them guidance as to how to ascertain whether a person is possessed and how to drive out the evil spirit. The latter should be done by reading Scripture and the use of the same exorcism that was used at baptism. There are only a few examples of possession from the history of this church, not to be confused with witches.

> In the Church Ritual of 1685 guidelines for the treatment of possession are put forth: If the pastor is called to someone who is held to be possessed, or in any other way is tormented by the Devil, one must not at all decline it; but he ought to, according to the duty of the office, in the name of the Lord, after serious prayer and calling upon God, go to the sick [sic] and investigate his condition.[33]

The pastor should not assume that possession is common "for such examples are at the present time rare in Christendom," neither should he think "that we now are totally free from these attacks by Satan." Together with doctors and other pastors whom the bishop appoints, the pastor of the area should evaluate the case, whether it is a natural disease or whether the person is "bodily possessed by the Devil, so that he either rules and governs in the whole body and all its members, as well as mind, reason and the attributes of the soul, or if he only has conquered for himself one or other limb on the body, in which he lives and lets his power be seen, as he did with the mute in the Gospel, Luke 11:14."

The ritual further makes it plain that it might be difficult to discern the spirits, but that servants of God do not easily err if they seek the guidance of God and test the case on the Word of God. Possession can either be caused by the possessed themselves, if they have made a pact with Satan or in any other way voluntarily given themselves to his service by sin or ungodliness, or it can be undeserved. The bishop should write a special prayer for possessed individuals to be prayed by the pastor and the relatives of the possessed.

Even though this ritual in some respects may seem a little strange to Christians today, it still reflects a biblical view of possession and exorcism. It shows that the Reformation church in Denmark-Norway did not look upon possession as a phenomenon that only belonged to the past, but reckoned it as a rare possibility to be handled by the servants of the church according to the Word of the Lord.

The Roman Catholic tradition

In its dogmas the Roman Catholic Church holds to the substance of the biblical views as reflected during the ancient church and the Middle Ages.[34]

From the third century the church has instituted the office of the exorcist, which in ecclesiastical language is a cleric who has received the third of the four minor orders.[35] "The order of exorcist invests the one who receives it with power and authority over evil spirits, deputing him to perform the exorcisms that are part of liturgical function." It is noteworthy that this office is not part of the priestly office instituted as a sacrament but is an ecclesiastical institution. The exorcist originally performed the exorcisms in the context of baptism.

The Catholic Church, however, is well aware that originally in the early church exorcisms of *energumens* (people possessed by evil spirits) were performed both by lay people and clerics. "This was true even after the institution of the order of the exorcist." This practice has changed over the years and "today the use of the power of exorcism is restricted by ecclesiastical law." The rite of solemn exorcism requires special permission that is given only to priests of piety and prudence. There is a need for "personal victory over the temptations of the evil spirits in those who receive the power to expel them from others."

As far as the understanding of possession is concerned, the Catholic Church distinguishes between "diabolical obsession," which is a "hostile action of the Devil or an evil spirit besetting anyone from without" (cf. 2 Cor. 12:7–8), and "diabolical possession," which is "the state of a person whose body has fallen under the control of the devil or a demon."

The great theologians of the Middle Ages (Thomas Aquinas and Bonaventure) maintain that what occurs in possession is the "entrance of the demon into the human body, the faculties (physical) of which he proceeds to control." The soul, however, cannot be entered or overcome and thus remains free – though its functions in respect to the body it informs, are, as it were, suspended.

The signs of possession were developed by P. Thyräus in the seventeenth century. He emphasised that the physical indications like spastic movements and hysterical convulsions were not to be considered decisive by themselves, but that the true criteria were knowledge of secret things and the knowledge of languages not learned by the possessed. All writers also mention lack of memory as a criterion. This means that it precluded normal human consciousness. It is also mentioned that maybe in the final analysis the effect of the exorcism settles the question.

As to why God permits possession, the Catholic Church has no final answer, but possession is an indication of the fact that God has not totally annihilated the evil spirits and that they remain capable of disturbing the normal processes of created matter. At the same time, exorcism is the ultimate weapon against the inroads of Satan.

As far as the practice of exorcism is concerned, there is the "Roman Ritual for Exorcism" ("Rituale Romanum"), which was issued in 1614 and still is valid and in use in official exorcisms in the Catholic Church.[36] The rules that must be strictly followed contain instructions for the exorcist, including prayers, biblical texts and formulas, and practices that should be used. Some of these go back to the fourth century, others may seem to border on magic and have been developed over hundreds of years of exorcistic practice in the church. The following could be mentioned.

The exorcist, who needs permission from the bishop, should be characterized by piety, prudence and personal integrity, he should not trust his own power, but rely on the power of God.

The exorcist should not jump to the conclusion that an evil spirit possesses or has possessed a person. He has to know the signs that make him able to distinguish between those who are possessed and those who suffer from a physical disease. In addition to the signs mentioned above, physical strength that goes beyond the age or ordinary condition of the possessed is mentioned. The exorcist should also be aware that the evil spirits use lies and deceit to lead him astray and that they only manifest themselves under pressure and otherwise let the person who is possessed look like he is not possessed to bring the exorcism to a halt. The exorcist should, however, not stop until he sees signs of deliverance.

Some spirits reveal that they have received the power over the possessed because of occult practices. This must not lead the exorcist to use similar means. He is not supposed to practice anything that is based on superstition. The exorcist is also warned against leading conversations with the evil spirit or asking unnecessary questions, especially not about hidden things and future events. Curiosity is dangerous. He should not believe the spirit even if it claims to be the soul of a saint or dead person or a good angel. The questions that may be asked concern the number and names of the spirits, when they entered the possessed and why they got power over him. The spirits should be treated with contempt.

The exorcism itself should be carried out with a command with authority, great faith, humility and eagerness. The exorcist should give no medicine to the possessed. That should be left to the doctors.

Then there are also some moral considerations. If the possessed is a woman, the exorcist needs to have well-reputed women present who may hold the possessed when she is tormented and convulsed by the evil spirit. These women should be patient and belong to the family of the possessed. The exorcist should be aware of the risk of scandal and avoid saying or doing anything that may harm him or others.

During the exorcism itself he should rather use the words of the Bible than his own or anybody else's. He should command the spirit to admit if it occupied the possessed because of any magic or sorcery symbol or occult document. If the exorcism is to succeed these things have to be turned over. If these are outside the body of the possessed, the evil spirit has to tell where it is. When the exorcist finds it, it should be burned.

If the possessed is delivered from the evil spirit, he should be advised to avoid sinful acts and thoughts. If he does not do this, he may give the evil spirit an opportunity to return and possess him anew.

These relatively detailed instructions in the Roman Ritual represent a long experience with exorcism and warn against dangers and mistakes which often have occurred when inexperienced Christians perform exorcisms on their own. Even though from a Protestant perspective there are some concerns in the Roman Ritual, there is no doubt that the ritual still holds great value as a guide for discerning possession and the practice of exorcism. This value is mostly due to the fact that it represents a tradition that goes all the way back to New Testament times and has stood the test in the encounter with possession in different areas and at different times.

In dealing with the question of spiritual conflict in today's mission we will do well in listening to the experience and words of the history of the universal church, in its Catholic, Orthodox and Protestant forms, and learn both from its mistakes and its successes. Only as we evaluate the history in light of the Scriptures and the experience of the church today will we be able to find a way forward.

New Testament texts

At the close of this historical overview we would like to take a look back at the New Testament texts in light of history.[37] At first glance it may seem that the comprehensive framework around possession and exorcism found in the literature of the ancient church is not prominent in the New Testament. Possession and disease appear to be regarded as of the same category. A "demonised" person may be associated with "all who were ill" (Matt. 8:16; Mark 1:32). People are said to be "troubled" or "afflicted" with unclean spirits (Luke 6:18; Acts 5:16). The expression "have a spirit" is used in one unusual case, namely, in Luke 13:11, where a woman is said to have a "sickness caused by a spirit." Jesus talks about this woman as being bound by Satan – not possessed. This is similar to where Paul speaks about his disease as a messenger of Satan (2 Cor. 12:7).

If one commences with the terminology that is used to describe the phenomenon of possession, the border between possession and disease seems to be unclear. It is different, however, if one begins with the phenomenon of exorcism.

There seems to be a relatively clear distinction between two types of miracle stories in the New Testament. On the one hand are the stories in which Jesus heals diseases, and on the other hand stories in which Jesus expels a demon. The differences are as follows:

1. In the healing stories Jesus addresses himself normally to the sick in a friendly, encouraging fashion. He praises the faith of the

sick persons (or the faith of those who bring the sick) and proclaims to the sick that they are healed and forgiven.

2. In the exorcism stories the whole structure is different. There we meet an angry and threatening Jesus, who does not address the possessed but rather the demon (or demons) in the possessed person. The possessed is talked about in the third person. The climax of the stories is not, as in the healing stories, a proclamation of forgiveness of sin but a powerful command to the spirit to come out of the possessed. All stories in the gospels seem to fall within one or the other of these two categories with the exception of Matthew 17:5ff. Here Jesus drives an evil spirit out of a *sick* boy and speaks to the sick, not to the spirit. If this account is compared with parallel passages in Matthew 17:14–21 and Luke 9:37–43, it can be seen that the Matthean version is an abbreviated rendering of a story which in Mark and Luke is a classical exorcism story, and that the dialogue is between Jesus and the spirit in the possessed boy. The story about the woman who had a spirit of sickness (Luke 13:10–17) is, for instance, clearly a healing story, not an exorcism story. Jesus does not in that case perform any exorcism. When Paul in 2 Corinthians 12:7 tells that he three times asked the Lord that the messenger of Satan might depart from him, it does not mean that he three times sought an exorcist or performed an exorcism on himself, but on three occasions he asked for healing from his disease.

We think it is useful to let the concepts of exorcism and possession mutually define and delimit each other, so that it is possible to speak about possession in those cases where the adequate response to the condition is exorcism. What then is characteristic of those cases where Jesus performs an exorcism?

Direct dialogue between Jesus and the demon in the possessed person is the normal style. This dialogue is always lacking in the healing stories but always present in the exorcism stories, with the one exception where it is a demon of muteness.

The dialogue contains some fixed elements. The demon knows who Jesus is and says clearly and precisely that Jesus is the Son of God and has come to make an end to the rule of the demons. The demons know this before any humans have acknowledged Jesus as Lord (Luke 4:34).

Few criteria are given in the Gospels for indicating the presence of an evil spirit in a human being, except that the demons in different ways hurt the possessed person. It is as if the symptoms of possession were obvious and recognised on the basis of previous experience. It was not necessary to have a special spiritual gift in order to determine possession. It had manifestations that were evident to all. The spiritual gift described as to "discern spirits" in 1 Corinthians 12:10 relates to the ability of testing prophetic messages (1 Cor. 14:29).

In the same way, with reference to the ancient church we want to address the framework of these exorcism stories.

1. The exorcisms of Jesus must be understood within a larger framework of conflict between God and Satan. Satan's goal is to lead people away from God and generally to destroy God's good creation. In this battle both God and Satan have at their command an invisible army of spiritual beings, angels and demons respectively. One of the means of Satan in his effort to destroy God's creation is demon possession. The fact that possession exists is evidence of the power of Satan in our world. Jesus clarifies this by using a picture: "How can anyone enter the strong man's house and carry off his property, unless he first binds the strong man? And then he will plunder his house" (Matt. 12:29). When Jesus expels demons from tormented people, it is visible evidence that the power of Satan is broken. Satan is bound by Jesus, and Jesus is plundering his house. He conquers and re-establishes that which Satan has destroyed. Hence, Jesus' conclusion, "But if I cast out demons by the Spirit of God, then the kingdom of God has come upon you" (Matt. 12:28). The exorcisms of Jesus lose their meaning if they are disconnected from this context.

Other people also performed exorcisms. Jesus himself speaks about Jewish exorcists who did not believe in him. Non-Christian exorcism did not free people from anything but the concrete sufferings that came with the possession. They were still fearful of demons and continued to appease them or scare them away. The whole culture of antiquity was dominated by fear of demons and possession, and the ancient practice of exorcism supported this fear rather than removed it. The exorcisms of Jesus were significantly different. He not only set people free from their sufferings, but he transferred them into a new reality where the power of the demons is finally broken and where there is no fear of demons. Several historians of religion have been struck by this peculiar characteristic in the oldest Christian writings.

2. The combination of demons and idols, of paganism and possession, is not explicitly stated in the New Testament. However, it is notable that the majority of recorded exorcisms take place in the "border area" of paganism such as in "the Galilee of the Gentiles." The

most profiled accounts are those of the daughter of the Syro-Phoenician woman (Mark 7:24–30) and the man in the tombs east of the Sea of Galilee (Mark 1:1–17), where the villagers owned pigs and were therefore pagans. The accounts in Mark 1:23–28 about the man in the synagogue of Capernaum, and Mark 9:14–29 with the boy with an unclean spirit leave the unanswered question whether paganism was involved. There is one exorcism story outside the Gospels – Acts 16:16–18. This story is especially interesting because it so clearly does not connect possession with disease but with a pagan cult.

We therefore believe that there is a large degree of continuity in all of this material. Ideas of the demonic found in Judaism in the "inter-testamental" period were carried forward and received a christological centre in the New Testament. This developed further in its Christian form in the literature of the ancient church. The central elements in this set of thoughts may be summarised as follows: (1) a connection between demons and idolatry, paganism and possession; (2) Christ as the conqueror of the demons who has "bound the strong man" and shows his resurrection power in Christian exorcism; and (3) exorcism is primarily on the church's border with paganism.

Conclusion

Two points may be emphasised in closing. First, the thoughts examined let the modern experience of the church with the phenomenon of possession appear as totally "normal" and exactly what one would expect: Exorcism takes place primarily on the border of the church with paganism, and we would add especially with the animistic paganism of today. That possessions "at present are rare in Christendom," as it was stated in the Church Ritual of the Lutheran Church in Denmark-Norway in 1685, would hardly have surprised a Christian in antiquity. This is only to be expected because Christians are members of a community upon whom Christ has placed his seal.

Second, the approach to the phenomenon of possession during the first time of Christianity does not primarily start from the problem of "disease," but from the problem of "idolatry" or "pagan worship." When people seek to contact the spiritual world in non-biblical cults, there is a danger of them being occupied by the forces they seek to contact.

Notes

[1] Oskar Skarsaune is responsible for the first part of this article, covering the ancient church, while Tormod Engelsviken is responsible for the last part. The comments on the biblical texts are generally Skarsaune's contribution. Both agree as to the main conclusions.

[2] Quotations are taken from Alexander Roberts and James Donaldson, eds., *The Ante-Nicene Fathers,* vol. 3 (Grand Rapids, Mich.: Eerdmans, reprint 1986).

[3] Ibid., 26.

[4] Ibid.

[5] Ibid., 36.

[6] Ibid., 37–38.

[7] Roberts and Donaldson, *The Ante-Nicene Fathers,* 1:209.

[8] Ibid., 1:236.

[9] Ibid., 1:241.

[10] Ibid., 2:97

[11] Roberts and Donaldson, *The Ante-Nicene Fathers,* 4:398.

[12] Ibid., 4:612.

[13] Engelsviken's translation.

[14] Engelsviken's translation.

[15] Engelsviken's translations.

[16] G. P. Goold, ed., *The Apostolic Fathers* (Cambridge, Mass.: Harvard University Press, 1975), 1:399.

[17] Roberts and Donaldson, *The Ante-Nicene Fathers,* 3:90.

[18] Ibid., 3:38.

[19] Augustine, *De Civitate Dei,* VIII-X: De divinatione daemonum.

[20] E.g., Thomas Aquinas, *Summa Theologica,* I q. 50–64; q. 106–14.

[21] Snorre Sturlason, *Norges kongesagaer* (Oslo: Gyldendal, 1988), discussed in Oskar Skarsaune, "Misjonstenkningen i oldtiden og middelalderen," in *Missiologi i dag,* ed. Jan-Martin Berentsen, Tormod Engelsviken and Knud Jørgensen (Oslo: Universitetsforlaget, 1994), 89–109.

[22] Snorre Sturlason, *Norges kongesagaer,* 316 (Engelsviken's translation).

[23] Skarsaune, "Misjonstenkningen i oldtiden og middelalderen," 103–4.

[24] Ibid., 105.

[25] Perhaps 40,000 to 50,000, not the millions that some claim.

[26] Oskar Skarsaune, "Myte og realitet i kristendomshistorien" ("Myth and Reality in the History of Christianity"), in *Religion og Livssyn* 2 (1998): 25–29.

[27] For Luther's view, see Paul Althaus, *The Theology of Martin Luther* (Philadelphia: Fortress Press, 1966), 161–78.

[28] Ibid.

[29] See W. C. van Dam, *Dämonen und Besessene* (Aschaffenburg, 1970), 105.

[30] See John Warwick Montgomery, ed., *Principalities and Powers: A New Look at the World of the Occult* (Minneapolis, Minn.: Bethany Fellowship, 1973), 196–205.

[31] See Theodore G. Tappert, ed., *The Book of Concord* (Philadelphia: Fortress Press, 1959): *Large Catechism*, explanation to the second commandment (on the name of God), 371–75 (note that Luther counts the commandments differently, the second being the third in other traditions).

[32] Ibid., *Large Catechism*, explanation of the Lord's Prayer, the prayer "Deliver Us from Evil", 435–36. Luther comments on the meaning of this prayer: "In the Greek this petition reads, 'Deliver or keep us from the Evil One, or the Wicked One.' The petition seems to be speaking of the devil as the sum of all evil in order that the entire substance of our prayer may be directed against our arch-enemy. It is he who obstructs everything that we pray for: God's name or glory, God's kingdom and will, our daily bread, a good and cheerful conscience, etc."

[33] J. C. Jacobsen, *Djaevlebesvaergelse: Traek af Exorcismens Historie* (København, n.d.), 148ff.

[34] See *Catechism of the Catholic Church* (Mahwah, N.J.: Paulist Press, 1994), "The Fall of the Angels" (nos. 391–95), 98–99.

[35] See *New Catholic Encyclopedia* (New York: The Catholic University of America, 1967), s.v., "Exorcism" by E. J. Gratsch, "Diabolical Possession (in the Bible)" by J. Jensen, and "Diabolical Possession (Theology of)" by L. J. Elmer.

[36] The ritual can be found, for example, in Malachi Martin, *Hostage to the Devil* (New York: Perennial Library, 1976), 557–64.

[37] See Tormod Engelsviken, *Besettelse og åndsutdrivelse i Bibelen, historien og vår egen tid* [Possession and exorcism in the Bible, in history and in our own time](Oslo: Lunde, 1978).

II.

Reflections from the front lines

6

Demonisation and exorcism in Ethiopian churches

AMSALU TADESSE GELETA

Ethiopia is a country with diverse cultures, languages and religions. In this essay I seek to examine the nature of spiritual warfare as it is practised and understood by Christians in that country.

Demonisation and exorcism

Demonisation is found throughout Ethiopia, among many, if not most, of its peoples. Various anthropological explanations have been suggested to account for these manifestations. Most offer a psychosocial explanation, which holds that socially induced depravity, low status and feelings of inadequacy produce psychological reactions in individuals. These may manifest themselves as unusual behaviour that accompanies spirit possession. It is claimed that this theory explains the high incidence of spirit possession among women who are socially disenfranchised, men of "downtrodden categories" and men with "frustrated status ambition."[1]

Individual or group deprivation is another explanation of spirit possession among the Sidamo of Ethiopia developed by John Hamer. Jan Brøgger disagrees, however, arguing that similar possession occurs among wealthy men with high prestige.[2] He prefers the explanation that this behaviour is a psychological mechanism of social cohesion that allows the release of frustrations through the redirection of hostility.

Herbert Lewis argues that spirit possession rests on the belief that there are incorporeal beings in the universe which are capable of and interested in seizing the bodies of human beings and using them for their own purposes.[3] Exorcism is practised as a means of providing relief to those suffering from such an invading spirit.

Zar spirit cult

The Zar is a spirit-possession cult in which the people worship a group of spirits believed to be invisible, capable of foretelling the future, and even capable of solving international problems. They may be courageous heroes in war, efficient doctors in time of illness (except for venereal disease) and capable of causing destruction, plague and death if people do not pay them due respect.[4] In this section I will consider some anthropological views before turning to the views of the church.

Atete is a fertility cult in honour of the spirit of motherhood found among the Oromo, and there is a similar practice among the Amharas.[5] Atete is a nonviolent female goddess mainly connected with fertility. The main clients are women who seek supernatural help to become pregnant and give birth to healthy children.

For example, a girl may be possessed by her mother's ayana, who will visit her once or twice a week.[6] She spends the day preparing things that are needed for the ceremony. She has to wear special clothes (often of the opposite sex), putting on beads and ornaments, wearing perfume and possibly carrying a whip, a steel bar, or an empty gun. Green grass (a reed from a riverside) is spread on the floor. Different types of food, including porridge, butter, lemons, dadhi (honey wine), farso (home-made beer) and coffee are prepared in advance. There might be a sacrifice prescribed by the ayana on its previous possession in which a chicken, sheep or goat of a certain colour is offered together with perfumes or different spices. If the offerings and the preparation please the spirit, it enters the one making the offerings.

People know that she is possessed when she starts yawning, stretching, salivating and becoming drowsy. Her body wavers, and she also cries, speaking as if she is in a dream. She often falls down and covers her face with her dress. She may jump and run away and climb trees, not coming down until people beg her. She may stand on glowing wood or eat embers, cut herself with a knife, or crush pieces of glass and eat them. She speaks in a strange voice, often using a language understood only by the zar themselves. She may sing a song reserved for the occasion or dance a peculiar dance associated with that ceremony. She has supernormal strength, talks in a different voice, and engages in abnormal activities to signify the spirit has possessed her.

This possession may last from a few hours to two or three days. The main function of the spectators is to appease the *ayana*, sing songs, clap, dance and beat a drum, and beg the spirit not to hurt her.

The equivalent man's *zar* cult is *seer*. The ritual expert *(qalicha)* dresses in special clothes for the occasion and summons his *zar*, that he has learned to control. As the *zar* takes possession of him, people begin to clap and sing the *zar's* song.[7] As the dancing continues, he does extraordinary things. At the pleas from his clients, he tells people the location of lost or stolen things. He is believed to know the right sacrifice needed to resolve calamities, cure diseases and deliver from death. He is also considered to have the ability to read the future by examining the fatty tissue around the stomach of a lamb or sheep.

The *qalicha* must not touch a corpse or enter a house where there is a dead body. He is not able to eat food that is disliked by his *zar*, nor is he able to cross the fields sown with certain crops.

The evil eye

The evil eye is considered to be a special ability of some people to harm others by looking at them. These people are known as *buda*, and the anthropologist Ronald A. Reminick records the Amharic myth of their origin.[8] This is not a well-known story and seems to be limited to the area or persons he interviewed. It may be one of a variety of myths found in the country. The major outline of the story is as follows.

It is said that Eve had 30 children, and one day God asked Eve to show him her children. Eve became suspicious and apprehensive and hid 15 of them from the sight of God. God knew her act of disobedience and declared the 15 children she showed him were to be his chosen children, but the other 15 God cursed. The 15 she hid were henceforth to go into the world as devils and wretched creatures of the earth. Some of the children begged God's mercy, and being merciful, he made some of them foxes, jackals, and rabbits, so that they might exist in a dignified manner. Some of the hidden children he left as human but sent away with the curse of being agents of the Devil, and these were the ancestors of the *buda* people.

Most people say that there is no way of recognizing *buda* by their physical qualities. Reminick has suggested that the *buda* have an eye deformity or suffer from discharge of puss from their eyes. They may tend to look sidewise at people, or they may have an ashen substance in their mouths that means they are unable to spit saliva. Even for Reminick these features are not enough to recognise them. *Buda* are considered to be possessed by an evil spirit and create problems for others to the extent of killing them.[9] It is believed that a person is most vulnerable to attack when the *buda* sees fear, worry and anxiety. Because of the power of the evil eye, *buda* are said to be able to change into hyenas and roam the countryside at night. This is a convenient form, for it conceals their human identity. Most people, including some Christians, are therefore fearful of them.

The second method of attack involves the *buda* finding a victim, twisting the root of a certain plant and forming a loop with this root as if tying a knot. The loop is then drawn smaller very slowly; while this is being done, the victim dies.

The third method of attack involves giving the evil-eye gaze to the victim and then waiting for his or her death. Explanations of the attacks of *buda* are commonly found not only among Amharas but also among the non-Amhara people of Ethiopia.

There are four traditional methods of diagnosis and exorcism of evil spirits. In the first the afflicted person is taken to a *debtera,* an ordained member of the Ethiopian Church who has knowledge of the rituals, literature and scripture. The *debtera* performs a rite using holy water, praying and pronouncing words in Geez, an ancient liturgical language. The drinking of holy water and the smoke from a burning root may effect the cure. If this fails the *debtera* may turn to magical incantations found in the *Magic Star Book.*

A second way of dealing with the affliction is to take the person to a *qalicha,* a person who has gained powers through being possessed by a *zar* spirit and is therefore able to communicate with the *zar* and effect cures for many kinds of illness. The *buda* spirit is exorcised by being possessed by a *zar* spirit.

A third way is through the use of smoke from a dung fire. If a person is recognised as being attacked by evil eye through showing signs such as biting his or her lips, the relatives may tie the victim's left thumb with string. The patient is then made to breathe the smoke of a dung fire. This causes the spirit that has possessed the person to speak. The attacking spirit may ask for compensation and leave with a shout when it is received. This is an immediate way that the family can use to exorcise the spirit and heal the afflicted.

A fourth means can take place in the very presence of the attacker. If a family recognises that the person is attacked by the *buda* spirit and have a suspect, they may call both the *buda* and non-*buda* people to one place. They then ask them to spit saliva on a glowing hot metal axe, a sickle or even a knife blade. When the *buda* spits the patient will get relief and be cured.[10] In these complex traditions the operation of evil spirits can be seen in both possessed and exorcist.

Demonisation in Ethiopia

Demonisation is not a new phenomenon. Ceremonies show that people deliberately prepare themselves to be demonised. The spirit can initially reward them, but finally it inflicts them with sickness or some dangerous condition. The demonised then come to church to seek exorcism. The Christian explanation of the *zar* and evil eye is that the people are oppressed by an evil spirit under various names.

Demonisation is not limited to a specific area, tribe, or religion. Tormod Engelsviken, a former missionary to Ethiopia, says, "Although the frequency may vary, reports of possession are found among most if not all tribes, in all areas of the country and in all religions, including traditional religions, Islam and Ethiopian Orthodox Christianity."[11]

The confrontation between Christianity and traditional religion is on the level of power encounter. This is continued in the daily experience of the Christian life. *Christus Victor* is the experience of Christians. Most prayer meetings and individual prayers concentrate on rebuking the evil spirits. Prayers are offered for protection against evil. The victory songs emphasise that Christ is victorious over all kinds evil spirits.

Non-Christians may first seek a cure by traditional methods. They may consult the seers (or *qalichas*), who require payment either in cash or kind. Often the relief is only for a while, and the person is forced to search for other cures. Modern medicine is not applicable to the cure of the demoniacs. As a final attempt victims either come by themselves or are brought by families or immediate neighbours to a prayer meeting.

Symptoms of demonisation

The afflicted may have various symptoms found in four groupings. The first is physical symptoms. Most demoniacs suffer illness when they are under the control of an alien spirit. As in the New Testament, demons are believed to cause muteness (Matt. 9:32f; Mark 9:17; Luke 11:14), blindness (Matt. 12:22), self-inflicted wounds (Mark 5:5), fever, headache and stomach aches. Demons can also give the ability to ignore pain or feel pain with no physical cause. These sicknesses have no medically discernible cause and do not respond to medical treatment.

The second group is that of various mental disturbances. The person may show

> unnecessary fears, unusual dreams or hallucinations (especially frightening and/or recurring ones), and mental problems that do not yield to normal treatment such as depression, extreme sexual perversion, unnecessary self-accusation, hearing sounds (footsteps, noises, and commands) that no one else hears, especially near the person at night, extreme passiveness, overwhelming fear of evil, extreme confusion, cloudiness of thought and unusual or inappropriate emotional reactions such as laughter, sadness, crying, anger.[12]

All forms of exaggerated passions, addictions to commit sin, temper, anger, quarrelsomeness and domineering personality are part of this group. These behavioral changes result in actions that are beyond the norm of the society. Screaming, crying, eating sour leaves, going out naked and deeds that are ethically evil are symptoms of demonisation.

A third class of symptoms can best be regarded as supernatural abilities. Demoniacs may have the ability to speak in a language they have not learned or even heard. There are several reports from different regions of demoniacs speaking in a language they don't use in their normal state. They may also know facts previously unknown to either the demoniac or to the exorcist.

Extraordinary strength is another characteristic in this group, as well as a change of voice. For example, a woman may speak in a man's voice or vice versa. It has been noticed that people have spoken with the voices of cats, hyenas, donkeys and dogs. There may be loss of body control, avoidance of eye contact, and breathing as if suffocating.

Spiritual symptoms are a fourth group of demonisation characteristics. This is usually understood by Ethiopian Christians as a reaction against the name of Jesus. There may be a loss of spiritual growth or the inability to concentrate on Scripture and prayers. On the other hand, an extreme sense of self-righteousness, visions directing a person to go against the will of God, "spiritual gifts" that are accompanied by negative effects like depression, and a sense of being unique are also symptoms.

CAUSES OF DEMONISATION

It is difficult to list all the causes of demonisation, but the following provides a general characterisation.

Ethiopians consider some places as particular dwellings for evil spirits. These may be ruined houses in which no one has lived for some time, so that anyone who enters is attacked by the spirit. Dirty areas, caves, thick forests and big waterfalls are suspected as dwelling places fit for spirits. Midday heat is believed to be a particularly opportune time for demons to do their activities. Eating delicious food in the sun or walking in the sun after a good meal may bring demonic attack. These beliefs are deeply rooted in the culture and are held also by Christians to some extent.

Personal involvement in the occult, especially with the *qalicha* or *zar* ritual, is a major cause of demonisation. Any involvement in magic, fortune-telling and astrology is also considered dangerous. Most of the people who come to church to get help were ritual experts or had excessive involvement in related ceremonies.

Evangelical Christianity is only a century old in the country. Some areas are newly evangelised and others have not yet been reached with the Good News. Often mediumistic powers of *qalichas* and traditional cults can be traced back over several generations in one family. So the influence can still be strong among Christians.

It is believed that there are times when people who come in contact with occult or demonic abilities are vulnerable to demonisation. This can be through laying on hands, holding hands, hypnotism, or some sort of magic treatment. There are many examples of demonised persons who speak in tongues, prophesy, and have the gifts of healing who are exorcised and are freed from deceiving evil spirits. Sometimes the reason may be a vow that the possessed has taken to achieve some advantage or help in a critical situation. Such a vow may involve a sacrifice to the spirits or the dedication of some pieces of property such as rings, pots or sticks.

Another cause of possession is believed to be extreme anxiety. This is seen, for example, when a person is frightened by a hyena or lion, when an individual insults or laughs at a demonised person, or when they are unreasonably afraid of being alone in the night. Demonisation can result from taking a shower or bath in a river.

Dealing with the demonised

In the third century the church instituted the office of exorcist to officiate at the service of exorcism for catechumens before their baptism. The office of exorcist is ranked higher than the office of reader, and exorcists are considered members of the clergy appointed by the bishop in the Greek Orthodox Church (see Canon 26, Synod Laodicea; Canon 10, Synod of Antioch). In the Greek Orthodox Church the exorcist is considered to have the gift of curing those who are demonised, but in the Ethiopian Evangelical Churches every Christian is considered able to exorcise. There is no special call to do it, and the gift of exorcism is given to all.

Sample case studies

There is no set formula to exorcise demons in the evangelical church. It is seen as a direct confrontation of the spirits in the name of Jesus. I have collected and analyzed 20 cases of exorcism, of which three are presented in detail. The following table lists the person possessed, the names of the possessing spirit, the place where the exorcism took place or where the demoniac came from, the year of the experience and the approximate age of the afflicted person. Out of the 20 cases given below, 16 are from my own experience; the remaining cases (10, 13, 17 and 20) are from reliable firsthand informants.

Table 6-1: Twenty cases of exorcisms

Case	Names of spirit		Place	Year	Approx. Age
1. Baby	High Fever		Boneya	1991	6 months
2. Boy	*Dache (Underneath)*		Boneya	1991	<15
3. Girl	Madness		Abdata	1991	15
4. Taye	Evil eye		Boneya	1992	30
5. Getachew	*Qalicha*		Mirkuze Mariam	1990	18
6. Carpenter	Jealousy		Naqamte	1984	<35
7. Girl	King of Aware[13]		Addis Ababa	1992	25
8. Man	Deception		Warqai-Dirre		>28
9. Woman from delivery room	evil eye		Naqamte	1984	30
10. Merchant	Disease		Asosa	1995	30
11. Mother of baby (case 1)	Headache		Boneya	1991	30

12. Alemayew	Madness	Naqamte	1995	>30
13. Woman	Disease	Jato	1997	
14. Endashaw	Unusual reaction	Addis Ababa	1991	>30
15. Adult	Of serpent	Naqamte	1997	35
16. Woman	*Dache*	Gara Hudha	1979	38
17. Ex-soldier		Fincha'a	1997	38
18. Wodaje	Idolatry	Boneya	1978	>40
19. Woman			1978	>40
20. Man	*Qalicha*	Ambalta	1996	45

These cases show that demonisation does not depend on the locality, age, sex or occupation. A six-month-old baby and adults over 45 are vulnerable to demonic attack. Neither age nor the social status of the person determines demonisation, so it does not seem to be a compensation for a lack of social status. All people seem to be open to demonic attack if they have no protection against it. The demonic attacks against the baby (case 1), merchant (10), carpenter (6), former *qalichas* (5, 20) and a small, private-company owner (14) demonstrate this.

As far as location is concerned, the cases given above cover different parts of eastern Wollega, Illu-Ababora, Asosa and Addis Ababa – areas of central, west and southwest Ethiopia. The settings for the exorcisms were in rural (3, 5, 16, 20), semi-rural (1, 2, 4, 8, 11, 13, 18) and urban areas (6, 7, 9, 10, 14, 17). They include unreached, newly evangelised and evangelised areas.

The exorcism ministry has many implications. The demoniacs become healthy, mentally normal, psychologically stable and socially accepted people. Some exorcisms provide opportunities for evangelising unreached areas. The exorcisms of cases 5 and 20 ended up establishing two congregations at Banbachi and Ambalta (EECMY Central Synod) respectively. In other cases unbelievers who followed the demoniacs to the prayer meetings became Christians because of the power of the name of Jesus in delivering people from bondage. The conversion of a Muslim husband (10), a sister of the demoniac (7) in Addis Ababa and the surrender of five people to Christ (15) at Naqamte show the breaking of the power of demons and the expansion of the kingdom of God.

CASE 15

For case 15 the event began around 6 o'clock in the evening. One of the evangelists of Naqamte congregation (EECMY Central

Synod) and I were at the main entrance of the church compound. A group of about ten people brought a man chained to a Land Rover. They were crying and struggling to hold him down. We stopped and asked what had happened. They told us that something was wrong with him and that no one could hold him, even with ropes. So we brought him to the church to see if we could get help. As there was no one in the church to pray for the man, we did. We rebuked the evil spirit, telling it to be quiet, and then we told the people to untie his ropes. They protested that the man could escape, but we assured them he would not. We then ordered the demoniac to walk into the church, and we told the demon not to disturb the gathering while we shared the gospel with those who brought the man. All of them were non-Christian neighbours who came to assist his wife in bringing him to the church. So we preached the victorious Christ, not only over the evil spirit, but also over the sins of the people.

Then we commanded the evil spirit to reveal itself and say who it was and why it had possessed the man. The spirit claimed that it was the spirit of the serpent *(hafura Jawe)*, and *Dache* (literally meaning "beneath" in Oromo language). These two spirits said that they attacked him because he had disturbed them while they had a coffee ceremony in the middle of the day. The spirits claimed that the person broke a cup and that made them angry, so they possessed him. In addition, the spirits said the person had no protection and so was vulnerable to their attack. Afterwards, he continued committing the sins that the spirits urged him to do.

The spirits aimed to kill the person that evening and make an offering. We continued to pray and give praises to God. Those who had brought the man were curious to observe what we did, and they were especially intrigued that no devices were used – we merely spoke in the name of Jesus. We rebuked the spirits and they said they would leave – and they did. The person stayed reclining for about five minutes before standing up, wondering how he had come to the church. He went home carrying the rope with which he was bound when he came. He came tied and went home free. The event was practical evangelisation for others.

This method is almost the same for all exorcisms practised by Ethiopian Christians. They usually include singing praise and victory songs, reading from the Scripture, prayer and confronting the spirit in the name of Jesus. Dialogue with the spirit is another important part of the exorcism ceremony. This helps the counsellor (exorcist) know how the spirit was operating in the life of the demoniac. The signs and events mentioned by the spirit are affirmed by the victim after deliverance. Sometimes the spirit identifies other people within the meeting who are afflicted. There are some exceptional cases in which the demoniac may call on other demonised persons from far-away places.

CASE 13

In this case a group of Christians was praying in a house meeting at Jato near Naqamte, which is 331 kilometres west of the capital. This was the usual morning prayer meeting led by Kedir Yasin, a converted Muslim. Suddenly a woman began to cry. Kedir commanded the spirit to tell her if there are other demoniacs in the meeting. The spirit responded that they occupied a man who was herding his cattle near the Jato River, which was half a kilometre away from where the meeting was being held. Kedir commanded the spirit to bring the demoniac from the riverside to the house. The people were praying and praising the almighty God, who does wonders. One of the group was watching while the possessed woman was telling how the demoniac was running to the prayer house. Within a couple of minutes the demoniac came, shouting that Jesus was tormenting him. They rebuked the spirit and both demoniacs were cured. Similar testimonies are reported from different directions.

CASE 10

There are times when exorcisms of demons are not so successful. Case 10 was that of a Muslim husband who brought his demonised wife to the Naqamte Wednesday prayer time, which is especially for healing. The wife had been sick for a long period, and they had found no cure. The prayer group tried to exorcise the spirits as they had done before, but this time it did not happen. The demoniac had extra strength and kicked all who tried to pray for her. The group decided to take its time and set up a program for two weeks, praying day and night. It was time-consuming and demanded patience to see any results. The demons got hosts of other evil spirits to empower her to resist the effects of their prayers. The prayer group resisted all oppression. After two weeks the demons inhabiting the woman left. She was cured, which resulted in the conversion of her husband and many people of her town of Asosa (500 kilometres west of the capital) where she was a known sorcerer. This was different from the other cases in that it demanded patience and perseverance.

DISCUSSION

In all cases the spirit is commanded to leave in no other name than that of Jesus. The exorcist tells of the redemptive work of Jesus on the cross, and whenever the blood of Jesus is called the demons shout that they are burned or tortured. The first case shows a typical type of exorcism that is often practised. The second account is rare. Calling the possessed from a far-away area and exorcising the demon is unusual, but it is sometimes done in newly evangelised areas as a power encounter. The third case indicates that exorcism is not always easy and may require a long period of prayer and intercession.

Not all exorcisms are successful. Alemayew, who lived in Naqamte, was possessed for a number of years and acted as if he was mad. The congregation finally took responsibility to minister to him in a holistic way for about five years. However, after five years of normal life, he was once again possessed and became mad.

Contemporary challenges

Because of the religious freedom in Ethiopia, various sects with extreme views about evil spirits have recently emerged. Some of them deny that Christians can be possessed. In practice, however, Christians who are baptised and confess their faith are sometimes possessed. The fast numerical growth of church membership and the lack of trained leadership are major challenges facing the evangelical church in Ethiopia.

Further, the influence of the traditional religions is still strong and produces syncretistic practices among some of the Christians. People still fear the power of the evil eye, and the notion of "fortune" is common among Christians. Traditional practitioners use particular techniques to exorcise spirits and some of these have influenced Christian practice of exorcism. These include slapping the demoniac and torturing those attacked by the evil eye by pouring cold water on them. Such violent acts are neither grounded in the Scripture nor beneficial to the person, as they can do harm to the former host.

Additionally, the political system is causing famine, war and environmental destruction. In addition to being unable to distribute food in times of famine and killing hundreds of thousands in war with Eritrea, Ethiopia was unprepared when a massive fire consumed thousands of hectares of forest in the southern areas in 2000. Several students who protested the government's handling of the fire were killed and farmers were imprisoned. Further, ethnic conflicts within the country have fragmented the nation and have had a negative impact on the unity and mission of the church in Ethiopia today. These, too, are areas of spiritual conflict in contemporary Ethiopia.

Notes

[1] See Herbert S. Lewis, "Spirit Possession in Ethiopia: An Essay in Interpretation," in *Proceedings of the Seventh International Conference of Ethiopian Studies, University of Lund, 26–29 April 1982*, ed. Sven Rubenson (Uppsala: SIAS, 1984), 419.

[2] Jan Brøgger, *Belief and Experience Among the Sidamo: A Case Study Towards Anthropology of Knowledge* (Oslo: Universtetsforlaget As., 1986), 289.

[3] Lewis, "Spirit Possession in Ethiopia," 420.

[4] E. Fuller Torrey, "The Zar Cult in Ethiopia," *Proceeding of the Third International Conference of Ethiopian Studies, Addis Ababa 1966* (Addis Ababa: Haile Selassie University), 217.

[5] Torrey, "The Zar Cult in Ethiopia," 219; Lambert Bartels, *Oromo Religion: Myths and Rites of the Western Oromo of Ethiopia* (Berlin: D. Reimer, 1990), 321.

[6] In this context *Ayana* refers to spirit.

[7] Torrey, "The Zar Cult in Ethiopia," 220.

[8] Ronald A. Reminick, "Evil Eye Belief Among the Amhara," in *Evil Eye*, ed. Clarence Maloney (New York: Columbia University Press, 1976).

[9] Ibid.

[10] Cf. ibid., 179f.

[11] Tormod Engelsviken, "Exorcism and Healing in the Evangelical Churches of Ethiopia," *Journal of Mission Theology* 1:1 (1991): 83.

[12] A. Scott Moreau, *The World of the Spirits: A Biblical Study in the African Context* (Nairobi: Evangel Publishing House, 1990), 152.

[13] "Aware" is an area name in Addis Ababa.

7

Umbanda in Brazil

Neuza Itioka

Spiritual conflict is the struggle between light and darkness and has been present throughout the history of God's people. Spiritual warfare can bring about the transformation of people, churches and cities, as the following case studies from Brazil demonstrate.

Brazilian spiritism

The powers of darkness are manifest in Brazil through the spiritism that is a mixture of beliefs in saints and spirits, divination and healing.

It was December 31, New Year's Eve. For many Brazilians this is the night for bringing in the new year, but it is also a night in which Iemanja, the spirit of the waters, is invoked. On this date between 1 and 1.5 million people go down to the beach to honour Iemanja, offering perfume, champagne, jewellery, flowers and food to the spirit of the waters in exchange for benefits in the areas of health, love and material prosperity.

A group of young people from an evangelical church decided to go to the beach for evangelism. They had prayed and prepared themselves, and even fasted, in order to be ready to face the difficult cases of evangelism that might arise. When they arrived at the beach, they parked their bus near the statue of Iemanja, which was already duly ornamented for her celebration. Nearby they saw a woman swirling in the sand, invoking the spiritual entities to become incorporated in her.

They began to pray quietly, forbidding the demons, as they understood them to be, to enter her body. After a while the woman stopped swirling and said, "What's going on here? I am invoking the entities, and they don't come."

The young people answered, "We are forbidding them to come to you, in the name of Jesus." She protested, "But I'm invoking them in the name of Jesus, too."

They began to share their faith, telling her about Jesus, the Son of the Almighty God, who wasn't just any Jesus, but Jesus, Lord of the Universe, who came in flesh and blood. And they told her about God's great love.

The woman knelt in the sand and opened her heart to receive the Lord Jesus. She revealed that she was a Mother of Saints, a priestess in Umbanda, one of the Brazilian religions, and she asked, "Please, come to my *terreiro* (spiritist temple) to tell my people about this wonderful Jesus."

Although Brazil is known as a Catholic country, in reality it is spiritist! This is a syncretistic religion based upon various traditions. The most ancient inhabitants of the land worshipped ancestors. When making any significant decision, the Indians consulted their family ancestors. Decisions concerning marriages, planting, harvest, hunting and migration were all decided after having consulted the ancestors.

Historical background

The European colonizers brought medieval Catholicism. When the black slaves were brought to Brazil they brought with them their African beliefs. Once the slaves arrived in Brazil, the Catholic Church baptised them in the name of Christ with little regard to the actual change of their beliefs. Thus, in their minds the slaves merged the African religion with the Catholic saints. The Virgin Mary was identified with the Yoruba deity Iemanja, the spirit of the waters. Saint George, who was often portrayed as mounted upon a horse fighting a dragon, was Ogun, the god of justice and violence. The pomp of the priests, with their colourful clothing, and the Latin ritual both attracted and excited the slaves.[1] Religious beliefs and practices were mixed to give birth to an Afro-Brazilian religion, which in the south of the country is called Candomble, and in the north and northeast, Xango. This religion was especially important among the poor and illiterate slaves.

Another element came with Denizard Hipolite-Leon Rivail, who introduced the ideas of a French spiritist named Alan Kardec. Kardec was influenced by the positivism of Augusto Comte, and he masterfully applied determinist and evolutionary ideas to form an elaborate religious system.[2] He said that God had created the universe and then abandoned it, leaving it at the mercy of the law of evolution (Darwin's theory of evolution was popular at the time). He taught that people are essentially spirits contained in a body, and these spirits continually evolve until they arrive at the level of Christ, who is the chief of planet Earth. As human beings are full of errors and sins, people often fail. They therefore transmigrate and are reincarnated.

The meeting of the Afro-Brazilian religions and Kardecism resulted in a second stage of syncretism with the formation of a low-level of spiritism called Umbanda. Pedro McGregor writes of Kardec's beliefs:

And here was the essence of religious and racial syncretism: Negro and white worshippers together, practising a more evolved form of African ritual, under the influence of Europe's Kardecism, under the leadership of an Indian spirit guide, and under the name of Our Lady of Piety! Yet, the spirit "appointed" by the Caboclo as "the great master," the spiritual leader of all, is none other than—Jesus Christ, whom he calls by the African equivalent, Oxalá.[3]

Renato Ortiz, an expert on the subject, says that Umbanda is the national religion of Brazil. Twenty years ago all of Brazil was immersed in some sort of practice of spiritism. Millions of people would go down to the beach and visit the lakes to invoke the spirit of the waters. The consequences in the lives of the people who practised low-spiritism were serious demonisation, oppression at all levels, broken families, divorce, death, sickness and bankruptcy.

A small sector of the church of Christ in Brazil became aware of the misery of the people and challenged the dominant principalities and powers. The church members were obligated to discover the authority and position of a disciple of Jesus Christ, based on his word, "Behold, I give you authority to step on serpents and scorpions, and on all the power of the enemy, and nothing will harm you" (Luke 10:19 and other declarations; see Matt. 10:1 and Mark 3:15). In light of this enormous challenge, and discerning what was really happening, they were obligated to become involved in the fight. The teachings on spiritual conflict and the practice of deliverance began to spread to many churches. In the last ten years thousands of Christians have participated in seminars on spiritual warfare, and many have experienced personal deliverance. Many leaders began to heal distraught people through deliverance and inner healing. As a result of this, the pioneers of this movement faced much criticism, especially from those leaders trained in Western theology.

During the last ten years many churches and ministries have been transformed, but other issues have arisen. Early in 1990, 70 disciples of Jesus met for the First National Consultation on Spiritual Warfare in the interior of the state of São Paulo. On that occasion, Iemanja, the reigning spirit in Brazil, one of the Brazilian versions of the queen of heaven, was dethroned.

The residue of the struggle remains. Her followers still dress as Iemanja in festivities and present themselves as her in parades and on stages. But the worship of Iemanja on the beaches has decreased drastically. Millions of people who used to go to worship her and ask favours no longer do so.

Thus many lives have been transformed by the power of the gospel. However, spiritual pride, triumphalism, boastful nationalism, immaturity, the search for the right method of warfare instead of sanctification, character and a life of authority have become problems in some areas of the church.

The transformation of people

Christian leaders now frequently minister to people in their churches. However, as the following stories will illustrate, they have the conditions that the individuals must be converted, that they be serious about their Christian life, and that they have a desire to be freed from their problems. Take the following case of a woman who was a priestess in Candomble.

She had been the wife of Beelzebub in Candomble. She sought us out because she was experiencing a very difficult moment. Recently her church, whose pastor was her husband, had been destroyed by a very unpleasant situation. She needed special help.

In Candomble she had discovered that she had the ability of a medium to hear the spirits, incorporate them, perform healings and divination, and resolve problems in the areas of love, marriage and finances. She became more and more involved, and later became the bride of Beelzebub. He would say that he was very happy with her. She had become a slave and was obligated to do anything that the spirit demanded, bringing false divinations. Instead of restoring marriages, the solution was only superficial, and in reality the spirits would separate the couples more and more. As for the healings, the spirits would just remove the symptoms and transfer them to other parts of the person's body. And she continued to obey them blindly, until one day Beelzebub asked her to offer her son as a sacrifice to him.

This woman fled from her master and found refuge in a Christian church. But she never received the ministration of deliverance. In this church she met a young worker, began to date him, and they got married. Her husband, who was from an evangelical family, became the pastor of the church. But then something strange began to happen. He began having sexual relationships with all the women of the church, and she, shocked, said that she had never seen anything like that, even in Candomble, became revolted, and began doing the same, sleeping with the men of the church. The church was destroyed, and she sought help. She was in despair, and her marriage had been destroyed.

Profound deliverance was necessary. She had made pacts with over 60 spiritual entities and had served each one. She had lived the illusion that she had controlled the spirits, but she was actually their slave. They controlled her. When Jesus came into her life, they carefully hid themselves and manifested themselves through her emotions – hate, anger, tears, loneliness, self-accusation, the desire to die, guilt and sadness.

After confessing her sins and renouncing the spirits, they began to manifest themselves. One by one they identified themselves and left, leaving her life forever.[4]

Deliverance of this ex-priestess required the following convictions. The first was a firm conviction of Jesus as Lord, that he had destroyed the power of Satan and his demons on the cross of Calvary and that the church had the authority to crush the powers of the enemy (Luke 10:19), to rebuke (Matt. 17:18) and to cast out (Mark 3:15).

Second, although she had been in the church for many years, she had never been ministered to in the area of deliverance. The pacts that this woman had made with darkness had never been clearly broken, and she had never formally renounced her former lords, whom she had served for many years (Acts 19:18–19). As they had not been recognised or cast out, they were hidden, so that they could make her life miserable.

Transformation of cities

Another aspect of this conflict is illustrated when the church has rejected the powers of darkness in an area.

In 1991 the mayor of the city of Florianopolis, together with some organisations, planned to transform the city into a great psychic airport, where witches from all over the country would perform magic, apparitions, levitation, and where the gods would manifest themselves through a Magic Festival. During this festival the island of Santa Catarina would be officially handed over to a spirit named Catarina of Alexandria, or Ewa. Beginning with this event, the city of Florianopolis, which is situated on an island, would be called by a suggestive name, The Magic Island.

The pastors were very concerned. They knew that if this festival took place the city would attract great curses to itself and would suffer great harm, and there would also be more confusion among the people. They went to the mayor to voice their concern, but they weren't taken seriously.

Three months before the festival the Christians displayed several billboards with the saying, "Florianopolis, Jesus' Island." The churches interceded 24 hours a day that the event would be a failure.

The first sign that God had heard the prayers of his children was the torrential rains the fell throughout the festival – dousing the candles lighted along the beaches to honor Ewa. The rains kept away the great multitude that had been expected.

The pavilion consisted of 62 stalls, where crystals, pyramids, candles, mystic decorations and straw witches were sold. There were stalls for the consultation of shells, tarot, numerology, astrology, psychic massages, cards, fortune-telling and all sorts of Umbanda consultation, where the people could chose any of the demons or spirits they wished.

Among all those stalls was one that received special attention, called Yeshua's stall. Those who entered received a word of comfort, consolation and a New Testament.

Almost every day the *orixas* were invoked, but thanks to the warfare intercession of the Christians, the spirits were hindered, bound and cast out, and did not answer the convocation of the witches.

Soon the organisers and owners of the stalls began to protest, saying that there had been interference in the spiritual world. The Christians were praying, forbidding any manifestation of the spirits at the festival. Then the media found out that the Christians were hindering the entities from appearing and decided to cause a scandal to denounce them. They went to the location armed with equipment and cameras, but God had told the warriors not to go on that day. Thus, alone, the press could do nothing.

A youth drama group also presented a play called "The Two Kingdoms," depicting the conflict between light and darkness. Amidst so many witches, Jesus was declared King!

In the last two days a different strategy was used to fill the pavilion with Christians, who brought with them the presence of Jesus. Pastor João de Souza recounts that at a particular moment there seemed to be more Christians than visitors at the festival. On the last day, Sunday, the Christians began arriving early. Some brothers and sisters spent all day there telling others about Jesus. The play "The Two Kingdoms" was presented again, and more people heard the gospel. There were Christians everywhere. When the mystics made one last attempt to invoke the presence of Ewa, the Christians made a circle around them and softly sang, "In the presence of the gods I will sing praises to You!" And then they sang, "Jesus, we enthrone you and declare that you are King!"

As a result of all this, the world saw, through the media, the difference between darkness and light. The church was strengthened, and the pastors more united. The witches were defeated, and not one demon landed on the island!

The Magic Festival turned into a great headache for the organisers. The local government, which had not heeded the advice of the pastors, had to assume a large debt, and the leaders of the festival became involved in court battles. They decided that they would organise the next such festival anywhere but in Florianopolis!

It was a great defeat for the world of darkness. It was proven, once again, that there is a name that is above all names, whose title is "the head of all principality and power" (Col. 2:10), and that all the powers are obligated to subject themselves to this name.[5]

Another example was the Congress on Cosmic Energy held in Brasilia.

In July of 1996, in the city of Brasilia, a large Congress on Cosmic Energy was also planned. Over 10,000 people were expected for the event. The event was advertised far ahead of time by the media and on posters.

The pastors of that city also took a position before God, forbidding, through prayer and intercession, the event to occur or to have any measure of success. The locale where the event was to take place was visited by the people, where they fasted and prayed, asking God to move and forbid the occurrence of the events. The locale was also duly anointed with oil.

In fact, the event did not take place, for of the 10,000 people that were expected, just 60 showed up, and all of these were either of the organising committee or were there to sell their products. The final result was disastrous, for the owners of the stalls and those who had meant to make a profit during the congress ended up suing the organiser of the event, and everyone ended up at the police station.[6]

What is common to all these stories is the need for prayer and intercession – of repentance, confession, renouncement and warfare (binding, rebuking, disconnecting, crushing, putting under the feet, casting out). All action must begin with the presupposition that God answers prayer and that the spirits submit themselves to the command of the people of God, done in the name of Jesus. However, it is also necessary to have unity among the pastors.

Carnival is an important feature of the life of many big cities, and this can result in much immorality. Many Christians have therefore opposed it in prayer.

When one of the members of my team read in her town's papers that the Pomba Giras (spirits of prostitution) would be honored during that Carnival, she sought to find out more about the subject. In fact, Santo Andre was making an allegoric float in honour of the spirit of sensuality, prostitution, and lust for the 1994 Carnival. And there would be naked women who would be parading in the streets also in honour of the Pomba Giras.

This information was brought to the deliverance team during a retreat, and so the team members interceded, asking God to intervene. There was repentance for the sins of the city, and they were confessed – sensuality, hedonism, exhibitionism, impurity. Forgiveness was asked especially for the permission that had been given to honour the spirit of prostitution. Other intercessors from the region joined in the prayer and intercession that continued in the following weeks. The intercessors prayed and asked God to send fire from heaven to burn all impurity. And God literally answered that prayer. The float caught on fire and was destroyed. There was no parade.[7]

The healing of the church

In order to see cities transformed, the church of Christ must be healthy and motivated to see the glory of God manifested in it. In reality, the situation in Brazil is shameful. The church could be described as a bride with torn clothing, dirty and fallen into a gutter. She is drunk from drinking in so much of the world. Paraphrasing Ezekiel 16, we could say that

the Brazilian church has forgotten that her origin was medieval witchcraft, her father Catholic and her mother spiritist. When she was born, no one paid much attention. She was small, ugly and covered with blood. No one passed by to help her. And the Lord, coming, even though she was dirty, rejected and despised, said, "Live." He cleaned her and washed her and made her beautiful and lovely. He made a covenant with her and dressed her in embroidered clothing of fine linen, and gave her shoes of marine animals, and decorated her with fine jewellery of gold and silver. But she began to trust in her beauty. The words of praise that came from many, such as, "The Brazilian church grows so quickly," "Brazil will produce many missionaries," led her to be prideful. Trusting in her beauty, she began to play the harlot. She began to seek other lovers – prosperity, the human empire, idolatry of ministries, numerology, egoism, deceit, hypocrisy, corruption, adultery, illicit sex, prostitution. Worse, she began to sacrifice her sons and daughters, which the Lord had given her, to strange gods. The little sheep were being sacrificed not for the building of the kingdom of God, but for the empire of men. The children began to die upon the altars of power, competition, radios, marketing and TV.

Here in the church the struggle is not against demons but against the enemy that abides within us, the flesh – pride, vanity, the search for power, control, manipulation, self-confidence, competition, envy, as well as idolatry and witchcraft (Gal. 5:19–21). I believe that the Lord has called the Brazilian church to repentance. In the midst of this corrupt church, there is a group of people who really are seeking to correct the situation through rending, repentance and sanctification.

Many churches are somewhat hindered from growing spiritually and are unable to be dynamic in evangelism. There is a multitude of unsatisfied people who flit from church to church but do not remain in any long enough to assume commitments. Where there is the life of the Holy Spirit, there should also be the birth of new lives, evangelism and conversions. If there is no expansion of the kingdom of God among the people of God, something is very wrong.

The vision of spiritual warfare has freed many people. A church where a seminar was taught on spiritual warfare has grown from about 200 members to 3,000 in two years. The members gained a vision of the struggle against the powers of darkness. They understood all of the consequences that Jesus triumphed over on the cross, not only against the power of sin and death, but especially over Satan and his demons. The Christians discovered their position of authority in Christ, that if they submit to the Lord and resist our enemy, he has to flee from them (James 4:7).

In another case the pastor called us saying that God had told him that he needed to thank me, because in six months his church of 200 members had grown to 500, and 10 new congregations were formed. We had taught a seminar on spiritual warfare and ministering to many people individually. The result was immediate.

A pastor came to see us. He said that he had been serving successfully as a pastor in another city, but that he had been transferred to a church that had existed for 50 years and had just 25 members. He wanted to know why that had happened.

In researching the history of that church, we discovered that it was formed as the result of a division. They had had some sort of disagreement in the other church and had divided. The first workers were domineering, and history shows us that there really was much dissension and misunderstanding. During the 50–year history of that church, the most members they had ever had at any one time was just 150.

Therefore we suggested that they choose a weekend in which the entire church could repent of its historical sins, as well as any others. There was a need to ask for forgiveness, for reconciliation and for restitution. The pastor understood what might be happening with his church, and he took this research into past sin seriously. So one weekend the members asked forgiveness for the sins of the church. Sin in the form of division, arguments, fights, pride, contention, dissension, and all others opens a breach through which the Devil can operate at will. They sought out the people who had been offended by the church and asked forgiveness.

After that day of repentance and after a period of reconciliation and restitution, the church, in fact, did begin to change. The pastor later said to me, "Neuza, it seemed as if there was a dark veil over our church. No one in the neighbourhood was able to see the church. Suddenly the neighbourhood became aware of its existence and began to visit us and give their lives to Jesus." In just a short time the church had around 200 members. He said, "I have already left that church and am going to heal another one."[8]

Just as a person can be free of demonic oppression and live a life of sanctification, and the church can be free from what binds it, so the city also can be transformed. The instrument for this transformation is the church.

A city in the northeast has a history marked by betrayal since its foundation – between the indigenous tribes of the land, between the whites and Indians, and between the two dominating families that disputed over the leadership of the city. This city received a new president of its pastors' council.

This city was considered to be cursed, for there were disputes among the churches, mutual betrayal among the pastors. They didn't speak to one another and avoided meeting each other. The churches were fruit of the many divisions that took place in the city. When a member was disciplined in one church, he was received with honour in another.

A spiritual warfare seminar took place, with the objective of claiming the city. The 15 churches that were invited to participate began to pray 40 days before the event. Much intercession preceded the event, and the actual days of the event were covered with prayer; afterwards, the churches continued to intercede for 15 days for the results. Thus the pastors brought their people and leadership to be taught. On this occasion there were all types of teaching and ministrations, from personal deliverance to the healing of churches.

At a given moment during the seminar, reconciliation was made between the indigenous peoples, between the whites and Indians, between the blacks and whites, and between the pastors of the various churches. God was working wonderfully among the people.

After the event we met with 40 pastors and made a few more suggestions. When we asked what they should do, they said, "We pastors have to set aside a day of repentance so that we can confess our sins and ask forgiveness of one another." Thus they defined, during those days, this priority: "Confess sins, take care of the families, reconcile divided churches, create an intercession movement, and begin spiritual mapping."

And that's what they did. The churches immediately began intercession campaigns of 21, 30, and 40 days. The pastors set aside a day of repentance, and God began to break them. The churches that resulted from separations sought out their original churches for reconciliation. The pastors that had not been speaking to one another were now praying together, thus bringing about a spiritual change. Then other things began to happen.

The son of an evangelical family was elected mayor, and he began to make things easier for the pastors, which brought about political change. As a result of intercession, the crime rate began to decrease, bringing about a social change. The churches began to experience new vigour and enthusiasm and began to grow. Eight months later the churches were seeing greatly accelerated growth, and many of them had to reform their temples and began having second and third services. And finally, the city was blessed financially. The city's coffee, which had previously been mixed with that of another state, was chosen as the better quality coffee, and they began to export a large quantity to other countries. The Northeast Bank began making loans to help small businesses.[9]

A long time before this transformation occurred, a pastor was praying that God would help the desperate situation of betrayal among the pastors and leaders of that city. His intercession, along with that of others, prepared the city for what would happen.

There are many changes taking place on the personal, church and city levels. This is occurring among historical denominations as well as some Pentecostal churches. Spiritual warfare is a significant issue for further prayer and study.

Notes

1 Neuza Itioka, *The Gods of Umbanda* (São Paulo: ABUB, 1988).

2 Harmon A. Johnson, "Authority over the Spirits." M.A. thesis (Pasadena, Calif.: Fuller Theological Seminary School of World Mission, 1969), 22.

3 Pedro McGregor, *Jesus of Spirits* (New York: Stein and Day, 1966), 169.

4 A case in which the author personally ministered.

5 Neuza Itioka, *God Wants Your City* (São Paulo: Sepal Editora, 1999).

6 Ibid.

7 Ibid.

8 In this case we were able to participate in the transformation.

9 Itioka, *God Wants Your City*.

8

A survey of North American spiritual warfare thinking

A. Scott Moreau

Spiritual warfare discussion in North America has developed into a bewildering array of thinking, practices, vocabulary and approaches. In this discussion we will briefly examine the types of approaches taken in spiritual warfare literature, a few questions related to terminology and some of the myths in our culture driving spiritual warfare practice and discussion.

Categories of spiritual warfare literature

When one takes into account the books, tapes, conferences, seminars and extension courses that are available on spiritual warfare, it is absolutely staggering. How do you sort the good from the bad? A quick overview of the types of books available will at least start us in the right direction. Recognizing the danger that in categorizing I may be placing people inappropriately in boxes, the broadly evangelical literature falls into seven general categories.

TRADITIONALISTS

Traditionalists are those who urge extreme caution. In this category demonic attack, especially on Christians, tends to be downplayed, and demonic confrontation is viewed with suspicion. Authors include John MacArthur, Thomas Ice and Robert Dean, Dan Korem, and David Powlison.[1] Korem's perspective is the most unique;

he looks at apparent displays of the supernatural (for example, for-tune-telling) and critiques them from the perspective of a stage magician.

EXPERIENCED-BASED WARRIORS

These authors relate sometimes startling testimonials of deliver-ance and integrate experience in testing doctrinal formulations. The reading is exciting, though there can be a naive attitude towards the real effect of some of the methods (for example, prayer against ter-ritorial spirits). Writers in this category include Peter Wagner, Chuck Kraft and John Wimber.[2]

EVANGELICAL CONFRONTERS

Evangelical confronters are those who recognise the reality of demonic work in Christians and advocate a direct confrontational deliverance approach. Books include Fred Dickason, Mark Bubeck, and Thomas White.[3]

THEOLOGIANS AND BIBLICAL SCHOLARS

Those who write as formal theologians and biblical scholars vary widely in perspective. The first "classic" author is Jesse Penn-Lewis.[4] Thomas McAlpine has written a good introductory survey of the types of theological paradigms in spiritual warfare.[5] Perhaps the most in-fluential series in academic circles is by Walter Wink,[6] for both the biblical discussion and the social side of spiritual warfare. Another outstanding scholar is Clinton Arnold, who comes to spiritual war-fare from the perspective of a sympathetic New Testament scholar.[7] Other authors in this category include Sydney Page, Anthony N. S. Lane, and Chuck Lowe.[8] Lowe takes to task on a biblical basis some of the teaching of strategic level spiritual warfare advocated by C. Peter Wagner. Finally, we may note authors working through a missiological frame, including Paul Hiebert, Robert Priest, and Scott Moreau.[9]

SPIRITUAL HEALERS

Spiritual healers explore the healing of deep hurts through a vari-ety of therapeutic means (prayer, counseling, medical intervention). Two of the better known in counseling circles are John White and Dan Allender.[10] Authors in this category also include the more char-ismatic authors such as John and Paula Sandford, Leanne Payne, and David A. Seamands.[11]

TRUTH-ENCOUNTER ADVOCATES

Those who advocate truth encounters focus on teaching people truth and its application rather than direct demonic confrontation. The most influential person in conservative evangelical circles is Neil Anderson, whose cognitive approach is presented in *The Bondage Breaker*. Anderson has also written *Living Free in Christ*, a compilation of devotions focused on our identity in Christ and *Setting Your Church Free* for those struggling in church settings.[12] Other authors advocating a type of truth-encounter approach include Jim Logan, Timothy Warner and Scott Moreau.[13] Steve Sjogren presents a refreshing orientation showing how practical works of kindness overcome Satan's work.[14]

CROSS-CULTURAL SPIRITUAL CONFLICT ANALYSTS

The final category is that of those who examine issues of spiritual warfare in light of cultural frames. They include Meg Kraft, Scott Moreau, and Gailyn Van Rheenen.[15] For a fascinating look through the eyes of a Yanamamo shaman, see Mark Ritchie's *Spirit of the Rain Forest.*[16]

New terms and new ideas in spiritual warfare

A wide range of relatively new terms and new ideas has been developed in contemporary discussions on spiritual warfare. We recognise the difficulty of terms employing the warfare metaphor among those who do not follow Christ, and though *spiritual conflict* is used as an appropriate substitute, we find it difficult to talk about the engagement of Christians with Satan without resorting to warfare-type terminology.

We talk about types of encounters *(power, truth* and *relational)*. We have developed a semantic domain of vocabulary relating to those who struggle: *afflicted, oppressed, harassed, demonised* and *demon-possessed*. We use a variety of terms for ministry among those who struggle: *binding, loosing, freeing, healing, delivering, exorcising, releasing* and *deep-level healing*. We see discussions on strategic thinking using such terms as *spiritual mapping, strategic-level spiritual warfare, identificational repentance* and *strongholds* (personal, corporate and cultural).

The presence of a growing, developing and changing vocabulary is a sign of the vibrancy of the field. With a plethora of perspectives, it seems unlikely that a consensus will be reached in the near future on appropriate terms or even on definitions of typically used words. It becomes more important, then, for practitioners and scholars to recognise the fuzziness in the vocabulary and the need to explain carefully the terms being used to describe the afflicted and ministry among them.

Driving images found in North American spiritual warfare

The imagery of a field of study and practice often gives important clues for future trajectories within the field. What are some of the significant contemporary images of spiritual conflict seen in the North American context? Here we will identify several of those images and their implications for spiritual warfare thinking and practice.

THE JOY IS IN THE FIGHT

The first contemporary image is the way we focus on the actual *fight* as opposed to the outcome of the fight.[17] Our myth structure glorifies violence to the extent that the "action" is all we want in action movies (and books, cartoons, and so on). We will have to think long before finding an example of an action adventure in our culture that gives as much space to the "happily ever after" phase as it does to the violent struggle that precedes the peaceful ending. The Rocky movie series, with its extended fight scenes, serves as a prime example. At the end of each movie the North American audience was left anticipating the next fight, the next challenge. The same is also seen in the question that comes at the end of every Super Bowl: "How about next year?" It is typically answered, "Let me enjoy this for a while, then I'll think about it." Even such a tacit admission implies that next year's game is never completely out of mind – even while enjoying this year's victory!

IF IT WORKS, IT MUST BE RIGHT

Americans tend to be pragmatic. Imagery related to this orientation shows up in several ways in spiritual warfare circles.

War story argumentation

One way this shows up in the spiritual warfare literature is in the reliance on war stories to prove assertions or buttress arguments. The impression received is that those involved in spiritual warfare ministry simply live from one confrontation to the next.

Full speed ahead

Another way in which this is seen is in what may be called a "full speed ahead" or a "put the pedal to the metal" mentality,[18] in which it is assumed that the demonic is the first consideration to be examined. As surprising as this sounds, the feeling I sometimes have in reading the literature is that for the authors it is easier (and more fun) to expel a demon than to walk through the realities of broken, shattered lives built on the foundations of relational disfunctionality.

Binding and loosing

There has been a tendency towards using binding terminology as a sort of fetish.[19] This is seen in prayer. If all the binding prayers I have heard have been answered according to the requests as spoken, then Satan would not have any influence in any area on earth! The tendency appears to be a reliance on a familiar term *(bind)* rather than an understanding of the theology of Jesus binding Satan throughout Jesus' ministry and finally on the cross. It is not inappropriate to use binding language,[20] but when we rely on it as a type of fetish or ritual or power word, we are practising Christian magic.

Ritual approaches

A second form of the chess game mentality is seen in the way so many of the strategies and techniques proposed in the literature have taken on ritualistic overtones. Unwittingly, some reproduce the pagan practices of New Testament times by thinking that they must know the names of demons to have power over them.[21] This applies to personal ministry[22] as well as to territorial spirits.[23] Though the danger of reliance on a ritualistic attitude is noted, at the same time pattern prayers are printed.[24] These include prayers to cleanse our homes, to test tongues, to enable the conversion of unbelievers, to renounce involvement in satanic rituals, and so on.[25] There is nothing inherently wrong with pattern prayers or even with rituals. However, if they are used as mechanical ceremonies in which every word must be spoken correctly and in the appropriate order, then we are moving towards a pagan worldview in which patterns of words replace a living relationship with a loving Father.

This is not seen just in patterned prayer, but also in Christian phrases such as "In Jesus' name" and "The blood of the Lamb," which some use as a (magical) means of protection and deliverance.[26] Hints of attributing power to formula or ritual also appear in the attitudes occasionally displayed towards verbal blessings and curses.[27] If the curse is seen to have power in and of itself, and is viewed as outside of the control of God, then one unintended implication is that we must know the curse to break its effects.

EXTRA VALUE MEALS AND ONE-MINUTE MANAGEMENT

Another tendency in the North American context is the desire for a quick fix to deal with the problems of life – even the intractable ones. It is attractive to North Americans to be able to blame abusive actions on a demon, for example, and then use a relatively quick ritual to get rid of the demon and the attached problem. This is not to deny the reality of release that comes when demons are expelled but to acknowledge the attraction in our culture of quick fixes to deal with problems.

THE NORTH AMERICAN HERO:
THE MARLBORO MAN AND COWBOY ROOTS

The myth of the hero permeates spiritual warfare literature and thinking in North American circles.[28] In the North American version, the hero, though tempted, *always* makes the right choice in the end. He (only rarely she) *always* snatches victory from the very jaws of defeat so that chaos will not overcome us. Sometimes the villain cheats (poison, use of banned weapons, breaking the rules of engagement, lying about the hero and turning society against him) to gain an unfair advantage. Then, just when it looks as though the hero cannot win, he discovers hidden inner resources or a new secret weapon which he uses to overcome the villain. Our mythic heroes are usually loners motivated by individual commitment to ideals (Superman, Lone Ranger) or revenge (Spiderman and Batman). They never question their own motivation; they always know they are doing right. The means by which they overcome their enemies are violent ones – they never seek to redeem the enemy, only to destroy him.[29] Their violence, however, is "good," while that of the villain is "bad." Good violence may be used to overcome evil violence, especially if the enemy has drawn first blood (for example, Rambo). There are several ways in which themes related to a hero mentality appear in the literature.

Outwitting the enemy

It is not difficult to find in the literature graphic transcriptions of demonic confrontations in which the counselor is portrayed as the hero who is able to outwit the enemy and set the captive(s) free.[30] Just as Superman never fails, I have yet to read in the literature or hear in a conference of a case that remained unresolved. Final failures are not allowed, though the reality is that they happen all too often.

Externalisation of the enemy

In concentrating on finding out the various forms of demonic attachments and focusing our attention on them, we ignore the fact that all too often the enemy is us. Some explore this reality,[31] but by and large the enemy is externalised, enabling us to avoid responsibility for our sin. If the enemy is both inside (for example, we need to repent) and outside, methodologies that ignore the inside are doomed to failure in the long run.

Unquestioned assumptions of heroism

Also overlooked too often in the literature is the possibility that it is the counselor, through the use of inappropriate methods, who is the real enemy. The danger of a form of "spiritual rape" in extended sessions during which a counselor abuses power or poses questions to demons simply to satisfy personal curiosity is not adequately treated. Instead, too much focus is placed on the length of the battles fought and the ultimate triumph of the counselor (as the hero) in delivering the oppressed. As in our mythic structure, authors rarely question their own motivations and integrity. The trap we may fall into is loving power rather than using the power of love.[32]

GOOD VIOLENCE MAY BE USED TO OVERCOME EVIL VIOLENCE

Implicit in this approach is the idea that right and wrong will always be clearly seen and easily judged (good guys wear white, bad guys wear black). Linked to this is the notion that good will always triumph simply because it is right. What Walter Wink calls the myth of redemptive violence pervades our thinking.[33] This myth enables us to justify violent methods against the demonic (demons, after all, are destined for hell). While there is little doubt that demons resort to violence, the fact remains that Jesus' response was to submit to the violence by going to the cross. Following Jesus' example in the midst of a violent world today is just as difficult as developing a Christian worldview in an anti-Christian environment, especially if the myth of redemptive violence is as pervasive as Wink maintains.[34] The issue is not developing a new Christian "mythic framework" as much as it is discovering the mythic framework God has already given us in God's Word. The core metaphor for spiritual conflict should not be that of conflict but that of God's rule and our resulting ethos of *shalom* built on the foundation of kingdom ethics.[35]

Notes

[1] John MacArthur, *How to Meet the Enemy* (Wheaton, Ill.: Victor Press, 1992); Thomas Ice and Robert Dean, *A Holy Rebellion: Strategies for Spiritual Warfare* (Eugene, Ore.: Harvest House, 1990); Dan Korem, *The Powers* (Downers Grove, Ill.: InterVarsity Press, 1988) and Dan Korem and Paul Meier, *The Fakers* (Grand Rapids, Mich.: Baker, 1981); David Powlison, *Power Encounters: Reclaiming Spiritual Warfare* (Grand Rapids, Mich.: Baker, 1995).

[2] C. Peter Wagner, *Engaging the Enemy: How to Fight and Defeat Territorial Spirits* (Ventura, Calif.: Regal Books, 1991), *Warfare Prayer* (Ventura, Calif.: Regal Books, 1992), *Breaking Strongholds in Your City: How to Use Spiritual Mapping to Make Your Prayers More Strategic, Effective, and Targeted* (Ventura, Calif.: Regal Books, 1993) and *Confronting the Powers* (Ventura, Calif.: Regal Books, 1996); Charles H. Kraft, *Christianity with Power* (Ann Arbor, Mich.: Vine Books 1989) and *Defeating Dark Angels* (Ann Arbor, Mich.: Vine Books, 1992); John Wimber, *Power Evangelism* (London: Hodder and Stoughton, 1986) and *Power Healing* (London: Hodder and Stoughton, 1986).

[3] Fred Dickason, *Demon Possession and the Christian* (Chicago: Moody Press, 1987); Mark Bubeck, *The Adversary* (Chicago: Moody Press, 1975), *Overcoming the Adversary* (Chicago: Moody Press, 1984) and *The Satanic Revival* (San Bernardino, Calif.: Here's Life Publishers, 1991).; Thomas White, *The Believer's Guide to Spiritual Warfare* (Ann Arbor. Mich.: Vine Books, 1990) and *Breaking Strongholds: How Spiritual Warfare Sets Captives Free* (Ann Arbor, Mich.: Vine Books, 1993).

[4] Jesse Penn-Lewis, *The War on the Saints* (Ft. Washington, Pa.: Thomas E. Lowe, 1912).

[5] Thomas McAlpine, *Facing the Powers: What Are the Options?* (Pasadena: MARC, 1991).

[6] Walter Wink, *Naming the Powers* (Minneapolis: Fortress Press, 1984), *Unmasking the Powers* (Minneapolis: Fortress Press, 1986) and *Engaging the Powers* (Minneapolis: Fortress Press, 1992).

[7] Clinton Arnold, *Ephesians: Power and Magic* (Grand Rapids, Mich.: Baker, 1989), *Powers of Darkness* (Downers Grove: InterVarsity Press 1992), and *Three Crucial Questions about Spiritual Warfare* (Grand Rapids, Mich.: Baker, 1997).

[8] Sydney Page, *Powers of Evil* (Grand Rapids, Mich.: Baker, 1995); Anthony N. S. Lane, ed., *The Unseen World* (Grand Rapids, Mich.: Baker, 1996); Chuck Lowe, *Territorial Spirits and World Evangelization* (Singapore: OMF, 1998).

[9] Paul Hiebert, *Anthropological Reflections on Missiological Issues* (Grand Rapids, Mich.: Baker, 1995); Paul Hiebert, Daniel Shaw, and Tite Tienou, *Folk Religions* (Grand Rapids, Mich.: Baker, 2000); Robert J. Priest, Ed Campbell and Tom Mullen, "Missiological Syncretism: The New Animistic Paradigm," in *Spiritual Power: What Are the Issues?*, ed. Ed Rommen (Pasadena, Calif.: William Carey, 1995), 9–87; Scott Moreau, "Religious

Borrowing as a Two-Way Street: An Introduction to Animistic Tendencies in the Euro-North American Context," in *Christianity and the Religions*, ed. Ed Rommen and Harold Netland (Pasadena, Calif.: William Carey, 1995), 166–82.

[10] John White, *Changing on the Inside* (Ann Arbor, Mich.: Vine Books, 1991); Dan Allender and Tremper Longman, *Bold Love* (Colorado Springs, Colo.: NavPress, 1992).

[11] John Sandford and Paula Sandford, *The Transformation of the Inner Man* (Tulsa, Okla.: Victory House, 1982); Leanne Payne, *Restoring the Christian Soul Through Healing Prayer* (Westchester, Ill.: Crossway, 1991); David A. Seamands, *Healing for Damaged Emotions* (Wheaton, Ill.: Victor Books, 1981).

[12] Neil Anderson, *The Bondage Breaker* (Harvest House Publishers, 1990).

[13] Jim Logan, *Reclaiming Surrendered Ground* (Chicago: Moody Press, 1995); while Warner's *Spiritual Warfare* (Westchester, Ill.: Crossway, 1991) advocates a more traditional confrontational approach, he is now serving as a vice-president for Neil Anderson's Freedom in Christ Ministries and largely relies on truth encounter; A. Scott Moreau, *Essentials of Spiritual Warfare* (Wheaton, Ill.: Harold Shaw, 1997).

[14] Steve Sjogren, *Servant Warfare* (Ann Arbor, Mich.: Vine Books, 1996).

[15] Marguerite Kraft, *Understanding Spiritual Power* (Maryknoll, N.Y.: Orbis Books, 1995); A. Scott Moreau, *The World of the Spirits* (Nairobi, Kenya: Evangel, 1991); Gailyn Van Rheenen, *Communicating Christ in Animistic Contexts* (Grand Rapids, Mich.: Baker, 1991).

[16] Mark Ritchie, *Spirit of the Rain Forest* (Chicago: Island Lake Press, 1996).

[17] Paul Hiebert, "Spiritual Warfare: Biblical Perspectives," *Mission Focus* 20:3 (September 1992): 41–46.

[18] A term used by Arnold in expressing his concerns with the Spiritual Warfare Network and its goal to get the strategy of praying against territorial spirits more broadly sown (Clinton Arnold, "Trends in Spiritual Warfare," speech given at the Third Biannual Conference on Spiritual Warfare. Sioux Falls, Iowa International Center for Biblical Counseling [March 1994]).

[19] See C. Peter Wagner, "The Key to Victory Is Binding the 'Strong Man,'" *Ministries Today* (November-December 1986), 84; Nigel Wright, *The Satan Syndrome: Putting the Power of Darkness in Its Place* (Grand Rapids, Mich.: Zondervan, 1990), 185 and 195; and John MacArthur, *How to Meet the Enemy: Arming Yourself for Spiritual Warfare* (Wheaton, Ill.: Victor Books, 1992), 146–47.

[20] Or restraining (see Thomas B. White, "Handling Spiritual Warfare," presentation at the North American Conference for Itinerant Evangelists [1994]; and Moreau, *Essentials of Spiritual Warfare*, 158–61).

[21] Clinton Arnold, *Powers of Darkness: Principalities and Powers in Paul's Letters* (Downers Grove: InterVarsity Press, 1992).

[22] C. Fred Dickason, *Demon Possession & the Christian* (Chicago: Moody Press, 1987).

23 Vernon J. Sterk, "Territorial Spirits and Evangelization in Hostile Environments," in *Engaging the Enemy: How to Fight and Defeat Territorial Spirits*, ed. C. Peter Wagner (Ventura, Calif.: Regal), 145–63.

24 For example, Grayson H. Ensign and Edward Howe, *Bothered? Bewildered? Bewitched? Your Guide to Practical Supernatural Healing* (Cincinnati: Recovery Publications, 1984), 271.

25 Thomas White, *The Believer's Guide to Spiritual Warfare*, 106–7; Ensign and Howe, *Bothered? Bewildered? Bewitched? Your Guide to Practical Supernatural Healing*, 294–300; White, *The Believer's Guide to Spiritual Warfare*, 123–24; and Neil Anderson, *Steps to Freedom in Christ* (La Habra, Calif.: Freedom in Christ Ministries, 1993), 5.

26 Ensign and Howe, *Bothered? Bewildered? Bewitched? Your Guide to Practical Supernatural Healing*.

27 Charles H. Kraft, *Christianity with Power: Your Worldview and Your Experience of the Supernatural* (Ann Arbor, Mich.: Vine Books, 1989), 130–32; Timothy J. Warner, *Spiritual Warfare: Victory over the Powers of This Dark World* (Wheaton, Ill.: Crossway Books, 1991), 103–4.

28 See Walter Wink, *Engaging the Powers: Discernment and Resistance in a World of Domination* (Philadelphia: Fortress Press, 1992), 18–20.

29 Ibid., 19.

30 Mark Bubeck, *The Adversary* (Chicago: Moody Press, 1975), 90–92; Ensign, *Bothered? Bewildered? Bewitched? Your Guide to Practical Supernatural Healing*, 20–24; Dickason, *Demon Possession and the Christian*, 194–97.

31 Thomas White, *Breaking Strongholds*; Wink, *Engaging the Powers*.

32 Wright, *The Satan Syndrome*, 173–86.

33 Wink, *Engaging the Powers*, 51–59.

34 Ibid., 13.

35 Hiebert, "Spiritual Warfare," 44.

9

Spiritual conflict among Western seekers

OLE SKJERBÆK MADSEN

The State Church in Denmark has for centuries had a monopoly on spirituality and religion. However, in the first part of the twenty-first century membership is decreasing, and in the larger towns the church will soon no longer be the major religion. In the inner city of Copenhagen, membership is now less than 66 per cent among adults and less than 33 per cent of the children (0–14 years of age). Less than 1 per cent of the urban population attends church services on a given Sunday. The church is there for baptism, confirmation, marriage and funeral, and perhaps Christmas. The church is a cultural institution and attended for concerts, but it is not considered the place to go for soul care, spiritual direction or guidance, healing, or the great questions on the meaning of life.

This trend is typical for modern Western society, but it does not mean an end of spirituality or religion. A great number of new religious or spiritual movements and cults have emerged, and many people are seeking new forms of spirituality and wholeness. It is a spiritual milieu of seekers in the quest for meaning to life that is often labelled New Age.

In *Conversations with God* Neale Donald Walsch describes those who will receive from God the truths for which they are ready as "those who truly want answers and who truly care about questions; . . . all those who have embarked upon the quests for truth with sincerity of heart, longing of soul, and openness of mind." They will know that leaders, ministers, rabbis, priests, books, even the Bible, are not authoritative sources of knowing God and self. The God of Walsch says:

> I cannot tell you My Truth until you stop telling Me yours. . . . Listen to your feelings. Listen to your Highest Thoughts. Listen to your experience. Whenever any one of these differs from what you've been told by your teachers, or read in your books, forget the words. Words are the least reliable purveyor of Truth.[1]

Such seekers do not respond to the gospel if Christians address them with a dogmatic vocabulary that is presented as the key to all questions. The church needs to understand the nature of this spiritual milieu that is the New Age movement. To this end I refer to the conclusions of Wouter J. Hanegraaff:

> New Age is not a unified ideology or world view or a centrally planned conspiracy. New Age is many different groupings, therapies, methods, spiritualities, teachers, and networks. But New Age nevertheless has some common goals and aspirations due to the fact that it arises out of a spiritual milieu, "the cultic milieu," which understands its practices, ideas and experiences as alternatives to dominant religious and cultural trends.[2]

In the first part of his conclusion Hanegraaff defines New Age as cultural criticism:

> All New Age religion is characterized by a criticism of dualistic and reductionistic tendencies in (modern) western culture, as exemplified by . . . dogmatic Christianity, on the one hand, and rationalistic/scientific ideologies, on the other. It believes that there is a "third option" which rejects neither religion and spirituality nor science and rationality, but combines them in a higher synthesis. It claims that the two trends, which have hitherto dominated western culture (dogmatic Christianity and an equally dogmatic rationalistic/scientistic ideology), have been responsible for the current world crisis, and that the latter will only be resolved if and when this third option becomes dominant in society.[3]

This outlines both possibilities of encounter in the process of communication and the distinctive between the church and the New Age movement. There are points of contact and co-operation in many of the areas of cultural criticism (scientific reductionism, materialism, consumerism, abuse of nature's resources, etc.), especially if we regain a fuller understanding of humankind's role in creation. However, Christians cannot share all of the criticism of the church – and certainly not the uniqueness of God's self-revelation in Jesus Christ.

The second part of his conclusion concerning New Age is that it is a secularised esotericism with historic roots in the Renaissance, the radical reformers (Schwärmgeister), romanticism and occultism. From the Renaissance comes the inspiration from neoplatonism and hermeticism, the interest in astrology, magic and alchemy and the theosophical speculations. Hanegraaff writes:

It adopts from traditional esotericism an emphasis on the primacy of personal religious experience and on this-worldly types of holism (as alternatives to dualism and reductionism), but generally reinterprets esoteric tenets from secularized perspectives. Since the new elements and "causality," the study of religions, evolutionism, and psychology are fundamental components, New Age religion cannot be characterised as a return to pre-Enlightenment worldviews but is to be seen as a qualitatively new syncretism of esoteric and secular elements.[4]

The esoteric legacy also provides some points of contact, especially in defining the inner meaning of creation, its wholeness as living nature and as a network of internal correspondences, creation and every single creature as signs of a greater reality. In this area evangelicals can be helped by the Eastern Orthodox tradition that speaks of the Logos and the Spirit as the uncreated energies of God made known to us in creation.

An important point of meeting with seekers of the new spiritual milieu is that of experiences. Their personal experiences are not far from the conversion experiences of many Christians and the ongoing process of sanctification. The challenge is how to avoid making experience itself the sole evidence of truth and instead point them to Jesus as the Way, the Truth and the Life, and the Holy Spirit as the one who leads one into all truth.

Hanegraaff's final conclusion is:

The New Age movement is the cultic milieu having become conscious of itself, in the later 1970s, as constituting a more or less unified "movement." All manifestations of this movement are characterized by a popular western culture criticism expressed in terms of a secularized esotericism.[5]

Area of conflict: Alternative culture

Since the seekers' milieu is to be understood as an alternative culture, the first area of spiritual conflict is to be found on the cultural level, including politics, economy and science. I have already pointed out the criticism of dualistic and reductionistic tendencies in "dogmatic Christianity" and the materialistic scientific way of thinking.

The danger for the church is to become hypnotised by the apparent criticism of the church and of our most precious doctrines. This can result in Christians withdrawing from constructive dialogue and co-operation in the many areas where there is agreement. Materialistic reductionism in the name of science is also our "enemy." It is too easy to avoid engaging in the work for world peace and justice, for the protection of nature, for animal rights, for a sound ecology in order not to be classified New Age or for fear of the church being infiltrated by New Age through these people of good will.

The second danger is that culture will be influenced by New Age paradigms, if Christians through fear of being identified with New Age withdraw from any contact with the new spiritual milieu and its ideologists as well as its seekers. Christians need to be involved in open dialogue, sharing the dreams of a healed Earth as a common quest and providing a biblical perspective of holism. They need to speak of a God who through his creative Word, the divine Logos, ordered the universe so as to find its meaning, goal and consummation in Christ.

The third danger has to do with a more or less conscious identification with the paradigms of the new spirituality. The conscious identification happens if a secularised church, which is in need of spirituality, indiscriminately adopts any religious practice that happens to fill the spiritual void of its members and clergy. As A. Scott Moreau states:

> The culture, and together with it the evangelical church, has moved in a spiritual direction in the sense that personal spiritual powers, once out of sight in our worldview, have now come into prominence. In one respect we can rejoice – a spiritual approach to the world is more in tune with the biblical worldview than an agnostic (or atheistic) scientific material-

ism. In another respect, however, we must be aware of the danger of shifting too far into what may be termed a functional evangelical animism and a corresponding set of "Christian magical" practices.[6]

Area of conflict: Anthropology, worldview and ethic

In the new spiritual milieu, humanity is understood from an evolutionary point of view. Human beings are understood as consciousness progressing through endless transformations of many incarnations towards true self-consciousness and the realisation of ultimate oneness with the ultimate. Human beings are their own saviours, who may or may not need the help of spiritual masters or guides. Human nature is often understood as a microcosmos which, like a fragment of a holographic plate, contains the whole picture. This is exemplified in the use of astrology.

In the New Age worldview, holism is not just the harmony of body, soul and mind/spirit but a monistic philosophy. This anti-dualistic stance of New Age dissolves the opposites of male-female, good-evil and true-false. The Christian will see a danger in this kind of relativism in the area of morals and truth. What will be the consequences for society if it abandons absolute values? Will this relativism endanger human responsibility? Gifts of discernment, wisdom and love are needed. For example, New Agers will understand the Christian concept of salvation and forgiveness as moral laziness and irresponsibility, because we do not take responsibility for our own life. They see the concepts of karma and reincarnation as opportunities of learning through experience and thus allowing them to take responsibility for their own lives. Christians need to explain that through recognition and confession of sin we really take responsibility and that through forgiveness the children of God are able to engage fully in loving care for our neighbour and for our fellow creatures without losing our energy in the effort of saving ourselves. This is an area of spiritual conflict, because human longing is for wholeness, and personal and social transformation are veiled in the illusions of monism and evolution.

Area of conflict: Religion

Christians are confronted with both practical and conceptual sides of New Age religion.

The most important spiritual conflict with New Age and the modern Western seekers has to do with conscious or unconscious teachings. These obscure, twist or contradict the saving truths of God's self-revelation in his eternal Logos and his Spirit, in creation, in the history of salvation and in the Bible. It is illustrated in that section of New Age that is influenced by Theosophy. Christ, or Maitreya, as he is often called, is understood as the leader of the Hierarchy, master of the second ray or emanation of the Solar Logos, the god of our solar system. Jesus is presented as a lower master who was overshadowed by the Christ. There are also many male and female masters in the Hierarchy. The Theosophy of Asger Lorentsen and the Shan-movement shows the fascination with Jesus, and Asger Lorentsen even claims that he wants his new work to be done under the Master Jesus.[7]

This interest in Jesus provides a starting point for dialogue and an exchange of the experiences of healing, salvation and peace. However, this does not mean that the Christian can agree with the assumptions of Lorentsen. First, there is no valid argument from the Scriptures in which the word *Christ* is anything other than the title and the function of the promised Saviour, born into the family of the great King David. Second, in the experience of the Christian and in the evidence of the New Testament, Jesus and Christ cannot be separated. Third, it is unhistorical to use Christ synonymously for the Maitreya. It is not true to either Jewish/Christian or Buddhist tradition. Seen from a Christian viewpoint, what is Christ if he is not the historic Jesus? It is not satisfying to the Christian that the Maitreya Theosophist states that his sources are not historic but esoteric.

What is also challenging is the understanding of the planetary or cosmic meaning of the death of Jesus on the cross. In the revivalist Christian tradition, concentration has been on what Jesus has done for me. Maitreya Theosophists challenge us to take up the wider Christology found in the letters of Paul to the Ephesians and the Colossians.

The sources of much New Age teaching often are channelled from the entities of the Hierarchy through the mind of human channels. They are sometimes conceived through visions or other intuitive means or faculties in sudden mystical experiences or a growing awareness of the spiritual dimensions of the world facilitated through meditation. Christians therefore have every reason to be suspicious of sources of spiritual information that speak of another Christ than Jesus. In January 2000 I heard a lecture on the Holy Grail in which the speaker said that Jesus in a former incarnation was known as

Melchizedek and was in fact the Babylonian god Ea, who created the first man out of clay. He now had to bring into order what he disturbed when he, through a wrong warning, hindered man from receiving the bread and water of life. The speaker also said that Ea was a fallen angel. Christians are opposed such notions.

Criticism of dogmatic Christianity has been evident in the New Age movement for many years, as illustrated in the writings of Alice Bailey:

> The presentation of divine truth, as given by the churches in the West and by the teachers in the East, has not kept pace with the unfolding intellect of the human spirit. . . . The Church today is the tomb of the Christ and the stone of theology has been rolled to the door of the sepulchre. . . . Christianity cannot be attacked; it is an expression . . . of the love of God, immanent in His created universe. Churchianity has, however laid itself wide open to attack.[8]

Another problem in the religion of modern seekers is elitism, the sense of having reached a higher level of consciousness, sometimes combined with the idea that those who have attained higher consciousness in the new era, the age of Aquarius, will have the right to execute a kind of consequence pedagogy towards those who have not attained the same higher consciousness. Also, some of the religious practices are dubious from a Christian point of view. What is the source of channelled messages? What does mediality do with the medium? How do mantic practices determine the life of the client, and what are the energies or entities behind the symbols of tarot and astrology? What happens to the person as a person if the techniques of healing or self-realisation blur personality?

In my practice as a pastor I have met several persons who were mentally and spiritually hurt through practices that left them in confusion. Some had to be helped through inner healing or deliverance, many through an act of confirmation and renewed commitment to their baptismal covenant. In short, they had to receive Jesus in their heart and turn to God as God has revealed himself in Jesus Christ.

Disciples of Jesus Christ in the milieu of Western seekers: Conflict and contact

Christians have many opportunities for being involved in spiritual conflict with modern seekers. However, the fear of demons and the fear of being demonised through contact with the new spirituality and the milieu of seekers is perhaps the greatest danger for us. I think that one of the strategies of the Foe is the blinding of our spiritual and mental faculties from recognizing the truths, the dedication and the insights of the quest for meaning, wholeness and fulfilment in our fellows. We must not be so preoccupied by our resentment to many of their wrong or strange practices or false doctrines that we forget that they are often sincere seekers, always loved by God, as well as potential disciples of Jesus and worshippers of the true God – if they meet the love of God in Jesus Christ and in the power of the Holy Spirit. I lost many opportunities to lead seekers into the presence of God by making right doctrines a condition for ministering to them. For example, I demanded that they renounce their past life experiences and their understanding of reincarnation before I would pray for healing. Now I want them to meet Jesus Christ and God in him first through love being presented to them in a way that will help them to interpret their experiences in a new way.

In the spiritual conflict in the milieu of seekerism our main strategy is not to discuss right doctrines opposing all that we conceive as dangerous, false, or even demonic. This would only estrange those to whom we would like present the gospel and leave them in their criticism of the church. Many people involved in New Age, and even occultism of the darker kinds, are victims of revivalist and fundamentalist Christianity.[9] Our strategy should be positive. We have to be among seekers as disciples of our Master and with the spirit of disciples.

The Master-disciple image is a dynamic image of what it is to be a Christian, and we learn through following our Master. A disciple is on a journey involving a process of learning. A disciple has not finished the quest because there is much more to explore; the depths of the love of God as revealed in Jesus Christ are inexhaustible. A disciple is committed to the Master. On our walk with our Master we accept any as co-disciples who begin to focus on Jesus as a source of meaning and direction in life. They may not understand all the formulations of the Nicene Creed or express themselves in standard Christian vocabulary. However, we travel a common road following the Master. The Master gives the unity and identity of the fellowship, and he is so wonderful and his words have such an authority and his love is so great that there is no room for the sectarian attitudes of Christendom.

It is the dynamic love-faith relationship between the Master and the disciples that will be the authentic answer to the quest of modern spiritual seekers. Another factor that attracts seekers is the charismatic dimension of the disciples as the body of Christ. The gifts of the Spirit are the authentic means of inspiration and healing. Charismatic fellowships and churches may become new spiritual centres because of the presence of the Master and because of the power of the Holy Spirit, which help the seeker to taste the true new age – that is, the kingdom of God.

In the Master's light

In the summer 1994 I was speaking with the Lord of my concern with many of my friends in the New Age milieu. Many seem to have been at the point of giving their life to Jesus and receiving him as their Saviour, but this had not occurred because they did not seem willing to drop their non-Christian concepts. Suddenly I heard Jesus speaking in my heart and mind. He told me how much he appreciated their commitment in their quest for wholeness and the meaning of life. He recognised their sacrifices in finding a new lifestyle, making progress in personal development and in caring for creation. However, he also indicated that he shared my sadness because their "light work" often ended up in darkness. Jesus then told me to start some spiritual meetings in the New Age milieu under the title *In the Master's Light*. These services started in May 1995. *In the Master's Light* recognises the quest of New Agers and shares many of their values, such as their reaction to materialism and self-interest. We respect their genuine quest for spiritual values in a materialistic age, but we are very specific in expressing that among all the spiritual masters in the seekers' milieu and over against the masters revered in Theosophy, Jesus is our only Master.

In the Master's Light tries to meet the longing to learn spiritual values with teachings inspired by the Holy Spirit. In meditation we advocate the use of the Jesus Prayer from Eastern Christianity as a kind of mantra: "Lord Jesus Christ, Son of God, have mercy on me!" They are also invited to meditate on a word from the Bible. We expect the Holy Spirit to inspire preaching and to come with prophecy and revelation. When Jesus spoke to me on *In the Master's Light* he promised a prophetic message for each teaching at the meetings, which we call "inspirations" or "the direct communication of the Master." We try to meet the longing for wholeness and healing by inviting people to come for healing of their heart.

We avoid adversarial arguments in speaking with those present and rather try to share experiences. We witness that the testimony of a disciple of Jesus is a seed of truth. To plant such seeds of truth we first have to listen to the other persons, their experiences, beliefs, values, needs. We try to use the seekers' language and forms to express our own spirituality and our own walking the way with the Master.

We have learned not to press seekers into conformity with ourselves or to start by correcting their opinions as if we understood their experiences better than they themselves do. They are invited to meet the Master and to taste his goodness and loving kindness. When they start reorienting their lives on their experience of Jesus, we accept them as fellow disciples. The more they focus on the Master, the more we trust them to correct what is not in accordance with the Master's teachings and his life, death and resurrection and presence through the Holy Spirit.

Today, there are branches of *In the Master's Light* in eight places in Denmark. In 1999 we prayed with more than 1,500 seekers for the healing of the heart in their relationship to God, their own inner being and the surrounding world. We have had disciple training classes for seekers in Copenhagen and Aarhus. We have had retreats and workshops and been present at New Age exhibitions such as "Body Mind and Spirit," and we have been invited to share our faith in New Age magazines, radio programs and societies. Many New Agers now come regularly for worship and pastoral care in the involved congregations.

Notes

[1] Neale Donald Walsch, *Conversations with God: An Uncommon Dialogue* (New York: Hampton Roads Publishing Company, 1995), Introduction and 8.

[2] Wouter J. Hanegraaff, *New Age Religion and Western Culture: Esotericism in the Mirror of Secular Thought* (New York: Brill Academic Publishers, 1996). Hanegraaff quotes Colin Campbell: "Whereas cults are by definition a largely transitory phenomenon, the cultic milieu is, by contrast, a constant feature of society" (15). Cults arise out of the cultic milieu. However different the cultic movements are, their spokesmen "have a common cause in attacking orthodoxy and in defining individual liberty of belief and practice. Arising from this there is a prevailing orientation of mutual sympathy and support, such that the various cultic movements rarely engage in criticism of each other. . . . Since this tradition emphasises that the single ideal of unity with the divine can be attained by a diversity of paths it tend to be ecumenical, super-ecclesiastic, syncretistic and tolerant in outlook."

[3] Ibid., 517.

[4] Ibid., 520–21.

[5] Ibid., 522.

[6] A. Scott Moreau, "Religious Borrowing as a Two-way Street: An Introduction to Animistic Tendencies in the Euro-North American Context," in *Christianity and the Religions: A Biblical Theology of World Religions*, ed. Edward Rommen and Harold Netland (Pasadena, Calif.: William Carey Library, 1995), 172.

[7] Ole Skjerbæk Madsen, "The Maitreya-Theosophy of Asger Lorentsen and the Shan-Movement," in *New Religions and New Religiosity*, ed. Eileen Barker and Margit Warburg (Aarhus, Denmark: Aarhus University Press, 1998), 191–203.

[8] Alice A. Bailey, *The Reappearance of the Christ* (New York: Lucis Publishing Company, 1984), 139–40.

[9] See John Warwick Montgomery, ed., *Principalities and Powers: The World of the Occult,* rev. ed. (Minneapolis, Minn.: Bethany Fellowship, 1981), 167ff.: "Converts to Church-of-Satan groups very often have a history of fundamentalist upbringing."

10

Case studies in spiritual warfare from East Asia

Hwa Yung

East Asia today is a land of economic miracles, scientific advances and technological innovations. Yet for many Christians living there, dealing with the demonic is not something novel and exotic, and certainly not an optional extra. The simple reason is that the whole spiritual realm is taken seriously and usually integrated (even if loosely at times) into our thinking about the physical world. Moreover, it is not always possible to draw a sharp line between certain religious and cultural practices. This is certainly true of those who practice folk religions, of which there remain large numbers in the region. But it is also true of those who practice the so-called higher religions. For example, many Chinese Confucian scholars are often well versed in fortune-telling, palmistry and the like.

One might think that the impact of modernity through Western-styled education, technological advancement and globalisation has led to a lesser attachment to traditional beliefs. That may be true to some degree. But what one scholar of Asian religions said of Japan probably is applicable throughout the region. Despite the surface impact of modernity, traditional religious beliefs persist in Japanese society. Thus he writes: "Kami, Buddhas, ancestors, and holy persons will probably remain at the core of Japanese religion and continue to form a distinctive pattern or 'sacred way' that has always been characteristic of the Japanese religious heritage."[1] What Paul Hiebert notes as "the flaw of the excluded middle" in the Western scientific worldview is generally not a problem in East Asia.

To give us a better understanding of the East Asian situation, we will begin with a brief summary of occult practices found in the region. We will then look at specific examples of how the advance of the gospel has often involved power encounters with the demonic realm. On the basis of these accounts some lessons will be drawn.

Occult practices encountered

Numerous types of occult practices are found in East Asia. For a start, traditional beliefs in the occult realm persist in many segments of Asian society. In Hong Kong and Singapore, for example, the belief in *fengshui* influences the location and structures of many buildings. Every time there is a major fall in the stocks of an overseas Chinese conglomerate, it is likely that the *fengshui* master will be brought to find out what has gone wrong. Fortune-telling and the choosing of "auspicious" dates and times for special occasions like weddings through various means are everyday occurrences. Involvement with palmistry, "spirit of the dish" or the ouija board, necromancy at graveyards and the like are widespread. One particularly common practice is giving a child for "adoption" to a deity who becomes the "god-parent" through a religious ceremony. The purpose of this is to seek the deity's lifelong protection over the child.

Mediumistic practices are also common irrespective of religious adherence, whether Buddhist, Chinese folk religion, Islam or other. In Malaysia, for example, *bomohs* or traditional Malay medicine men are often employed to ensure fine weather during important soccer matches or Formula One *Grand Prix* races. Alternatively, regular visits are made to temple mediums when a child is sick to ensure recovery. Interestingly, it should be noted that one does not usually choose to be a medium. Rather, experience from a variety of backgrounds shows that one is often chosen by the spirits instead.[2]

Together with this is the use of charms or amulets, which are usually hung in vehicles or in houses or worn on the person for protection. If one travels around the region, these can often be seen hanging in taxis or buses to ward off accidents. Similarly, soldiers, police personnel, gangsters and others whose work constantly involves fighting with knives or guns are known to wear powerful amulets, obtained from temple priests or medicine men. There is an abundance of anecdotal evidence that points to their efficacy in protecting the wearers from injury in fights or battle.

Apart from the more overt manifestations of the occult listed above, a strong resurgence of traditional religions in different forms is observed in many parts of the region today. One of the clearest examples is the rise of the *Soka Gakkai*, which is probably the fastest growing and largest Nichiren Buddhist sect in Japan today. It even has under it *Komei-to*, the party for clean government in Japan. Moreover, its influence has spread to other parts of East Asia as well. But this is only one among many similar resurgent groups.

Overall, there is in general a vivid awareness of the spiritual realm. The deities and spirits are real and must be served, placated or feared. Only the foolish will mess around with them. Related to this is the ultimate fear – what the spirits can do to humans at death, the great unknown. This is clearly seen in traditional Chinese culture. Few will wear black because it symbolises death (hence many Chinese do not like being soccer referees!). Moreover, many rich Chinese will pay the Daoist priests tens of thousands of dollars at funerals for a few nights of religious rituals to ensure that the "souls" of the deceased are taken safely to "heaven."

Examples of power encounters

The above gives a brief summary of the types of practices linked with the powers of darkness in the region. Although sometimes people have become Christians merely through the preaching of the Word, more often the advance of the gospel results from healing through prayer or some form of power encounter with the demonic. Such power encounters are common all over East Asia.

For example, one of the latest studies of the recent rapid church growth in China draws attention to the important role that signs and wonders play.[3] This is not surprising, because church growth in China has always been associated with these occurrences historically. Three examples may be cited.

One well-documented case comes from James O. Fraser's work among the Lisu people in southwest China, near the border with Burma (now Myanmar). An engineering graduate of Imperial College, London, he began work in 1909 as a CIM missionary. He encountered a tribal people who had practiced idol worship for centuries. The demonic powers held the people in fear through inflicting illnesses, attacks by wild animals, spirit possession of individuals, demonstrations of special powers through mediumistic practices like climbing the "sword ladder" without being cut, and the like. Over the next 25 years or so, he gained much experience in dealing with the powers of darkness. He found that only what he termed the "prayer of faith" could bring breakthroughs in the evangelistic work among the Lisu.[4] He also came to realise that he needed urgently the backing of as many intercessors as possible, who need not however be physically near. "I should very, very much like a wider circle of intercessors. . . . I know enough about Satan to realise that he will have all his weapons ready for determined opposition. . . . I shall feel greatly strengthened if I know of a definite company of pray-ers holding me up."[5] Over the years, hundreds and thousands came to faith as the bondage of Satan was broken through healing prayer, deliverance ministries and the demonstration of the superior power of Christ.

Another example is recounted by Watchman Nee, one of the leading Christian leaders of China in the mid-twentieth-century period.[6] He tells of an evangelistic trip to a large island off the coast of China, where in spite of much prayer and effort, there was no breakthrough. In frustration, one 16-year-old member of the team asked the locals why they persisted in their unbelief. Someone in the crowd responded: "We have a god – *one* god – Ta-wang (Great King), and he has never failed us."[7] The person went on to say that the islanders hold an annual festival procession for this Ta-wang on a day chosen by divination. And there has never ever been rain on that chosen day in 286 years! On asking when the procession day would be that particular year, they were informed that it would be on January 11, in two days' time. In a moment of unguarded enthusiasm, the 16–year-old team member blurted out, "I promise you that it will certainly rain on the eleventh." Watchman Nee was elsewhere at the time. When he was informed, it was already too late. The news spread like wildfire among the 20,000 islanders. The gauntlet had been thrown down.

Watchman Nee goes on to share how they agonised in prayer over what happened. And then the word of the Lord came to him: "Where is the God of Elijah?" With this assurance the whole team together thanked and praised God. Standing on the victory of Christ, they then continued in earnest prayer for rain. On the morning of the January 11, as Nee describes it, "There was no cloud in the sky, but we knew that God was committed." No sooner had they finished saying grace over breakfast than the first rain drops fell. Soon the streets were flooded. When the islanders tried to proceed with the procession carrying the image of Ta-wang on a sedan chair, three of those carrying stumbled in the waters. The idol fell and broke. With that the bondage of almost 300 years was broken, and many in the village came to faith in Christ.

A third example is more recent and illustrates the type of power encounters that is fuelling the advance of the church in China today.

In a certain village in northern China one of the homes was thrown into chaos because of a demonic attack in the house. The family tried everything but to no avail. Finally they turned to an old "Bible woman" (a woman evangelist) for help. The Bible woman came and stayed in the home for about two weeks. During that time she prayed for the family and taught them about the Christian faith. At the end of the two weeks there was much rejoicing because the whole family had found faith in Christ and the demon had been driven from the house. But the next door neighbours were not happy – because the demon entered their house instead! The Bible woman was then invited into the next home, and the whole process was repeated until the second family also found faith and deliverance in Christ. But now the third family was not happy because the demon had launched his next attack on its house. One can imagine the rest of the story. The demon was driven from house to house over a period of eight months until every family in the village turned to Christ. The place is now called The Village of the Jumping Ghost.[8]

The above accounts drawn from China at different periods of history can be repeated over and over again in the experiences of the church in other parts of East Asia. This was clearly the case with the revivals in Indonesia in the 1960s and the subsequent rapid growth of the church there through the 1970s. There have, of course, been questions over the accuracy of some of the accounts. But to suggest that much of what has been reported is mere exaggeration fails to do justice to the great number of corroborating reports,[9] and to the fact of the spectacular growth of the Indonesian church among animists and Muslims in that period. Much of the growth was accompanied through signs and wonders, not least power encounters with demonic forces exercised through sorcery.

The last example, of which I have personal knowledge, should serve to warn us that not everything is smooth sailing in this type of ministry. A certain Christian in Malaysia had a vivid dream one night some years ago that a friend, who was a pastor in another part of the country, had been run over in an accident and nothing was left of him except the skeleton. When he called the pastor concerned to tell him about the dream, he was informed by the pastor of what had happened in the latter's church. There had been some real advances in evangelism among the local people. In one year the church had been involved in bringing some 40 families to faith and had helped in removing the family altars dedicated to idol worship in all their homes. A few weeks earlier, a group from the church was going to yet another new convert's house to remove the family altar. On the way the bus met with an accident and caught fire, and 4 members were killed and burned to the bones! The pastor of the church concerned was not on the bus because he had been called away at the last minute to attend to some urgent matters. The long and short of this was that those concerned came to realise that this was Satan's backlash and that the dream was the Lord's warning to the pastor to be doubly watchful.

Some lessons to be drawn

There are of course lessons to be drawn from all these. The first and most important is that both history and present-day pastoral experience demonstrate again and again that the advance of the gospel of Christ in Asia has often been achieved through power encounters with Satan and his minions. The latter seek to hold individuals and communities in spiritual bondage through the religious traditions and social and cultural structures of the communities. But by standing on Christ's victory, persistent prayer and faithful proclamation of the gospel, Satan's bondage is repeatedly broken. Thus it is the forms of the Christianity which take power encounters seriously that have been and are making the most headway all over Asia. One may well ask with respect to places like Japan and India whether one of the key reasons that has prevented a more effective penetration of the gospel in these societies is precisely the failure to appreciate the strong demonic bondage in which they are being held? Unfortunately, many Christians have failed to pay sufficient attention to this.

This leads to the second lesson that may be drawn. Where Christianity has begun to become properly indigenised in Asia and the church is effectively penetrating the community, more often than not it takes on a Pentecostal-charismatic form. It may not be locked into the classical Pentecostal doctrine of spirit-baptism linked with tongue-speaking. But it will emphasise the manifestation of spiritual gifts and the ministry of signs and wonders, including power encounters. For without this recovery of the power of the Holy Spirit in the ministry and mission of the church, the penetration of the gospel in Asian societies has often been slow and sometimes even superficial. But it should also be noted that these Pentecostal-charismatic versions of Christianity are not always derivatives of Pentecostalism from the West, as such, but are rather proper indigenous expressions of biblical Christianity in their own right in different parts of Asia.

A final lesson that may be drawn relates to the question of whether Christians can be demonised, meaning by that either some form of intense spiritual oppression or, more seriously, demonic possession. Pastoral experience shows that it is possible for Christians to be demonised under certain conditions. Many Christians are converts from non-Christian backgrounds. Invariably, many of them have been involved in idolatrous or occult practices in their pre-Christian days. For example, they may have been given for adoption to the deities or consulted mediums or used talismans and amulets. Some have made certain vows in response to healings at temples or answers to prayers. Others have made pacts with the spirits, for example, in secret society initiation ceremonies, and so forth. Invariably, unless such past involvements are confessed and specific renunciations made, the person remains in spiritual bondage.

The degree of the seriousness of such bondage does vary with the level of involvement with such practices in an individual's pre-Christian (and sometimes post-Christian, as well) days. There is no simple formula to gauge this. But as a rule of thumb, the more extensive and prolonged the involvement, the stronger is the demonisation. This is particularly the case where there is also serious or persistent sin in a person's life. The most serious form of bondage, with which there is no hesitation to speak of possession even in Christians, is found in those who in their pre-Christian days have been heavily involved in the occult as mediums, witch doctors and the like. If there was no definite deliverance at the time of their conversion to Christ, some form of exorcism must invariably be carried out before the persons are freed.

Notes

[1] Byron H. Earhart, *Religions of Japan: Many Traditions Within One Sacred Way* (New York: HarperCollins, 1984), 133.

[2] Daniel L. Overmyer documents one example from Taiwan in *Religions of China* (New York: HarperCollins, 1986), 96–101.

[3] Tony Lambert, *China's Christian Millions: The Costly Revival* (London: Monarch, 1999), 109–20.

[4] Eileen Crossman, *Mountain Rain: A Biography of James O. Fraser* (London: OMF, 1982), 48–73.

[5] Quoted in Chuck Lowe, *Territorial Spirits and World Evangelization?* (Sevenoaks, Kent: OMF, 1998), 136. See also pages 129–41 for a summary discussion on Fraser's approach to prayer and spiritual warfare.

[6] Watchman Nee, *Sit, Walk and Stand* (London: Victory Press, 1957), 57–63.

[7] Nee, *Sit, Walk and Stand*, 59.

[8] I owe this account to Rev. Raymond Fung of Hong Kong, who was the secretary for evangelism of the WCC from 1981 to 1991. This merely illustrates the point made by Tony Lambert's book (*China's Christian Millions*).

[9] See, for example, Kurt Koch, *The Revival in Indonesia* (Grand Rapids, Mich.: Kregel, 1971). Similar happenings are also reported in the autobiography of Petrus Octavianus (*My Life for the Lord and My Neighbours: A Forty-One Years of Service to the Lord* [1957–98], privately published [1998], 57f.), one of the key leaders of the Indonesian revival. J. Edwin Orr (*Evangelical Awakenings in East Asia* [Minneapolis, Minn.: Bethany Fellowship, 1975], 146) relates a similar example of such power encounters by an Indonesian team of the same historical period.

Issues from the Indian perspective

Juliet Thomas

In 1992 the Intercession Working Group of the LCWE expressed concern with the contemporary trends and consequent practices of spiritual warfare. Tom Houston captured the concerns of the consultation in the published statement on spiritual warfare.[1] At the consultation papers were presented from various regions including India. When it comes to discussing this subject from the Indian context there are many issues, of which I want to mention two: Western Imperialism and Power Encounter.

Western imperialism and exploitation

I first want to recognise and thank God for our Christian brothers and sisters from the West. Many have served sacrificially and even given their lives on our soil so that the gospel of Jesus Christ can take root. I appreciate all those who have carried a deep burden, prayed and given generously to help the Indian church in its mission.

Unfortunately, the Indian church has recently seen many come without the same servant spirit that characterised earlier missionaries. These newer missionaries seem to exalt and serve themselves rather than exalt Jesus Christ and serve the kingdom cause. Men and women who come from the West regard themselves as "experts" in spiritual conflict, even though they have only very recently come in contact with this dimension of the powers of darkness. Furthermore, without taking into account the national scene or listening to national workers, they have worked out programs in a Western style and have bombarded the developing world with their methods of spiritual conflict.

In so doing they have been insensitive to our social, cultural and religious contexts. Their language and approach have often been very offensive to people of other faiths. Their attitude has been arrogant and triumphalistic. I do not think I am wrong in saying that our present persecution in India has been sparked by exaggerated, distorted reports and statistics published widely in newspapers and journals and on the Internet. Some of these reports are not even true, and this brings confusion and divisions in our churches. Multitudes of independent ministries, many of them without any accountability or integrity, have also come in and divided the church even further.

It seems that all too often Westerners can see things only from the Western perspective. They need to look at things from the Indian perspective. For example, honest, sincere, simple evangelists, who are obeying the call of God with total commitment, are being tempted to affluence by offers to become champions of different Western schools of thought and individualistic ministries! Much pressure is put on them to produce results so that these can be used to bring in more funds. There is great temptation to exaggerate and falsify reports. These so-called champions now lord it over their national colleagues because of the funds at their disposal. Money buys. Money speaks. Let me give two examples. I have changed names for the sake of anonymity.

First, a pastor from North India, let us call him David, has been working in that region for many years. An organisation from the West was after him for several months with offers of a house and an office of his choice. He was given access to the kind of money he had never seen before. He was persuaded that with these facilities and assets he could reach North India more effectively. However, still a little doubtful, both David and his wife took a one-year leave from their respective jobs. David was offered a salary much higher than their previously combined salaries. They moved to the city where they were asked to set up the new office, and moved into a lovely home. Everything seemed to be going well for him until his boss from the West presented a master plan for evangelising North India.

The Westerner had no clue about the North Indian context and would not listen to David's counsel because the plan was already set. The strategy was thoroughly Western, and David was simply compelled to implement it. He was very upset, because he knew the way things were planned would not work well. Finally, after all his pleas failed, he resigned. David was broken and disillusioned. He and his wife had to leave the city and return to their former home and jobs.

The second Christian worker, I will call James, had an extremely effective ministry among an important unreached people group. For such people as James, the struggle for funds and tools is always part of the task.

Then came a "big man" with "loads of money," and that was actually how he described himself! He approached James, asking him to leave his present location and work among the same people group in another region of the country. He offered great personal and financial benefits. James was deeply offended. He rejected the offer, replying, "Who told you that I was for sale?"

These are only two cases out of many that I could give. They represent a large number of men and women who face distressing situations. From the West, and more recently from Korea, a vast number of wealthy and powerful ministry leaders are sweeping into India. They cause more damage to Christian mission and testimony than you can ever imagine. Uncaring, they leave broken lives in their trail!

Where is accountability and integrity? The individual's success, popularity and self-exaltation are all that seem to matter. Money has become the bottom line to control and manipulate the weak and the powerless. It has a name. We can label it spiritual exploitation and abuse. This is not Jesus' way.

Power encounter

National workers in India have confronted demons for centuries. They have testified that by the power of God they have been able to deliver those possessed from the bondage of Satan to life and freedom in Christ. Even so, in the Indian context some believe that perhaps the church needs to engage in more serious power encounter for more effective results. There are dangers in using power encounters in this way.

First, there is a preoccupation with statistics and reports. Some emphasise spectacular accounts of deliverance that often give rise to exaggerated stories. Often psychological, cultural and social factors are not taken into consideration. Thus, the final account is not actually completely true.

Second, triumphalism can lead one to presume that any deliverance that has taken place is to their credit. What about all the prayer that has been made for so many years before for that same deliverance? There is also sometimes the feeling that the West has *all* the answers to *all* the problems in the developing world. But has it?

Third, today there is a frenzy for bringing people into the kingdom. We hear many success stories of deliverance ministries and power encounters causing many people, sometimes even whole villages, to turn to Christ. But are these genuinely converted? If genuine, what follow-up plans of discipleship are made for the new converts? Lack of follow-up results in many returning to their old faith.

The issue here really is that the people in India worship many gods, sometimes Christ among them. Whichever god they feel answers their prayers and heals their diseases is the god they follow for that time. Later, when this same god does not answer their request, they turn to a different god. In this context, turning to Jesus Christ needs to be evaluated to see if it is really genuine and the work of the Spirit in their lives. In evangelistic campaigns, many who raise their hands to mark belief in Jesus fall into this category.

Fourth, prayer trips have become popular. Much labour, time and money goes into organising these prayer journeys to distant cities. I accept that praying on site can help us understand the people and the situation better, but such intercessors often shut themselves up while on site, giving themselves to prayer without any effort to understand the people or their problems. Do they believe that praying on site while closeted in a hotel gives more power in prayer?

Others go out and stand in front of temples and mosques during their prayer walks to pull down the strongholds of the gods worshipped there. This again causes much offence. In Calcutta, as in other places, local Christians were angry because such events cause hostility towards Christians who are trying hard to reach others in compassion with the love of Jesus Christ.

Did not Jesus pray for those who would believe in him through the ministry of the disciples in John 17? Did not Paul often pray for those he had not seen or even known? Did not Jesus say that we are to worship in "spirit and in truth" and that the place does not really matter?

Fifth, high-powered, high-tech evangelists from overseas often conduct evangelistic and healing crusades. I am sorry to say that they look very similar to show-business performances. The spectacular keeps the audience spell-bound. Occasionally the government actually has stopped these meetings (in Punjab, Bombay and Orissa), and the evangelists were asked to leave immediately. The government has accused them of deceiving our people by promising them healing that did not happen. The name of Jesus is thus defiled, not glorified! In spite of the publicity and crowds, there is a growing disillusion in such deliverance ministries! Furthermore, national evangelists undergo training in power evangelism through videos released by the hundreds. They demonstrate power when they blow into the mike and the people all fall down. They throw hankies over the choir, and they all fall down. A proud evangelist related this to me. Personally, this appears more of the flesh than the Spirit!

Jesus never induced disciples to believe in him or follow him through the spectacular. In fact, he talked of denying oneself and carrying the cross. Paul takes this thought further: "We preach Christ crucified who is the power of God and the wisdom of God" (1 Cor. 1:22–24).

Sixth, the various kinds of teaching regarding the powers of darkness and how to conquer them through strategic-level spiritual-warfare prayer seems to set up an elite class of Christians who have special powers of intercession. I believe that every Christian is a *pray-er* and is called to be an intercessor (2 Chron. 7:14), with the power of the indwelling Christ to overcome all forms of evil.

Seventh, in India during a certain Hindu festival millions of Hindus make their way to the Ganges to make their sacrifices and find cleansing by dipping in their holy river. During the most recent festival, 25 million Hindus made this pilgrimage. During this time there was a terrible fight among them and several *sadhus* (Hindu holy men) were killed.

There were many intercessors there. These intercessors actually rejoiced greatly, praising God that he had answered their prayers. This attitude is painful to us. Should not the compassion of Jesus Christ be the motive for reaching those who do not know him? How could we then exult over the death of others, whoever they are?

Conclusion

I agree with Charles A. Hoole, who, writing out of the Indian context, advocates a return to the more classical model of spiritual conflict. He sharply criticises the newer methodologies being imported from the West.

The third wave Pentecostal movement seems uncritical of its own worldview. Kraft and Wimber advocate a third world type of perspective which they identify as supernaturalistic. This perspective is more pagan than Christian. Third wave deliverance teaching appears to adapt the Gospel to popular (folk) culture; producing thereby a form of cultural Christianity that has elements of New Age and Little Traditions of Hinduism and Buddhism. This has made the third wave both relevant and appealing. Such an approach to culture is similar to the efforts made by the liberals over one hundred years ago in adapting the Gospel to high culture. Liberals in effect graft Christian elements onto an underlying naturalistic worldview, creating a hybrid religion acceptable to modern minds. Similarly, the third wave mentality grafts Christian elements onto on underlying demonic, superstitious and supernaturalistic worldview, creating a hybrid religion acceptable to pre-modern and post modern minds.[2]

He therefore rejects the strategic-level spiritual warfare in favour of the classic mode of evangelism. He continues:

The former is a misunderstanding of the nature of Christian power. The Apostle Paul wrote his letter to Ephesus when it was in the grip of pagan power. He wrote about Christian counter-action against the "principalities and powers" (2:2, 3:10, 6:12). He did not prescribe shouting in ruined amphitheaters, but the declaration of the Gospel, and through it, the creation of a Christian community where the power of the love of Christ could be incarnated (Act 19:8–10). This classic mode led to the establishment of a church at the centre of Diana's kingdom in Ephesus which was to last over a thousand years.[3]

I would appeal to those advocating strategic-level spiritual warfare to be wise and to recognise that it is through his Word that God speaks and acts, judges and saves. There are no powers that can stop the progress of the gospel (Matt. 28:18).

Notes

[1] "Lausanne Statement on Spiritual Warfare," online at http://www.gospelcom.net/lcwe/statements/spwar.html (accessed December 4, 2000).

[2] Charles A. Hoole, "Territorial Spirits: An Indian Perspective," *Dharma Deepika* (December 1998), 49–50.

[3] Ibid., 50.

12

Spiritual conflict
in the Indian context

V. Ezekia Francis

India ranks second by population among the countries of the world. It is estimated that there are just over one billion people there today, about 16 per cent of the total world population. India's rich tradition dates as far back as 4000 B.C. to the earliest civilisations centred around Mohanjadharo and Harappa in the north and the Dravidians in the south.

As early as the first century (ca. A.D. 52), Thomas, one of the apostles of the Lord, came to India to preach the gospel. He died there as a martyr. Some historians estimate that there were nearly 300,000 Christians in Mylapore area at the time of his death. In the subsequent centuries other Christian missionaries came from Syria, and still later more came from the West.

Though India is one country, it actually consists of people from many different ethnic, religious and linguistic groups. Before its independence from the British in 1947, it was estimated that there were more than 560 kingdoms, both large and small. This wide variety of different ethnic groups has now been grouped together under the word *Indian*.

The predominant group today is the Hindus. About 80 per cent of the total population is categorised as such. However, included in this group are tribals, Buddhists, animists, and even atheists, as well as several other groups which are not strictly Hindu in their beliefs and practices. This naturally leads to internal tensions within the Hindu group. At the same time, out of this group has emerged the

Hindutva concept, which has as its goal the "Hinduisation" of India through communal cleansing and the restoration of *Manu-dharma* (the ancient law code of *Manu*) over the land.

Since independence India has progressed fairly rapidly on the economic front, and great strides have been made in raising the literacy rate in the country. Nevertheless, some 30 per cent of the people are still living below the poverty line. Thus, in spite of the existence of many wealthy people, there remains a vast disparity in wealth distribution between the rich and poor. India has also produced many well-known thinkers, philosophers and scientists, including S. Radhakrishnan, C. V. Raman, Abdul Kalaam, Ramanujam and Bose, who have been widely acknowledged for their erudition. Yet many people still live under much superstition.

The above factors indicate that India is a highly heterogeneous country. Against this background we will now examine some of the spiritual realities that are hindrances to the effective evangelisation of India.

Spiritual realities in India today

The people of India are generally God-fearing. In their lives a very important place is given to God, religion and its practices. As already noted, the predominant religion is Hinduism. S. Radhakrishnan, a former president of India and well-known philosopher, described it as a "way of life." Hinduism is therefore not just a religion but a distinctive approach to life. This explains the pervasive influence of religion today. We will now examine further how this expresses itself at the ground level in everyday life in India.

GODS AND GODDESSES

Initially in Indian religion people were encouraged to see God as one of the five elements: earth, water, air, fire and sky. Therefore, in the early history of Hinduism as practised in South India, there were no deities. Ancient literature in Tamil, a language spoken in South India, makes no reference to idol worship. The worship of gods and goddesses came in later through other influences, including the desire to worship the personification of human virtues, which led to a proliferation of deities.

In Hindu belief there exists a pantheon of some 330 million gods and goddesses, at the head of which is the *Tirumoorthy*.[1] These deities are represented visually by idols of various shapes and sizes. There is a general resurgence in the worship of Hindu deities today.

More and more new idols of huge sizes are installed at vantage points all over the country. Religious festivals for particular deities are also on the increase.

For example, Ganpat is a major festival which has been growing in importance in recent years. Originally from North India, it has now spread to the other parts of the country as well. As part of the celebration huge idols of the deity are made and installed all over the cities and villages where the people gather. In one particular incident a few years back, there was a competition to build the largest idol in the Bombay-Pune area. Huge idols were made that year. But on the last day of the festival a terrible earthquake rattled that area, and many people at the celebrations perished.

One unfortunate observation that can be made about the worship of Hindu deities is that sexual perversion is sometimes given religious sanctions through its myths. For example, the story of Sivalingam is found in the book *Hindu Manners, Customs and Ceremonies*.[2] The *lingam* (phallus), the symbol of Siva, is an object of deep veneration throughout India. In the mythological story, Siva and his wife were surprised in the act of intercourse by some other gods. But so concerned was he with his own sensual gratification that he continued to indulge in the act in the presence of his visitors. The gods were so angered that they killed both Siva and his wife. The account goes on to say that "Siva desired that the act which had covered him with shame and which had been the cause of his death should be celebrated among mankind. . . . Accordingly he ordained that men should thereafter offer sacrifices and worship to his *lingam*."[3] Similarly, the story of Ayyappan tells of his being born out of a homosexual union between Siva and Vishnu, thereby giving religious sanction to the practice.

Within Hinduism, devotion to Sivalingam, Ayyappa and such other idols exemplifying moral and sexual perversions abounds and is often on the increase. This, in turn, has given rise to the proliferation of all sorts sexual sins and perversions, including temple prostitution.

TERRITORIAL SPIRITS

Another observation concerning the practice of such worship is that devotees of a particular deity tend to acquire the characteristics of that deity. This appears to tie in with what we read in Psalm 115:8, "All those who make them (idols) and those who trust in them are also like them." Moreover, since particular deities are associated with different geographical areas, the peoples of different regions tend to take on the characteristics of the respective deities. This is consistent with what many believe to be the teachings of the Bible concerning territorial spirits.

For example, in Andhra Pradesh the presiding deity is Venkata-chalapathy, who is known for his romantic adventures and sexual perversions. Consequently, the incidence of prostitution, polygamy and other sex-related problems appears to be higher there than in other places. In West Bengal, Saraswathy, the goddess of learning, is worshipped. Thus there are more men of letters there. At the same time, Bengalis are often considered intellectually arrogant by others. And in Bihar, the goddess Kali is venerated. Kali is cruel, ferocious and bloodthirsty, and she delights in blood sacrifices. It is observed that her devotees tend to take on similar characteristics.

Occult practices, magic and superstitions

The Bible specifically forbids anyone to pass through the fire; practice witchcraft; interpret omens; conjure spells; be a soothsayer, sorcerer, medium or spiritist; or call upon the dead (Deut. 18:10–12). Yet in India many are involved in such occult practices.

One of the most common practices is the use of astrology to determine the most auspicious times for various things. Right from the birth, at every important stage in a person's life – naming, commencement of education, transaction of property and so forth – auspicious times are sought. This is particularly important when it comes to marriage, wherein the compatibility of the groom and bride is examined in great detail by an astrologer before a match is agreed to and the time of the wedding finalised. The whole process is based on the Hindu almanac and astrological charts.

There have been repeated cases where people in the highest offices, including prime ministers, have sought the aid of astrologers for the moment of assumption of office. To ensure success, *pujas*, *yagas*, and other religious ceremonies are further carried out. But again and again these people have fallen from office. Yet such occurrences have not deterred the common people, including sometimes Christians, from these practices. The overall result is that both the educated and uneducated persist in following such practices by tradition, and many remain mired in superstitions.

God-men and their influence in the socio-political field

In India, God-men,[4] gurus and religious teachers exert great influence. Most Indian political leaders, whether in state or central politics, have their own "god-father" or "god-mother." Therefore it is common to see many god-men and god-women establishing ashrams and seeking to exercise their authority through influencing the leaders.

The story of Chandra Swamy, a god-man who wielded a lot of influence and authority over Rajiv Gandhi and Narasimha Rao, both former prime ministers, is well known. He was able to establish a separate centre of authority and power through which he could even change the decisions of the cabinet. In the assassination of Rajiv Gandhi, Chandra Swamy's name was mentioned widely and the newspapers carried many stories suggesting his involvement.

The power these god-men exert on the politicians is such that they are able to rule by proxy, thus becoming "centres of extra-constitutional power." But the situation is changing even further. Not being satisfied with the indirect power some of them have exercised, these god-men now desire direct political power of their own. More and more saffron-clad *sanyasis* and *swamijis* are seeking elected office for themselves today.

ATTACKS ON RELIGIOUS MINORITIES, ESPECIALLY CHRISTIANS

Finally, there is a rising militancy in the name of religion, ostensibly to protect the culture and religion of India. In fact, it is a spirit of murder, chaos and confusion that is being activated. We find different kinds of groups, ranging from the apparently peace-loving (who carry out their nefarious acts under cover) to the openly militant. Their actions have brought much misery to the people and destruction to property. Some of these groups have their own political wings that are slowly attempting to gain power. Further, Hindu militant groups actively support the present BJP government in India.

The attacks of these people have been directed especially at Muslims and Christians. But because the Christians in general have not responded to violence with violence, they are seen as easier targets. Those who are active in persecutions and anti-Christian attacks consider themselves the guardians of India's culture. Under the guise of championing its cause, they persecute the church. Their work follows a pattern. They initially seek to restrain people from following God by lure of money, office, prestige, and so on. When these fail, they try to manipulate the facts and also to intimidate. Finally, they may resort to violence to achieve their goal. Among the allegations that have been used are that Christian social services are only a cover for proselytising; Christianity is a foreign religion; and Dalits and tribals are converted by Christians, who take advantage of their ignorance, gullibility and deplorable socio-economic conditions.

In recent years a systematic propaganda campaign against Christians (and Muslims) has been let loose. The writing, production and distribution of hate literature to incite and inflame communal animosity and to provoke attacks on Christians are identical to methods used in Nazi Germany. Numerous acts of anti-Christian violence have been reported. More than 50 churches have been burned in Gujarat, Maharashtra, Tamil Nadu, Karnataka, Orissa and Andhra. Ten or more bomb blasts have been reported. Several pastors and Christian workers had been killed in addition to Graham Staines and his two sons, who were burned alive. Innumerable cases of assaults on believers have been reported. Christian hospitals in Latur and Maharashtra have been damaged.[5]

To sum up, for those who believe in spiritual warfare as a reality, the various observations above show how Satan maintains a powerful grip over the peoples of India. These are some important spiritual factors that prevent many from coming to the knowledge of the true God in Christ.

Selected testimonies

In this concluding section I offer three cases of spiritual warfare from India. The first is my own story, followed by two other cases.

WORK IN NORTH INDIA

When God first gave me a burden for North India many years ago, I went there with much zeal, thinking that I would shake North India. But instead, I was shaken. We fasted and prayed as a team but could not see any results. A senior pastor said that he had distributed three truckloads of gospel tracts and not even a single soul was won. We were depressed and discouraged when nothing happened.

But as we fasted and prayed, God spoke to me. He told me that preaching alone would not suffice. Rather, the people had to be transformed into a mighty army. I heard the audible voice of God saying, "Raise me an army!" When we started training young men and women, we saw the fruits of our labour. They went out to win souls, delivering people from the evil clutches, healing the sick and doing signs and wonders. Mere preaching was not enough. Power encounters were needed to break the enemy's bondage.

Since then I have travelled all over the country conducting seminars for full-time ministers and others. We have conducted sessions on fasting and prayer, and run short-term courses on spiritual warfare, prayer, praise and worship, exercising the gifts of the Holy Spirit and learning more about the supernatural realm. Thousands have since been raised up. I conclude with some examples of power encounters in our ministry in India over the years.

BINDING THE STRONG MAN OF SALEM

Salem, a city in Tamil Nadu, is known for prostitution and sexual perversions. Several earlier attempts to conduct evangelistic crusades had met with stiff resistance. Attendance at these meetings was negligible. The Lord showed us that the entire place was under demonic influence. The strong man of that area thwarted all attempts at prayer. The Holy Spirit, therefore, led us to bind the strong man first. We arranged for a chain prayer accompanied with fasting. After this was done, there was a breakthrough. There was a big ingathering of more than 5,000 people.

DELIVERANCE FROM SPIRITS OF IDOLATRY

Once in Muscat a lady came forward for prayer. She had been suffering from severe headaches for some years since her youth. No amount of medical treatment helped. After praying for her, I counselled her to spend more time with the Word of God and to be in God's presence. At that, she broke down and told me that whenever she tried to do that, the severity of her headache multiplied greatly, so much so that she could not even read.

Then I inquired about her past. Her parents were Hindus, and she too had participated in all the religious ceremonies. She had even carried the *Kavadi* (a kind of frame carrying an idol) on her shoulders. It was then that she started getting headaches. It was clear that the spirit behind the idol was tormenting her. I then took authority in the name of Jesus and commanded the Devil to release his hold on that lady. Within minutes she vomited some black stuff and that was the end of the headache.

Another time, during one of our short-term intensive ministerial courses in 1992, I was teaching on the authority of a believer. I explained that a demonic spirit which had possessed a person who was a non-believer would not loosen its hold on the person after he or she becomes a believer unless the spirit is cast out. I also explained that the spirits behind idols could possess their devotees.

I pointed out that even nominal Christians from some traditional churches, where statues are venerated, could become victims. When I mentioned the worship of statues of Mary and other saints, one of the participants rushed forward. One of his hands was bent backward and could not be straightened. We found out that prior to his salvation he was a peddler. He was a nominal Roman Catholic and also a devotee of Mary of Velankanni (a place of pilgrimage for Catholics where Mary is supposed to have appeared). When he was delivered in the name of Jesus, his hand was immediately straightened and became normal. Subsequently he became a full-time minister and today is preaching the word of God in different countries.

Conclusion

From my experience of more than 25 years in the Lord's vineyard, I can now boldly say that the power of the Holy Spirit is *the* answer for effective evangelisation and building up God's kingdom.

Notes

[1] Alternately spelt Trimurti, meaning "triple form." This refers to Brahma the Creator, Visnu the preserver, and Siva the destroyer, a perceived trinity of Hinduism.

[2] Abbe J. A. Dubois, *Hindu Manners, Customs and Ceremonies*, 3d ed. (Oxford: Clarendon Press, 1906).

[3] Ibid., 630.

[4] Religious leaders who are perceived to be *avatars*, that is, incarnations of the gods, e.g., Sai Baba.

[5] See Vishal Mangalwadi, Vijay Martis and Maganbhai Bhagwanji Desai, *Burnt Alive*, rev. ed. (Mumbai, India: GLS Publishing, 1999), 144; they report that the Indian home minister told Parliament that there have been 116 reported incidents of attacks of Christians, including five killings, since January 1998.

13

African traditional religions as a basis for understanding spiritual conflict in Africa

Yusufu Turaki

African traditional religious systems

TYPES OF SPIRITUAL POWERS IN TRADITIONAL RELIGIOUS BELIEFS

There are four types of spiritual powers found in traditional religions: (1) impersonal forces, (2) spirit beings, (3) divinities or gods and (4) the Supreme Being. Understanding the beliefs related to these spiritual powers is essential to our theological interpretation and analysis of the traditional religions.

Belief in impersonal forces

Belief in impersonal forces is pervasive in traditional African religious thought. The whole of creation is endowed with this impersonal power, which has been given various names in Africa, such as life force, vital force and life essence. The source of this impersonal force is usually attributed to the activities of higher powers. The potency, efficacy and durability of such powers vary from object to object. The belief in the impersonal and its impact on social roles and functions have theological bases, which Christians must recognise and seek to understand in order to apply the Bible and the Christian gospel to this deep-seated religious belief.

What do traditional Africans feel about the pervasive and dominant presence of the mystical forces? A biblical theology that addresses the traditional theology of impersonal forces must go beyond matching biblical texts with specific traditional beliefs. It must address the theological, philosophical, moral and ethical bases and foundations of these beliefs. When beliefs in the potency of mystical forces are condemned as demonic, the traditional African needs to know why. Africans often have personally experienced their power and efficacy, and simplistic Bible verses given in response will not change their thinking.

Belief in spirit beings

Traditional African concepts of reality and destiny are deeply rooted in the spirit world. Spirit beings are seen to govern all social and spiritual phenomena. There are two types of spirit beings in this category: non-human spirits and spirits of the dead. Non-human spirits are regarded in hierarchical order, depending on the power they wield and the role they play in the spirit world.[1] First in the hierarchy is the Creator, followed by the deities, object-embodied spirits, and finally the ancestral and non-human spirits. Humanity stands between this array of spiritual hosts and the world of nature.[2]

What constitutes the spirit world? Byang H. Kato lists the following beliefs about the spirit world in Nigeria: (1) the whole world is full of spirits; (2) the abodes of spirits are numerous, including trees, rivers, burial grounds, and so on; (3) spirits can be good or evil; (4) people can come back through reincarnation; (5) spirits can possess people and be exorcised; (6) life after death, future reward and future punishment are all real; and (7) evil spirits are associated with Satan.[3]

Spirit possession. John S. Mbiti stresses that the spirit world of the African people is densely populated.[4] There is a very close relationship between the spirit beings and the impersonal forces. This realm of the supernatural empowers magic, witchcraft and sorcery. The spirit realm is, in a sense, a battleground of spirits and powers that use their power to influence the course of human life. These mystical powers can be used positively or negatively.

If people knew how to master and control the realm of the supernatural, the world would be a much happier place. Belief in the mystical powers, the spirit beings behind them and the human quest to control or influence them results in a variety of specialists such as medicine men, rain makers, mediums, diviners, sorcerers, magicians and witches. Superstitions, totems, taboos and rituals also grow out of such beliefs.

The ancestral spirits are close to the living and serve as their custodians. All spirit beings are endowed with powers that they apply towards humans for good or harm. Because the spirit beings can be benevolent, capricious or malicious, people must be wise in dealing with them. To do so, we need human specialists who have experience and access to the spirits to help us live successful lives. The specialists are able to manipulate spirit beings to serve the humans, but they can also manipulate humans to serve the spirits.

Belief in many divinities

African scholars over the past three decades have changed their orientation towards what were initially called gods.[5] Some reject that traditional religions were polytheistic and debate whether African divinities were worshipped as gods or simply recognised as intermediaries or mediators. To date this debate is inconclusive.

There are many African divinities, each with specific areas of influence and control. Some were originally mythological figures from legends and primordial histories, while others were human tribal heroes or heroines. Divinities covering different aspects of life, society and community were usually recognised as exercising power over oceans, waters, rain, thunder, fertility, health or sickness, planting or harvest, tribe and clan or family. The plurality of the divinities with their varying roles and powers, even within a single ethnic group or community, explains the African openness to religious accommodation, assimilation and even syncretism.

Belief in a Supreme Being (God)

The works of African scholars for the past three decades have established that Africans conceived a universal God.[6] Most Africans agree that traditionally Africans did not actively worship this Supreme Being. Instead, the African divinities and the ancestors were actively sought in everyday life through offerings and prayers. The Creator God seemed "not to be intimately involved or concerned with man's world."[7]

The religious activities, then, of the traditional Africans revolve mainly around the lower powers, spirits and ancestors. The basic theological system growing around this reality is holistic. The material and the spiritual are totally integrated, with a resulting focus on balancing the powers by rituals that manipulate them and thereby provide fulfillment.[8]

Hierarchy of spiritual beings

In the traditional religious worldview all spiritual beings are in a hierarchical order. The Supreme Being is the highest. The lesser beings occupy lesser positions but are higher than humans. The authority, power, influence and legitimacy of spirit beings depend on their position within the ontological order. Spirits, by virtue of their positions and roles, dispense and control the activities of the impersonal forces and thereby influence the morality and ethics of the human societies.

Traditional Africans respond to these spirit beings according to their place of hierarchy. Religious values, activities, practices, morality and ethics are accorded to each spirit in proportion to the position of that spirit. This has important consequences on the traditional conceptions of morality and ethics.[9]

Foundational religious practices

There are four foundational religious practices in the traditional religions related to the spirit realm. They are the practices related to (1) establishing relationships with the cosmic powers, (2) religious and social rituals, (3) establishing communication with the spirit world and (4) traditional specialists.

ESTABLISHING RELATIONSHIPS WITH THE POWERS

In the quest to establish links with the powers, Africans developed a variety of practices, rituals and ceremonies intended to exercise control over the powers and/or to restore cosmic harmony or balance.

Means of exercising control

Control can be exercised through the use of the power of such things as incantations and words, symbolism, magic, fetishes, witchcraft and sorcery.[10] While many of these practices are condemned, the Bible does not deny their power.

For the Christian, the theological issues centre on (1) the belief in the usefulness of such powers and the means of obtaining power and (2) the act of giving oneself to the authorities. A biblical theology should address the nature of the practices, behaviours, and feelings involved in obtaining the desired power; and also the act of submitting to the powers.

The powers are not acceptable substitutes for God. In Christian theology only God can exercise control over the entire universe. Thus, a theology of God's providence and Christ's mediatorial work on the cross are relevant.

Means of restoring cosmic and spiritual harmony

Humanity's delicate dealings with the spirits have rules that are manifest in religious practices. When our expectations are not met, harmony must be restored through reconciliation with the powers. This harmony is maintained through observing of taboos. When a taboo is broken, harmony can be restored through offering sacrifices and gifts.

When things go wrong, specialists have the role of doing something so that harmony can be restored. This raises many questions. What are violations against the spirit world? If wrongs are admitted, what feelings are generated? Who gets hurt when humans sin? Why is maintaining cosmic harmony important? What specific religious practices are efficacious in reconciling humans and spirits? Christianity has to address these questions and provide biblical solutions. In Christian theology God alone can restore cosmic harmony over the entire universe, and a Christian theology of reconciliation provides an important foundation here.

PRACTICES RELATING TO RITUALS AND CEREMONIES

The purpose behind traditional rituals and ceremonies must be ascertained, including the rules and regulations that are the means of linking traditional Africans with the spiritual realm. A Christian theology should examine the religious rituals to see what the underlying beliefs are and address those beliefs in relevant Christian ways.

MEANS OF SPIRITUAL AND MYSTICAL COMMUNICATION

There are various means of communication with the spirit world, including dreams, visions, vision quests, divination and ordeals. The Bible has much to say in this area. All aspects of this communication must be examined theologically in developing an African approach to spiritual conflict.

PRACTICES OF SPECIALISTS

Traditional Africa has a host of specialists who are professionals in their various disciplines. The theological, practical and ethical foundations for these specialists must be examined.

Philosophical foundations in traditional worldview

There are four basic philosophical foundations in African traditional worldviews:[11] (1) holism/organism, governed by the law of harmony; (2) spiritualism, governed by the law of the spirit; (3) dynamism/power-consciousness, governed by the law of power; and (4) communalism, governed by the law of kinship.

The foundational religious beliefs discussed previously combined with these four philosophical foundations produce a worldview that dominates traditional African thought. The philosophical foundations discussed below complement the theological foundations of the previous section. From the philosophical foundations we can also understand traditional moral laws.

HOLISM/ORGANISM AND THE LAW OF HARMONY

Africans stand face to face with the physical, material and spiritual dimensions of their world, interacting with all elements holistically. Traditional Africans seek to live in a harmonious and peaceful existence with this integrated world.

We can understand how a Western dualism that separates physical from spiritual creates serious theological problems for the traditional Africans' holistic view of life. Here, Christianity faces not a specific religious belief with creeds but a philosophical worldview that covers the totality of life, both in the human and spirit realms. This is not to be learned as much as lived, caught and passed on, and Christianity has to address this orientation to the world.

Traditionally, all of nature is related to the mysterious powers and spirit beings.[12] The Creator creates nature. Nature, humanity and the spirit world constitute one fluid coherent unit. Hence the conception of the traditional African worldview as a unity. It is not a confused world of non-integrated parts. Life, in general, is holistic and remains mysterious.

The law of harmony, unfolding naturally from a holistic and organic worldview in which "the universe, the spirit world and man are all part of the same fabric,"[13] deals with the theological questions of reconciliation, restoration, reverence, awe, a sense of wonder and the accompanying ceremonies and rituals. Moral and ethical questions are also raised in the area of a relationship between the humans and spirit beings. The theology of redemption and reconciliation in the work of Christ addresses the questions of cosmic harmony and must be brought to the questions raised in the African context.

SPIRITUALISM AND THE LAW OF THE SPIRIT

Spiritualism reflects the preponderance of spiritual reality in traditional African beliefs. "This world in essence is spiritual rather than material" and "life is saturated with supernatural possibilities."[14] The question of meaning in life is dominated by the spiritual emphasis. Because of this spiritual view of life, "when personal resources fail, religious specialists will divine and supply satisfactory meanings."[15]

Traditional Africans recognise this quest for meaning in the every-day happenings of life and want to find out what lies behind every incident. The penetrating power of the law of the spirit gives the traditional worldview a pantheistic conception of the source and effects of the forces, while the presence of a myriad of spirits and divinities results in a polytheistic conception of the universe. These must both be addressed if a theology of spiritual conflict is to be relevant to Africans.

DYNAMISM/POWER-CONSCIOUSNESS AND THE LAW OF POWER

The dominance of the impersonal, the unseen and the unpredictable spirit powers makes people search for power which can help in this dangerous world, where fate, evil and death abound. Steyne notes that "the search for and acquisition of power supersedes any commitment to ethics or morality. Whatever is empowering is right."[16]

Many terms are used to describe power, such as *life force, vital force, life essence* and *dynamism.* Power can be obtained by rituals, charms, fetishes, ceremonies, witchcraft and sorcery, or directly from powerful people or the spirits.[17] And it is transferable.

This all-consuming concept of power is critical in our understanding of how traditional Africans assess the potency or the efficacy of any new religion. Christianity must develop a theology of power that addresses the traditional theological conception of power and recognises how this law of power operates in traditional Africa.

COMMUNALISM AND THE LAW OF KINSHIP

Africans see humanity as a community, people in relationships to other people, nature and the spirits. This communal concept defines how a person becomes a member of society and relates to other humans, to nature and to the spirit world. B. J. Van der Walt lists as values of this African communalism interdependence, communal self-respect, survival of the community, group assurance, co-operation and harmony, affiliation and shared duties.[18]

The African concept of community is founded on kinship. The relationship is defined in terms of the physical and blood linkage to the progenitor. The community traces its roots from this human source and builds a network of relationships around this ancestral nucleus. Even the integration of tribal groups into modern African states has not eradicated this foundational concept of kinship.

The life of the community is controlled and protected by the ancestors. The communal life in this kinship system is "ancestrally chartered." Steyne observes that personhood is meaningless apart

from these ancestral relationships.[19] Within this network of relationships, a person is not held

individually responsible for his actions. Because he believes
himself to be the extension of the spirit world, the corporate
family and the tribe, these must all share responsibility and
blame for what he is and does. He is acted upon by powers he
believes are beyond his control.[20]

The task for Christianity is to define the African within the context
of this communal network of relationships which is governed by the
law of kinship, the law of harmony, the law of power and the law of
the spirit.

The spirit realm

As noted at the outset, the traditional African believes in spirit
beings as well as impersonal mystical forces. Understanding the twin
beliefs in (1) the spirits and (2) the mystical forces, together with
their profound influence on traditional African life, is essential to any
understanding of the traditional African religious worldview.

It is important to control, or at least work with, these powers
through magic and religion.[21] Thus, people have developed rituals
and ceremonies to enable specialists to communicate with and control the powers and meet their needs in life.

Scholars have observed that the concept of worship as it relates
to both the Supreme Being and the divinities in the traditional religions has not been as fully developed as it is in Christianity. They
suggest that the dominant motive in African religion is not worship
of God, or profession of faith in God, but securing well-being in the
face of the forces through religious manipulation.[22]

THE QUEST FOR SPIRITUAL AND MYSTICAL POWERS

In the face of the spirits and powers, humanity is not completely
powerless or without responsibility. Because people are dependent
on the powers, and at times anxious about their apparently capricious nature, they seek ways to control the powers and bring their
own universe under control.[23]

How is control over powers acquired?

One may be born into a family of power or have special powers
at birth, though that is rare. Others gain power through disciplines

(vision quests, arduous tasks and physical acts of purification) or drugs designed to heighten awareness of the powers.[24] Others seek power through linking with the ancestors or persons of power (heroes, diviners, religious leaders, and so on) who impart their energy. Still others seek power through regular participation in religious celebrations, liturgies and rituals. These include laying on of hands; anointing with sacred oils; painting or marking the body; wearing sacred objects, drinking or eating blood, sacred drinks or food; burying animals or sacred objects; and incantations, recitations and singing. The quest for power through religious celebrations and rituals is prevalent among some Christian groups in Africa. Finally, we note that some gain power through the use of charms, sacred objects, weapons and other paraphernalia. Objects empowered with vital force can be manipulated as means of protection and attack. At times they will be worn on the person being protected or buried near the home or workplace of one being harmed.

How is control over the powers exercised?

Having the ability to control the powers is not the same as exercising that control. There are numerous methods by which control may be exercised. The more common are listed briefly below.[25]

Word power (incantations). Words are perceived to have innate power and are vitally connected with what happens in life – and this applies whether people are traditionalists or Christians.[26] Thus, blessings and curses are taken literally, and prayers and oaths as well as the words used in rituals of possession are thought to be extremely powerful.

The African traditional belief in the power of words has been reinforced by the theologies of some of the Independent Churches as well as the nontraditional and new Christian Pentecostal and charismatic groups. In some cases the theological words and terms used are couched in Christian language but fundamentally rooted in African traditional beliefs. Thus, the continuity between the pre-Christian religious and cultural heritage is assumed, not in terms of Christian theologisation, but in terms of traditional and cultural praxis.

Symbolic power. Symbols are also seen as sources of control over spiritual forces. Steyne notes:

> Symbols serve to secure and protect places, people and times from the attacks of evil spirits and to invite the benevolent spirits to exercise their good offices on behalf of the supplicants.

Under the protection of the symbol, devotees feel secure, endued with power and confident.[27]

Symbolic power is often linked to items such as charms or masks or other objects of power and may include gestures and acts (for example, making the sign of the cross). Religious symbols are particularly powerful, and include the use and sprinkling of blood, colours, clothing and designed objects or shapes.

Magic. Magic is a deliberate attempt to use occult powers to influence future events. Several categories of magic may be noted,[28] including divine, natural (for example, the evil eye), black, white, homeopathic (making a doll that resembles the victim and injuring or destroying the doll), and contagious (magic through physical contact). Each has associated rituals to engage the magic and enable it to do that for which it is called.

Charms, amulets and talismans. A charm is an empowered object worn by the person it is intended to protect. Types of charms include animal parts, consecrated cords, stones, leather pieces, metal objects, Scripture portions, ointments, and so on.[29]

Fetishes. A fetish is typically a shrine for a spirit. This may be a symbolic object such as a carved idol, a stool, a tablet, and so on. It is often thought to be the residence of a spirit, or that a spirit may be called to it because of magical attachments that have been made by a person of power.

Witchcraft. Those who engage in these evil practices are called witches and sorcerers. Their powers may be hereditary or acquired from a source other than family.

Sorcery. In contrast to witchcraft, sorcery involves a conscious manipulation of power to harm.[30] Sorcery is often used for revenge or against perceived attack or threat.

Both the belief and the dread of witchcraft and sorcery in Africa are pervasive and very powerful. The death of young people, mysterious deaths, accidents and incurable diseases are usually attributed to witchcraft or sorcery.

A biblical theology should address these beliefs and practices as they affect African expressions of Christianity. The Bible has much to say about magic, sorcery and witchcraft. These mystical powers are real in African experience because there exists behind them a spiritual reality. And this spiritual reality, as far as Christians are concerned, in Africa or elsewhere, must be resisted for the sake of the gospel.

MEANS OF COMMUNICATING WITH THE SPIRIT WORLD

Traditionally, Africans seek to communicate with the spirit realm through, among other things, divination and ordeals. These are means by which the unseen and the future are known.

Divination. Divination relies on specific religious occult techniques to determine the answers to questions we could otherwise not answer: to find out about the future, to connect with the powers in order to make requests, to determine the source of a problem, to overcome human limitations and to send and receive messages from the spirit realm in order to determine the source of disharmony and restore balance.

Ordeals. An ordeal is a trial or test used to discover the answer to a question, often to determine the guilt or the innocence of someone accused of a societal violation. Often the ordeal is impossible to endure with human strength alone (for example, taking a rock from a pot of boiling water without being burned) under the assumption that the spirits will protect the innocent from harm or judge the guilty.

MEANS OF MAINTAINING HARMONY WITH THE SPIRIT WORLD

Africans see communication with the spirit world as reciprocal in that we send *and* receive communication. This reciprocity needs to be maintained by means of fellowship or communion.

Unfortunately, the human world is unstable. It looks chaotic and fragile and is subject to invasion and capriciousness by powerful forces. Thus the harmony that is desired appears as a mirage. It is constantly under siege and attack. Efforts must always be made at restoring harmony. Reconciliation for breached relationships must be sought. Without these efforts, the person and even the community are stifled and even endangered. There are two major elements that are used to maintain harmony. The first is the establishment of taboos and means dealing with violations. The second is that of the sacrificial system.

Taboos

Taboos in an African setting are the sacred moral codes. They foster correct social religious behaviour. They are seen in religiously defined prohibitions of conduct. The purpose of these prohibitions is to protect people from being harmed by an object, place or action that has power associated with it.[31] Taboo violations upset the harmony of the powers, and the person who violates taboo without protective power will be harmed in turn, even to the point of death. Steyne notes:

> Taboo is a legal system which dictates how life shall be lived in order to realize salvation and blessings. . . . It is an all encompassing system calling on the spirit world to either validate, restrict or censure human behavior.[32]

Taboos are applied to sacred places, land use, proscribed food, sexual behaviour, social behaviour, status-related obligations, religious actions, and so on. The taboo system has continuing moral, ethical, social and religious consequences, and a theology addressing the taboo system of a particular people is important in understanding its concept of sin and its consequences.

Sacrifices and offerings

Sacrifices and offerings abound in traditional religions, serving many purposes. They cement cordial relationships and communion between the spirits and people. They can placate angry spiritual powers after taboo violations. They please the powers, paving the way for requests. They maintain communion between sacrificer and spirit power and remind the powers of their obligations to watch over people. They send off the dead in ways that show how beloved they were.[33]

There are numerous types of sacrifices and offerings, ranging from plants to animals, and in rare cases, even humans. Offerings are usually thought of as presents to the powers, without formal obligation, while sacrifices are usually given after violation or taboo as a means of restoration.[34]

Conclusion

Understanding the background of African traditional religions is essential to any application of Christian spirituality in Africa. The demonic is just a part of the whole, and Christian warfare in Africa must focus on and address the totality of the traditional spiritual worldview.

Christian spirituality will have to address the various aspects of the traditional religious system that have been outlined. This is primarily to engage the Christian spiritual worldview with that of the traditional spiritual worldview.

Christian confrontation with the demonic within the traditional spiritual worldview arises when the demonic features as a stumbling block to Christian spiritual transformation of the traditional spiritual worldview. The demonic and spiritual forces and powers are dealt with in their encounter with Christianity as they stand in opposition to the presentation and proclamation of the gospel of Christ as well as obstacles to Christian spiritual transformation of lives.

The stories of Christian encounter with the demonic and spiritual forces abound everywhere in Africa. There is an increasing revival of manifestations of the demonic and spiritual forces and thus an increasing need to understand what traditional ideas are driving those practices.

Notes

[1] E. D. Oji, "*Ikpu Alu* (Atonement) in Igbo Traditional Religion," B.A. thesis, Jos ECWA Theological Seminary (1988), 17.

[2] E. Ikenga-Metuh, *God and Man in African Religion: A Case Study of the Igbo of Nigeria* (London: Geoffrey Chapman, 1981), 125–44.

[3] Byang H. Kato, *Theological Pitfalls in Africa* (Nairobi: Evangel, 1975), 36–41.

[4] John S. Mbiti, *African Religions and Philosophy* (London: Heinemann Educational Books, 1971), 75; Ikenga-Metuh, *God and Man in African Religion*, 103–79.

[5] E. Bolaji Idowu, *Olodumare: God in Yoruba Belief* (London: Longman, 1962); John S. Mbiti, *Concepts of God in Africa* (London: SPCK, 1970).

[6] Ibid.

[7] Philip M. Steyne, *Gods of Power: A Study of the Beliefs and Practices of Animists* (Houston, Tex.: Touch Publications, 1989), 35.

[8] See ibid., 39.

[9] Ikenga-Metuh, *God and Man in African Religion*, 243–59.

[10] Steyne, *Gods of Power.*

[11] Adapted from ibid.

[12] Oji, "*Ikpu Alu*," 15.

[13] Steyne, *Gods of Power*, 58.

[14] Ibid., 59.

[15] Ibid., 37.

[16] Ibid., 60.

[17] Ibid.

[18] B. J. Van der Walt, *A Christian Worldview and Christian Higher Education for Africa* (Potchefstroom, South Africa: Potchefstroom University for Christian Higher Education, Institute for Reformational Studies, 1991), 29–44.

[19] Steyne, *Gods of Power*, 64–65.

[20] Ibid., 67.

[21] Victor B. Cole, "The Christian and African Traditional Religion and Culture: Some Basic Principles of Understanding and Approach," unpublished paper (1989), 3.

[22] See Steyne, *Gods of Power;* Richard J. Gehman, *African Traditional Religion in Biblical Perspective* (Nairobi, Kenya: East African Educational Publishers, 1989).

[23] See Langdon Gilkey, *Maker of Heaven and Earth: The Christian Doctrine of Creation in the Light of Modern Knowledge* (Lanham, Md.: University Press of America, 1959), 6.

[24] Steyne, *Gods of Power*, 90–92.

[25] Following ibid., 100.

[26] See discussion in ibid., 100–106.

[27] Ibid., 106.

[28] Ibid., 107–13.

[29] Ibid., 115.

[30] Steyne, *Gods of Power*, 119.

[31] Steyne, *Gods of Power*, 140.

[32] Ibid., 140–41.

[33] Ibid., 137–38.

[34] Ibid., 137–40.

III.

Reflections on contemporary issues

14

Contemporary trends in the treatment of spiritual conflict

CHARLES H. KRAFT

Some of the contemporary trends in the treatment of spiritual warfare among evangelicals, especially in the United States, are worthy of attention. By "contemporary," I mean twentieth century. By "evangelicals," I mean those faithful to the Bible but not involved in the Pentecostal movement of the early twentieth century or the charismatic movement of the mid-century. This is one of the geographical constituencies represented by the Lausanne movement until the latter part of the century, when Pentecostal Christianity was admitted into the evangelical mainline.

I know little of what was going on in the Roman Catholic Church in this regard, except that many Catholics were early participants in the charismatic movement that started in the mid 1960s and continue to be renewed through the continuance of that movement. Nor am I knowledgeable about what has been going on in Europe and other areas outside the United States. I apologise for this and welcome additions and corrections in these or any other areas.

I need to make it explicit that I am tackling this subject from a particular perspective. I am not an unbiased observer of the discussion this conference is dealing with. I am one of those carrying the label Third Wave.

I have been a missionary and a trainer of missionaries for some 43 years now. I have come from an evangelical, non-charismatic background, attended Wheaton College and Ashland Theological Seminary, both of which would be considered mainline evangelical institutions. I went to Nigeria in 1957 with no charismatic or Pentecostal influence in my life, but found that I had no ability to deal with the demonic or even to discuss it intelligently. This ignorance stayed with me after I left the mission field and began my career as a trainer of missionaries. Then, in the early 1980s, we on the Fuller School of World Mission faculty, feeling keenly the failure in our own missionary experience in dealing with spiritual conflict, invited John Wimber to teach a course on signs and wonders within our curriculum.

Starting in January 1982, then, I began to go through a shift in my life, my teaching and my involvement in ministry that has taken me into the area of spiritual warfare both as a practitioner and a theoretician. Now I have authored five books and a number of articles on subjects related to spiritual conflict and have a regular ministry of inner healing and deliverance both in the United States and internationally. In addition, I regularly teach several courses in these areas within the Fuller School of World Mission curriculum.

History

TIME LINE

Spiritual conflict was very obvious in the ministry of Jesus and of the early church. The early church Fathers record that in post-Apostolic times churches were so concerned about demonisation that they appointed exorcists to their pastoral staffs. One such church is reported to have had more than 50 officially recognised exorcists.

Through the Middle Ages credulity concerning what were believed to be spiritual manifestations reached such a high level that the Reformers and their followers reacted against belief in supernatural manifestations. This, plus the rise of the universities, the influences of the Enlightenment, the Industrial Revolution and other human being-centred focuses led in Western societies to the widespread abandonment of any belief in spiritual reality, except for a belief in God, sometimes accompanied by a vague belief in angels.

United States

In the early twentieth century, however, the movement we know as Pentecostalism arose in the United States, alerting the Western Christian world once again to the existence of spiritual beings antagonistic to the Christian cause. This movement, though shunned by evangelicals for several decades, understood that Jesus provides his followers with spiritual power to heal and cast out demons. We sometimes refer to this movement as the First Wave in

Western Christianity of a focus on the Holy Spirit and the Spirit's activities in spiritual warfare.

In mission lands, even before the rise of Pentecostalism, Western missionaries and their converts often recognised spiritual conflict in the form of demonisation countered by deliverance in Jesus' name and breakthroughs following intense intercessory prayer. Many missionaries, however, made the mistake of assuming that the cultures of non-Western peoples are so infested with satanic power that they are unredeemable. They, therefore, established schools and other Western institutions designed to convert people from their own cultures to Western understandings of reality that did not include any but superficial belief in the spiritual reality of the Bible.

In the mid-1960s, then, a second wave of emphasis on the Holy Spirit and the Spirit's power swept through certain segments of American Christianity. This charismatic movement, unlike the Pentecostal movement, took place largely in established churches, including Roman Catholic and mainline Protestant churches. It did not, therefore, result in sizeable denominations, as did the Pentecostal movement. Though it enlivened many individuals and congregations, it was widely rejected by the evangelical mainstream.

In the early 1980s, then, a third wave of focus on the Holy Spirit and the Spirit's power began. This movement is primarily within evangelical churches and seems to be growing today.

All three of the waves continue, though the charismatic wave may have been largely swallowed up in the Third Wave. There are great similarities between the waves, but some significant differences as well. Each is similar in focusing on the activity of the Holy Spirit in warring against the powers of darkness. Enthusiastic worship, believed to be effective in countering satanic activity, also characterises all three movements. The Third Wave, however, has the advantage of widespread acceptance of such worship in churches outside of the movement. This fact provides some opportunity for this latest wave to be regarded more positively than the other two in mainstream evangelicalism.

Evangelicalism largely rejected Pentecostalism and the charismatic movement because of their focus on speaking in tongues and their emotionalism. The Third Wave has muted the emphasis on tongues, focusing more on healing and spiritual warfare. Meanwhile, many Pentecostal churches have become less focused on their distinctives and more like mainline evangelical churches.

Though Pentecostalism has traditionally attracted a working-class, not highly schooled constituency, both the charismatic movement and the Third Wave have received much of their acceptance among the more educationally privileged classes. Indeed, Third Wave emphases are now being taught in prestigious seminaries and Bible colleges.

All three waves have challenged the Western worldview that characterises most Western Christian churches concerning such things as the existence of a spirit world (especially demons and angels), the presence and power of the Holy Spirit, satanic activity in human affairs, faith healing, spiritual gifting and worship. As mentioned, Pentecostalism, in order to focus on its distinctives, largely isolated itself from mainstream evangelicalism. In mid-century, though, both evangelicals and Pentecostals began to discover that they had more in common than they had previously recognised. Pentecostal denominations, then, were admitted into evangelical organisations such as the National Association of Evangelicals and increasingly referred to as evangelicals. More recently, certain Pentecostal scholars have won a great deal of respect among evangelicals, even rising to prominence as leaders of previously anti-Pentecostal seminaries such as Gordon-Conwell and Fuller. Often, however, this respectability has been achieved at the cost of the muting of Pentecostal distinctives on the part of these leaders.

Pentecostals have often taken a dim view of the Third Wave movement. Possibly some have felt that we of the Third Wave are "stealing" some of their distinctives. Or, perhaps, in their drive towards evangelical respectability, some have adopted a good bit of Western scepticism towards spiritual reality. They may also be reacting against some of the emotional excesses of early Pentecostalism and the tendency of the movement to go to certain extremes with regard to the spirit world (for example, a demon under every bush).

For whatever reasons, more non-Pentecostal Western evangelicals have become open to the concept of spiritual warfare and other emphases that were once limited to Pentecostals and charismatics. It is probable that the wide popularity within evangelical circles of the 1980s novels *This Present Darkness* and *Piercing the Darkness* by Pentecostal Frank Peretti had something to do with the move towards openness.[1] So also did the early Calvary Chapel emphases, springing out of the Jesus People movement, the healing seminars and teaching at Fuller Seminary of John Wimber and his disciples in the 1980s and 1990s.

Two-thirds World

While these things were happening in America, we can point to at least two major developments in the Two-thirds World. On the one hand, in many places missionised people, most of whom were or are deeply into spiritual power assumptions and practices, began to see discrepancies between the largely powerless Christianity brought by evangelical missionaries and that portrayed in the Bible. This factor played a major part in the splitting off of literally thousands of groups from mission-founded churches to establish independent brands of Christianity, most of which focused a good bit of attention on spiritual conflict.

In Africa, for example, 5,000 or more such churches have been identified in South Africa alone, with many hundreds more in East and West Africa. Healing and deliverance from demons are often major emphases in these churches, though excesses abound.

Not entirely unrelated to the independency movement is the fact that Pentecostalism has, from the beginning of the twentieth century, mounted the largest missionary thrust in evangelicalism. The Pentecostal emphasis on spiritual warfare has clicked with the concern for spiritual power of most of the peoples of the world and resulted in rapid spread and growth of Pentecostal Christianity.

Whether they are Pentecostal or influenced by the recent openness to charismatic emphases, numerous churches in each country in the Two-thirds World include spiritual conflict among their major emphases. And some of these churches are among the largest in the world today.

Innovator categories

Before turning to the topic of publications and conferences, it might be well to focus on the process of innovation of a concern for spiritual conflict among American evangelicals. Everett Rogers and others have pointed to several stages in the process of the acceptance of innovations.[2] Given the virtual captivity to Western worldview assumptions concerning the spirit world on the part of evangelicals, we can helpfully point to such steps in the emerging consciousness of sizeable numbers of evangelicals to the reality and scriptural appropriateness of a focus on spiritual warfare.

When a new idea is introduced, the research shows that about 2.5 per cent of those exposed to it will accept it. These are the *innovators*, people who are frequently way ahead of the majority of their group in accepting new ideas. As these innovators practice the idea, another group watches and soon adopts it also. These are the *early adopters*. They make up 13.5 per cent of the population of those who will eventually accept the idea (we are not counting those who will never accept it). This group is followed by the *early majority* (34 per cent), the *late majority* (34 per cent) and eventually by those who do accept but only after everyone else who will accept has come in. These are what are called the *laggards* (16 per cent).

My assessment would be that many American evangelicals are in the early adopter stage of this sequence with regard to the acceptance of the innovation, spiritual warfare. Theologians, of course, are mostly either ignoring the movement or negative towards it. The "common people," however, are much more likely to see the relevance of spiritual power issues, with pastors somewhere in between.

The innovators in dealing with spiritual warfare among evangelicals cover a wide spectrum of time. This period would seem to extend up to the 1980s. Though Pentecostals were practising and doing some writing early in the twentieth century, evangelicals pretty much isolated themselves from Pentecostal influence.

PUBLICATIONS AND CONFERENCES

Before 1970

Prior to the 1970s, there were few publications dealing with our subject that attracted evangelical attention. There were, of course, more on the Pentecostal side of the fence. And the rise of the charismatic movement during this decade added a few publications. One of the books that attracted a very limited amount of evangelical attention was Jesse Penn-Lewis's 1912 volume *War on the Saints*,[3] but often in its abridged edition. More attention was given to this book at a later stage, however.

Merrill Unger at Dallas Seminary was active in teaching concerning demonology in the 1940s and 1950s, publishing his classic *Biblical Demonology* in 1952.[4] In that volume he contended that Christians could not be demonised, a position that personal experience plus the experiences of former students led him to abandon in his later books.

An example of the typical evangelical attitude during this time was the experience of R. A. Torrey. Though he had written extensively on the person and work of the Holy Spirit even before the Pentecostal movement began (for example, his 1897 work entitled *Baptism with the Holy Spirit* and a long section on the Holy Spirit in his *What the Bible Teaches* 1898[5]), the great respect that was his among evangelicals did not include the acceptance of his ideas on the Holy Spirit. I have even heard that the section on the Holy Spirit was omitted in a Moody Press reprint of *What the Bible Teaches* but have been unable to verify that rumour.

Two startling books by Lutheran James Kallas, *The Satanward View* (1966) and *Jesus and the Power of Satan* (1968), attracted some attention, though they deserved more.[6] In these books Kallas contends that there are two very distinct themes in the New Testament, the "Godward view" and the "Satanward view." These views are both there, apparently contradictory at various points; for example, the Godward view is high on human responsibility for what goes wrong, while the Satanward view implies that we are victims of a power much greater than ours. He contends, then, that in spite of the nearly total concern of evangelicals with the Godward view, some 80 per cent of the teaching of the synoptic Gospels concerns the Satanward view. At a later date, this understanding fed into Wimber's teaching and thus into the Third Wave perspective.

The charismatic movement, starting in the mid-1960s began to produce some writings. These, however, were largely devoted to personal experience and apologetics for distinctive charismatic emphases.

A book of this period that attracted later attention, especially in Vineyard and Fuller circles, was George Ladd's *Jesus and the Kingdom*.[7]

The 1970s

The 1970s saw attention to our subject growing among evangelicals, though it was still considered by most to be a subject that only fringe groups such as Pentecostals and charismatics took very seriously. There were a few practitioners who broke away from evangelical unconcern such as Ernest Rockstad and Frank and Ida Mae Hammond, each of whom had Baptist roots.[8] These were largely written off as defectors by mainstream evangelicals, although the Hammonds' book *Pigs in the Parlor* (1973) attracted some evangelical attention. Zondervan, a thoroughly evangelical publishing house, published *A Manual of Demonology and the Occult* by Kent Philpott in 1973. And two more volumes by Merrill Unger of Dallas Theological Seminary were published, one in 1971 and the other in 1977.[9] Mark Bubeck's helpful book *The Adversary* appeared in 1975.[10]

A significant scholarly event during this period was a conference convened by the Christian Medical Society in 1975 at the University of Notre Dame. It was entitled "A Theological, Psychological, Medical Symposium on the Phenomena Labeled As 'Demonic.'" Twenty-five invited specialists tackled the subject of demonisation from their various perspectives. Most of the papers were then published in the 1976 volume entitled *Demon Possession*, edited by John Warwick Montgomery.[11]

In missionary training, Alan Tippett made frequent mention of what he called "power encounters." He defined these as encounters between the power of God and that of Satan similar to the encounters between Elijah and the prophets of Baal and between Moses and Pharaoh at the time of the Exodus. Tippett's research showed that such encounters played a major part in the conversion to Christ of the peoples of the South Pacific. His book *People Movements in Southern Polynesia* documents the place of such encounters in the turning to Christ of groups, sometimes large groups, of southern Polynesian peoples.[12]

In Europe and also in America a medical doctor named Kurt Koch attracted some attention among evangelicals through his books and lectures. Several of his books were translated from German and published during the 1970s.[13]

The 1980s

We date the beginning of the Third Wave to the early 1980s. In mid-1981, the School of World Mission faculty at Fuller Seminary discussed the possibility of offering a course on healing to be supervised by C. Peter Wagner, with John Wimber doing most of the teaching. The feeling of need for such a course sprang from a deep sense of failure in this area in the ministries of those of us on the missions faculty. We knew and trusted Wimber. So, in January 1982 we started a once-a-week course entitled "Signs, Wonders and Church Growth," with 85 missions students and two of us faculty couples.

This course has continued from that day to this, and the impact it has had on us and our students in the School of Mission and on many of the theology students has been profound. It resulted in a great deal of controversy both on and off campus, and administrative decisions resulted in Wimber being dropped as the teacher, the course being officially discontinued for one year (though the students put it on as a student activity that year) and a change in the course number. But Wagner and I have been able to teach that basic course and to add several other courses dealing with various aspects of spiritual power and conflict, some of which attract very large enrolments.

Through exposure to our Third Wave approach to spiritual warfare, many missionaries, pastors and international church leaders have moved from ignorance and/or apathy concerning these issues into openness and/or active ministry. A steady stream of American and international pastors also has recognised the need to be active in taking people and places from the enemy. In addition, whether through contact with what we are doing at Fuller or through some other influence, several evangelical seminaries and Bible colleges now offer courses dealing with healing and/or deliverance.

Publications in the 1980s

The 1980s saw an increasing number of publications by evangelicals dealing with healing, inner healing, prayer, deliverance and cosmic-level warfare.

In the area of physical healing and the availability of spiritual power in general, John Wimber and Kevin Springer's books *Power Evangelism* and *Power Healing* have been prominent.[14] So was Francis MacNutt's *Healing*.[15] Influenced by Wimber, other Third Wave books began to appear, including those by Ken Blue, Don Williams, Wagner and myself.[16] Part of Williams's book is devoted to a critique of the position taken by the committee set up to evaluate the Fuller signs and wonders course, published in Smedes.[17]

In inner healing, the books by David Seamands and John and Paula Sandford led the way, with books by Dennis and Matthew Linn attracting some interest to this approach on the Catholic side of the fence.[18]

In the area of spiritual warfare and deliverance, Michael Harper published *Spiritual Warfare* in 1984.[19] C. Fred Dickason, a professor at Moody Bible Institute, published *Demon Possession and the Christian*, a helpful approach to proving that Christians can and do carry demons.[20] Another book by Mark Bubeck dealing with spiritual warfare appeared in 1984.[21] But by and large, evangelicals were not yet into dealing seriously with spiritual warfare. On the Catholic side, Scanlan and Cirner published *Deliverance from Evil Spirits* in 1980.[22] A Pentecostal reaction against the possibility of Christians carrying demons was put together by Opal Reddin in 1989 in response to some of the discussion that occurred at the Fuller conference in 1988.[23]

Among academics, Scott Peck's *People of the Lie* paved the way for many, and Morton Kelsey's *Psychology, Medicine and Christian Healing* also attracted attention.[24] In a series on psychological issues, Word Books included Rodger Bufford's *Counseling and the Demonic*.[25] Clinton Arnold's excellent and pioneering commentary on Ephesians, in which he sees spiritual warfare as the core of the epistle also appeared at the end of this decade.[26] From an unlikely direction, then, came Susan Garrett's *The Demise of the Devil*.[27] And, for those of us who read anthropological literature, it was interesting to find in Goodman a secular author who takes demons seriously.[28]

Perhaps the most important academic approach of this decade was Walter Wink's trilogy.[29] These were significant from a number of points of view. First, since Wink comes from a liberal theological background, it is surprising that he tackles this subject at all. And second, his attempt to wrestle with evil as it has infested the institutional aspects of Western societies is truly original. Even though he seeks to deal with the demonic without admitting the personal nature of evil spiritual beings, his approach embodies much insight and his 1992 volume shows a bit of movement in that direction.

On the missiological scene, a truly significant article was published in 1982 by Paul Hiebert entitled "The Flaw of the Excluded Middle."[30] This article helped alert many to the importance of dealing with our Western worldview with regard to spiritual reality.

As mentioned above, the 1980s also gave us two volumes by the Pentecostal Frank Peretti that were widely read by evangelicals.[31] Though he wrote these books as fiction, those of us who have become practitioners in the spiritual warfare arena find a ring of truth in much of what Peretti wrote. The function these books played in alerting evangelicals to the need to take spiritual warfare seriously is a contribution of major proportions. It is unlikely that the Third Wave movement would be having anywhere near the impact it is having had not Peretti's volumes gained wide attention in evangelical circles.

Though consciousness of cosmic-level warfare was just beginning to be a factor among evangelicals at this time, John Dawson's 1989 *Taking Our Cities for God* is still a major contribution.[32]

Conferences in the 1980s

At least two important conferences on this subject took place in the 1980s. The first, convened by C. Peter Wagner, took place at Fuller in 1988. Quite a number of the major players in the Third Wave met there with some Pentecostals and charismatics. The papers and responses presented there have been published in Wagner and Pennoyer's *Wrestling with Dark Angels*.[33]

The second and more significant conference was the 1989 Manila Lausanne II Congress. This was a gathering of 6,000 or more evangelicals (now including Pentecostals and charismatics) to follow up on the 1974 Lausanne meetings. In it a new openness was shown to charismatic influences. The worship was contemporary, people like Jack Hayford (a classical Pentecostal) played a prominent role in plenary sessions, and the three most heavily attended workshops all dealt with spiritual warfare. One of my publications includes several of the papers that were presented in the workshop I led on spiritual warfare.[34]

THE 1990S

The 1990s saw a major increase in publications and an increase in the offerings at Fuller (at least) in this area. In addition to our basic healing course, we began to offer courses in power encounter, deep-level healing and cosmic-level healing.

As a result of the blurring of the formerly clear dividing lines between Pentecostal and charismatic groups on the one hand, and non-charismatic evangelical groups on the other, many from the latter groups regularly attend conferences and events (for example, Toronto Airport Christian Fellowship and Brownsville, Pensacola) sponsored by Pentecostal and charismatic groups.

Significant books were published during this decade by Wagner, White, Silvoso, Otis, Grieg and Springer, C. Kraft, M. Kraft and many others.[35] Several representative titles appear in the bibliography.

Approaches to spiritual warfare

WHAT IS INCLUDED IN SPIRITUAL WARFARE

The traditional evangelical understanding of spiritual warfare included little more than recognising that Satan is involved in tempting us to do wrong things. It has been common to deal with temptations as basically a human problem, for which we are completely responsible, but to see God's enemy as behind the temptations seeking to entice us into disobeying God.

Liberals, to the extent that they acknowledge an evil presence at all, tend to go along with behavioural scientists in seeing that presence in cultural structures. The recent writings of Walter Wink are a more sophisticated approach to portraying this position than anything heretofore published. His approach interprets demonisation as a characteristic of structures rather than as infestation by spiritual beings.

Pentecostals and charismatics have from the start of their movements dealt with demonisation (incorrectly labelled *demon possession*). Their tendency has been to assume that if a person is having great difficulty, the major if not the only cause is demons living inside a person and that the problem will go away when the demons are expelled. For these groups, demons are seen as independent spiritual entities under the authority of Satan, very common and very active in tempting and pushing people to do evil. Spiritual warfare for these groups, then, includes both dealing with temptations and expelling demons. These groups also regularly engage in praying for physical healing, dedication of buildings and intercessory prayer as acts of spiritual warfare. The charismatic movement added inner healing to the list.

The Third Wave has focused on healing (both physical and inner) and deliverance (both of which we include in "ground-level" warfare) and added cosmic-level warfare. Not that cosmic-level warfare had never been spoken of previously, but the Third Wave has moved into a greater emphasis on it than the previous two waves.

Concerning cosmic-level warfare, evangelicals have always focused on the need for such basic things as righteousness, repentance, intercession, unity in prayer, forgiveness and the like. But Third Wave thinkers (for example, Wagner, Otis, Dawson, Jacobs and Silvoso) have connected these important ground-level activities with the breaking of cosmic-level spiritual power over territories, institutions, vices and the like.

In accord with Third Wave thinking, I will divide the following into what we call ground-level warfare and cosmic-level warfare (Wagner refers to this as "strategic-level warfare"[36]). My own classification of the types of spirits follows. In each category the assumption is that there are spirits assigned by Satan and competing spirits (angels) assigned by God. On God's side we have names such as angels and archangels (Dan. 10:13, 21). On Satan's side we have names such as "wicked spiritual forces in the heavenly world"; rulers (principalities, KJV), authorities (powers, KJV), cosmic powers (rulers, KJV) of this dark age (Eph. 6:12, GNB).

I assume that cosmic-level spirits have a good bit of authority over ground-level spirits, probably assigning them and ruling over them. I assume also that cosmic-level spirits gain and maintain their rights only through human permission. I doubt that Satan is interested in territory or institutions for their own sake. I believe he is interested in people and the power over such things granted by people, to whom God originally gave authority over everything in the world. In Luke 4:6, then, Satan, in tempting Jesus, can boast that he can give to Jesus all power over the kingdoms of the earth and all their wealth because "it has all been handed over to me, and I can give it to anyone I choose . . . if you worship me."

CATEGORIES OF SPIRITS

1. *Cosmic-Level spirits* (Eph. 2:2, in "the air," living outside of persons)
   a. Territorial spirits: assigned to territories: nations, cities regions
      i. God's: assigned to enhance God's plan for territories
      ii. Satan's: assigned to disrupt God's plans
   b. Religion/institutional spirits: assigned to religions and organisations
      i. God's: assigned to churches, parachurch organisations, Bible schools, seminaries
      ii. Satan's: assigned to non-Christian religions and organisations (e.g., Freemasonry) and to disrupt churches and others of God's organisations
   c. Vice Spirits: assigned to deal with vices
      i. God's: assigned to prevent vices such as divination, prostitution, abortion, gambling, homosexuality, pornography
      ii. Satan's: assigned to encourage such vices

2. *Nature, household and object spirits:* assigned to nature, cultural objects (e.g., artifacts, music) and homes
   a. God's: assigned to protect these places and objects
   b. Satan's: assigned to inhabit dedicated objects and places

3. *Ancestral spirits*
   a. God's: assigned to take people to God at death
   b. Satan's: assigned to behave like dead ancestors in order to deceive people into believing the dead are still active in human affairs

4. *Ground-level spirits* (demonic, living in people—the Godly counterpart is the Holy Spirit living in God's people)
   a. Family spirits: demons inhabiting those dedicated to them and inherited from generation to generation in families
   b. Occult spirits: demons inhabiting those involved in false religions and occult allegiances (e.g., Scientology, witchcraft)
   c. Ordinary spirits: demons inhabiting those wallowing in sinful attitudes and emotions (e.g., fear, anger, rebellion, lust, hatred, shame)

VARIETIES OF GROUND-LEVEL WARFARE

I will deal with ground-level warfare first, since it is less controversial than cosmic-level warfare. Jesus spent a good bit of his time and energy healing and casting out demons. Most of us find, however, that our record for healing is not as good as Jesus'; simply commanding demons out as the Gospels show Jesus doing is often not sufficient to get people free. There are, therefore, a variety of styles extant among those of us who are active in healing and deliverance ministries.

To state my own credentials, I have personally led a large number of healing sessions (probably more than 1,500) with at least 1,000 of them involving deliverance from demons. Most of what I have learned has been published in five books and an article in response to some critics (see the bibliography for these titles).

As mentioned, both Pentecostals and charismatics have been active for some time in ministering healing and deliverance. Inner (or "deep-level") healing was introduced during the charismatic movement. Few, however, seemed to connect inner healing with deliverance in any formal way, though it must have been connected informally by some. Until recently, then, ministries of physical healing, inner healing and deliverance have been looked at as quite separate types of ministry.

Traditional evangelical approaches

Traditional evangelical (non-charismatic) approaches to spiritual warfare have tended to see Satan's activity limited largely to tempting people to sin. The antidote, therefore, was to learn more about the kinds of temptation employed and how to combat them. Combating them is seen as a matter of recognising temptation, looking to the Bible for the things to say to ourselves and to Satan, and praying to overcome the temptation. If a person seems unable to resist temptations, he or she is advised to pray and study the Bible more fervently. If a person seems to be having emotional difficulties, he or she is advised to see a Christian counsellor or, often, simply to forget the past. The latter advice is often based on an out-of-context misinterpretation of Philippians 3:13, "forgetting those things that are behind."

Truth-oriented approaches

Two truth-oriented approaches are those of Neil Anderson ("freedom in Christ") and Ed Smith ("theophostic").[37] Anderson's approach focuses on dealing with self-image and works quite well with those who are able to take cognitive control of their emotional wounds and to tell themselves the truth of who they are. He has observed what we all see: Satan's primary attack on Christians is in the area of self-image. Satan doesn't want us to discover who we really are. The answer as Anderson sees it, then, is to go through certain steps towards freedom that involve learning and assimilating basic scriptural truths concerning who we are in Christ. He assumes that when certain truths are believed, emotions get healed and if there are any demons, they leave.

Another truth-oriented approach is that of Ed Smith. From this "theophostic" perspective, healing is attained through discovering the lies we have been believing and then allowing Jesus to come and speak truth to us, thus healing the wounds left by the lies. Though dealing with lies and truth appears on the surface to be quite cognitive, theophostic practitioners are given to encouraging people to feel deeply the emotions associated with the beliefs and to let Jesus heal the emotional wounds as well as the cognitive ones. This takes people well beyond Anderson's approach and often stirs up demons that have to be dealt with.

Deliverance-based approaches

Deliverance-based ministries are those that assume that demons are the major problem and that simply casting them out is the way to get people healed. They note that Jesus seemed to do nothing to help the demonised other than to free them from their demons. So they go after the demons and try to blast them out. This has tended to be the approach of Pentecostals and charismatics. It often results in violence, vomiting and other disagreeable things, sometimes resulting in damage to the demonised person in the process of getting the person free.

In addition to Pentecostals and charismatics, certain evangelicals have taken this position. In our day we can mention Frank and Ida Mae Hammond and Ernest Rockstad (now deceased). Rockstad had an interesting and controversial twist on dealing with demons that were especially difficult to get out. He sometimes had one of his team members call the demons into him/herself as a means of freeing the client. The team member then casts out the demons. Rockstad called this method "pouring the demons through" the team member.[38] It apparently worked.

Doris Wagner fits here, though she, like those of the next group, recognises the need to do or advise the client to do inner healing to get completely healed.[39] Wagner uses a long questionnaire to discover in prayer what demons are present. She then goes after them one by one without seeking further information from them. She prefers to do any inner healing after the deliverance, though she recognises the need sometimes to do some inner healing earlier in order to weaken the demons.

Inner-healing approaches

Inner healing-based ministries may focus almost exclusively on dealing with emotional and/or spiritual "garbage," as John and Paula Sandford do, or, after dealing with the garbage, go on to tackle any demonic "rats" that might be attached to the garbage, as I do.[40] The Sandfords do not completely neglect demons, but seem to deal with them only if they make their presence obvious.[41]

My own approach is to look for them (and usually find them) if the amount of garbage the person has been carrying seems to predict that there may be rats attached. We have observed that the strength of demons is calibrated to the amount and kind of garbage in the client's life. Thus, if we do not want to have to fight with the demons, the best thing to do is to use inner-healing techniques to deal with the garbage, then to free the person from the demons later. With this approach we almost never have any violence, vomiting, or other disagreeable happenings.

What I mean by garbage includes the following: generational or contemporary dedications; curses or vows/pacts made with enemy spirits or gods; dedications to spirits or gods by persons in authority over the client or by the client; self-cursing; wallowing in negative emotions such as anger, unforgiveness, hatred, shame or the like; having death wishes or inviting spirits of death in through abortion, suicide attempts or the like; inviting in spirits of homosexuality; and so on.

Those who use my approach assume that there may be a double cause underlying the person's problems: a human one (garbage) and a spirit one (demons). We find that if there are demons, we can assume there is a human cause, the garbage. If there is human garbage, though, there are not necessarily demons, especially if the amount of garbage is small.

We recognise, then, that the demons are a secondary problem, not the primary one. In order for them to be there, they must have legal rights given them by those who created the garbage. These can be ancestors, those in authority over the person, or the person himself or herself. Taking away the demons' legal rights through inner healing takes away all of their power, cancels their right to stay, and makes it easy to kick them out. Ed Murphy has developed a similar approach.[42]

COSMIC-LEVEL WARFARE

Fairly recently there has been an increased emphasis on cosmic-level warfare among Third Wavers. In the forefront of this emphasis have been C. Peter Wagner, George Otis Jr., John Dawson, Cindy Jacobs and Ed Silvoso. Each has written one or more books on the subject and on related subjects such as intercession, repentance, dealing with territorial spirits and strategies for taking cities. Prominent in these discussions has been the experience in Argentina, where evangelists and pastors such as Carlos Annacondia, Omar Cabrera, Claudio Friedzon and Victor Lorenzo have been very successful in winning people to Christ by employing the principles of cosmic-level warfare.

These principles parallel the principles outlined above for my approach to dealing with ground-level demons. That is, cosmic-level warfare approaches the breaking of the power of cosmic-level rats through dealing with cosmic-level garbage. This garbage includes sin on the part of human populations (both present and in the past); the breaking of satanic power gained through past dedications and/ or sinful use of a place; disunity and competition among spiritual leaders; and neglect of godly use of a place or territory.

The approach, therefore, includes the fostering of unity among the pastors in a given area (including repentance for critical and competitive attitudes). It proceeds with the development and increase of intercessory activity aimed at specific geographical areas and/or spiritual problems. It often requires the breaking of satanic power achieved through dedication and/or sinful use of a place by specifically claiming authority over that place in the name of Jesus Christ.

Along with intercession and the taking of authority in prayer goes the practice of *spiritual mapping* – the researching of the kinds of both God's and the enemy's activity both historically and in the present in the area to be attacked. The findings from this research become the focus of the intercession and the calls to repentance that follow. A major part of the repentance, based on the historical analysis of spiritual problems, is what is called *identificational repentance*. This involves the present generation accepting responsibility for the sins of its predecessors and representing them in repenting to the representatives of the wronged group(s), as did Ezra (Ezra 9), Nehemiah (Neh. 1) and Daniel (Dan. 9).

There will also usually be *prayer walks,* involving the intercessors in walking around and praying over the territory to be taken, thus claiming it for Christ and/or other *intercessory events* designed to break the power of Satan over the area in focus. These will sometimes be held on mountaintops overlooking the area to be captured. Bob Beckett is fond of claiming areas by driving into the ground stakes that have been empowered through prayer. Ed Silvoso employs a combination of techniques designed to take whole cities for God. John Dawson is strong on discovering and focusing on the "redemptive gift" of a city, by which he means God's reason for the founding of the city.

With all the emphasis on technique, it needs to be underlined that those involved in cosmic-level warfare are primarily concerned about evangelism. The stated aim of these techniques is to break the power of the Evil One over people and territory for the specific purpose of winning the lost and enabling people to grow in Christ. The point is made that both Satan and God are interested in people, but that people cooperate with either God or Satan to empower places and activities (e.g., rituals, dedications), thus giving one or the other spiritual advantage in that place or activity. Through asserting spiritual power wielded authoritatively in the name of the other power, the ruling power can be broken and the other power put in control.

Since, according to Scripture, the whole world is under the power of the Evil One (1 John 5:19), the wielding of God's authority to break that power can give great opportunity for the light of Jesus to flow into the consciousness of people whose minds have been darkened by the god of this world (2 Cor. 4:4). And this has been the experience in Argentina and elsewhere that cosmic-level warfare has been employed. The conversion records of Annacondia and the other Argentine evangelists are truly impressive.

Controversies

In dealing with spiritual conflict, there are a number of issues that are disputed. The reasons for dispute are usually claimed to be theological, though I suspect that a closer look would show that it is underlying worldview assumptions more than theological perspectives that are to blame, since the disputes are usually between practitioners with considerable experience and theoreticians with little or no experience.

An example of such is the rather wide-ranging critique of Third Wave approaches to spiritual warfare launched by Priest, Campbell and Mullen from Columbia Seminary at the meetings of the Evangelical Missiological Society in 1994. This was published with my response in the volume entitled *Spiritual Power and Missions*.[43] The exercise of replying to these authors was a good one for me in many ways. For example, they forced me to clarify the differences between animism and God-given authority. We find in spiritual warfare that on the surface, much of what we do in the power and authority of Jesus Christ looks very similar to what Satan and his followers do. Satan heals, blesses, empowers dedicated objects, infects through inheritance and in many other ways imitates God. The main differences between what Satan does and what God does lie in the source of the power flowing through the activity rather than necessarily in the activity itself.

Priest and colleagues challenged our use of anecdotal evidence without being able to give counter evidence of their own. They were able to disprove one example and to call a few others into question, leading them to conclude inappropriately that there is no evidence for the claims made for cosmic-level success and to dismiss all claims for such success as if these are the only examples available. Though we have had to stop citing the example from the Philippines once claimed by Lester Sumrall, there are plenty of other examples that point to effectiveness of cosmic-level efforts. As for such evidence being anecdotal, Scripture is made up of just such anecdotal reporting.

These critics challenged our claim that demonic influence can be passed down from generation to generation. Had they any experience with dealing with demonised people, however, they would have discovered that a major difference occurs in freeing people whose forebears have been in occult organisations when God's power is asserted over the spiritual inheritance possibly acquired from those forebears. When one has dealt, as I have, with hundreds of persons with such a characteristic and seen the positive results from speaking against generational demonic inheritance, one becomes a believer.

Their other areas of critique showed equally that they neither have experience in this area (a fact I have confirmed in face-to-face discussion with Priest) nor are able to distinguish between God's activity in spiritual power and that of the enemy. This puts their critique perilously close to those of Dave Hunt, Hank Hanegraaff (of Christian Research Institute) and John MacArthur, whose rationalistic worldviews keep them from understanding differences between God's and Satan's activities in the spiritual realm.[44]

An area of controversy that has been around longer is the question of whether or not Christians can be demonised. Certain Pentecostal groups hold strongly that when a demonised person comes to Christ, he or she is freed from demon possession. There are two problems to be addressed here: the concept of demon *possession* and the possibility of Christians continuing to carry demons after coming to Christ. The first of these problems is raised by the mistranslation in many English versions of the Greek terms *daimonizomai*

and *echein daimonion,* each of which means merely to have a demon, not to be possessed by a demon. Nothing in the Greek allows
the translation "possessed." I believe it is misunderstanding concerning the concept of possession that has led these Pentecostals to
take such a strong stand against Christians being demonised (see
Reddin for a defence of the Assemblies of God position[45]).

With regard to the possibility of Christians carrying demons, the
problem is again lack of experience versus experience. Anyone who
has dealt with demonised people to any extent soon discovers that
there are a lot of people whose salvation experience cannot be denied who are, in fact, carrying demons. It is interesting that the scholar
Merrill Unger, who taught at Dallas Theological Seminary for some
time and wrote several books on demonisation, was forced to change
his opinion on this issue when a member of his own family was
found to be demonised. This was after he had published his classic
Biblical Demonology. Ed Murphy, who had become a practitioner in
deliverance already, was also shocked into recognizing that Christians can have demons when his 14–year-old daughter began manifesting demons.

There is no doubt that Christians can be demonised. I have dealt
with over one thousand myself. A useful book on this subject is that
by C. Fred Dickason, *Demon Possession and the Christian.* Dickason
gives an exhaustive presentation of the scriptural evidence for and
against the possibility and contends that one cannot prove the case
either way from the Scriptures. He concludes, therefore, that we must
appeal to experience. His experience, mine and everyone else's lead
us to the conclusion that Christians can indeed carry demons.

One possibility that Dickason doesn't address adequately is the
probability (in my estimation) that most of the people Jesus healed
and delivered from demons were people of faith. He continually says
to them that their faith has made them whole (e.g., Matt. 9:22, Mark
10:52, Luke 17:19). I believe the meaning of this statement is that
the person has come in faith to the right source, Jesus. This coming
to Jesus in faith is, I believe, salvific.

The situation with respect to demons in Christians is, in my understanding, parallel to that concerning sin. When a person comes
to Christ, the spirit part of that person is renewed and called our
New Nature (1 John 3:6, 9). I believe this New Nature is free from sin.
But sin remains to be dealt with in our body, mind, emotions and will.
When a demonised person comes to Christ, then, any demons living
in that person's spirit have to leave that central part of the individual
that has become a New Nature. They may, however, continue to live

in the person's body, mind, emotions – and will unless dealt with specifically.

One of the things Priest, Campbell and Mullen do not like about my and others' approach to demons is that we talk to them to get information that we can use against them. We find that demons are like "hostile witnesses" in court. They can be questioned to obtain insight into the kinds of things they have a grip on in the person they inhabit. Under the power of the Holy Spirit, they frequently reveal things that we could not have discovered, such as persons that need to be forgiven. We can then use that information to lead the demonised person to take care of the garbage that gives the demon rights. Even though we must always be careful not to trust what demons tell us, we find the information God gives us through them to be very helpful and to often greatly speed up the process of deliverance.

Those without experience who critique this approach assume that we should simply command the demons out as Jesus seemed to do, without any further interaction with them. Those of us who recognise that it is the garbage that is the biggest problem, however, want to find out what that garbage is. We therefore seek to use the demons to reveal what they are connected to in order to do the inner healing that will make the person well, since our aim is getting the person healed, not just delivering him or her from the demons.

There are some who work in deliverance who are also against talking to demons. Doris Wagner and Cindy Jacobs are among them. Doris uses a questionnaire to obtain all the information she needs. She prays over the information on the questionnaire to determine what demons are there and commands them out on that basis. This approach works relatively well for her. We, however, have a steady stream of people coming to us who have received ministry from people who simply command demons out without getting information from them. We usually find that the demons did not leave when simply commanded to go.

A further controversy surrounds what to do about cosmic-level spirits. Few who take the Scriptures seriously doubt that there are spirits "in the air" (Eph. 2:2). There are those, like Clinton Arnold and the late John Wimber, who contend that we have no scriptural warrant for challenging these higher level spirits. They point out that neither Jesus nor his followers seem to have challenged these spirits.

Those in favour of challenging cosmic-level spirits, however, note that the demons in the Gerasene demoniac begged Jesus not to send them out of that region (Mark 5:10). This, they assert, probably means that the legion of demons inhabiting the demoniac had a territorial assignment, even though they were lodged in a single human being. It is also possible that Jesus' encounter with Satan at the temptations (Luke 4:1–13) had territorial implications.

Wagner, Otis, Dawson, Silvoso, Jacobs and others (including the Argentineans), however, feel there is enough evidence of the success of direct challenges to cosmic-level spirits that we should continue and escalate our efforts in this regard. Wagner has even suggested that this approach may be part of a new technology God is giving us in these last days.

Whatever one's position in this controversy, I would like to suggest that the ways in which the cosmic-level garbage is being dealt with are scriptural enough to justify most of what the advocates of direct confrontation are into. That is, we know it is scriptural to advocate repentance, unity of spiritual leaders and intercessory prayer. I see no reason to quibble over spiritual mapping or identificational repentance or prayer walking if they enable us to do these things better. Unfortunately, there are those involved in cosmic-level confrontation who are looking for a "fast foods" approach to spiritual warfare, in which they do a few things quickly and declare victory over the enemy. These give the scripturally solid features of this approach a bad name.

Conclusion

We recognise that this is an area of considerable unfamiliarity within evangelicalism. It therefore occasions much discussion and debate. I regard the fact that the subject is out in the open as a very good thing. The emergence of the Third Wave and the inclusion of Pentecostals and charismatics within evangelicalism promise to encourage the continuance of dialogue concerning these matters.

In the present situation, then, we find a series of polarizations among evangelicals. It is probable that the vast majority of evangelicals are showing little concern for the discussion, and a fairly significant segment follow those leaders who speak out against a concern over spiritual warfare. These either deny or ignore the reality of spiritual warfare, often claiming that Jesus took care of everything on the cross, so we do not need to be concerned at all about this area. At the other end of the spectrum are those who see "a demon under every bush" and go completely overboard in their attention to both ground-level and cosmic-level spiritual warfare. These draw appropriate criticism both from opponents of this emphasis

and from those who are more balanced because by blaming demons for everything, they avoid assigning much, if any, human responsibility for negative behaviour.

Both of these positions are to be regretted. Those of us who attempt to take a balanced position are, however, frequently stereo-
typed into the latter position and regarded as extremists, especially
by those who wish to ignore the reality of the conflict.

A polarity that often plays a part in the negative approach of the
conservatives to discussions concerning spiritual warfare is how to
use the Bible. Those who are negative frequently call for chapter
and verse support for all approaches to our topic. If there are not
specific scriptural commands and guidelines, they feel justified in
condemning the whole emphasis. Those in favour of an emphasis
on spiritual warfare are at another pole in their use of the Bible,
claiming that this emphasis fits well within biblical boundaries even
if we cannot cite specific scriptural texts supporting specific activities. We point out that there are several activities in which
evangelicals regularly engage for which there is no specific scriptural support. Among these are citywide evangelistic crusades,
Sunday Schools, three-point rationalistic sermons, denominations,
Bible schools and seminaries, even the ways we go about interpreting the Scriptures and the like. We would contend, however,
that these and other helpful activities are neither unscriptural nor
anti-scriptural.

A second set of polarities centres around the focus in dealing with
spiritual warfare. One of these involves the opposition between those
in favour of the emphasis and those against it. The latter, of course,
choose to focus on other things altogether. Among these might be
any of a number of good things related to such things as evangelism
based on rational presentations of the gospel, church growth, worship, discipleship and the like. Those at the opposite pole into a
focus on spiritual warfare would add that dimension to all of these
other good things.

A set of polarities within the emphasis is that between those who
focus on deliverance and those whose focus is on inner healing. A
further set is that between those who focus on ground-level warfare
and those who focus on cosmic-level warfare. As mentioned, there
is disagreement among those who accept the reality of cosmic-level
spirits regarding what to do about them. This sets up a polarity between those who seek to attack cosmic-level spirits and those who
hold that there is no scriptural precedent and so we should not be
involved in attacking at that level.

Notes

[1] Frank Peretti, *This Present Darkness* (Westchester, Ill.: Crossway Books, 1986); idem, *Piercing the Darkness* (Westchester, Ill.: Crossway Books, 1989).

[2] Everett Rogers, *Diffusion of Innovations*, 4th ed. (New York: Free Press, 1995).

[3] Jesse Penn-Lewis. *War on the Saints* (New York: Thomas E. Lowe, 1912).

[4] Merrill Unger, *Biblical Demonology: A Study of the Spiritual Forces behind the Present Unrest* (Wheaton, Ill.: Scripture Press, 1952).

[5] Reuben A. Torrey, *Baptism with the Holy Spirit* (New York: Fleming H. Revell, 1897); idem, *What the Bible Teaches* (New York: Fleming H. Revell, 1898).

[6] James Kallas, *The Satanward View* (Philadelphia: Westminster, 1966); idem, *Jesus and the Power of Satan* (Philadelphia: Westminster, 1966).

[7] George E. Ladd, *Jesus and The Kingdom* (New York: Harper, 1964).

[8] Ernest Rockstad, *Demon Activity and the Christian* (Andover, Kans.: Faith and Life, 1976); Frank Hammond and Ida Mae Hammond, *Pigs in the Parlor* (Kirkwood, Mo.: Impact Books, 1973).

[9] Merrill Unger, *Demons in the World Today: A Study of Occultism in the Light of God's Word* (Wheaton, Ill.: Tyndale, 1971); idem, *What Demons Can Do to Saints* (Chicago: Moody, 1977).

[10] Mark I. Bubeck, *The Adversary: The Christian Versus Demon Activity* (Chicago: Moody Press, 1975).

[11] John Montgomery, ed., *Demon Possession* (Minneapolis, Minn.: Bethany Fellowship, 1976).

[12] Alan Tippett, *People Movements in Southern Polynesia* (Chicago: Moody, 1971).

[13] See, for example, Kurt Koch, *Occult Bondage and Deliverance* (Grand Rapids, Mich.: Kregel, 1971); *Christian Counseling and Occultism* (Grand Rapids, Mich.: Kregel, 1972); *Demonology Past and Present* (Grand Rapids, Mich.: Kregel, 1973); and *Occult ABC* (Grand Rapids, Mich.: Kregel, 1978).

[14] John Wimber and Kevin Springer, *Power Evangelism* (London: Hodder and Stoughton, 1986); idem, *Power Healing* (London: Hodder and Stoughton, 1986).

[15] Francis MacNutt, *Healing* (Notre Dame, IN: Ave Maria Press, 1988).

[16] Ken Blue, *Authority to Heal* (Downers Grove, Ill.: InterVarsity Press, 1987); Don Williams, *Signs, Wonders and the Kingdom of God* (Ann Arbor, Mich.: Servant Publications, 1989); C. Peter Wagner, *How to Have a Healing Ministry in Any Church* (Ventura, Calif.: Regal Books, 1988); Charles H. Kraft, *Christianity with Power: Your Worldview and Your Experience of the Supernatural* (Ann Arbor, Mich.: Servant Books, 1989).

[17] Lewis B. Smedes, *Ministry and the Miraculous* (Dallas, Tex.: Word, 1987).

¹⁸ David Seamands, *Healing for Damaged Emotions* (Wheaton, Ill.: Victor, 1981) and *Healing of Memories* (Wheaton, Ill.: Victor, 1985); John and Paula Sandford, *Transformation of the Inner Man* (Tulsa, Okla.: Victory House, 1982) and *Healing the Wounded Spirit* (Tulsa, Okla.: Victory House, 1985); Dennis Linn and Matthew Linn, *Healing of Memories* (New York: Paulist, 1974) and *Healing Life's Hurts* (New York: Paulist, 1978).

¹⁹ Michael Harper, *Spiritual Warfare* (Ann Arbor, Mich.: Servant Books, 1984).

²⁰ C. Fred Dickason, *Demon Possession and the Christian* (Chicago: Moody Press, 1987).

²¹ Mark I. Bubeck, *Overcoming the Adversary* (Chicago: Moody Press, 1984).

²² Michael Scanlan and Randall J. Cirner, *Deliverance from Evil Spirits* (Ann Arbor, Mich.: Servant Books, 1980).

²³ Opal Reddin, ed., *Power Encounter: A Pentecostal Perspective* (Springfield, Mo.: Central Bible College Press, 1989).

²⁴ M. Scott Peck, *People of the Lie: The Hope for Healing Human Evil* (New York: Simon & Schuster, 1983); Morton T. Kelsey, *Psychology, Medicine and Christian Healing* (New York: Harper, 1988).

²⁵ Rodger K. Bufford, *Counseling and the Demonic* (Dallas, Tex.: Word, 1988).

²⁶ Clinton E. Arnold, *Ephesians: Power and Magic: The Concept of Power in Ephesians in Light of Its Historical Setting*, Society for New Testament Studies Monograph 63 (Cambridge: Cambridge University Press, 1989).

²⁷ Susan R. Garrett, *The Demise of the Devil* (Philadelphia: Fortress Press, 1989).

²⁸ Felicitas Goodman, *How About Demons?* (Bloomington, Ind.: Indiana University Press, 1988).

²⁹ Walter Wink, *Naming the Powers: The Language of Power in the New Testament* (Philadelphia: Fortress Press, 1984); *Unmasking the Powers: The Invisible Forces that Determine Human Existence* (Philadelphia: Fortress Press, 1986); and *Engaging the Powers: Discernment and Resistance in a World of Dominion* (Philadelphia: Fortress Press, 1992).

³⁰ Paul G. Hiebert, "The Flaw of the Excluded Middle," *Missiology: An International Review* 10 (January 1982): 35–48.

³¹ Peretti, *This Present Darkness* and *Piercing the Darkness*.

³² John Dawson, *Taking Our Cities for God: How to Break Spiritual Strongholds* (Lake Mary, Fla.: Creation House, 1989).

³³ C. Peter Wagner and F. Douglas Pennoyer, eds., *Wrestling with Dark Angels: Toward a Deeper Understanding of the Supernatural Forces in Spiritual Warfare* (Ventura, Calif.: Regal Books, 1990).

³⁴ Charles H. Kraft, ed., *Behind Enemy Lines* (Ann Arbor, Mich.: Servant Books, 1994).

³⁵ C. Peter Wagner, ed., *Engaging the Enemy: How to Fight and Defeat Territorial Spirits* (Ventura, Calif.: Regal Books, 1991); idem, *Warfare Prayer: How to Seek God's Power and Protection in the Battle to Build His Kingdom* (Ventura, Calif.: Regal Books, 1992); idem, ed., *Breaking Strongholds in*

Your City: How to Use Spiritual Mapping to Make Your Prayers More Strategic, Effective and Targeted (Ventura, Calif.: Regal Books, 1993); and idem, *Confronting the Powers: How the New Testament Church Experienced the Power of Strategic-level Spiritual Warfare* (Ventura, Calif.: Regal, 1996). Thomas White, *The Believer's Guide to Spiritual Warfare* (Ann Arbor, Mich.: Vine, 1990) and *Breaking Strongholds: How Spiritual Warfare Sets Captives Free* (Ann Arbor, Mich.: Vine Books, 1992). Edgardo Silvoso, *That None Should Perish* (Ventura, Calif.: Regal, 1994). George Otis, *The Last of the Giants: Lifting the Veil on Islam and the End Times* (Grand Rapids, Mich.: Baker, 1991). Gary Grieg and Kevin Springer, eds., *The Kingdom and the Power* (Ventura, Calif.: Regal, 1993). Charles H. Kraft, *Deep Wounds, Deep Healing* (Ann Arbor, Mich.: Servant Books, 1994); *Defeating Dark Angels* (Ann Arbor, Mich.: Servant Books, 1992); and *I Give You Authority* (Grand Rapids, Mich.: Chosen/Baker, 1997). Marguerite G. Kraft, *Understanding Spiritual Power: A Forgotten Dimension of Cross-Cultural Mission and Ministry* (Maryknoll, N.Y.: Orbis Books, 1995).

[36] C. Peter Wagner, *Confronting the Powers: How the New Testament Church Experienced the Power of Strategic-level Spiritual Warfare* (Ventura, Calif.: Regal, 1996).

[37] Neil Anderson, *The Bondage Breaker* (Eugene, Ore.: Harvest House Publishers, 1990); Ed M. Smith, *Beyond Tolerable Recovery,* rev. ed. (Campbellsville, Ky.: Theophostic Ministries, 2000).

[38] Ernst B. Rockstad, *Triumph in the Demonic Crisis,* cassette series (Andover, Kans.: Faith and Life, 1976).

[39] Doris Wagner, *How to Cast Out Demons* (Ventura, Calif.: Regal, 2000).

[40] Sandford, *Transformation of the Inner Man* and *Healing the Wounded Spirit;* Kraft, *Defeating Dark Angels.*

[41] See John Sandford and Mark Sandford, *A Comprehensive Guide to Deliverance and Inner Healing* (Grand Rapids, Mich.: Chosen/Baker, 1992).

[42] Ed Murphy, *The Handbook for Spiritual Warfare* (Nashville, Tenn.: Thomas Nelson, 1992).

[43] Edward Rommen, ed., *Spiritual Power and Missions: Raising the Issues* (Pasadena, Calif.: William Carey Library, 1995).

[44] Dave Hunt, *The Seduction of Christianity* (Eugene, Ore.: Harvest House Publishers, 1985); Hank Hanegraaff, *Counterfeit Revival: Looking for God in the Wrong Places* (Dallas, Tex.: Word Publishing, 1977); John MacArthur, *How to Meet the Enemy: Arming Yourself for Spiritual Battle* (Wheaton, Ill.: Victor, 1992).

[45] Reddin, *Power Encounter.*

15

Spiritual conflict in light of psychology and medicine

JERRY MUNGADZE

The reality of spiritual conflict in our world is a given to those who believe the Bible, but sometimes those who are convinced of the reality of spiritual conflict deny or minimise the reality of psychological and psychiatric illness. Often Christians suffering from psychological or psychiatric illness have been treated as if they were demonised. Those who have demonic problems in addition to their psychological and psychiatric illness often get their demonic issues attended to and not their psychological and psychiatric illness.

The approach that attempts to balance the spiritual and the natural needs of people is referred to herein as *holistic*. Jesus' use of Isaiah 61:1–3 shows that his ministry took into account the natural aspect of humanity's suffering. In the passage, people are "brokenhearted, in mourning, grieving, despairing, captives and prisoners in darkness." It is clear that the ministry of the Lord Jesus went beyond preaching good news. It included meeting other needs that people had.

The reality of spiritual conflict

To those who believe the Bible, the reality of evil spiritual forces is undisputed in both Old and New Testaments. Paul points out in Ephesians 6:10–12 that the believer is already involved in the conflict. The evil forces, consisting of Satan and his fallen angels, wage war against the angels of God and God's people. In Daniel 10:10–13, 20–21, an angel of God informs Daniel of the war that was being fought over countries, regions and nations. Daniel was involved in the conflict by his prayers, but he may not have realised that the answers to his prayers were held up due to the war the fallen angels of Satan were waging against the angels of God and the Israelites.

In the New Testament there are several examples of demonic forces causing physical and mental illness. Perhaps the real question is not whether spiritual conflict exists, but what is the best way of dealing with spiritual conflict when it co-exists with psychological, psychiatric and physical illness. This is further complicated by the fact that there are times when psychological and psychiatric illness exists with no direct link to spiritual conflict. In such cases assuming the presence of spiritual conflict may lead to serious mistakes in helping others.[1]

The reality of psychological, psychiatric and physiological illness

Genesis 3 outlines the Fall and the entrance of sin, death, pain, suffering and illness into the world. The fallen world we live in is subject to natural laws. Psychology and medicine help us deal with our problems related to the natural laws. Our minds or souls contain our decision-making capacity, our desires, our will and our emotions. The mind or soul is the realm where psychological processes take place. Our bodies, including the brain, interact with our mind/soul, and physical medicine helps us with problems related to the body. The following diagram may be helpful in understanding the relationships and the interconnectedness of our being (Gen. 2:7; Heb. 4:12).

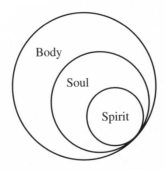

The human being comprises body, soul and spirit. The spirit is the part that communes with God. It is the place of regeneration. Upon the occurrence of the new birth, the spirit of God indwells our spirit. The process of spiritual growth or sanctification is really the influence of salvation into our mind, which controls the body. The body has many organs, including the brain, which is the powerhouse of most bodily functions. The brain regulates certain chemical processes in the body for our survival and sustenance.

It is very unfortunate that the Western worldview seems to split the human being into separate parts, namely, body and mind or material and immaterial. It appears from a biblical viewpoint that body, soul and spirit are so intertwined that they can't be separated. Doing so can only harm the process of maintaining unity of the body. The same unity of the body also makes it difficult to tell when certain problems are largely psychological, psychiatric, physical or spiritual. This brings us to the discussion on correct discernment and diagnosis.

Discernment and correct diagnosis when dealing with spiritual conflict

One of the fundamentals in dealing with people is that no harm should be done to them in the name of deliverance or help. If someone is having problems with physical manifestation, he or she could have a physical condition that needs a physician's attention. What may be appearing as spiritual conflict could be a physical problem based in a physical disease. Ignoring this could lead to death or physical impairment for the person seeking help. As a rule of thumb, physical manifestations need to be followed up with questions concerning the presence of a history of physical disease in the person or the family, and also by a visit to a physician. This area may not be the hardest one to discern.

The next area, which presents possibly the hardest challenge, is the manifestation of what could be demonic or mental illness. The safest approach is first to rule out mental illness or psychological problems before assuming that it is a spiritual conflict. The following steps are helpful in that process.

First, we need to ask for a history of mental problems. That should be followed by a check for distress of an emotional or mental nature in the person's life. We also need to find out if the person has sought psychological or psychiatric help before or even help from traditional healers. Additionally, we need to know if the person is using psychiatric medications or has ever had them prescribed. Finally, we should ask if the individual has been hospitalised for emotional or mental problems in the past. If the information given seems to contain these natural situations listed above, then the person needs psychological or psychiatric care, even if he or she has already been through deliverance or prayer.

There is a mental illness that is perhaps the most misunderstood as demonisation in the Christian deliverance ministry. This illness is called dissociative identity disorder, formerly known as multiple personality disorder.[2] This illness is characterised by the afflicted person hearing voices; seeing people and things no one else sees; speaking in different voices; having memory lapses too great to be accounted for by ordinary forgetfulness; and exhibiting self-destructive behaviours and unexplainable physical symptoms.[3]

Sometimes people with this illness are convinced that they are demon possessed. The voices they hear do claim to be demons when they are actually not. In North America this mental illness is well understood and successfully treated.[4] In the majority of Third World countries, it is largely seen as spirit possession or ancestral mediumistic activity. Usually in these societies people with this condition go through traditional healing or traditional Christian exorcism, which actually antagonises the created personas and makes them more angry and destructive towards the person who is afflicted.[5] The following are helpful guidelines when dealing with people who claim to be demonised.

First, if the person who claims to be demonised is also a victim of childhood trauma, the person may have this disorder. Doing an exorcism without a good understanding and acceptance by the person's created parts can lead to harming the person emotionally.[6] Second, the created parts are not foreign beings or spirits of grandparents but parts of the mind the individual created unknowingly to deal with the trauma. Therefore these parts need to be embraced rather than cast out.[7]

Third, although these created parts claim to be separate people, they are really parts of the person's mind. The person must be encouraged to realise that there is only one real person.[8]

Fourth, this type of disorder needs to be treated by specially trained professionals. When ministering to a person with dissociative disorders, it is best to work with such a trained professional.[9]

Fifth, occasionally these created personas do not share the same beliefs, behaviours and perceptions of the main person. As a result, some type of conflict arises. If the person is a Christian, it is important to know that this does not mean that he or she is automatically going to hell. The person is just very unstable.

Sixth, and finally, every so often this illness will exist with spiritual conflict. In such cases deliverance is not effective if the existence of the illness is ignored.

A man in seminary believed that he was possessed by a legion of demons that yelled obscenities to him daily and told him to get out of seminary. Sometimes he heard little boys crying and adult voices screaming. He had been through numerous deliverance sessions. According to some of his ministers, he had been delivered from the spirits of anger, hate, suicide and lust. But he still heard voices. Once in a while he would experience the same problems with anger, hate, suicide and lust. After encouragement from his wife, the man sought therapy from the seminary counselling centre and was referred to a trauma specialist. Here he discovered that the voices belonged to created parts inside called "alter personalities" not demons. The personalities carried different emotions that developed because of early childhood abuse. Some acted out in anger and some in hatred. Some even wanted to die because they were so wounded by the abuse.

Some of the other chapters speak to discerning whether some of these problems are a direct result from a spiritual conflict. However, given the controversial nature of this particular topic, we mention here a few appropriate cautions. Various deliverance approaches diagnose demonic problems when the people actually have emotional and psychological problems. Some even go as far as to believe that any emotional problem invites demonic forces. We have heard of demons of anger, lust, eating, suicide, depression, anxiety, and so on. Some of these "demons" are actually psychological and psychiatric diagnoses. Other approaches make it sound as if it does not take much for demonic forces to invade people's lives. It is helpful to realise that demonic strongholds are often connected to covenants and pacts with evil forces rather than fleeting brushes with evil. The overboard emphasis on demonising seems to cheapen the validity of the safety that is found in the blood and name of the Lord Jesus Christ. It can also lead to an over-spiritualisation of emotional and psychiatric problems.

When considering the possibility of demonisation, it is important to obtain the following information from those seeking help:

• Do they have any involvement in the occult or cultic practices? This is an important factor because most of these groups practise making covenants or pacts with demonic forces.

- Did anyone in the family line practise occultism or cultic arts?
- Have they willingly, under any circumstances, vowed to follow Satan?
- Did anyone dedicate them to Satan or some other god, spirit or any being when they were a child?

These types of experiences indicate that the person may indeed be subjected to a spiritual conflict, which would need attention immediately.

COMBINING SPIRITUAL WARFARE HEALING AND SPIRITUAL GROWTH

If it becomes obvious that the person is in spiritual crisis, then the person needs to be empowered to fight his or her own battle instead of relying on an outsider to do it. The person needs to take responsibility over the situation, even if it is an ancestral one. Those in spiritual crisis need to recognise fully what happened, how it happened and repent from it. They must renounce their pact or whatever covenants were made or possibly made for them. This helps them realise that as believers, they have the authority to remove their loyalty from Satan and turn it over to God. Furthermore, it lets them know that it is their responsibility to stay close to God.

It has been said before that getting delivered is the easy part; it is the resisting the Devil that is hard. One needs to know how to walk with God when the deliverance ministers are gone.

COLLABORATION BETWEEN MENTAL HEALTH AND SPIRITUAL MINISTRY

The seeming conflict between theology and psychology is nothing new. It appears, though, that recently there seems to be a growing understanding that the two can be in collaboration.[10]

Collaboration is needed today in the world in which we minister. As the church seeks to evangelise the world, it faces challenges in the people it seeks to reach. Woundedness is a common reality in the world today. Abuse, poverty, war, disease and serious occult practices cause all kinds of spiritual and emotional problems for people. Mental-health sciences have done helpful research in this area. The research can help the church better understand wounded people and how they react to certain situations. Research has shown that when people are traumatised during childhood, certain biological alterations occur in the way their brain processes information.[11]

These alterations can severely affect the way they function in society, which includes the church. Some of the following problems are examples of what wounded people may experience: inability to control emotions and negative behaviours, inability to rationalise, severe panic attacks and memory problems.[12]

Research has discovered that the structures in the left hemisphere of the brain process our rational thinking, organisation and analyzing. These are significantly reduced in activity, thus making trauma victims unable to be rational when they are reminded of past trauma. When victims are in those situations, they are extremely emotional, making it hard to reason with them.[13]

If the people who are going through deliverance prayer happen to be victims of trauma, chances are they may respond to any threatening or disturbing stimuli as if the trauma were happening all over again. In such a case, the person becomes re-traumatised by the deliverance instead of receiving help.

For example, a 45-year-old man who has struggles with anger most of his adult life seeks deliverance. The minister says there may be a spirit of anger. The minister addresses the spirit of anger in prayer. The man goes into a trance and an entity manifests and shouts, "I am angry!" People move to restrain the man. This goes on for over an hour. The man goes in and out of the trance while the minister calls the anger spirit out. The man is tired, in pain, and very afraid. Finally, he calms down and goes home, believing he was delivered. For several months he has no problems with anger, but it eventually comes back. The man goes to see a psychologist for marriage counselling because his marriage is in trouble due to his anger. His children are afraid of him. The psychologist takes a history of the man's life. He finds out that this man was molested as a young boy and that the spirit of anger was a split-off part of the person who held the anger from the abuse. This part of him begins weeping, then begs the psychologist not to cast him out as the preacher did several months prior.

This is a typical scenario when dealing with wounded people who may seem to present as angry, aggressive and demon-possessed. Given this situation, it would appear that to approach wounded people effectively, especially in the light of world evangelism, we need collaboration between mental health and spiritual ministry. These two disciplines look at people and the world a little different from each other. Each can contribute to the other.

There are certain details we need to know about people and our world in order to reach people successfully. We need to know that people are complex. They cannot be easily explained in one dimension, either spiritual or psychological. People are influenced by their heredity, culture, environment, geography and new birth. We also need to know that people are not always aware of the processes at work in them. Therefore, denial of certain realities could be due to unawareness instead of pure denial or resistance. Finally, we need to bear in mind that people are more than what we can see and touch. There is an element of spiritual essence that science cannot put a finger on.

Because our world helps shape who we are, we need to realise some things about the world itself, especially parts of it where the people we minister live. The world is a complex place. Cultures, societies, governments and climates do influence people. The way people understand life around them is greatly influenced by their worldview. The world also consists of the seen and the unseen. If we ignore the unseen, we reduce our understanding of the world to the seen only, which diminishes our ability to reach people who are open to the reality of the unseen. The world has become a global village. In other words, there is a lot of interaction among countries, cultures and worldviews. It is imperative that we be aware of other worldviews besides our own.

A comprehensive understanding of people and the cultures they live in can only enhance whatever type of ministry or secular work one does. The church should be no exception. It needs to develop an awareness of people and their different worlds.

Those who live in metropolitan areas know that large cities have become melting pots of diverse cultures and ethnic groups. These ethnic groups bring unique social, spiritual and psychological issues when seeking help. For instance, a young woman who lives in a Haitian area of Miami, Florida, goes to a deliverance service for her problems. She informs the minister about voices in her head telling her to kill herself. The minister suggests that these are probably evil spirits and proceeds to question her about involvement in the occult. She denies this and states that she is a Christian. The minister begins praying for her. The woman jumps up and starts wiggling on the floor like a snake while hissing. The confrontation goes on for two hours, but nothing happens in terms of relief. Furthermore, the woman is disappointed. Later on, she attends a seminar on trauma survivors, knowing that she grew up in an abusive home. While there, she reveals that she hears voices. The seminar leader, who is a Christian therapist, encourages the young woman to discuss her early life experiences. She reveals that her father was both verbally and physically abusive. The therapist asks her what the voices inside are saying besides "kill yourself." She replies, "They sound like my parents and the things they used to say to me when they hurt me." Then the therapist suggests that she ask these voices who they are, where they come from, and what they want or if they have any concerns or fears. The young woman went home and asked the voices. When she came back the next day, she brought several pages of communication from the voices in her mind which she had created to deal with the abuse. One of these parts claimed to have supernatural voodoo powers. The therapist questioned this particular part about why she needed the power, and the answer was that she could avoid feeling the pain of the abuse. This specific part went through the deliverance, which meant letting go of the dependence on evil power and withdrawing the agreements made with the voodoo gods.

Concluding remarks

Although the church has sought to use worldly means to reach people as they are in their complexity, without the power of God this is futile. Other times the church fails to recognise human complexity and over-spiritualises, thereby not producing lasting results. I propose a strong collaboration between Christian mental-health workers and evangelists to help meet the needs of the whole person in a holistic way.

This collaboration can be done efficiently in several different ways. Christian mental-health workers can hold seminars on issues related to spiritual growth and the mental-health field, in conjunction with theology. Churches can offer classes on emotional well-being. Further, churches can employ a full-time mental-health person to minister to the wounded people who are members in the church.

Many of these ideas already exist and are being put into practice in other countries. If we are to minister to the deepest needs of people in ways that honour them as created in the image of God and respect them in that light, these ideas need to spread to those countries that do not yet practise them.

Notes

[1] Jerry Mungadze, "Is It Dissociation or Demonization? Sorting Out Spiritual and Clinical Issues in the Treatment of Dissociative Disorders," *Journal of Psychology and Christianity* 19:2 (2000): 139–43.

[2] James G. Friesen, *Uncovering the Mystery of MPD* (San Bernardino, Calif.: Here's Life Publishers, 1991).

[3] Jerry Mungadze, "Multiple Personality Disorder: No Longer a Rare Diagnosis," *Treatment Centers Magazine* 9 (1992).

[4] Colin Ross, *Satanic Ritual Abuse: Principles of Treatment* (Toronto: University of Toronto Press, 1995).

[5] Ibid.

[6] Dennis L. Bull, Joan W. Ellason and Colin A. Ross, "Exorcism Revisited: Positive Outcomes with Dissociative Identity Disorder," *Journal of Psychology and Theology* 26:2 (1998): 188–96.

[7] George A. Fraser, "Exorcism Rituals: Effects on Multiple Personality Disorder Patients," *Dissociation: Progress in the Dissociative Disorders Special Issue: Possession* 6:4 (1993): 239–44.

[8] Colin A. Ross, "Response: Critical Issues Committee Report: Exorcism in the Treatment of Patients with MPD," *ISSMP-D News* 11:2 (1993): 4.

[9] Christopher H. Rosik, "Some Effects of World View on the Theory and Treatment of Dissociative Identity Disorder," *Journal of Psychology and Christianity Special Issue: Dissociative Identity Disorder* 19:2 (2000): 166–80.

[10] Richard Noll, "Exorcism and Possession: The Clash of Worldviews and the Hubris of Psychiatry," *Dissociation: Progress in the Dissociative Disorders Special Issue: Possession* 6:4 (1993): 250–53.

[11] Bessel A. Van der Kolk, "The Psychological and Biological Processing of Traumatic Memories," symposium conducted in Seattle, Wash. (1995), TMs [photocopy].

[12] Bessel A. Van der Kolk, "The Body Keeps the Score: Memory and the Evolving Psychobiology of Posttraumatic Stress," in *Essential Papers on Posttraumatic Stress Disorder*, ed. Mardi J. Horowitz, et al. (New York: New York University Press, 1999), 301–26.

[13] Bessell A. Van der Kolk, Jennifer A. Burbridge and Joji Suzuki, "The Psychobiology of Traumatic Memory," in *Psychobiology of Posttraumatic Stress Disorder*, ed. Rachael Yehuda and Alexander C. McFarlane (New York: New York Academy of Sciences, 1997), 99–113.

16

Spiritual conflict
in socio-political context

KNUD JØRGENSEN

As I write, the media are telling me:

- Today we remember the fifth anniversary of the massacres of Srebrenica in Bosnia, where 7,000 Muslims were killed in an act of ethnic cleansing.
- Today a major slide from the man-made garbage hills in Manila has drowned a whole block in human waste and killed more than 150 people.
- Statistics at the opening of the global AIDS-conference in South Africa reveal that 34 million people are sick with AIDS, most of them in Sub-Saharan Africa.
- A Norwegian bishop and friend of mine charges all Christians and congregations to lift up to the Lord of history the Middle East peace negotiators at Camp David.

For most of my life I have worked for the media and for humanitarian organisations. There is anger and grief within me – an anger that has followed me for many years. I first felt it as a young radio reporter was sent to Wollo and Tigre in Ethiopia in 1974 to report on a famine that killed more than 1 million. This was a famine caused by human greed and ignored by the celebration of the Organization of African Unity tenth anniversary in Addis, less than 100 kilometres away. This anger has overwhelmed me and made me cry out in the midst of the genocide of southern Sudan and Rwanda. It has travelled with me to the poverty-stricken metropolises of Bangladesh and India and Peru and Ecuador. It gripped me in the midst of ethnic terrorism in Ethiopia and the white prisons of apartheid in Johannesburg. And it then followed me to the "ignorance" and indifference of Western globalisation, whether in Scandinavia, America or Hong Kong. This anger lies underneath the following pages.

My brief is to focus on evil and Satan as they are manifested in the socio-political realm, both collectively and individually, in such evils as injustice, exploitation, oppression, materialism, war, ethnic hatred, persecution and destruction of humans and of creation. How can sin and the Evil One be identified and fought in this realm?

Kingdoms in conflict

Evangelical theology usually views the conflict between Jesus and his adversary as a conflict between two kingdoms. Casting out evil spirits was part of the conflict, but so was also preaching in the synagogues (Mark 1:39). Preaching the Good News, healing and exorcism were all signs of the presence of the kingdom of God (see Matt. 12:28 and Luke 11:20, where exorcism is viewed as a sign of the kingdom). In evangelical theology this usually points to the reality of a hostile realm in conflict with the kingdom of God.[1] This hostile realm has several dimensions or fronts, including what Scott Moreau calls "the systemic front," where the agenda is warfare against the domination systems that make up our cultures and societies.[2] We shall later discuss and explain the term *domination system* as Walter Wink uses it. Suffice it to say in this connection that these systems (cultural, economic, political, religious) are manifestations of what John calls "the world" (*kosmos*: the whole world is under the control of the evil one" [1 John 5:19]; see also John 12:31 and 14:30, where Jesus talks about Satan as "the prince of this world"). This concept of kingdoms in conflict is also illustrated by Satan's claim of dominion when he offered Jesus the kingdoms of the world (Matt. 4:8–9). The point is clearly that even though God ultimately is the sovereign king of heaven and earth, Satan does exercise significant influence over the world and its power structures.

The conflict is evidenced in a tension between the two often overlapping kingdoms. Our allegiance is to the kingdom of God, and as citizens of this kingdom we are part of the new creation. Nevertheless, we see the impact of evil all around us, in the form of violence, poverty, crime, racism, ethnic strife, betrayal and brokenness.

This way of looking at the kingdoms in conflict was also central to the Reformation. Try to sing the battle hymn of the Reformation, "A Mighty Fortress Is Our God," and you will realise that the *leitmotif* is the battle between God's kingdom and Satan. This is not just in an internal, personal manner but is on a cosmic scale, in the midst of life in society and as an attack on the church. For Martin Luther, the truth that "God is for us" implies that "the devil is against us." One may therefore claim, as Heiko Oberman does, that if this Reformation understanding of the powers hostile to God is left out, the entire gospel of incarnation, justification and forgiveness is reduced to vague ideas rather than experiences of faith.[3]

It is therefore essential that we perceive of evil and spiritual warfare in a broad way. It has to do with the common struggle as Christians, and it touches every area of our lives – family, relationships, neighbours, communities and work. All these areas of life are battlegrounds for the kingdoms in conflict. And we no longer need the Bible to tell us. At different levels we have been forced to recognise that the biblical worldview corresponds to a reality of Auschwitz, Rwanda, Cambodia, Bosnia, Kosovo – or even closer, the reality of a drug culture, a divorce culture, a culture of ethnic and racist strife, and the devastating effects of a globalised culture marginalising major parts of the world.

As we pursue this topic, we need to bring along a balanced view of evil influences: the biblical perspective highlights the interconnectedness of *flesh, world* and *Devil.* In this context we use the term *world* to signify the ungodly aspects of culture, values and traditions, that is, the prevailing worldview assumptions that stand contrary to the biblical understanding. Satan attempts to exert influence on the societal and cultural levels. This influence may come through idolatry and occult practices and beliefs (for example, Acts 13 about the magician Elymas). Or it may come through what Sherwood Lingenfelter calls "prisons of disobedience" found in all cultures.[4] In a sense every culture and system may be used by the Evil One to hold us in bondage by entangling us into a life of conformity to shared values and beliefs that are fundamentally contrary to God's purpose and will for humanity. Thus Satan has worked on a corporate level, says Lingenfelter, to blind people to the gospel. We shall come back to this topic when we look at Walter Wink and his assertion that we need to be "reborn" from our primary socialization in a culture, for example, a culture that has "convinced" us of the need for violence as a solution (redemptive violence).[5]

This link between culture/society and bondage illustrates and emphasises by the same token that how that bondage is experienced will vary greatly from culture to culture. In some parts of the world there is great fear of the spirits, and the gospel is heard as the good news of deliverance from these spirits. In other places there is evidence of powerful occult undercurrents with overt demonic activity. In some Latin American countries major parts of the population are caught up in witchcraft, voodoo and magic. Likewise, in Hindu cultures there is a pervasive fear of the spirit world. In the West, discarding Christianity has taken off the lid of the ancient jungle of religiosity. As the animals of the jungle reappear, we call them new (New Age) even though they are as old as the Fall. However, the main bondage most Westerners – or should we say "the westernised/globalised world" – experience is still the desire for affluence. The globalised culture has allowed the pursuit of the "good life" to shape its perspective, values, and psychology so profoundly that Lesslie Newbigin is right in viewing the Western culture as the most non-Christian culture ever.[6]

In the kingdom conflict we are, Paul says (Eph. 6:10–20), confronted by *principalities (archai), authorities (exousiai), world rulers (kosmokratores)* and *spiritual forces (pneumatika)*. Among evangelicals these terms are usually understood to refer to satanic forces.[7] Paul's focus is here on the day-to-day struggle of the believer in the midst of culture and society, not on territorial spirits. Neither do the terms seem to describe a hierarchy of spirits. As Arnold says: "The terms appear to come from a large reservoir of terminology used in the first century when people spoke of demonic spirits."[8] As we focus particularly on the works of Walter Wink in the next section, we shall meet a theologian who looks at these powers in a different way – namely, as created, fallen, but redeemable.

Engaging the powers

Engaging the Powers is the title of the third volume in Walter Wink's trilogy on the powers. The first two books of the trilogy are *Naming the Powers* and *Unmasking the Powers: The Invisible Forces that Determine Human Existence*. In addition, Wink has published a condensed and popularised version of the trilogy under the title *The Powers That Be*.[9] Wink's aim, particularly in the condensed version, is to help us reformulate ancient concepts, such as God and Satan, angels and demons, principalities and powers, in light of the world today. Thus the theological thinking is clearly shaped as much by his involvement in the civil rights movement and the fight against apartheid in South Africa as by the study of Scripture. This combination becomes even more evident in his 1998 analysis of the powers as they appear on the global scene, *When the Powers Fall.*[10] The refreshing and provocative aspect of Wink is his contextualisation of powers and principalities in the midst of our contemporary social institutions. He is as concerned with salvation as with justice.

Wink's point of departure is that everything has both a physical and a spiritual aspect. Therefore the powers are not simply people and their institutions; they also include the spirituality at the core of those institutions. If we want to change those systems – social, economic, cultural, political – we must address not only the outer form but the inner spirit as well. In the likeness of those management experts who highlight organisational culture, Wink claims that every business, corporation, school and bureaucracy is a combination of visible and invisible, outer and inner, physical and spiritual. However, this spirituality is not always benign. The sole purpose of the institutions is to serve the general welfare; when they refuse to do so, their spirituality becomes diseased (demonic). Against this background Wink views our time as a time of hope and of despair:

> We live in a remarkable time, when entire nations have been liberated by non-violent struggle; when miracles are openly declared, such as the fall of the Berlin Wall, the collapse of communism in the Soviet Union and Eastern Bloc, and the transformation of South Africa. . . . Yet these are also times of endemic violence, ethnic hatred, genocide, and economic privation around the world, as the super-rich hoard increasing shares of the world's wealth and the poor drown in poverty. . . . I believe that even these rebellious Powers can be transformed in the crucible of God's love.[11]

Wink advocates, as already indicated, an integral view of reality that sees everything as having an outer and an inner aspect. In this worldview God is within everything (*panentheism* means God in everything and implies that all creatures are potential revealers of God). This view opens up the spiritual reality. Latin American liberation theology made good efforts to reinterpret the powers and principalities, not as disembodied spirits, but as institutions, structures and systems. But it did not see the spiritual dimension – that the powers at the same time are visible and invisible, spiritual and institutional (Col. 1:15–20). Furthermore, we must reverse the process of projecting these spiritual dimensions onto the screen of the universe. Rather, the spiritual force that we experience in a system emanates from that actual system. In other words, the demons are not up there but over here, in the socio-spiritual structures and political systems (cf. the demonised pigs of Mark 5 and the political systems of Rev. 12–13). And when these powers (which may be personal or impersonal) network around idolatrous values, we get what Wink calls "the domination system," whose master is Satan. In this way the powers are everywhere around us and their presence is inescapable. The primary issue is therefore to learn to identify them (Paul's gift of discerning the spirits). When a power pursues a vocation other than the one for which God created it and makes its own interests the highest good, then that power becomes demonic. The task is to unmask this idolatry and recall the powers to their created purposes in the world. This, however, requires the ministry of the church (Eph. 3:10) and not just an individual. Wink lifts up as an illustration how corporations ignore God's humanising purposes by making profit the bottom line. This is a capitalist heresy to which not even Adam Smith would agree. It is therefore the task of the church to remind corporations that as creatures of God they have as their divine vocation the achievement of human well-being (Eph. 3:10).

On the one hand, Wink views evil as profoundly systemic; on the other hand, the powers are not intrinsically evil in his view. Rather, they are at once good and evil, though to varying degrees, and they are capable of improvement. He therefore works on the basis of three theses as his theological framework:

- The powers are good. They are good by virtue of their creation to serve the humanising purposes of God.
- The powers are fallen. They put their own interests above the interests of the whole.
- The powers can be redeemed. What fell in time can be redeemed in time.

This applies in a temporal sense; that is, the powers were created, they are fallen, and they shall be redeemed. But it is also to be viewed as something *simultaneous*: God at one and the same time *upholds* a given system (since we need some such system to support human life), *condemns* that system (it is destructive of human life), and *presses for its transformation* into a more humane order.[12]

This view sets us free from demonising those who do evil. We can love our enemies or nation or culture – critically, yes, calling them back to their purposes. The view also implies that God does not endorse any particular power. He did not create capitalism or socialism, but human life requires some sort of economic system. Some institutions and ideologies, says Wink, can only be transformed by being abandoned or destroyed or replaced.

Against this background Wink sees us as being involved in a threefold activity: *Naming the powers* identifies our experiences of these pervasive forces that dominate our lives. *Unmasking the powers* takes away their invisibility, and thus their capacity to coerce us unconsciously into doing their bidding. *Engaging the powers* involves joining in God's endeavour to bend them back to their divine purposes.[13]

So, the evil is not intrinsic but the result of idolatry, and therefore the powers can be redeemed. This, in turn, means that the task of redemption is not restricted to changing individuals but also applies to changing the fallen institutions. And Wink takes even one more step: the gospel is not the message about the salvation of individuals from the world but news about a world transfigured, right down to its basic structures. This cosmic salvation will take place when God will gather up all things in Christ (Eph. 1:10).

It is not difficult to question some of Wink's assumptions and views. How does he understand the Fall? Is it a structural aspect of all personal and social existence and/or a temporal myth? What then does he mean by saying that the Fall affirms the radicality of evil?[14] He may describe evil with terrible "human" examples, but one wonders whether evil really stands in contrast and absolute opposition to the living God: "Fallenness does not touch our essence, but it characterises our existence."[15] In the same way one is left uncertain in Wink's theology whether the human being, after the Fall, is totally alienated from God. True, he talks clearly about the need for the individual to be changed. Human misery is caused by institutions, but these institutions are maintained by human beings; in other words, the institutions are made evil by us. Yet, I lack a more clear understanding and description of the gulf between God and humanity caused by disobedience and sin.

At the same time his view of the powers as created, fallen and redeemable may help us negotiate a truce between the Anabaptist and the Calvinist traditions. The first one may argue that all social and cultural systems are intrinsically evil (though capable of doing some limited good). The other position may insist that governments and public institutions are intrinsic elements of God's creation and therefore capable of being "christianised." The first position may abandon the powers to secularity while the other installs a sort of theocracy. Wink's view does neither. Instead, it leaves open the door for running for political office or working to overthrow the political system, depending on the state of disobedience of the system. Furthermore, his thinking challenges us to bring together evangelism and social struggle and to include in our evangelistic task the proclamation to the principalities and powers of the manifold wisdom of God.

When an entire network of powers integrates around idolatrous values, we get a domination system, the system of the powers. In this way the domination system is equivalent to what the Bible often means by the terms "world," "aeon" and "flesh." For example, a farming family in Bangladesh loses everything to crafty lawyers and hired guns and is forced into city slums devoid of labour opportunities but full of crime, prostitution and starvation. And it is true that approximately 16 million people die of starvation and poverty-related diseases every year. Another example is that of blacks struggling against apartheid, or rather the apartheid system, because that was how it was perceived. A third is the consumer sickness of wealthy societies, fuelled by belief in endless progress and by a commercialised information society saying less and less to more and more. A fourth is the sick combination of violence and sexual perversion available for all ages on the Internet and video that cripples the minds of old and young. The domination system is characterised by unjust economic relations, oppressive political relations, biased race relations, patriarchal gender relations, hierarchical power relations and the use of violence to maintain them all.[16]

The basic structure of this system has persisted since the rise of the great conquest states of Mesopotamia in about 3000 B.C. At that time the horse and the wheel together make conquest lucrative, and the plunder and conquest includes females as slaves, concubines, wives, resulting in female subordination and a system of patriarchy. Wife-beating and child-beating develop as a male right. Evil is blamed on women. In addition, plunder and conquest give rise to new classes of aristocrats and priests – people producing nothing but dominating others through a spiral of violence.

To uphold the domination system a myth of redemptive violence comes into being, a myth that lifts high the belief that violence saves, that war brings peace, that might makes right. Violence in this way becomes the nature of things. It becomes inevitable, the last, and increasingly through history, the first resort in conflicts. This myth is the Babylonian creation story (Enuma Elish from approximately 1250

B.C.) in which the young god Marduk kills the mother god Tiamat in a terrible manner and then splits her skull and stretches out her corpse and from it creates the cosmos. In this way, and in stark contrast to the Bible, creation is an act of violence. The world is created from the cadaver of a woman. Chaos is prior to order, and evil precedes good. The gods themselves are violent. In contrast, the Bible portrays a good God who creates a good creation in which good is prior to evil and neither evil nor violence is a part of creation but enter later as a result of the serpent and human sin (Gen. 3).

It is, however, the Babylonian myth that has dominated much of history and has spread everywhere. Human beings are created from the blood of a murdered god, our origin is violence, killing is in our genes, life is combat, peace through war, security through strength, and the common people live to perpetuate the advantage that the gods have conferred upon the kings, aristocrats and priests – because religion exists to legitimate power and privilege. Here are the core values of the domination system as it is found in every society.

It is not difficult to see the traces of the myth in contemporary Western media, sports, nationalism, militarism, foreign policy, and so on. The TV cartoons and comic books of the Western world can be stark illustrations of violence, anger and scapegoating. In a similar way the American western makes the law suspect and weak compared to the hero with the gun. Rambo and James Bond become the messiahs in a world where justice is lodged in the gun.

The reason why we swallow this is that the myth of redemptive violence is the simplest, laziest, most exciting, uncomplicated, irrational and primitive depiction of evil the world has ever known. It strikes the cords of original sin and opens the door for the demons of hell into a culture that has lost its point of departure. Both in Western culture and to some extent also and increasingly in other cultures we socialise our children through this myth, by making violence pleasurable, fascinating and entertaining. In this way the powers are able to delude people into compliance with a system that keeps them in bondage – the domination system. As one illustration, consider that an average child in the United States is reported to see 36,000 hours of television by age 18, viewing some 15,000 murders. Just think what this does to an entire civilisation. And this does not even address the sadistic combinations of sex and violence available on videos – and available everywhere and in all major cities around the world. Youngsters in Addis Ababa watch the same demonic stuff as youngsters in New York. There are boys who receive their first introduction to sex by watching on video women being raped, decapitated, dismembered and cannibalised. Even the Devil seems to have abandoned sophistication!

It is the same myth of redemptive violence that we make use of in international conflicts, whether in Bosnia and Srebrenica or on the border between Ethiopia and Eritrea, where teenage soldiers last year were being used as a shield against the tanks of the opponent. The myth gives divine sanction to the nation's imperialism. In this way the Cold War was a satanic trick to make both sides believe religiously in the terror balance of violence. I think Wink is right in claiming that "the myth of redemptive violence serves as the inner spirituality of the national security state. It provides divine legitimisation for the suppression of poor people everywhere, and the extraction of wealth from the poorer nations."[17] The result is that nationalism becomes idolatry and ethnicity becomes demonic.

> The myth of redemptive violence . . . speaks for God; it does not listen for God to speak. . . . It misappropriates the language, symbols, and scriptures of Christianity. It does not seek God in order to change; it embraces God in order to prevent change. Its God . . . is a tribal god worshipped as an idol. Its metaphor is not the journey, but the fortress. Its symbol is not the cross but the cross-hairs of a gun. Its offer is not forgiveness but victory. Its good news is not the unconditional love of enemies but their final elimination. Its salvation is not a new heart but a successful foreign policy. It usurps the revelation of God's purposes for humanity in Jesus. It is blasphemous. It is idolatrous.[18]

Based on Revelation 12—13 Wink outlines the delusional apparatus of the powers and the domination system.[19] If it had not been for the powerful delusions, why would people, why would we all, tolerate the powers and the domination system? Therefore, exposing this system of delusion must be a central task in the discernment of the powers, for the powers are never more powerful than when they can act from concealment (see the imagery in Scripture of wolves in sheep's clothing). True, the system may use violence, but even more effective is to drop out of sight, to masquerade as the permanent furniture of the universe, to make oppressive structures appear to be of divine construction. This is illustrated when John strips off the mask of Roman imperial benevolence and reveals the true spirit of Rome. It looks like a prosperous peacemaker but conceals a monstrous deformity aiming at supplanting God or a harlot inviting intercourse with the kings she has intoxicated with power (Rev. 17).

At the centre of the delusions John sees that the Dragon creates another Beast (Rev. 13:11) – a beast that imitates the lamb, a beast that proselytises by means of a civil religion that declares the state and its leaders divine. This element of *power worship* is central in John's vision – because it represents *the manufacture of idolatry*. So deception and propaganda are not enough for the Evil One. Misinforming people about the nature of the system may not last. But if one can cause people to worship the Beast, one has created a public immune to truth, Wink claims.[20]

Since the beginnings of the domination system some 5,000 years ago, it has deceived people by means of a series of delusional assumptions; these assumptions are what Colossians 2 calls the *stoicheia tou kosmou*, in Wink's opinion. They may come and go, but they continually have reasserted themselves:

• The need to control society and prevent chaos requires some to dominate others.
• Men are better equipped by nature to be dominant than women, and some races are naturally suited to dominate others.
• Violence is redemptive, the only language enemies understand.
• Ruling is the most important of all social functions.
• Rulers should therefore be rewarded by extra privileges and greater wealth.
• Money is the most important value.
• The production of material goods is more important than the production of healthy and normal people and of sound human relationships.
• Property is sacred.
• Institutions are more important than people.
• There is no higher value or being or power than the state. God is the protector of the state.
• God is not revealed to all but only to select individuals or nations and their rulers and priesthood.

May it not be claimed that for Christians and the church to expose these delusionary assumptions is a central part of spiritual warfare in society and culture? The trouble is, however, that we do not have much training in so doing.

But also at a personal level we remain responsible for what we do with the demonic delusions and propaganda. Telling the truth and living the truth remain the most forceful danger to any system of falsehood. The fundamental threat to a system of lies is the threat *that just one is living the truth*; we know this from the recent history of Nazi and Communist domination. We even know it from a fairy tale where a single child cried out, "The emperor is naked!"

Along the same lines a sense of powerlessness may hide a spiritual disease deliberately induced by the powers to keep us afraid. The sense of political powerlessness in some of our countries represents in my view a demonic deception to keep us believing that politics are dirty and that we do not make any difference. Could it be that the victory of faith over the powers lies, not in being immune to them, but in being set free from their delusions? And to break the spell of lies and delusions we need a vision of God's domination-free order.

Fighting the powers

The fight against the powers has already been under way a long time by our engaging them and diagnosing their strategies and delusions. We may take one step further by adding the vision of God's domination-free order, to show the clear distinction between a domination system and a partnership society, between the myth of redemptive violence and the story of Jesus. Rather than doing this in a general way, let me show the contextual chart Wink has developed to clarify the differences between the domination system and God's domination-free order.[21]

We may disagree on several counts with Wink's interpretation of God's reign – at least I do – but there is for us evangelicals a serious challenge in his attempt to place God's reign in a socio-political and cultural setting. Without such daring contextualisation we run the risk of transforming the gospel into a timeless, placeless, eternal nowhere. The same may then happen to the powers. The challenge for us as we fight the powers is to proclaim the gospel as a context-specific remedy for the evils of a society and a culture dominated by the powers.

The primary weapon against the powers has always been and will always remain *the liberating message of Jesus*. That small word or testimony is sufficient to bring down the whole army of powers and principalities. The gospel is the most powerful antidote for domination that the world has ever known. It was that antidote that inspired the abolition of slavery, the women's movement, the non-violence movement, the civil rights movement, the human rights movement, the fall of Nazism, Fascism and Communism, the break-up of apartheid.

Table 16-1: The domination system and God's domination-free order

Societal Mode	The Domination System	God's Domination-free Order
Gender differences	Patriarchal; superiority/inferiority	Equality of sexes; differences in specialization
Power	Power over; power to take life, control	Power with, to give, support
Politics	Conquest, autocracy, authoritarian	Diplomacy, democracy, enabling
Economics	Exploitation, greed, privilege, inequality	Sharing, sufficiency, responsibility
Religion	Male God-jealous, wrathful	Inclusive God-images, punishing loving/judging Compassionate/severe, merciful/demanding
Relationships	Ranking, Domination hierarchies, slavery, classism, racism	Linking, Equality of opportunity
Transformative mode	Violence, force, war Suppression of conflict	Non-violent confrontation, negotiation Non-violent conflict resolution
Ecological stance	Exploitation, control, contempt	Harmony, co-operation, respect
Role of ego	Self-centered	Affiliation-oriented
Education	Indoctrinating	Enabling
Sexual responsibility	Subordination of women's reproductive capacities and sexual expression to male control	Control of sexuality by individuals in the light of community values
Eschatology	Status quo, holding and keeping power, Preoccupied with this world Eternity in the future, injustice in the present	Cultural transformation, the reign of God, the coming aeon Eternity in the present, justice in the future

Source: Engaging the Powers: Discernment and Resistance in a World of Domination *by Walter Wink, copyright © 1992 Augsburg Fortress. Used by permission.*

In our fight against the domination system we shall lift up the biblical focus on *servanthood and servant leadership* (Luke 22:22–27), not just as a principle, but because the central core of the gospel is the slave or servant of the Lord who took upon himself our transgressions. The consequence of this gospel truth is the repudiation of the right of some to lord it over others by means of power, wealth, shaming or titles. The man on a donkey is the master of God's people in their fight against powers and principalities in this world.

Does this challenge not also include *a call for equity*? Breaking with domination means ending the economic exploitation of the many by the few in a local social setting and at a global level. Is not the growing gulf between rich and poor a satanic abomination in the eyes of the Lord? Are we not challenged to change the economic order and to shout to our consumer cultures, "Enough is enough!"?

And what about *the redemptive violence* surrounding us, even after the demise of the Cold War? True, a society with an unfair distribution of goods requires violence. And violence is the only way some are able to deprive others of what is justly theirs. And do we not need means of violence to keep the rest of the world away from our meat pots in the rich world? Along these lines some think to themselves or even boldly proclaim, "All these heathen immigrants." Jesus rejects violence as far as I can read – not resistance – but violence. And Paul tells us that the weapons we use in our fight are not the weapons of the domination system *(kosmos)* but God's powerful weapons which we use to destroy strongholds (2 Cor. 10:4).

My intention is not to make Jesus a reformer or revolutionary, attempting to replace one oppressive power with another. Rather, we may view his ministry as *a struggle against the basic presuppositions and structures of oppression, against the domination system itself, against Satan himself.*

The first serious lessons in spiritual warfare I received as a young Scandinavian missionary derived from the East African Revival. These lessons changed my life and they still follow me, also in relation to fighting the powers:

• Do not become too preoccupied with analyzing demons and the tricks of Satan. With the occult people do their utmost to catalogue demons, their name, colour, smell, origin, taste, etc. When people come to faith in Jesus, they refrain from this. Jesus has conquered the demons, and we do not need to study their activities to gain control over them.

- Lift up Jesus and him crucified. All spiritual gifts are to be used to lift up the cross – also signs and wonders.
- The decisive mark of the power of the Holy Spirit is a contrite heart, not speaking in tongues or mighty deeds; they may appear, but the central sign of God's power is repentance.
- The only way to break the power of Satan in everyday life, in society and in culture is by walking in the light with all of your life so that Satan may not get a chance to bind you in the darkness. And to walk in the light means to live in openness with others, in small groups where intercession and healing are central.
- The gifts of grace belong in relations and contexts that are cleansed by the blood of Christ. The power of the Lord is the blood that cleanses from all sin.
- The person who is cleansed and walks in the light renounces the Devil and all his works absolutely and totally.
- The witness to the power of the Lord and the spiritual gifts needed for the journey grow out of being cleansed and of walking in the light, in close communion with sisters and brothers.

Notice how central the cross is in this East African understanding of spiritual warfare. In the same way Paul claims that it was not primarily through the Resurrection that the powers were unmasked, but on and through the Cross: "Unmasking the principalities and powers, God publicly shamed them, exposing them in Christ's triumphal procession by means of the cross" (Col. 2:13–15). Jesus died because he challenged the powers. But something went wrong for the powers. Their use of violence exposed their own illegitimacy. Their nailing him to the cross meant the end of the domination system. The powers that led him out to Golgotha are led in God's triumphal procession. When they tried to destroy him, they stepped into a divine trap, as Luther says: "The devil saw Jesus as his prize, snapped at the bait, and was pulled out of the water for all to see." Therefore, on the Cross the powers themselves are paraded and made captive. And so the Cross marks their failure and the failure of violence. The power of God is here hidden under seeming powerlessness *(sub contrarie specie).*

And so the Cross continues to challenge the entire domination system, because the Cross reveals the delusions and deceptions and reveals that death does not have the final word. Jesus entered darkness and death and made it the darkness of God; it is now possible to enter any darkness and trust God to wrest from it resurrection. And the Cross proves that truth cannot be killed. The mighty forces of deception cannot ever kill the truth any more. After Good Friday it will continue to survive, even in a single Chinese student standing alone before a column of tanks in Tiananmen Square. "Killing Jesus was like trying to destroy a dandelion seed-head by blowing on it. It was like shattering a sun into a million fragments of light."[22]

So let us continue to lift up the cross of Christ because we know that where the cross is lifted high, the powers are losing strength. I mean this in a very literal sense. Proclaim the Cross to the leaders of this world, whisper the name of the Crucified in the dark prisons, shout it out in the midst of our modern consumer temples, walk into the battle zones of Ethiopia and Eritrea with the cross of reconciliation, challenge the ethnic fighting in Eastern Europe in the name of *Christus Victor.*

And then let us die with Christ to the fundamental assumptions of the domination system – the *stoicheia tou kosmou* that Paul talks about in Colossians 2:20: "Why do you let yourselves be dictated to as if your lives were still controlled by the *kosmos*?" I sense in my own life and ministry a need for understanding better what Jesus meant by losing my life: "Those who try to make their life secure will lose it, but those who lose their life will keep it" (Luke 17:33). Does it also have something to do with my bondage under social and cultural values invented by the powers? I know that I need to die to my private egocentricity, but is there also a call here to die to the hubris of Western culture? Do we evangelicals need to be more radically social-oriented when we talk about dying with Christ?

And let us build bridges from our daily lives to him who has all power and honour, through praying in the name of the crucified and risen Lord – because we know that the act of praying is itself one of the primary means by which we engage the powers. Here their secret spell over us is broken. Intercession can affect the shape the future takes. Therefore the gift of intercession must be encouraged and given room. In Scripture we see that intercession changes the world, and it changes what is possible to God. It creates islands of freedom in a world in the grip of the powers. And it rattles God's cage and wakes God up and sets God free. Praying is joining God on the battlefield in the conflict between the kingdoms. The drastic and unexplainable changes in the former Soviet Union or in South Africa or the Philippines would not have happened had it not been for people praying so that God found an opening and was able to bring about change. The answer to prayer may take time, maybe because the powers are blocking God's response. But when we fail to pray, God's hands are tied.

Conclusion

The primary task of the church with reference to the powers and principalities is to unmask their idolatrous pretensions, to identify their dehumanising values, to strip from them the mantle of credibility and to set free their victims. This includes the testimony to the Crucified to the rulers and powers. It does not include a commission to create a new society; rather, we are, in the midst of society, to call the powers' bluff, to de-legitimate and ridicule the domination system.

Central in calling the powers' bluff stands our offer of praise and worship to the one true God. It stands because in and through that praising of the one true God, the bluff of all idols is revealed. So as we fight the powers, we shall ascribe to God glory and strength.

Notes

[1] See Clinton Arnold, *Three Crucial Questions About Spiritual Warfare* (Grand Rapids, Mich.: Baker, 1997), 20ff.

[2] A. Scott Moreau, *Essentials of Spiritual Warfare: Equipped to Win the Battle* (Wheaton, Ill.: Harold Shaw Publishers, 1997), 18f.

[3] Heiko A. Oberman, *Luther: Man Between God and the Devil* (New York: Doubleday, 1992), 104f.

[4] Sherwood Lingenfelter, *Transforming Culture: A Challenge for Christian Mission* (Grand Rapids, Mich.: Baker, 1992).

[5] Walter Wink, *Engaging the Powers: Discernment and Resistance in a World of Dominion* (Philadelphia: Fortress Press, 1992).

[6] Lesslie Newbigin, *Foolishness to the Greeks: The Gospel and Western Culture* (Grand Rapids, Mich.: Eerdmans, 1986).

[7] See, for example, David F. Wells, *God the Evangelist* (Grand Rapids, Mich.: Eerdmans, 1987), 76ff.; Gary Greig and Kevin Springer, eds., *The Kingdom and the Power* (Ventura, Calif.: Regal, 1993); and Clinton Arnold, *Powers of Darkness: Principalities and Powers in Paul's Letters* (Downers Grove, Ill.: InterVarsity Press, 1992).

[8] Arnold, *Three Crucial Questions*, 39.

[9] Walter Wink, *Naming the Powers: The Language of Power in the New Testament* (Philadelphia: Fortress Press, 1984); idem, *Unmasking the Powers: The Invisible Forces that Determine Human Existence* (Philadelphia: Fortress Press, 1986); idem, *Engaging the Powers: Discernment and Resistance in a World of Dominion* (Philadelphia: Fortress Press, 1992); idem, *The Powers that Be: Theology for a New Millennium* (New York: Doubleday, 1998).

[10] Walter Wink, *When the Powers Fall: Reconciliation in the Healing of Nations* (Philadelphia: Fortress Press, 1998).

[11] Ibid., 10.

[12] Ibid., 32f.

[13] Ibid., 34–35.

[14] Wink, *Engaging the Powers*, 59.

[15] Ibid., 72.

[16] Wink, *When the Powers Fall*, 59.

[17] Ibid., 57.

[18] Ibid., 61–62.

[19] Wink, *Engaging the Powers*, 47–48.

[20] Ibid., 94.

[21] Ibid., 46–47.

[22] Ibid., 143.

Worship, praise and prayer

Juliet Thomas

The Christian life can be best described as a love relationship with God. Through the death and resurrection of Jesus Christ, sinners have been brought into a living relationship with a righteous and holy God, saved by grace and not works. God has called us to live a life of sanctification growing into the likeness of Jesus Christ (Eph. 3:19) through the Holy Spirit, who empowers us to "work out our salvation" by obedience to his ways and surrender to his will. Because God's ways are not our ways and his thoughts are far above our thoughts, we constantly need to learn to align our will and ways to his. In this process we deal with three enemies: the world, the flesh, the Devil. We are not to be conformed to this world but to crucify the flesh and its desires and constantly resist the Devil.

We find ourselves caught in a conflict between two kingdoms. We suffer wear and tear as we rub shoulders with the world. We are sometimes bruised as we come in conflict with the Devil. And often times we find an erosion of values, a lowering of standards, a shifting of focus from God to self and from faith to works. We need to be restored and renewed continually, lest we burn out when the going becomes too tough; as noted in Psalm 23:3, "He restores my soul. He guides me in paths of righteousness for his name's sake."

Worship and prayer are vital for our wholeness. As we come to God in worship, we regain focus and put things into right perspective. Jesus appointed his twelve disciples to *be with him* before he sent them out. This learning to be with Christ is what worship is all about. Worship, praise and prayer are therefore crucial to living out the Christ-life in our broken world.

Present trends

Paul warned Timothy that in the last days people would become entangled with the world. They would substitute love of God with love of self, money and pleasure. They would be people "having a form of godliness but denying its power" (2 Tim. 3:5).

The church today is in grave danger of pursuing the popularisation of Christianity, hoping to attract sell-out crowds but in danger of compromising the gospel. Ideas deviating from the Word of God have crept in. We need to submit to the Scriptures' incessant demand that all new teaching be carefully assessed. This is especially difficult today, because we have shifted from exposition to experience as arbiter of truth.

A genuine experience of Jesus is not found in the works of the flesh. Rather, it is found in a life of obedience and surrender, walking in the Sprit as we rediscover the joy of genuine worship, a passion for prayer and praise, and the proclamation of the Word that will bring others into that living transforming relationship with Jesus Christ.

A. W. Tozer calls worship the missing jewel in modern evangelicalism – the longing for God that releases "the rivers of living water from within us."[1] May the Lord help us to be seized by a new God-consciousness, as together we begin to taste and hear and feel the God who is our life and our all, filling us with the wonder and glory of his Presence. We need again the fire of Pentecost! It cannot be earned, worked up or simulated. Can we draw near enough to God until the Shekinah fire begins to transfigure our vessels of clay and we see glimpses of his glory?

What is worship?

Worship defies adequate definition. The meaning of the term, like *grace* and *love*, is like the perfume of a rose or the delightful flavour of honey – it is more easily experienced than described. Worship comes from the overflow of a grateful heart under a sense of divine favour. The emphasis is on spontaneous worship. It is not something that has to be laboriously pumped up, but that which springs up and overflows from a heart filled with a sense of the greatness and goodness of God.

Worship is the outpouring of a soul at rest in the presence of God. It is the occupation of the heart, not with its needs or even blessings, but with God himself (2 Sam. 7:18–22). In the visions of worship in heaven there is not a single mention of a request – the focus is on God's worthiness.

Worship is the quickening of the conscience by the holiness of God to feed the mind with the truth of God, to purge the imagination by the beauty of God, to open the heart to the love of God and to devote the will to the purpose of God.

In summary, worship is all that we are responding to all that God is. I do not worship only because God has blessed me or because I want God's blessings. In those non-Christian religions that depend on "works" to find favour with God, this concept of coming to God *in order to* receive his blessings is the motivation to worship. We need to recognise that God is not obligated to anyone. God is sovereign and can give or withhold as it pleases him. Like Job, in true worship we learn to worship simply because God is God. We can perhaps draw these distinctions among prayer, praise and worship: prayer is the occupation of the soul with its needs, praise is the occupation of the soul with its blessings, and worship is the occupation of the soul with God himself.

We can see an example of worship when Mary anointed Jesus (John 12:1–11). Mary did not come for blessings. The greatest teacher the world has ever seen was there. She often sat at his feet. But as she came into the presence of the One she loved above all others, she desired to occupy herself with this One alone. She made no request. She did not seek to refresh herself but to refresh the Lord and fill his soul with joy.

Mary did not withhold her best but poured it all fully, joyously and with humility at the feet of the Lord. The whole house was filled with the exquisite perfume. The Lord was given the supreme place and all the occupants benefited by it. She herself would long bear the fragrance wherever she went. All present would carry on their person traces of the sweet perfume.

So it is in Christian worship. Individually and collectively in such an act of worship the whole company is affected. The fragrance of their worship is then carried to others, who will realise that they have been with Jesus.

The nature of worship

Several passages from the Scriptures note the true nature of worship (for example, 1 Chron. 16:29; Ps. 95:6; Ps. 96:9; Ps.100:4–4; and Matt. 4:10). Perhaps John 4:23–24 states it most clearly:

Yet a time is coming and has now come when the true worshippers will worship the Father in spirit and truth, for they are the kind of worshippers the Father seeks. God is spirit, and his worshippers must worship in spirit and in truth.

God wants a very special kind of worship. God dictates exactly how he is to be approached and worshipped: *in spirit* and *in truth*. Let us note three significant facts about this type of worship. First, Christ changed the very nature of accepted worship. Before Christ, people worshipped God in special sacred places. Christ opened the door into God's very presence, so *place and locality mean nothing* – we can now worship God from any place at any time.

Second, we are to worship "in spirit and in truth." To worship God *in spirit* means with the spiritual drive and ability of one's soul, seeking the most intimate communion and friendship with God; and with the spiritual core of one's life and being, trusting and resting in God's acceptance and love and care.[2] To worship God *in truth* means to approach God in the right and true way, through his son, Jesus Christ. It means to worship God sincerely and truthfully without need for location or physical symbols such as the temple or the altar.

Third, God created people to worship him and to share fellowship with him. He is a Spirit, and therefore he seeks people who will worship him in spirit and truth. He has chosen to make our bodies his dwelling place, the temple of the living God, so that worship is very intimate and personal.

WORSHIP AND THE HUMAN PERSON

The human person is an integrated being. We are to worship God with all our heart, mind and strength. Paul tells us to be transformed, a process that takes place through the renewal of the mind (Rom. 12:2). This is crucial, as the battle is for the renewal of the mind. Christ's attitude of obedience even to death is what God wants to find in us (Phil. 2:5). This is done through disciplining ourselves to focus on what is true (Phil. 4:8) and setting our minds on heavenly rather than earthly things (Col. 3:2). In addition to the renewal of the mind, the body has to be a living sacrifice, holy and acceptable to God (Rom 12:1). Worship does not just involve the spirit and mind; our bodies are also to be deeply engaged.

WORSHIP AND THE HOLY SPIRIT

The Holy Spirit, the wonderful gift, has been sent by our risen Lord to indwell and empower us. God did not set before us the ideal of a life filled with worship and praise and leave us to struggle to achieve it on our own. We have the Holy Spirit to empower us to turn away from the distractions of flesh, trials and self-love (Rom. 8:26). He is within us, as a fountain of water, springing up to fill us with fresh life – life that is full and meaningful.

Through him we can know the refreshing that comes from the presence of the Lord. Through the Spirit we can understand the Scriptures and experience the marvellous things God has freely given us in Christ. Through him we are linked in vital oneness with the Father and the Son, and have all we need for life and godliness. Thus we have all we need to inspire praise – comfort, encouragement, inexpressible joy, overflowing hope, strength in our innermost being and power to love and serve.

WORSHIP AND THE CHURCH

Hebrews 10:24–25 exhorts us to continue motivating each other to love and good deeds as well as continuing to meet together. Some had apparently forsaken the church even in those days. This attitude can be found in every generation! The author tells us to exhort one another, and even more as we see the Day approaching. What Day is this? It is the day of the Lord's return, which is immediately upon us. Genuine believers need one another – the presence, fellowship, strength, encouragement, care and love of each other. All of this is found in a very special way when believers come together for worship.

The concept of worship and prayer

The essential biblical concept of worship is service. Service originally signified the labour of slaves or hired servants. To offer this worship to God, his servants must prostrate themselves and manifest reverential fear and adoring awe and wonder.

In the Old Testament there are instances of individual worship (Gen. 24:26f. and Exod. 33:9—34:8). But the emphasis is on worship in the congregation (Ps. 108:3–5; 1 Chron. 29:20). To the Jew, worship of God was central to all of life.

In the New Testament, temple and synagogue worship are also found. Christ participated in both, but he always exemplified the worship that is the love of the heart towards a heavenly Father. In his teaching, he explained that the approach to God through ritual and priestly mediation is not merely unimportant, it is now unnecessary. Furthermore, he also taught that worship is true, a service offered to

God not only in terms of temple but of service to one's fellows (Luke 10:25ff.; Matt. 5:23f.; John 4:20–24; James 1:27) However, Jesus' emphasis was on the Spirit and the inner love and devotion of the heart rather than on external forms and symbols.

PRAISE AND PRAYER

Worship is more than an emotional "turn on."[3] It includes offering ourselves to God to be his servants and to do his will – nothing more, nothing less and nothing else. It means that we radically change our goals. We choose basic life goals that are centred in God: to know him better, to love him with all our being, to do his will at any cost, to glorify him, and to please him.

In the Bible, prayer is worship that includes all the attitudes of the human spirit as we approach God. We worship God through adoration, confession, praise and supplication. This highest activity of which the human spirit is capable may also be thought of as communion with God, so long as due emphasis is laid upon divine initiative. A person prays because God has already touched his or her spirit.

Prayer in the Bible is not a natural response – it is borne of God's Spirit (see John 4:24). Consequently, the Lord does not "hear" every prayer (Isa. 1:15, 29:13). The biblical doctrine of prayer emphasises the character of God, the necessity of a person's being in saving or covenant relation with God, and that person's entering fully into all the privileges and obligations of that relationship with God.

IMPERATIVE OF A CLEANSED LIFE

God is a holy God. Nothing unholy can come into God's presence. So our communion with God will be conditional based on an attitude of repentance and confession of all known sin. "If I cherish sin in my heart the Lord will not hear me" (Ps. 66:18).

Sin has clouded our perspective. Our vision is distorted. Our values are corrupt. Only as we let the word of God sink deep into our will are we able to see sin for the horror it is! Only then will we know that no step is too drastic to deal with it.

James says, "The prayer of a righteous man is powerful and effective" (James 5:16). God outlines the way to find forgiveness and healing of the nation through prayer: "If my people, who are called by my name, will humble themselves and pray and seek my face and turn from their wicked ways, then will I hear from heaven and will forgive their sin and will heal their land" (2 Chron. 7:14).

PRAYER AS SPIRITUAL WARFARE

In 2 Corinthians 10:3–4 Paul writes that we have been given "divine power to demolish strongholds." A stronghold is founded when we believe a lie, implanting it in our minds. When we justify and strengthen it with reason and argument, it soon becomes a stronghold. Strongholds can only be pulled down through prayer and obedience. We must replace them with truth and destroy the arguments supporting the strongholds. Prayer, in this sense, is therefore warfare against all that is deceitful and false.

The whole of the Christian life is spiritual warfare. Thus we are called to take up the whole armour of God and stand (Eph. 6:10–17). Each piece of armour stands for a Christian characteristic or discipline: truth is the belt, righteousness is the breastplate, and so on. Prayer, however, is not mentioned as a piece of the armour. The exhortations to prayer (vv. 18–20) indicate that prayer is the attitude in which warfare takes place rather than a weapon. This passage, then, should not be understood as a basis for a type of warfare prayer against territorial spirits as advocated by some, nor can Paul's actual prayers in Ephesians (1:17–19 and 3:14–19). These prayers are instead traditional humble petitions addressed to God rather than aggressive attacks on Artemis, the alleged territorial spirit of Ephesus.

We recognise that there is of course much more about spiritual warfare in Scripture than what is found in Ephesians. Revelation reflects at length on our battle against Satan. But God has already won the battle in Christ. We are called upon to hold the ground that Christ won at such cost. "Christians are not working towards victory, but from victory already achieved."[4] This is beautifully illustrated by an event in Billy Graham's ministry. While the choir was singing at a crusade in Chicago, several hundred Satan worshippers sought to force their way to the stage to disrupt the event. The mayor of Chicago offered police assistance, which is against Graham's policy for crusades. Instead, he interrupted the choir to inform the audience of the attempt. As the Satanists came forward, Graham asked the people to surround them and love them. Graham relates:

> I will never forget that moment! Hundreds of young Christians rose to their feet and did exactly as I had asked. Some grabbed hands and began to sing. Others put their arms around the Satan worshippers and began to pray for them. Others calmly shared their faith with them. Everyone else in McCormick Place sat praying as God's Spirit moved through his people

to confound the work of Satan in our midst. I stood watching in silence. I waited and prayed until peace was restored and the service could resume.[5]

The same think happened again in Oakland, California, with the same results. Graham concludes:

The power of those Christian young people came not in the impact of evil and violent force, but in their quiet, loving, prayerful resolution.[6]

Tozer's test of all religious experience

It is critical that Christians take full advantage of every provision God has made to save us from delusion, including worship, prayer, faith, constant meditation on the Scriptures, obedience, humility, disciplined thinking and the illumination of the Holy Spirit.

Strange as it may seem, the danger today is greater for fervent Christians than for the lukewarm and the self-satisfied. Seekers after God's best things are eager to hear anyone who offers a way by which they can obtain them, particularly if it is presented by someone with an attractive personality and a reputation for superior godliness.

How do we test contemporary experiences and teachings? Tozer explains a series of questions for this purpose. The way to check an experience or impulse spiritually is to query how it affects our attitude toward and my relation with (1) God, (2) Christ, (3) the Holy Scriptures, (4) self, (5) other Christians, (6) the world and (7) sin.[7]

The first vital question of all religious experience is, How does it affect our relation to God, our concept of God and our attitude towards him? Any doctrine, any experience that serves to magnify God is likely to be inspired by him.

The second question is, How has this new experience affected our attitude towards the Lord Jesus Christ? He must stand at the centre of all true doctrine, all acceptable practice and all genuine Christian experience. Christless Christianity sounds contradictory, but it exists as a real phenomenon in our day.

The third question is, How does it affect our attitude towards the Holy Scripture? Did this new experience, this new view of truth, spring out of the Word of God itself? Whatever originates outside the Scriptures should for that very reason be suspect until it can be shown to be in accord with them. The Spirit of truth cannot and does not operate apart from the letter of the Holy Scriptures. For this reason a growing acquaintance with the Holy Spirit will always mean an increasing love for the Bible

The fourth question is, How has this affected our life? We can prove the quality of religious experience by its effect on the self, on our life. A good rule to apply is to examine the experience in light of humility. Those that serve to humble us are more likely of God. Those that give us a feeling of self-satisfaction are more likely false and should be dismissed as originating from self or the Devil.

The fifth question is, How has it affected our relation to and our attitude towards our fellow Christians? Any religious experience that fails to deepen our love for our fellow Christians may safely be written off as spurious (1 John 3:18–19; 4:7–8; 5:1; John 13:35).

The sixth question is, How has it affected our relation to and our attitude towards the world? Here "the world" refers to the world of carnal enjoyments, of godless pleasures, of the pursuit of earthly riches and reputation and sinful happiness.

The final question to test the genuineness of Christian experience is, How has it affected our attitude towards sin? Whatever makes holiness more attractive and sin more intolerable may be accepted as genuine (Titus 2:11–13).

The heart of worship and prayer

Moses spoke to God face to face. John White comments that two things dominated his prayer: his tender concern for the nation he led, and his passionate jealousy for the reputation of his God.[8] He was a man torn between his love for God and his love for his people. Worship and prayer, then, can be said to cause us to reflect God's heart and also to reflect God's glory.

Reflecting God's heart

On Mount Sinai, covered with mist and smoke, Moses was in the immediate presence of God. The people had fallen into idolatry. Appalled at their fickleness, Moses sent the Levites slashing through their ranks, killing 3,000 of them in a horrible, bloody orgy. He heard God say, "Now leave me alone so that my anger may burn against them and that I may destroy them. Then I will make you into a great nation" (Exod. 32:10). Was God testing him? What a temptation to get rid of the undisciplined mob and begin afresh with Moses!

Moses was, however, determined to plead for mercy, even if he had to give his own life for them. "O LORD," he said, "why should

your anger burn against your people, whom you brought out of Egypt
with great power and a mighty hand?" He continued: "Why should
the Egyptians say, 'It was with evil intent that he brought them out,
to kill them in the mountains and to wipe them off the face of the
earth'?" (Exod. 32:12).

Have we ever prayed like this? More often we have gone our way
totally unconcerned by the judgements of God that threaten our
people. Have we experienced the burning holiness of God, who is a
consuming fire? How we need to pray with the boldness and passion
of Moses! Our faith rests not in anything we can do, but upon the
unchanging, covenant-keeping God. And God delighted in his servant Moses, in whom he had found one who reflected the compassion of his own heart.

And so through history God has found men and women who have
interceded powerfully for the people and moved God to intervene
and act strongly on their behalf. One was Abraham, called the friend
of God, who dared to stand before the Angel of the Lord to plead on
behalf on Sodom and Gomorrah. Another was Hannah, who brought
forth a priestly son in answer to prayer. A third was Job, who, in an
age where prayers were self-centred for self-gratification, stands out
as one who, stripped of everything that he owned, could declare
"The LORD gave and the LORD has taken away; may the name of the
LORD be praised" (Job 1:21).

We have similar saints of God today who make us hang our heads
in shame at the coldness of our heart for our Saviour. Gladys Staines
was the wife in the Australian missionary family recently martyred
in India. When the burned bodies of her husband and sons were
brought to her, she said: "I forgive the murderers of my husband and
sons." The expression of the reality of her faith had a greater impact
than all the preaching preceding it in India.

REFLECTING HIS GLORY

I am amazed by the prayer of Moses, "Now show me your glory"
(Exod. 33:18). What a prayer! Did he not have much prayer with
God? Did he not commune with God often on Mount Sinai? Did not
God work mighty signs through him? Yet he was called the meekest
man in all the earth. He could not have enough of God. He wanted
more and more! I have made this my prayer ever since. "Lord, show
me too thy glory. Never let me be complacent in my walk with you.
Show me more and more of thy glory!"

Then a wonderful thing happened. When Moses came down from
the mountain, unknown to him, his face shone with the glory of the

Lord with whom he had been (Exod. 34:29). He reflected the glory of God. As we spend time in God's presence, it is God who gives us that seal and the stamp of his own presence with us, so that others take heed we have been with Jesus (2 Cor. 3:18). John White remarks that the church today "could do with a few men and women with shining skin on their faces"![9]

Conclusion

In worship and prayer we struggle and learn to transcend and overcome the wiles of the Devil, the snares of the world and the lusts of our own fleshly desires. We Christians can lose if we do not give God preeminence in our life, or if we switch sides or quit.

We will face many struggles, and perhaps even death, but we can face them knowing our victory in Christ is secure. Let me close by illustrating this reality with a story from India told to me by a friend. Mr. Das, her father-in-law, was a high-ranking government officer in the days of the British in India. He was out on an inspection tour of the forest reserves, and it was getting late. He decided to spend the night in one of the government rest houses. As he arrived there, the caretaker came running out trembling with fear. He stuttered "Sahib, you cannot stay here. A huge python has entered the living room and is still there! I have fastened all the windows and doors."

Mr. Das always carried a rifle with him. Now he took it and saw that there was just one bullet in it. He gave it to the caretaker and said: "There is only one bullet. Take careful aim and shoot the python in the head." Opening a window, the caretaker saw the python coiled around the furniture. With bated breath and nervous fingers, he took aim and shot the python in the head.

The wounded python reeled and thrashed out. It was dying! But in its death throes it destroyed every bit of furniture in that room. Terrified, they watched. For one hour the violence and destruction they saw was incredible. Finally, the python's energy subsided and it dropped dead.

Mr. Das explained the events as a parable. The python is like Satan, the serpent. Christ shot the fatal bullet by his death on the cross. Satan, now dying, is furious and violent. Though defeated, he is still destructive. But his time is limited – his final hour is almost up.

Jesus is the victor. Since we belong to him, we no longer strive for victory. I praise God that as I continue to learn to appropriate this wonderful truth in my own life, I am entering a new dimension of worship and prayer. As the whole of creation proclaims in Revelation 5:3, "To him who sits on the throne and to the Lamb be praise and honour and glory and power, for ever and ever!"

Notes

[1] A. W. Tozer, *Gems from Tozer: Extracts from the Writings of A. W. Tozer (1897–1963)* (Harrisburg, Pa.: Christian Publications, 1979), 13–15.

[2] Leadership Ministries Worldwide, *What the Bible Says to the Minister* (Chattanooga, Tenn.: Leadership Ministries Worldwide, 1991), 56.

[3] Ruth Myers, *Thirty-one Days of Praise* (Singapore: The Navigators, 1992).

[4] Leon Morris, *The Book of Revelation*, Tyndale New Testament Commentaries (Leicester, England: Inter-Varsity Press, 1987), 157.

[5] Billy Graham, *Storm Warning* (Dallas, Tex.: Word Publishing, 1992), 146.

[6] Ibid., 146–47.

[7] Tozer, *Gems from Tozer*, 57–64.

[8] John White, *Daring to Draw Near: People in Prayer* (Downers Grove, Ill.: InterVarsity Press, 1978), 48.

[9] Ibid., 40.

18

Spiritual conflict
and folk religion

David G. Burnett

Suffering, misfortune and evil are part of human life. How these are understood and explained varies, as do the methods used to alleviate the problems. The major world religions have addressed the matter in philosophical arguments, but for most people in the world these explanations fail to address the practical aspects of daily life: Why is my wife sick? Why did my well run dry? Why did this accident happen to my son? For these people, answers are sought in the realm of the non-empirical. Important questions are then raised concerning the whole issue of spiritual conflict as understood by Christians. In looking at folk religion and the way it has been addressed by Western missionaries, we should explore some of the causes of misfortune assumed in many folk communities and consider some common means of protection used in folk religion against evil forces. These raise significant issues that Christians must address in the current discussion of folk religion and strategic-level spiritual warfare (SLSW).

Folk religion

During the late nineteenth century, Western scholars categorised religious traditions into major collections labelled Hinduism, Mohammedism (later, more respectfully, Islam), Buddhism, and so on. These religions of major civilisations were therefore considered world religions based partly upon a respect for these civilisations and the literacy of the religious tradition. However, such categories created gaps, and into these gaps were gathered heaps of intransigent phenomena. Rosalind Shaw argues that in religious studies, these residual categories were classed as "tribal religion" or "primitive religions"; later "traditional religion" and "primal religion" were employed in this typology.[1] The category *traditional religions* therefore tends to be the catch phrase for all "other" religious expressions, from whatever part of the world they may originate. Harold Turner made deliberate use of such a distinction when he defined primal religions as those that "have preceded and contributed to the other great religious systems."

In the 1950s Robert Redfield pointed out that peasants in Latin America, whilst stating their allegiance to the Roman Catholic Church, manifested many of the beliefs and practices of traditional religions.[2] In order to discuss the religious nature of peasant society, Redfield employed a two-tier model with the concepts of the "great" and the "little" traditions. The great tradition is the culture of the priests, theologians and literary people who live mainly in the great cities. Although it is the most respected and authoritative, it is usually only followed by the educated elite. In contrast, the little tradition is the religion of the majority of villagers who are essentially illiterate and have little access to the teaching of the Bible.[3] Redfield never suggested that these traditions were totally separate, but he argued that they were like "two currents of thought and action, distinguishable, yet ever flowing into and out of each other."[4] One may understand this as three permeable bands: *philosophical world religion, folk religion* and finally *traditional religion*. The latter two bands are distinguished by whether or not the people acknowledge an allegiance to a world religion. The middle band is usually a reworking of long-existing beliefs within the confession of the major religion.

This model has become popular among Christian missionaries because it is a simple way of explaining the differences they have observed between philosophical and local aspects of major religious traditions.[5] Norman Allison, for example, proposed the following characterisation of "high" and "low" religion (see Table 18-1).[6]

High religions are essentially philosophical in their explanation whilst folk beliefs are based upon the existing worldview into which the teaching of the world religion is incorporated. Thus, as far as this chapter is concerned, many of the issues relating to spiritual conflict in traditional religions are found in folk religion. The people look for explanations and answers different from those offered by

Table 18-1

High Religion	Low Religion
Answers cosmic questions: origin of the universe, meaning to life	Answers everyday issues: sickness, drought, war
Written texts with fixed system of beliefs	No written text – myths and rituals
Specialist leadership roles	Informal leadership, no specialists
Central institutions: church, mosque, temple, and formal training of leaders	Few formal institutions
Formalised moral code	Pragmatic

Source: Norman Allison, "Make Sure You're Getting Through," Evangelical Missions Quarterly *20 (1984): 167–68*

the philosophical religion. For example, when some misfortune comes to villagers in India, their neighbours will attribute this to bad actions *(karma)* in a previous life in accordance with the teaching of the higher tradition. However, frequently the person concerned may reject this explanation and attribute the misfortune not to bad *karma* but to sorcery or the evil eye of a jealous neighbour. One of the common influences of the world religion is the introduction of new symbols of spiritual power that can be applied to traditional methods. The use of the sacred text of the great tradition is often adopted into the folk tradition, as are distinct religious symbols and rituals. This religious syncretism occurs within all major religions, including Christianity.

Paul Hiebert raised the issue of the excluded middle.[7] The Enlightenment worldview resulted in a distinction between mind and body, spirit and matter. "The result was a secularisation of science and a mystification of religion."[8] Science dealt with the empirical

Figure 18-1

High religion	➤	Formal Christianity
Folk beliefs	➤	?
Traditional science	➤	Modern science

Source: Paul Hiebert, "The Flaw of the Excluded Middle," Missiology *10 (1982): 35–48.*

world using mechanical analogies and religion became based upon private faith. The middle zone became marginalised as superstition. Western missionaries adopted the Enlightenment worldview in the nineteenth and twentieth centuries. Missionary work therefore became focused along two levels: arguing that Christianity is the most rational of religions, and providing education and technology to meet social needs. Magic and folk beliefs were generally discounted, and it was assumed that they would die out with further education.

The surprise was that these traditional beliefs did not die out but often became compartmentalised. While much of life is lived as a member of the global technological society, when things go wrong the people turn to traditional practices. In recent years scholars have shown how political, social and economic changes have often given rise to beliefs and practices centred on occult forces.[9] It is in the realm of folk belief that much of the discussion of spiritual warfare has its context, and it often revolves around theodicy – the problem and cause of evil.

Causes of misfortune in folk religion

Why do bad things happen? I am going to use the general term "misfortune" for those things that people consider to be evil, bad and are the cause of suffering. There is always a danger of oversimplifying the situation and imposing alien categories upon other societies. However, there are two common causes of evil found in most societies: those attributed to spiritual beings and those to human beings. It is important that these aspects always be seen as part of the wider culture and not as distinct elements. To fail to appreciate this means a failure to appreciate the underlying fears and beliefs that are inherent within the society as a whole.

SPIRITUAL BEINGS

Although a belief in a Supreme Being who is the creator is common to most traditional religions, that being is usually considered as distant and unconcerned with human affairs. It is the lesser gods and spirits that are bound up with human experience and require shrines, images, priests and rituals to placate them. These deities are neither totally good nor totally evil. Some of the spirits are regarded as of greater importance than others, and some may be more popular at one time than others. These beings may range from powerful spirits, which must be treated with respect, to relatively insignificant spirits of the forest, field or water, who may merely cause a nuisance. Often such deities are associated with certain geographical areas or natural phenomena. A river may be associated with a particular god, or a tree perceived as the dwelling of a specific spirit, or even a dark valley feared as the abode of demons. Occasionally, there is a territorial association of the spiritual beings, as described by David Lan in his study of the Dande of Zimbabwe.[10]

Ghosts and ancestors are a class of spiritual beings that are often believed to cause harm. Harm often results from a "bad death," such as death as a result of suicide, murder, execution or untimely death. This may lead to considerable fear so the house may be abandoned in case the ghost will return and cause harm. However, more often a diviner is called in to identify the cause of death. Once the cause has been identified some offering may be necessary to pacify the ghost and encourage it to leave and cause no more harm to the people. Amongst the Bimoba of Ghana, one of the worst forms of bad death is that of a woman dying during childbirth with the baby undelivered. In this case the woman's room is broken down, every trace of it is cleared, and all her belongings are thrown away. No funeral ceremony can be performed in such cases, for the (ghost) refuses to go to the high god; it just wanders about.[11]

Many societies believe that ghosts may materialise in some form that can be seen by the living. In northern India, for example, the *bhut* are believed to be able to appear at night in the form of human beings. There are two notable differences: first, they do not cast a shadow, and second, their feet point backwards. In the villages of India the fear of ghosts is strong and people avoid being in isolated fields when night has come. It is easy to consider this a result of superstitions and a lack of education, but many Western people have similar fears in dark and isolated areas. Another common belief is the possibility of a person becoming possessed by a wandering ghost. A *bhut* may lay hold of any passer-by that may have unwittingly trespassed within its domain or roused its interest. The ghost is said to "lay hold of" the person, and the victim has to resort to exorcism for deliverance.

Francis X. Hezel, S.J., recounts the following story of a young women from Chuuk (the most populous state of the Federated States of Micronesia) who was possessed by an ancestor:

An incident involving Fermina, the 15-year-old daughter of devout Christian parents, is rather typical. One evening a few years ago she went to bed complaining of a pain in her stomach. By the next morning her body was twitching uncontrollably and she was seized with convulsions. As the family gathered around her mat to comfort her, they heard her suddenly reprimand a much older male relative, angrily telling him, "Leave the house, because I don't like what you are doing." The words came from Fermina's mouth, but the voice was that of her mother, who had died a year or two earlier. Fermina recovered within two or three days of the incident, but she has had similar experiences a few times since this one.[12]

Possession by a spirit or ghost is an important aspect of spiritual conflict and will be returned to later.

An important question that must be considered is how these spiritual beings are conceived within Christian theology. Paul addresses this issue in 1 Corinthians 8 and 10. He affirms that there is no God but the one true God (8:4). However, he recognises the existence of other gods and lords, but in a qualitatively different way.[13] Christians have generally regarded local gods and spirits to be manifestations of Satan and his demons. This does not necessarily mean that a local deity is a demon in some symbolic form. As with culture, there is that which is good and bad and even demonic in all religions. The demonic may well contextualise itself to each religion taking on forms and expressions that will cause the greatest degree of evil and destruction.

One cannot deny the real sense of fear and awe found among adherents of religious traditions; thus the cultural reality of these deities must be acknowledged. However, this does not mean that these deities have an ontological reality. A distinction must be made between the "cultural truth" believed by the local people that particular deities exist, and "ontological truth" that assumes the existence of the demonic that contextualises itself to specific cultures.

Often when a society has converted to a major world religion the "High God" has been associated with the deity of the world religion. Christian translators have often used the name of the High God to translate the word Yahweh in the Scriptures, and the lesser deities have often been ignored, being considered as some manifestation of demons. Likewise, occasionally, a particular deity has been associated with Satan. For example, among the Yoruba, the Supreme Being, Olodumare, is often seen as similar to a traditional king who works through his ministers.[14] Within Yoruba tradition there is no marked duality between good and evil. Esu is the messenger to the world above and is everywhere observing and reporting to the divine. He may deceive people into doing wrong, thus necessitating that they offer sacrifices in order to regain the favour of the gods. He is often represented in the form of a human figure with horns and a nearby club or knife. Esu is considered as the power of mischief and has been aligned by Christians and Muslims with Satan.

In her study of the Ewe of Ghana, Birgit Meyer showed the confusion missionaries caused to the Ewe by claiming that God was good and that the Devil was responsible for all the evil in the world.[15] This made little sense to the people, because they had always thought of spiritual beings as ambivalent beings:

> In the Ewe's encounter with Pietist missionaries conversion did not bring about what professional theologians and social scientists tend to expect, namely rationalisation and disenchantment. . . . In the context of Pietist (and also Pentecostalist) missionaries who approach the world in terms of the dualism between God and Satan, new converts tend to adopt a variant of Protestantism, emphasising the image of the Devil and transforming gods and ghosts into "Christian" demons.[16]

The missionaries therefore demonised the lesser gods and spirits and brought about a radical dualism in the cosmology of the Christian converts. This seems to have actually increased the fear of demons, and many people attribute to spirit influence their own failure to achieve economic progress.

Human beings

A common starting point for the discussion of witchcraft and sorcery has been the observations of E. E. Evans-Pritchard among the Azande of Southern Sudan. Evans-Pritchard noted a distinction between witchcraft and sorcery.[17] Although this distinction is useful, it is necessary to recognise that in many societies no such simple separation can be made. It does, however, provide a vocabulary to start discussing this subject.

Among the Azande, witchcraft is seen as the cause of most misfortunes that can affect an individual. Witchcraft can be the cause of sickness, accident, failure of the crops, failure in hunting and general lack of success. For example, if a man is careful to take all the normal precautions but still wounds himself with his cutlass whilst clearing a field, he assumes that this must be the result of witchcraft. The notion of coincidence, or probability, is not a sufficient answer. There must be a reason why this has happened to this individual, and for the Azande, witchcraft is the obvious answer. However, this does not mean that the people are unaware of a technological element to the whole incident. Imagine that two people sat under a small food granary, which suddenly collapses, killing them. A Western perspective may say that termites had eaten the supports, which unfortunately gave way while the two men were seated under it. The Azande would say that while witchcraft is not necessarily the cause of the collapse, it is responsible for the conjunction of the collapse and the people sitting underneath. As Evans-Pritchard says, "The attribution of misfortune to witchcraft does not exclude what we call its real causes, but is superimposed on them and gives to social events their moral value."[18] The Azande believe that witchcraft is inherited from one's parents. If a man is a witch, the substance will be passed on to his sons; likewise a mother to her daughters. The witchcraft substance, called *mangu*, is considered to be a definite physical part of the body that resides near the liver or gall bladder of the person. This substance can be discovered by autopsy.

The Comaroffs have shown that most of the missionaries who came to sub-Saharan Africa from Europe in the nineteenth century were imbued with a secular perspective, especially with regards to witchcraft.[19] According to Western missionaries, sickness and disease were caused not by witchcraft but by bacteria, parasites and viruses. A cure was effected by Western medicine and education. Witchcraft was considered not to exist, so Christians were to ignore it. Where Christianity became the dominant force in a region, this view was outwardly accepted, but often belief in witchcraft was merely driven underground. This is another example of the flaw of the excluded middle.

A second position that has been adopted by Christian missionaries mainly from Pentecostal churches is that witchcraft is demonic and the accused need to be delivered. Today, among the Charismatic churches in Africa and many other areas of the world, witchcraft is dealt with by vigorous prayer leading to the exorcism of the spirit. Witchcraft is perceived as one of the manifestations of the work of Satan in the community, and it is part of the spiritual warfare that the Christian is obliged to carry on. This is considered as a direct encounter between the power of God and the power of evil. Public confession of sin is required, after which the person is encouraged to receive the cleansing blood of Christ and the enduing power of the Holy Spirit.

Harriet Hill, a missionary who has worked for many years in Côte d'Ivoire, has proposed a third option.[20] She argues that witchcraft concepts correspond to what in the West are regarded as psychic powers that may be dealt with by living a pure life:

It can therefore be considered neutral in the same way that intellectual power, physical power, and emotional power are accepted as neutral. We do not automatically assign them to God or to the devil. . . . If this is an accurate assessment of witchcraft, then we need to speak out against the evil use of witchcraft rather than against witchcraft itself. The key message, then, is, love thy neighbor, live a pure life, and renounce evil in all its forms. Do not give Satan a foothold. . . . In the end, then, we find we are no different from our African brothers and sisters after all. Do we not all struggle with jealousy, envy, and hatred?[21]

Christians must address the issue of witchcraft, but not merely in terms of spiritual warfare. Witch-crazes result from social trauma, as seen in the witch trials of Medieval Europe and Salem as well as Africa. Christians need also to engage with the social issues that are afflicting a society by finding ways of helping the poor and by challenging corrupt and unjust systems.

Sorcery is Evans-Pritchard's second category. He considered it to differ from witchcraft in that it is a deliberate, conscious act of an individual, or group of individuals, to harm another by non-empirical means. It can express itself in various forms including the evil eye, curses and black magic.

Alan Dundes defined the evil eye as "a fairly consistent and uniform folk belief complex based upon the idea that an individual, male or female, has the power, voluntarily or involuntarily, to cause harm to another individual or his property merely by looking at or praising that person or property."[22] All over the Muslim world the evil eye *(nazar)* is considered to be a frequent cause of misfortune. According to Arab proverbs, the evil eye empties the house and fills the graves (or, the evil eye owns two-thirds of the graveyard).[23] The eye is regarded not only as an instrument for transmitting evil wishes but also as an originating source of injurious power. This power need not be a voluntary act but can work automatically from a person desiring something of another. Thus, a man blind in one eye is assumed to be envious of another man with two good eyes, and a barren woman envious of a woman with many children. The danger is considered to be even greater if it is accompanied with speech that expresses admiration or envy. A mother would feel great fear if a European woman was to smile at her baby and compliment her on a lovely baby. This may be normal practice in Europe, but in North Africa it could be regarded as the exercise of the evil eye.

The concept of uttering curses or blessings appears universal among human societies. To appreciate the concept behind these oral expressions, it is necessary to realise that in the traditional worldview words are not viewed merely as vibrations in the air. Words which are said deliberately and with intention take on a reality of their own that can bring about the desires of the speaker. India, especially, has developed an elaborate cosmology of sound in the use of mantras that are considered to establish a relationship between the cosmos and the magician. The effectiveness of the curse is dependent upon several factors: the intensity of the desire, the manner of its expression and the personality of the curser. Behind the spoken word stands the personality of the one who expresses the words. The greater the personality of the speaker, the greater the effectiveness of the spell. Thus, if a god, or his devotee, utters a curse in his name, the effect will be very great indeed. This is reflected in the Old Testament passages in which God says to Adam, "Cursed is the ground because of you" (Gen. 3:17). The curse here is God's judgement against sin. For this reason, calling upon the name of a deity, often strengthens a curse, or blessing.

Among some Christians there is a growing tendency to ascribe certain events and circumstances to the influence of curses. Derek Prince's *Blessing or Curse: You Can choose!* is an example. The comment on the back cover reads, "Blessing and curses . . . are vehicles of supernatural spiritual power. . . . They tend to continue from generation to generation."[24] Is this a biblical position or, as some would suggest, a distortion of the Scriptures?[25]

These beliefs often result from the jealousy one person may have towards another. This is why anthropologists have often considered witchcraft and sorcery to act as a means of social control as well as to explain misfortune. The possibility of these spiritual powers generates intense fears even in the hearts of Christian converts and raises the question of how people achieve protection from these sources of evil.

Protection from evil

Misfortunes are part of everyone's life, and they usually leave us perplexed and uncertain as to the cause and the appropriate actions to take. Decisions have to be made, and the results have to be accepted, whether good or ill. How are such decisions made? First, common sense tends to be used to deal with the multitude of little matters, that are part of everyday life. But often people feel the need to draw upon additional resources from some non-empirical source, so they turn to divination.

DIVINATION

The methods used for divination are many, but most involve some sort of ritual or spirit possession.[26] Generally missionaries have dismissed divination as evil but have failed to address the question of with what to replace it. Christians have therefore been left with secularised methods of healing, education and agriculture. However, various methods of divination and foretelling the future continue in all societies. In the UK, 40 per cent of the people regularly read their horoscope.

CHARMS AND RITUAL PROTECTION

Various means are used to protect vulnerable members of the community. Children may, for example, be protected from the evil eye by some ruse. A child may be left unwashed or dressed in rags; a baby boy may be dressed in girl's clothing.[27] These things seek to make the child less attractive, less open to envy, and so divert the evil eye. Another means of protection is the use of charms, of which there are a great many in the Muslim world. Charms made of iron or the claws of a tiger or a bear are thought to be able to resist the influence of the evil eye by some inherent property of the material itself. Muslim women often wear a charm that has the hand of Fatima: an open hand with an image of an eye on the palm. The symbol of the eye itself is regarded as having great power in throwing back evil and is often used in patterns and designs.

These practices are based upon an inherent belief in and fear of the evil power of magic in its various forms. Frequently the Bible comes to take the role of a new powerful charm for the young convert. What is required is not merely a response to one aspect of magic but a radical change in worldview that sees Jesus Christ as Lord over all – visible and invisible (Col. 1:16).

EXORCISM

Where possession is known within a society, there is usually some indigenous means of exorcism to deal with the affliction. There are often recognised exorcists who know appropriate rituals and claim to be endowed by a more powerful spirit. A common aspect of exorcism is the transference of the spirit from the patient to an animal or object. This form of exorcism may provide some cure, but this may only be temporary.

An alternative treatment is to initiate the person into a possession cult.[28] In possession cults the individual comes into a working relationship with the afflicting spirit. The individual remains free from sickness so long as he or she takes part in the periodic cult festivals. During these festivals the person becomes possessed by the spirit, which acts out its particular character. In the course of time, individuals may graduate to a position in which they are in full control of their own spirit and capable of controlling and healing others with similar afflictions.

In folk societies these healers, whether witch doctors, shamans, exorcists or other healers, are considered to play a socially positive role. When people are sick and have no money for Western medicine, or the medicine is ineffective, indicating deeper causes, to whom do they turn? Missionaries have often considered these healers their main opponents, and in some cases they have been. But they have also sometimes been the first to recognise the power of God. How should Christians relate to such healers? Do they cast out Beelzebub by the power of Beelzebub?

Christians have often taken the role of these healers and exorcists. "Demonisation and deliverance" has therefore become an important issue alongside territorial spirits in the debate of SLSW. Some practitioners have made a distinction between possession and demonisation. They would say that non-Christians may be possessed and controlled by spirits. Christians, however, are possessed by Christ but may be demonised and in need of deliverance. Care needs to be exercised in ascribing all such manifestations as being simply demonisation and not psychological or physical.

Current issues for ongoing discussion

First, forces of evil and misfortune are an integral part of folk tradition, and the people need to see Christianity not merely as a satisfying theology but as the power of God to deal with the issues they face in their world. Teaching on spiritual warfare must be part of a holistic approach to mission and theology. Just as in the 1970s the Lausanne movement did much to unite evangelism and social action into a more holistic approach to mission, now there is a need to integrate spiritual warfare into the whole. It should be word, works and wonders!

Stephen Hayes writes:

Over 200 people who were accused of being witches were burnt to death in South Africa between the beginning of 1994 and mid-1995. These killings were not legal executions, but took place at the hands of lynch mobs, mostly from the communities in which the accused lived.[29]

Hayes concludes that this increased fear of witchcraft is a result of the social tensions that have been experienced in South Africa in recent years. Bawa Yamba made a similar observation in a recent study on witch-finding in Zambia in the face of HIV-transmitted disease and AIDS.[30] There is a need for an approach that relates the social, economic and personal, not merely seeing the demonic as the sole cause of evil.

Second, Christians have to relate to the beliefs of their own particular cultural context. Although we accept the influence of Satan within all human societies this does not mean he works in the same way. Local river gods, mountain spirits and village deities are common in folk societies and may all be categorised as "territorial spirits." However, in some societies witchcraft is considered the greatest source of evil, and it not helpful to the people to seek some local territorial spirit as the centre of demonic activity. Christians must accept the ontological truth of the reality of the demonic but must also appreciate the beliefs of the local people as "cultural truth." When Western Christians write and speak about SLSW, these ideas must not be imposed unilaterally upon Christians throughout the world. The members of the church worldwide must humbly listen to one another and place themselves under the authority of Scripture, so avoiding overt speculation.

Third, the New Testament shows that converts who have been involved in magic should destroy the paraphernalia they have used. A frequently quoted example is that of Paul on his visit to Ephesus, where the sorcerers were famous for a particular form of charms known as Ephesian letters. This power encounter is an essential rite of separation from old ways and entry into the new life in Christ. However, there is a danger of this being perceived as Christian magic or stimulating an unnecessary interest in spirits. God is not merely more powerful than Satan but has a radically different nature. As Paul Hiebert has continually argued, when Christ was suffering on the cross he could have called down legions of angels to establish his kingdom. The Cross is the demonstration of victory through weakness, of love over hate and of God's way over that of Satan.[31]

Fourth, Christians should be aware of the changing social context throughout the world. Frequently those accused of being witches were people at the fringes of society, such as an old widow living on her own, or minority groups who had become scapegoats for the social tensions. However, there are major changes occurring, as illustrated in Nigeria.

> In the past elderly women with ugly wrinkled skin were more likely to be accused of witchcraft. The belief was that the older wife acquired witchcraft to attack her husband because he no longer cared for her now that he had a younger wife or a more attractive and fertile co-wife. Today the story is different as all categories of people – young and old, male and female, students and civil servants – are believed to be involved in witchcraft.[32]

The Christian message should result in the restoration of social harmony through reconciliation and mutual acceptance.

Fifth, there is a danger of Christians becoming preoccupied with spirits and developing an unhealthy interest. Mary Douglas tells a sad story of the Roman Catholic mission working among the Lele of the Republic of Congo.[33] The mission had associated the god of the Lele with Satan of Christian traditions. Whereas before the Lele had believed in one god, the universe now seemed to be controlled by two deities, one good and one bad. The priests of the old religion, including the herbalists, were classed as sorcerers and seen as Satan's servants. As most of the younger people had been baptised in the church and educated in the mission schools, the youth increasingly derided the traditions of their parents and grandparents. This resulted in a tension between younger and older generations. Newly ordained Catholic priests began persecuting the practitioners of the traditional religion. Eventually the mission began to run its own anti-sorcery cult to detect and expose all sorcerers. The practice of the movement resulted in physical abuse and accusation of the old, the handicapped and mentally defective. When the anti-sorcery activities came to the attention of the bishop, he promptly suspended the young priests from their duties and sent them overseas for two years. Douglas concludes with a significant warning.

> Contemporary Western theology is not attuned to answering the questions that plague Africans about the causes of evil in the world, the causes of sickness and death, questions which their pagan traditions answer all too plausibly in terms of sorcery. On this there is a block, or a gap, a pregnant silence.[34]

Sixth, one must recognise that within our global society, literature, video, and the Internet are allowing the exchange of ideas from East and West, North and South. This is resulting in new movements in the teaching on SLSW, which are at times highly speculative. The booklets and videos made by Christians in West Africa demonstrate popular beliefs that are found among Christians in that area. Christians must maintain a balance between secular scepticism and the adoption of animistic beliefs.[35]

Conclusion

Christians from a background of folk religion need to develop a worldview and theology that acknowledges the demonic. However, the demonic should not preoccupy them. They, like all Christians, need to have their eyes fixed upon the Lord Jesus Christ, who has all power and authority. There is a radical nature of the kingdom of God that manifests not merely the power of God but the *shalom* of God that transforms people and societies.

Notes

[1] Rosalind Shaw, "The Invention of African Traditional Religion," *Religion* 20 (1990): 339–53.

[2] Robert Redfield, *Peasant Society and Culture* (Chicago: University of Chicago Press, 1956).

[3] Robert Redfield, *The Little Tradition* (Chicago: Chicago University Press, 1955).

[4] Ibid., 72.

[5] Bill Musk, *The Unseen Face of Islam* (Eastbourne: Monarch 1992).

[6] Norman Allison, "Make Sure You're Getting Through," *Evangelical Missions Quarterly* 20 (1984): 167–68. Recently Paul Hiebert, Daniel Shaw and Tite Tienou have developed this perspective (*Understanding Folk Religion* [Grand Rapids, Mich.: Baker, 1999], 73–89).

[7] Paul G. Hiebert, "The Flaw of the Excluded Middle," *Missiology* 10 (1982): 35–48.

[8] Hiebert, Shaw and Tienou, *Understanding Folk Religion*, 89.

[9] Rosalind Shaw, "The Politician and the Diviner: Divination and the Consumption of Power in Sierra Leone," *Journal of Religion in Africa* 26 (1996): 30–55; Umar H. D. Danfulani, "Exorcising Witchcraft: The Return of the Gods in New Religious Movements on the Jos Plateau and the Benue Regions of Nigeria," *African Affairs* 98 (1999), 167–93.

[10] David Lan, *Guns and Rain: Guerrillas and Spirit Mediums in Zimbabwe* (London: James Curry, 1987).

[11] Peter Barker, *Peoples, Languages, and Religion in Northern Ghana: A Preliminary Report* (Accra, Ghana: GEC, 1986), 164.

[12] Francis X. Hezel, "Spirit Possession in Chuuk: A Socio-cultural Interpretation," *The Micronesian Counsellor Occasional Papers* 11 (July 1993).

[13] Clinton E. Arnold, *Powers of Darkness* (Leicester, England: Inter-Varsity Press, 1992), 94–98.

[14] E. Bolaji Idowu, *Olodumare: God in Yoruba Belief* (London: Longmans, 1962).

[15] Birgit Meyer, *Translating the Devil: Religion and Modernity Among the Ewe in Ghana* (Edinburgh: Edinburgh University Press, 1999).

[16] Ibid., 110.

[17] E. E. Evans-Pritchard, *Witchcraft, Oracles and Magic Among the Azande* (Oxford: Clarendon Press, 1976).

[18] Ibid., 70.

[19] John and Jean Comaroff, *Of Revelation and Revolution: Christianity, Colonialism and Consciousness in South Africa* (Chicago: Chicago University Press, 1991).

[20] Harriet Hill, "Witchcraft and the Gospel: Insights from Africa," *Missiology* 24 (1996): 232–344.

[21] Ibid., 337.

[22] Alan Dundes, "Wet and Dry: The Evil Eye," in *The Evil Eye: A Casebook*, ed. Alan Dundes (London: Garland, 1981), 258.

[23] Edward Westermarck, *Pagan Survivals in Mohammedan Civilization* (London: McMillan, 1933), 24.

[24] Derek Prince, *Blessing or Curse: You Can Choose!* (Milton Keynes: Word, 1990).

[25] Mary J. Evans, "'A Plague on Both Your Houses': Cursing and Blessing Reviewed," *Vox Evangelica* 24 (1994): 77–90.

[26] For a detailed list of Bunyoro (Uganda) divination practices, see David G. Burnett, *World of the Spirits* (Tunbridge Wells: Monarch, 2000), chap. 7.

[27] Violet R. Jones and L. Bevan Jones, *Women in Islam* (Lucknow, India: Lucknow Publishing House, 1941), 359–60.

[28] Raymond Prince, "Indigenous Yoruba Psychiatry," in *Magic, Faith and Healing*, ed. Ari Kiev (New York, Free Press, 1974).

[29] Stephen Hayes, "Christian Responses to Witchcraft and Sorcery," *Missionalia* 23 (1995): 339.

[30] Yamba C. Bawa, "Cosmologies in Turmoil: Witchfinding and AIDS in Chiawa, Zambia," *Africa* 67 (1997): 200–223.

[31] Paul G. Hiebert, "Spiritual Warfare and Worldview," http://www.gospelcom.net/lcwe/dufe/Papers/Hiebert.htm (May 2000).

[32] Danfulani, "Exorcising Witchcraft," 170.

[33] Mary Douglas, "Sorcery Accusations Unleashed: The Lele Revisited, 1987," *Africa* 69 (1999): 177–93.

[34] Ibid.

[35] Robert Priest, Thomas Campbell and Bradford A. Mullen, "Missiological Syncretism: The New Animistic Paradigm," in *Spiritual Powers and Missions: Raising the Issues*, ed. Edward Rommen (Pasadena, Calif.: William Carey Library, 1995).

19

Gaining perspective on territorial spirits

A. Scott Moreau

In North American Christian circles the novels of Frank Peretti did not so much chart a new direction in thinking as they described the path many were already walking. Over the past several years, as I have spoken to various groups on spiritual warfare, I have taken informal polls. In every group I have polled, at least one-half of the people have read one or more of Frank Peretti's novels – *This Present Darkness, Piercing the Darkness, The Prophet, The Oath,* or *The Visitation.*[1] His works vividly portray angels and demons in fierce battles over schools, towns and whole territories. His best-selling depictions captured the imaginations of many, selling well in both Christian and secular markets.

This follows the North American growing cultural fascination with spirit beings, including angels. Attraction to the demonic among youth was popularised with the rise of the dungeons and dragons type of fantasy games, now in computer game format, as well as in movies which ranged from comedy *(Ghostbusters)* to horror *(The Haunting).* The fascination has not been limited to the demonic; angels (and the afterlife) have also been the subject of movies, television specials and regular network series. Whole sections of secular bookstores have been given over to new titles related to the spirit realm. Web pages advertise psychic angel contacting services (an interesting combination of technology and spiritism which echoes the rise of materialistic magic portrayed by C. S. Lewis in 1961[2]), and angel paraphernalia is being widely sold as good luck charms and protective icons.

Parallel to this development in our culture is the development in Christian and especially mission circles of a fascination with territorial spirits. Peter Wagner even goes so far as to say that in engaging territorial spirits as part of our ministry of setting people free to respond to the gospel, we have introduced a "spiritual technology" which will bring the greatest power boost in the mission of the church since William Carey started the Protestant missions movement at the end of the eighteenth century.[3] Wagner is not alone in advocating strategic-level spiritual warfare prayer against territorial spirits as the single most important strategy we can utilise in reaching the unreached,[4] though he is the most commonly cited authority on the topic.

Here we present the position of those who advocate a more aggressive approach to spiritual warfare through engaging territorial spirits. After presenting their position, we respond with points of appreciation as well as critique in the hopes that we may forward the discussion and ensure biblical integrity in this particular arena of spiritual warfare.

Theological orientation

What do proponents of engaging territorial spirits teach? In a nutshell, what Wagner and others are calling "strategic-level spiritual warfare" (SLSW) is praying against territorial spirits, seeking to "map" their strategies over given locations by discerning their names and what they use to keep people in bondage, and then binding them so that evangelism may go unhindered. "Spiritual mapping" is researching an area and identifying the spirit(s) in charge so that "smart-bomb" praying may loosen their hold over the people, who may then freely come to Christ.[5]

In building a theological foundation, they argue that Satan is not omnipotent or omniscient. Thus, he must delegate responsibilities to spirit rulers who do his will in local contexts.[6] These spirit rulers are also limited and need help in turn. The Bible gives no information as to how many layers this may extend. It is argued that these spirit rulers must be organised in some fashion or else chaos would dominate Satan's efforts to rule the world.[7]

Advocates note that Paul was not unaware of Satan's schemes – he knew them in order to combat them (2 Cor. 2:11). They remind us that Jesus had to bind the strong man before he could plunder the strong man's house. Wagner interprets: "The 'house' is the territory

controlled by Satan, or his delegated spirits, and that territory cannot be taken unless he is bound. But once the territorial spirits are
bound, the kingdom of God can flow into the territory and 'plunder
the strong man's goods,' as it were."[8]

Biblical examples of the types of demonic attachment are report-
edly seen in people (through demonisation), animals (for example,
the pigs in Mark 5:11–13), and idols (1 Cor. 10:20). There are several passages that appear to relate demons to territories. In the Old
Testament, the concept of gods of the nations exercising power in
specific geographic localities, such as the gods of the high places
(some 63 times in the NIV, including Num. 26:30; Deut. 33:29; 1
Kings 3:2; 2 Kings 21:3; 2 Chron. 11:15; Ps. 78:58; Isa. 15:2; Jer.
7:31; Ezek. 6:6; Hos. 10:8; Amos 7:9); the "gods" of the hills vs. the
"gods" of the plains (1 Kings 20:23); the idea that gods could be
established in new locations (2 Kings 17:29–31), and the linking in
Deuteronomy 32:17 of all false gods to demons. The most commonly cited example is Daniel 10–11:1, in which the princes of Persia and Greece appear to be demons in charge of the respective
geopolitical units.[9] We see other possible examples in the LXX of
Deuteronomy 32:8, which states that the nations set according to
the number of angels of God. Finally, we note that another example
given is the demons begging Jesus not to send them out of an area
(Mark 5:10).

More recently, the existence of territorial spirits as defined by the
spiritual-warfare movement has been strongly challenged. Perhaps
Chuck Lowe provides the most thorough and irenic critique. He concludes:

> The evidence cited for SLSW is unconvincing. Scripture pro-
> vides no support, animism is an unreliable guide, and the "case
> study" evidence is anecdotal rather than verified. If arguments
> were counted rather than weighed, the point might be carried.
> But the evidence simply does not pass scrutiny. The absence
> of proof makes it easy to devise exciting hypotheses, but con-
> siderably harder to develop convincing ones. . . .
>
> In the end, it is likely that tutelary spirits exist, and that they
> are not territorial (at least they are not in Scripture, or, for the
> most part, in animism). Probably some are angelic, and others
> demonic. Due to spotty and inconsistent evidence, it is not
> possible to determine how their respective jurisdictions are dif-
> ferentiated.[10]

The Core Ideas and Strategies

A whole new vocabulary has been coined to distinguish strategies, characters, practices and issues related to territorial spirits. Before evaluating such practices associated with territorial spirits, we need to explain them. Wherever possible in the discussion below, we use definitions given by those advocating SLSW and engaging territorial spirits.

IDENTIFICATIONAL REPENTANCE

In its most basic form, this involves corporate repentance for corporate sins. In the case of sins committed by people now dead against people now dead (for example, the slave trade), living representatives of the corporate sinners repent for the sin committed to representatives of those sinned against. Four steps are involved: (1) identify the national sin; (2) confess the sin corporately and ask God for forgiveness; (3) apply Christ's blood; and (4) walk in obedience and repair the damage, a step that may involve changing laws or making suitable payments to effect restitution.[11]

RECONCILIATION WALK

Originated by Lynn Green of YWAM (Youth with a Mission), the reconciliation walk was designed to incorporate the ideas of identificational repentance and prayer journeys (see below). Envisioning thousands of Christians tracing the path of the Crusades and repenting on behalf of the original Crusaders to Muslim populations,

> the aim of the Walk is to bring Christians face to face with Muslims and Jews with a simple message of regret and confession. It is important that the Walk is done in an attitude of reconciliation, without a trace of the arrogant spirit that characterised the Crusades. We must go to pray for the lands crossed by the Crusaders.[12]

LEVELS OF SPIRITUAL WARFARE

Wagner developed an approach to spiritual warfare that involves three levels.[13] The first is *ground-level spiritual warfare*, which refers to casting demons out of believers. The second is *occult-level spiritual warfare*, which refers to "dealing with powers of darkness that are more coordinated and organized than one or more demons who might happen to be afflicting a certain person at a certain time."[14] The third is *strategic-level spiritual warfare*, which

> involves confrontation with the high-ranking territorial spirits which have been assigned by Satan to coordinate the activities of the kingdom of darkness over a certain area in order to keep the people's minds blinded to the "gospel of the glory of Christ" as we read in 2 Corinthians 4:3–4.[15]

PRAYER JOURNEYS

Prayer journeys are essentially field trips to practise prayer walking and, in some cases, to enable better spiritual mapping. Taken as short-term mission trips, they include short visits to strategic cities or sections of cities within a country or continent.

> A prayer journey is a trip taken by believers into one of the 10/40 Window countries [a part of the world from ten degrees north to forty degrees north of the equator, from West Africa to East Asia] to pray for the lost. Team members spend extended time prayerwalking, asking God to bring the Gospel to your Unreached People Group. Prayer journeys focus on praying on-site for your unreached peoples and does not entail evangelism or mercy ministries.[16]

SPIRITUAL MAPPING

One result of this emphasis on territorial spirits is the development of a strategy for evangelism known as spiritual mapping. George Otis, who coined the phrase, notes:

> Spiritual mapping . . . involves . . . superimposing our understanding of forces and events in the spiritual domain onto places and circumstances in the material world. . . .
> Spiritual mapping is a means by which we can see what is beneath the surface of the material world; but it is not magic. It is subjective in that it is a skill born out of a right relationship with God and a love for His world. It is objective in that it can be verified (or discredited) by history, sociological observation and God's Word.[17]

Harold Caballeros concisely summarises the underlying thinking:

We have learned that it is to our advantage to know who the strongman is in order to bind him and divide his spoils. Spiritual mapping helps us identify the strongman. In some cases, spiritual mapping will give us a series of characteristics that will guide us directly to the territorial prince or power. In other cases, we will find ourselves facing a natural person whom Satan is using. In still others, we will find ourselves face-to-face with a corrupt social structure.[18]

Wagner advocates on a city-wide level that we "work with the intercessors especially gifted and called to strategic-level spiritual warfare, seeking God's revelation of: (a) the redemptive gift(s) of the city; (b) Satan's strongholds; (c) territorial spirits assigned to the city; (d) corporate sin; (e) God's plan of attack and timing."[19] Finally, some emphasise a need to discover the names of the territorial spirits as part of the spiritual-mapping process, whether through historical or religious research or by revelation through prayer.[20]

THE QUEEN OF HEAVEN

The most recent development has been Wagner's emphasis on confronting the Queen of Heaven. Originally manifesting and receiving worship as Diana (or Artemis) of Ephesus, he advocates that the Queen of Heaven has taken on many forms in history around the world; she is known in Japan as the Sun Goddess, in Mexico as the Virgin of Guadalupe, in Nepal as Sagarmatha and in Calcutta as Cali.[21] Perhaps most controversially, he maintains that one of her current disguises is that of the Virgin Mary as venerated by Roman Catholics.[22] Ultimately, according to Wagner,

> she is the demonic principality who is most responsible under Satan for keeping unbelievers in spiritual darkness. It could well be that more people are in Hell today because of the influence of the Queen of Heaven than because of any other spiritual influence.[23]

The Queen of Heaven is also said to be "'the great harlot who sits on many waters' in Revelation 17. What are the 'waters'? 'The waters which you saw, where the harlot sits, are peoples, multitudes, nations, and tongues' (Rev. 17:15),"[24] and Beelzebub (Luke 11:22) is a "high ranking principality in the order of the Queen of Heaven."[25] Wagner's most recent emphasis has been the Celebrate Ephesus event, an event orchestrated by revelation given to Wagner through several prayer and ministry partners. In it a variety of forms of SLSW against the Queen of Heaven were practised over the course of several years,[26] culminating in a four-hour praise and worship service in the amphitheatre in Ephesus which held the demonstration for Artemis described in Acts 19. Wagner anticipated that this series of events would break this top-level territorial spirit's stronghold on uncounted millions of people in the 10/40 Window and free them for fruitful harvest.[27]

Approaches to confronting territorial spirits

For those who assert that the concept of territorial spirits is biblical and that we have a responsibility to work against their efforts, a spectrum of prayer approaches may be described.[28]

CONFRONTERS

The more aggressive advocates promote direct and public confrontation of the identified territorial spirits to weaken their hold on the location and enable greater evangelisation. In addition to personal prayer against such spirits by specially anointed individuals, they organise spiritual-mapping projects, prayer journeys and sometimes local praise marches or rallies as means of confrontation.

MODERATES

The more moderate emphasise unity of local leadership, centrality of prayer and priority of dealing with strongholds within the church as preconditions for aggressive prayer against the strongholds.

CONSERVATIVES

Though acknowledging that there is strong scriptural evidence of territorial spirits, conservatives maintain that we do not see in Scripture or church history specific SLSW encounters of the type being described today. They advocate an approach closer to truth encounter in which the local body of Christ manifests repentance and reconciliation in a way that speaks destruction to the powers of darkness, modelled on Paul's letter to the Ephesians.

Response

POINTS OF APPRECIATION

Several points of appreciation for those who advocate SLSW are worthy of note.[29] First, SLSW and the emphasis on territorial spirits take Satan and the powers more seriously than traditional Western approaches.[30] If nothing else, they focus on the power of prayer rather than planning and strategy, and the strategic focuses are not built on finding new ways to generate decisions but on dealing with the demonic. This is a healthy corrective for Western missiology that tends to be too managerial in its orientation.

Second, because of the focus on the spiritual, advocates of SLSW recognise that divisiveness weakens prayer and as a result stress the unity of the church in fulfilling its mission. They seek co-operation rather than competition.

Third, there can be no doubt that SLSW advocates focus on the ultimate goal of saving the lost. Many of the proponents emphasise that the ultimate goal is not casting down spirits, but bringing the lost to Christ.

Fourth, another helpful feature is the recognition of the evil spiritual dimension of culture. All cultures have elements which together work as domination systems that entrap people and keep them blinded to spiritual realities.

Fifth, one of the emphases of those engaged in this type of ministry is to discern areas in which the church needs to repent. Often this comes together with the call for a public gathering to express corporate repentance. Certainly this is a positive action which unleashes the power of God to work in a location or people, and one in which we should be delighted to participate.

Sixth, and finally, there is generally an explicit recognition that this concept/strategy is new and pioneering rather than proven. Advocates see themselves in some respects as experimenters who are following God's leading rather than sensationalists who simply want to make names for themselves.

POINTS OF DISAGREEMENT

First, whatever our conclusion as to whether or not spirits are assigned territories, perhaps the biggest obstacle to SLSW is that the fundamental strategy is not found biblically or in church history, at least not without some serious stretching of the accounts.[31]

Second, the emphasis on discerning and *naming* demons before we can have power over them is approaching a form of Christian animism (as Paul notes in Ephesians 1:18, we have power over any name that can be named). Tom White points out:

> The same angelic beings that tempted Israel tempt us today and even use the same tactics. There is nothing new under the

sun. These demons may merely change their names and create a new "front of operation" suitable to modern sophistication. And I do not believe that learning the name of a ruling Spirit [sic] is necessary to overcome its influence. *Seeking to know names is a speculative and slippery matter.*[32]

The requirement to find out the names of territorial spirits is dangerously close to what could be called Christian magic.[33] The idea of needing the names to have power over spirits is found in magical thinking around the world. An Indian friend of mine who has long been involved in spiritual warfare on a personal and corporate level has told me that one of the most difficult problems he faces in sharing the claims of Christ with his Hindu friends has come after they see well-intentioned Christians engaging in what they believe to be simple magical practices. As they observe teams of Christians on short-term prayer walking mission trips, they see Christians engaged in practices that are familiar to them as magical ceremonies, and as a result they feel that Christianity has nothing new to offer. In my friend's case, this type of warfare prayer has been more damaging to the ministry than helpful.

The concept of "discerning" the names and the functions will *always* be subjective at best. The model Scripture provides is that demons do indeed have names or designations, but knowing those names does not appear necessary for expulsion (Acts 16:18). Additionally, Scripture urges caution in approaching the spirit realm and the extent of our authority as granted in Christ is debated in the area of territorial spirits.[34]

Third, the orientation towards prayer as "smart bombs versus scud missiles" borrows too heavily on what Walter Wink explored as the myth of redemptive violence that pervades human cultures.[35] Prayer is not intended to be a vehicle of violence, but a means of fellowship, growth and strength. One danger of an attitude of "spiritual violence" is that we may become the very thing we are fighting against. White, one of the more cautious advocates, comments:

> The primary activity envisioned in strategic warfare is *intercession* before the throne of God, not *interaction* with fallen principalities. We *are not* called to wield laser beams of biblical authority to destroy heavenly strongholds. We *are* called to destroy in the lives of people (Christian and non-Christian) "strongholds . . . arguments and every pretension that sets itself up against the knowledge of God" (2 Cor. 10:4, 5). We are called

to faithfully reflect the glory of Jesus Christ through our obedience to his commands.[36]

Fourth, as important as informed prayer is, seeking information about the spirit realm as a means of overcoming spirits or gaining special knowledge does not appear to be portrayed as necessary (or even significant) in Scripture. Indeed, the majority of the warnings against the occult in the Bible focus on unwarranted explorations into the spiritual realms for knowledge or power.

Fifth, ultimately a focus on this strategy as *the* key to effective evangelisation demeans the Scriptures: if this strategy is *so* significant, then why is it not found in the Bible? Additionally, support for the advocacy has tended to come through eisegetical reading into biblical texts the meanings that advocates of SLSW want.[37] For example, "rulers" and "authorities" (NIV) in Ephesians 6:12 perhaps indicates territorial spirits, but Paul's statement is more of an ontological aside than advocacy of warfare directly against such spirits.[38] Further, the statement comes in the context of the Christian's daily struggle, not the church's SLSW strategy.[39] Additionally, passages such as Ephesians 3:10 cannot be used as a mandate for proclaiming the gospel to the powers (the verb is passive; that is, the *existence* of the church is the issue, not the *action* of the church).[40]

Sixth, another possible danger is that we detach demons from people, which de-emphasises our own participation in the rebellion against God. In concentrating on finding out the various forms of territorial demonic attachments and focusing our attention on them, we ignore the fact that all too often the enemy is us. Some explore this reality,[41] but by and large the enemy is externalised, enabling us to avoid responsibility for our sin. If the enemy is both inside (we need to repent) and outside, methodologies that ignore the inside are doomed to failure in the long run. White again has a pertinent question:

> How can we know if the negative influence in a given spiritual environment originates primarily from the heavenlies downward or from the corrupt leaders hearts of men outward? Before we plunge into projects designed to weaken "territorial spirits" (we hope to be agents of positive change for the populace) we must consider the possibility that the greater bondage may rest with the wickedness of human hearts.[42]

Finally, the idea of serving notice, evicting and binding spirits over territories does not have biblical warrant,[43] and there is too much emphasis on a "bottom line" of technique and effectiveness.[44] How can we serve notice to a spirit over a territory if the people themselves continue to invite control by the way they live? Perhaps the idea that they cannot change until the power of the ruling spirit is broken has merit, but that is significantly different than advocating complete freedom once the powers have been broken.

SOME SUGGESTIONS FOR REFINEMENT

The first suggestion for refinement in this area is that we must be more cautious in the use of exaggerated claims and anecdotes as the means by which SLSW is established. We must be careful in analyzing the success stories given in the literature not to confuse coincidence with causation.[45] While there may be reports of crime rates declining over a period coinciding with a particular prayer struggle, this does not prove that it was the struggle itself that resulted in the decline.[46] For example, one often-quoted example is that of the border town straddling Brazil and Uruguay in which people are responsive to the gospel on one side of the street (in Brazil) and unresponsive on the other (in Uruguay). This is attributed to the power and influence of territorial spirits.[47] When Priest, Campbell and Mullen tracked down the story, however, they discovered that the missionary from whom it originated did not even remember the name of the town and his impressions came from one afternoon of witnessing during a four-month evangelistic trip in 1947![48]

A second suggestion is that advocates of SLSW emphasise spiritual diagnosis over spiritual mapping and be more cautious in their pronouncements. We must enable Christians to develop a worldview that acknowledges the powers without capitulating to them or being captivated by an unhealthy interest in them. Paul's approach was to give Satan and demons what might be called a selectively appropriate inattention. The best means for doing that is to keep our attention on God's sovereign control and to use God's sovereignty as a lens through which we examine demonic activities. Surely this is a significant theme in Ephesians, as Paul notes Christ's authority over any name that can be named in any age (1:21) and prays that the Ephesians would be filled with God's power not to confront demons but to know the depths of God's love for them (3:14–21). Along these lines, we should find appropriate ways to stress more strongly the need for discipleship rather than warfare alone. Additionally, we must not overlook the need to die to the powers rather than follow the desire to overcome them. As Wink notes:

> One does not become free from the Powers by defeating them in a frontal attack. Rather, one dies to their control. Here also the cross is the model: we are liberated, not by striking back at what enslaves us – for even striking back reveals that we are still determined by its violent ethos – but by dying out from under its jurisdiction and command.[49]

We need to die not only to our privatised egos but also to the outer network of social beliefs. In self-denial, the task is not a conquest of ego by ego, but ego-surrender to God's redemptive initiative. In the social arena the task is not one social structure conquering another social structure, but the human beings who inhabit the social structures surrendering those structures to God's redemptive initiatives.

Finally, our goal must be to integrate the spiritual, the personal, the cultural and the social, and to stop placing all the blame on the spirits and start recognising the human side of choice to rebel against God's established order.

DEVELOPING AN ONGOING DISCUSSION

What are some suggestions for moving forward? The following points may be noted. First, our goal should be to give Satan and demons a selectively appropriate *inattention*. Do not let the flaw of the excluded middle become the flaw of the expanded middle; major on God and minor on demons, not the other way around.

Second, if you are an advocate of SLSW, be cautious in the use of claims and anecdotes to establish the validity of SLSW. Note the dangers of the language of advocacy and apologetics. If you are a critic, some room must be given for the "eyes of faith" to see things that may not be empirically provable.

Third, whatever your perspective, beware of the emotional attachment to the method and how that can influence both your advocacy and your response to criticism.

Fourth, if you are an advocate, work hard not to confuse coincidence with causation. While there may be reports of crime rates declining over a period coinciding with a particular prayer struggle, this does not *prove* that it was the prayer that resulted in the decline.

Fifth, develop a more robust vocabulary/interdisciplinary framework (advocated in spiritual mapping but not yet seen in the case

Table 19-1: Disciplines and vocabulary

Discipline	Typical vocabulary available for discussion
Spiritual warfare	Demons/spirits, casting out, deliverance, authority, prayer, repentance, domination, "possession," forgiveness, healing, praise, faith and strongholds.
Psychology	Psychosis, release, hysteria, dissociation, stress, compensation, co-dependency, projection, repression, ego development, reward, regression and defense mechanism.
Biology/medicine	Hormonal/chemical abnormalities (e.g., dopamine), dietary deficiencies, sleep deprivation and brain damage.
Sociology	Social stress, social roles, institutionalisation, renewal movements, change agentry, power, innovation, conflict negotiation and politics.
Anthropology	Culture, cultural conformity, mores, permission, kinship, institutions and law.
Economics	Social classes, surpluses and shortages, barter, politics and power.
History	Precedent, trends, traditions, exemplar and case study.

studies or reports). *If spiritual warfare is ever to be seen as a type of science, it will have to develop a multi-disciplinary vocabulary.* The following table illustrates types of disciplines that can assist in developing a more interdisciplinary vocabulary.

Sixth, if you are a critic, demonstrate an understanding of what is being said and lovingly prod – that will go much farther than blanket condemnations. Further, do not stereotype. Accept what is acceptable; do not feel you have to disprove every point.

Seventh, if you are an advocate, do respond to honest critique by doing your homework rather than just brushing off the criticism.

Eighth, and finally, if you are an advocate, do not stereotype. Do not simply dismiss people who have not had your experiences as not having the ability to critique your theology or methodology. It is easy to project an air of elitism that stifles genuine dialogue.

Conclusion

While it appears that for the immediate future this particular area of spiritual warfare will itself be something of a battleground, that does not mean that the discussion cannot move forward. For that to happen, however, advocates and critics alike need to keep apprised of each other's discussions, listen to each other and continue to go back to the Scriptures for guidance.

Notes

[1] Frank Peretti's vivid portrayals of encounters with evil spiritual powers as given in his novels *This Present Darkness* (Wheaton, Ill.: Crossway Books, 1986), *Piercing the Darkness* (Wheaton, Ill.: Crossway Books, 1989), *The Prophet* (Wheaton, Ill.: Crossway Books, 1992), *The Oath* (Nashville, Tenn.: Word, 1995) and *The Visitation* (Nashville, Tenn.: Word, 1999) seem to be almost mandatory reading in Christian circles.

[2] C. S. Lewis, *The Screwtape Letters* (New York: Macmillan Publishing Company, 1961), 33.

[3] C. Peter Wagner, *Confronting the Powers: How the New Testament Church Experienced the Power of Strategic-Level Spiritual Warfare* (Ventura, Calif.: Regal, 1996), 46.

[4] See, for example, George Otis, *The Last of the Giants* (Tarrytown, N.Y.: Chosen Books, 1991); John Dawson, *Taking Our Cities for God* (Lake Mary, Fla.: Creation House, 1989); Cindy Jacobs, *Possessing the Gates of the Enemy* (Grand Rapids, Mich.: Chosen Books, 1991); Larry Lea, *The Weapons of Your Warfare* (Altamonte Springs, Fla.: Creation House, 1989); and the chapters in C. Peter Wagner, ed., *Breaking Strongholds in Your City: How to Use Spiritual Mapping to Make Your Prayers More Strategic, Effective and Targeted* (Ventura, Calif.: Regal Books, 1993).

[5] The term *spiritual mapping* was popularised by George Otis and is summarised in "An Overview of Spiritual Mapping," in Wagner, *Breaking Strongholds in Your City*, 29–48.

[6] God "chairs" a council of angels (2 Chron. 18:18–22; Job 1–2; Ps. 89:5–8), apparently pointing to an angelic hierarchy, which Satan may duplicate. While extra-biblical speculations abound, biblical evidence is scanty. Evidence used in favour of territorial spirits from the Old Testament is that there are powers in heaven which appear to correspond to kings (Isa. 24:21) or nations (Deut. 4:19; possibly Deut. 32:8 and Dan. 8:9–12) on earth, which correlates with the idea of territoriality. In the New Testament, the fact that the demons did not want to leave a particular area may be significant (Mark 5:10), as may the hierarchical spirit listings (e.g., Eph. 1:21; Col. 1:16).

[7] Timothy Warner relates, "Satan does indeed assign a demon or corps of demons to every geopolitical unit in the world, and . . . they are among the principalities and powers against whom we wrestle" (*Spiritual Warfare: Victory over the Powers of This Dark World* [Westchester, Ill.: Crossway Books, 1991], 135).

[8] C. Peter Wagner, "Territorial Spirits," in *Engaging the Enemy: How to Fight and Defeat Territorial Spirits*, ed. C. Peter Wagner (Ventura, Calif.: Regal, 1991), 280.

[9] Though Priest, Campbell and Mullen argue quite strongly against this view, see Robert J. Priest, Thomas Campbell and Bradford A. Mullen, "Missiological Syncretism: The New Animistic Paradigm," in *Spiritual Power and Missions: Raising the Issues*, ed. Edward Rommen (Pasadena, Calif.: William Carey Library, 1995), 9–87.

[10] Chuck Lowe, *Territorial Spirits and World Evangelization?* (Kent, Great Britain: OMF International, 1998), 144. Lowe also notes the difficulty the movement has with defining the concept of territories: "On closer examination it turns out that territorial demons are purportedly assigned not only to geographical regions, but also to geopolitical institutions, such as nations or states; to topographical features, such as valleys, mountains or rivers; to ecological features, such as trees, streams and rocks; or to smaller physical objects, such as houses, temples or idols."

[11] C. Peter Wagner, *The Power to Heal the Past*, <http://www.pastornet.net.au/renewal/journal8/8d-wagnr.html> (January 24, 2000).

[12] "The Reconciliation Walk," <http://www.reconciliationwalk.org/walk.htm> (January 24, 2000).

[13] See, for example, C. Peter Wagner, *Confronting the Queen of Heaven* (Colorado Springs, Colo.: Wagner Institute for Practical Ministry, 1998), 11–13; idem, *Warfare Prayer: How to Seek God's Power and Protection in the Battle to Build His Kingdom*, (Ventura, Calif.: Regal Books, 1992), 16–18.

[14] Wagner, *Confronting the Queen of Heaven*, 11.

[15] Ibid., 12. For multiple examples of this type of prayer, see Wagner, *Engaging the Enemy*; and idem, *The Third Wave of the Holy Spirit: Encountering the Power of Signs and Wonders Today* (Ann Arbor, Mich.: Vine Books, 1988), 94–96.

[16] "What Is a Prayer Journey?" <www.globalharvest.org> (January 24, 2000). Information on prayer journeys is available at a number of sites.

[17] Otis, "An Overview of Spiritual Mapping," 32–33.

[18] Harold Caballeros, "Defeating the Enemy with the Help of Spiritual Mapping," in Wagner, *Breaking Strongholds in Your City*, 136.

[19] C. Peter Wagner, "Summary: Mapping Your Community," in Wagner, *Breaking Strongholds in Your City*, 223–32.

[20] "I cannot be too emphatic. In dealing with the princes and rulers of the heavenlies, they must be identified. Even the ancient Greeks know how to approach their gods (whom we now identify as 'principalities'). They were always approached by name and title" (Dick Bernal, *Storming Hell's Brazen Gates, Isaiah 45:2: Through Militant, Violent, Prevailing Prayer!* [San Jose, Calif.: Jubilee Christian Center, 1988], 57).

[21] Wagner, *Confronting the Queen of Heaven*, 20.

[22] Ibid., 31–33.

[23] Ibid., 17.

[24] Ibid.

[25] Ibid., 23.

[26] See the story as portrayed in Wagner, *Confronting the Queen of Heaven*.

²⁷ As of this writing, I have been unable to find any literature noting the effectiveness of the Celebrate Ephesus event except the reports on the personal lives of the participants and their certainty that something significant happened. Several websites discuss the event.

²⁸ Adapted from Tom White, *Breaking Strongholds: How Spiritual Warfare Sets Captives Free* (Ann Arbor, Mich.: Vine Books, 1992), 142–44.

²⁹ Clinton Arnold has been a mentor to my thinking more than any other person; over the years it is hard to remember where his suggestions end and my own begin. In any event, these are my own points that rely on his perceptive comments made over the years.

³⁰ As Chuck Lowe notes, "We must not forget that proponents of SLSW have performed an important service in alerting evangelicalism to its recently insipid and careless attitude toward prayer and toward demons, as well as its lethargy in the practice of spiritual warfare" (*Territorial Spirits and World Evangelization?* 112).

³¹ See the critique of Wagner by A. Scott Moreau, "Broadening the Issues: Historiography, Advocacy and Hermeneutics," in *The Holy Spirit and Mission Dynamics*, ed. C. Douglas McConnell (Pasadena, Calif.: William Carey Library, 1997), 132.

³² White, *Breaking Strongholds*, 141, italics added.

³³ The strongest critique in print is found in Rommen, *Spiritual Power and Missions*. See also A. Scott Moreau, "Religious Borrowing as a Two-Way Street: An Introduction to Animistic Tendencies in the Euro-North American Context," in *Christianity and the Religions: A Biblical Theology of World Religions*, ed. Edward Rommen and Harold Netland (Pasadena, Calif.: William Carey Library, 1995), 166–82. Wagner responded to the critique in his own book, *Confronting the Powers*.

³⁴ See Clinton E. Arnold, *Three Crucial Questions About Spiritual Warfare* (Grand Rapids, Mich.: Baker, 1987), 164–65.

³⁵ Walter Wink, *Engaging the Powers: Discernment and Resistance in a World of Dominion* (Philadelphia: Fortress Press, 1992). See also the discussion on mythic frameworks pervading North American thinking on spiritual warfare in A. Scott Moreau, "Religious Borrowing as a Two-Way Street," 166–83.

³⁶ White, *Breaking Strongholds*, 141–42.

³⁷ See, for example, Moreau, "Broadening the Issues"; Lowe, *Territorial Spirits and World Evangelization*; and Arnold, *Three Crucial Questions About Spiritual Warfare*, 143–99.

³⁸ Lowe, *Territorial Spirits*, 30–43.

³⁹ Arnold, *Three Crucial Questions About Spiritual Warfare*, 156–57.

⁴⁰ Ibid., 167–68.

⁴¹ For example, White, *Breaking Strongholds;* Wink, *Engaging the Powers.*

⁴² White, *Breaking Strongholds*, 150.

⁴³ See the warnings in Jude 8 and 2 Peter 2:10–11; see Arnold, *Three Crucial Questions About Spiritual Warfare*, 165.

⁴⁴ Sociologists note that emphasis on technique is a secularising influence rather than a spiritualising one; see the discussion on this in Lowe, *Territorial Spirits*, 147–51.

[45] See Lowe, *Territorial Spirits*, 114–27.

[46] The distortion that can happen when anecdotal proof-texting is used is discussed in Priest, Campbell and Mullen, "Missiological Syncretism," 36–41.

[47] Warner, *Spiritual Warfare*, 136.

[48] Priest, Campbell and Mullen, "Missiological Syncretism," 40, especially note 16.

[49] Wink, *Engaging the Powers*, 157.

20 _____

Spiritual conflict and the mission of the church: Contextualisation

Marguerite Kraft

Even today most Christians in the West and often those non-Western Christians trained in the West or trained by Westerners have limited understanding of spiritual powers. This involves how spirits affect human activity, the power of curses and blessings, the need for harmony with the spiritual forces, and the constant battle being waged in the spirit world. Furthermore, the Western church, under great pressure from rationalism and science, has failed to teach and practise a theology of the spirit realm. This has resulted in a lack of awareness of God's power, including the Holy Spirit's power within Christians, and its relation to other existing spiritual powers.

Many societies of the world are spiritual-power oriented. In these cases the world is seen as dynamic, with one power pitted against another in daily living. However, Christianity as carried by emissaries from the West has not focused on a God of power as clearly presented in the Bible. This has caused problems for new believers and the established church as well as for the future growth of the church.

To gain a greater understanding of the spiritual dimensions of the receptor's society in cross-cultural missions, I will first examine spiritual conflicts. Only then will I make suggestions for carrying out a contextualised ministry. The result, I hope, will be allowing God to be God in all his power rather than God being limited by the worldview of the West.

The influence of worldview on spiritual-power concepts

The field of anthropology has provided many definitions for *worldview*, the central control box of culture. *Worldview*, as I am using it, refers to the basic assumptions, values and allegiances of a group of people. It can be seen as the way people perceive of such things as the self, the in-group to which they belong, outsiders, nature around them and the non-human or supernatural world. Worldview is formed unconsciously as we learn our culture. It enables us to feel comfortable in our environment; it is a picture of what is and ought to be and permeates all of our customs and behaviour. Since we are usually not aware of these basic assumptions, values and allegiances, the natural way to proceed in cross-cultural situations is to follow our cultural ways.

THE WEST AND POWERLESS CHRISTIANITY

A Navajo Christian explained his Native American life experiences: born and raised on the reservation; moving to the city and suffering further oppression; and finally living on the inner-city streets of Skid Row. He joyfully spoke of his faith in Christ and his faithful family, who helped rescue him from the streets. But he reported that when he tried to interest other Navajos in following Christ, they were uninterested, saying, "There is no power in Christianity. We need power to survive in this world." He was aware of the Navajo worldview with lots of spirit activity, and he had not been taught how to handle this as a Christian.

Lesslie Newbigin has pointed out that Christianity is the most secularising force in recent history.[1] The reason behind this is that a form of Christianity that is comfortable in the West has been transferred to other parts of the world. It fails to deal with the whole person as a spiritual being. The categorising of life influences the establishment of institutions to provide for various areas of life: church for religious life, schools for the educational area, hospitals and clinics for the physical/medical area, organisations promoting developmental technology for the production and health areas.

For the Westerner, faith in and commitment to science give humans control over the material universe. Charles H. Kraft describes the situation well:

> Western societies passed through the Renaissance, the Reformation, the Enlightenment, and a wide variety of ripples and

spin-offs from these movements. . . . The result: God and the church were dethroned, and the human mind came to be seen as savior. It is ignorance, not Satan we are to fight. And our weapons are human minds and technology. God, if there be a God, only helps those who do it all themselves. Thus, by the nineteenth century, God had become irrelevant to most Westerners.[2]

Christians in the West, then, struggle to combine a secular worldview and the God of the Bible. Spiritual powers and their place in the universe are given very little attention or relevance in daily living.

A HOLISTIC APPROACH TO LIFE

In many societies of the world supernaturalism is the centre of life and the integrating factor. Humans are seen as weak and needing increased strength to survive in a world full of spirit activity. In such societies spiritual power is viewed as necessary for success, wealth, guidance and meeting daily crises, such as illness, accidents, barrenness and drought.

The Navajo illustrate clearly a holistic approach to life with the concept of harmony as a central focus. They believe that everything was brought into being in perfect harmony – a balance between human beings and the physical world around them, between human beings and the spiritual powers around them. Unity in the spirit realm generates a feeling of understanding, concern, peace and identity with the surroundings – in nature, people and animals. When disharmony arises (for example, sickness, misfortune, strained relationships, breaking of a taboo), harmony must be restored. Disease and injury are often perceived as of spiritual origin, caused by witchcraft, sorcery, or contact with ghosts. "Positive health for the Navajo involves a proper relationship to everything in one's environment, not just the correct functioning of one's physiology."[3] Because of this belief, the traditional and Peyote ceremonies deal with the whole person: family, clan, animals, fields, origins and the spirit powers around the person.

My own experiences living in a Nigerian village and since then interacting with people from many other countries have raised many questions in my mind. Should all Christians have the same concept of God? How does God respond to other spiritual powers that are so real to those of other societies? How can the God of Scripture be the God of power for the everyday lives of Christians in spiritual-power-oriented society? How can the God of the Bible become the integrating factor in life?

Other questions, however, I hear coming from the minds and hearts of Christians or potential Christians from other societies. Does the foreign doctor know how to take care of the spirits who are making me ill? How will I know when to plant my crops if I do not go to the local diviner? Does the pastor have enough spiritual power to deal with my wife's barrenness? How can I survive the curses of my father when he hears of my Christian faith? Where within the church is there power to protect me from witches? In fact, when discussing Christianity with a non-believer from another society, the question raised is often not, Who is this Jesus? but What can Jesus do? In my reflecting I consider the validity and significance of this question.

SPECIFIC NEEDS FOR SPIRITUAL POWER

Basic needs include the needs for food, shelter, protection, identity, communication, belonging and security. These are common to all human beings and have been described and categorised in a variety of ways by a number of psychologists and anthropologists.[4]

Perceived needs are the source of motivation to action. To illustrate, the need for wealth motivates some to work hard, others to steal, others to make things right with spiritual powers and still others to have large families. In one society the belief is if you work hard you will be rich. In another group the belief is that you deserve more than you have, so you can take from others to get your due. In another society you do not get rich without the gods making it so with their blessing. Still another society defines wealth as the extended family, so the larger the family, the wealthier you are. Perceived needs motivate, but the societal beliefs and values shape the resultant action.

Human beings seem to know they have limitations and seek help beyond their own capabilities. Each society has its own way of obtaining spiritual power for times and events that are filled with unknown dangers and for situations that are beyond human control. In many societies of the world the quest for spiritual power for daily living is at the forefront of people's minds. I use the term "spiritual-power-oriented" to describe such societies. Seeking spiritual power in Africa has been described by Diedrich Westermann:

> This craving for power is the driving force in the life of African religion. . . . Man is weak, and what he needs is increased strength. . . . The absorbing question for him is how to acquire

some of this power so that it may serve for his own salvation or that of the group for which he is responsible.[5]

The need for the spiritual to enable human beings who are perceived as weak and limited to survive each day is real in many parts of the world today.

In my research of concepts of spiritual power in three different societies, I found that spiritual power was sought for common basic human needs.[6] *Perpetuity* needs included ensuring fertility for reproduction within the family and also as it relates to the land, crops and livestock. *Prosperity* needs included the dangerous transitions through life (for example, childbirth, puberty, marriage, death), building a new house, opening a new business, and so on. *Health* needs drive one to spiritual power depending on the society's theory of sickness and accident. Spiritual causes and the need for harmony demand attention to spiritual power. *Security* needs include the dangers perceived when venturing into new territory or travelling, natural disasters such as floods and droughts, and the dangers of sorcery and witchcraft. *Restitution* needs deal with the prescribed ways to restore order after someone has broken the rules. This includes dealing with the ancestors and with other human relationships. *Power* needs for situations humans cannot control or explain drive one to seek help from the spiritual realm also.

Worldview and human needs are interrelated. Worldview shapes a people's needs; needs shape the worldview. To illustrate, the human need for safety influences people to form basic assumptions and values that will result in action that meets that perceived need. In Western societies, safety was at one time conceived of as in the hands of spiritual powers. Belief in God's protection and belief in the power of prayer were important assumptions. As worldview changed over a period of many years, with science replacing belief in spiritual power, the basic need for security persisted, resulting in law enforcement agencies, insurance policies and locks and safety alarms on houses, businesses and cars. The assumption now is that safety is provided by using material means and is under human control.

The church and spiritual conflicts

For many peoples the world is seen as dynamic, with one power pitted against another. Often there is no sharp dividing line between sacred and secular because the material and spiritual are intertwined.

Power encounters, the confrontation between two or more spiritual powers, are common. The spiritual powers that are involved when there is a power encounter may be personal or impersonal, evil or good, greater or lesser, within a person (demonisation) or outside a person. When people destroy their fetishes, they are recognising that they have available to them a power stronger than that in the fetish. Among the Navajo, when lightning, which is perceived as a malevolent spiritual power, strikes a house and the people refuse to abandon it, but pray to God for protection, this is a power encounter. Whether or not a particular event is perceived as a confrontation between two spiritual powers is, however, in the mind of the beholder and is dependent on his or her worldview.

Alan R. Tippett reports:

> When Christianity arrived the religious encounter was not between a pagan deity and the Christian God. . . . The encounter had to take place on the level of daily life against those powers which dealt with the relevant problems of gardening, fishing, war, security, food supply and the personal life crises. . . . In the eyes of any potential Melanesian convert to Christianity, therefore, the issue was one of *power in daily life*. The convert could not stand with the missionary and conceptualise in terms of psychology and Western thought-forms. Rather the missionary had to stand with the convert and help him to understand what Christ meant in terms of power encounter.[7]

For Christ and the church to be relevant to life, missionaries must be aware of the active existing spiritual powers and on what occasions they are called on for assistance.

The mission of the church is to introduce people to Christ, make them aware of God's purposes for all human beings (the creation, the Fall, and reconciliation) and assist them in responsibly becoming bearers of God's good news. Spiritual conflicts are involved at all levels. God's design has always been to meet human beings where they are and then gently move them closer to himself. With most of the world heavily involved in spiritual-power activities, the initial communication of the gospel must deal with spiritual power. When people give allegiance to Christ, spiritual conflicts will arise over spiritual power for each day's needs. The form and corporate practices of the church will need to be shaped to meet the needs for spiritual power. Christian theology must give creedal attention to specific areas where spiritual powers are involved.

THE CHURCH NEEDS TO MEET NEEDS
IN THE INITIAL COMMUNICATION OF THE GOSPEL

Communication theory affirms the importance of the receptors, because they are the ones who decide the credibility of the message and the communicator. The message must be relevant to the receptors' values and practical for their context. In fact, it is the receptors who construct the meaning of the messages according to their worldview, experiences and conditioning.

To illustrate, for the Navajos nature is very sacred and harmony between humankind and nature is paramount in their thinking. Christians should emphasise the biblical relationship between humans created in God's image and the created universe. Harmony among all he created was in the heart of God as he gave humans the responsibility to keep creation alive (Ps. 104; Gen. 1—2). Many passages in the Old Testament speak of the physical environment and of how God works and speaks through it. He demonstrates his power to keep nature in balance. Inclusion of these concepts in presenting the gospel could very well catch the attention of the Navajo and enrich their journey of faith in God.

When something goes wrong (for example, sickness, death, accident) it is often perceived to be the action of evil spirit power. The cross-cultural communicator must recognise the activity that takes place between the spirit world and humans (Eph. 6:12) and be ready to let God be victorious. For example, when a non-Christian child is ill (whether the perceived cause is offending a tree spirit or germs), the one bringing the message of Christ needs to be ready to pray audibly for healing from God, to claim the power and authority God gives us (Luke 9:1) and to recognise his power over the spirit world. Being aware of the difference in causality in the worldview of the receptor allows the outsider to show God's relevance and position in the universe and in daily living.

Consciously seeking common ground is important in reaching out to spiritual-power-oriented societies. Some of the basic assumptions provide fertile ground for establishing a vibrant, all-encompassing Christianity. First, in these societies people recognise the existence of both good and evil spiritual powers apart from human power. Good spiritual power is needed due to human power being limited and in order to ward off the evil powers. Second, spiritual powers, both good and bad, are active and involved in human daily experiences. However, often more attention is given to rituals for warding off the evil powers who bring harm and danger. Third, human beings have access to spiritual power and may use it to harm other human beings or for their own safety and health. Fourth, some spiritual powers are stronger than others, and the strongest one wins when there is an encounter or spiritual conflict. Fifth, the struggle with spiritual powers continues throughout life. God's pattern of outreach is to meet people where they are and move them to faith in and obedience to himself. Recognition of the starting point will assist us greatly in our involvement in the task. Furthermore, those who accept Christ and sincerely study God's Word from *these* basic assumptions will have great insights to share with Christians who have science-humanistic basic assumptions. Due to the Westernising and secularising effect of Christianity in the past, we have failed to reap these benefits.

THE CHURCH NEEDS TO MEET NEEDS
IN BRINGING ABOUT SPIRITUAL GROWTH

The worldview of the convert is important because people interpret new truth from their own viewpoint, looking through their own worldview lenses. We must recognise that it will require considerable time to bring the basic assumptions and values in line with what the Bible says. This can be illustrated by how difficult it is to have a biblical view of wealth in America even today. For instance, for Christians wealth should be used to meet immediate needs and shared with others (Luke 6:30; 2 Cor. 9:11; 1 Tim. 6:9–11).

The problem of "dual allegiance" is a very serious problem in worldwide Christianity today as Christians have found themselves without the spiritual power to handle life's crises.[8] This happens often when people come to Jesus but continue to depend on other spiritual powers for protection, healing, guidance (for example, shamans, diviners, amulets, sacrifices) or when they add to their Christian commitment a dependence on occult powers (for example, fortune-telling, New Age, astrology, psychic healing).

Most important for spiritual-power-oriented societies is solid instruction on the greatness of the power of God and the existence of the powers of evil. Passages to be studied and learned include 1 John 4:4; 5:4–5, 19. God at work in the Old Testament reveals his power over other gods and spirits (for example, 1 Sam. 5; 1 Kings 18; Isa. 44:6–20).

Since warding off evil spirit attack is real in the daily lives of those in spiritual-power-oriented societies, the new believer needs to learn to employ the power of God to overcome (not simply placate) these spirits. Passages that speak of God's protection should be studied, memorised and used (Ps. 27:1–6; 28:7; Luke 10:19–20; 1 Pet. 4:11;

and Col. 1:9–14). Jesus gave all Christians the Holy Spirit (Acts 1:8; 1 Cor. 12:13) and also the power and authority over all demons and all diseases (Matt. 10:1; Luke 9:1; 10:17–19). Christians must realise that the greatest spiritual power in the universe is available to them through the indwelling Holy Spirit.

God's power is given not for protection only but for enabling his people to do his work. Christ in each Christian in the form of the Holy Spirit is the source of power for doing God's work (Rom. 15:13–17). Wayne Dye points out how the power God gives is to serve his purposes:

> God gives power to be the right sort of spiritual person, to be morally strong and to react as a Christian should to the trials of life. (Col. 1:10–11; Phil. 4:3; 1 Cor. 10:13; Eph. 6:10–12; Luke 22:32; Acts 16:5)
>
> The second biblical purpose of spiritual power is to be able to do God's work more effectively. This means to speak prophetically and also to see healing and other miracles in answer to prayer and to serve other believers in practical ways. (Micah 3:8; 2 Cor. 13:4; Eph. 3:7; 2 Cor. 12:12)[9]

Those who convert to Christ must know in practice that the Holy Spirit within them empowers them for living and confronting the spiritual powers that exist around them.

The church needs to be shaped to meet perceived needs

Cultural voids often emerge if perceived needs for spiritual power are not reckoned with and met in the structure and practice of the church. Since areas of life in which a person feels the need for spiritual assistance still exist after conversion, the church must seriously consider how to meet these needs. If there is a cultural practice that needs to be rejected when one accepts Christ, the church needs to deal with two questions: What were its functions in society? What kind of Christian substitutes could take its place?

Functional substitutes must be designed by the insiders of the society if they are to become permanent. When the church leadership senses that members of the church are struggling with unmet needs or when followers of Christ continue to seek assistance from non-Christian practitioners, it is time for the church leadership to consider a functional substitute:

The concept of functional substitute permits amazing diversity in application. A functional substitute may be a form, a ritual, a symbol, a role, an idea, a craft, an occupation, an artifact, an economic pattern, or it may even be the Christian religion itself under certain ideal circumstances.[10]

The missionary can assist in this process by helping the church become aware of the freedom to change current practices to meet current needs. Whereas the first-generation converts to Christianity were often most harsh in rejecting old customs having to do with power, later generations no longer see those customs as sacred but only as cultural symbols. Sometimes practices that were prohibited by the first Christian missionaries and their converts are years later revised with Christian meaning by the local pastors in order to meet perceived needs.

In societies where spiritual powers are perceived as the cause of illness, the church needs to have in its structure a means of dealing with physical illness. This could be a regular part of worship, a prayer team available to go to homes, or even separate prayer teams for each extended family group in the church. It might be good to have a member of the pastoral staff who is trained and gifted in healing and deliverance available at all times. Familiarity with power encounter is essential training for Christians. Tippett emphasises the fact that Scripture demands that the people of God be willing to be involved in power encounter:

> The works of the devil have to be *destroyed*. Sinful man is bound. Christ came to *unloose* him. . . . I have given you . . . power – with authority . . . over the power of the enemy. . . . If the Christian takes up his place in the world, he is involved as a soldier of Christ both defensively and offensively.[11]

Christians are told to be on the watch and ready to defeat the powers in faith and loyalty to God (1 Pet. 5:8). Even though Christ unmasked and disarmed the powers at the cross and the victory is certain (Col. 2:13–15), yet the battle continues (Eph. 6:12; 1 Cor. 15:24).

Rosalind Hackett, who has researched new religious movements in Nigeria, notes that African independent churches have allowed women a great deal of independence in religious activities. The emphasis on healing attracts women especially because of their needs:

Given the pressures on women to perpetuate the lineage and the problems surrounding childbirth and rearing healthy children in a developing country whose medical facilities are still far from adequate, it is not surprising that women turn to these churches for total or supplementary support. We should not ignore the supernatural beliefs or fears which surround conception and childbirth and which the independent churches treat as existential realities.[12]

These churches are meeting women where they are in their needs and worldview. Hackett also notes that the independent churches provide opportunity and an acceptable place in society for women who have become "displaced persons" (through childlessness, divorce or accusations of witchcraft).[13] Mission churches can learn from the independent churches in the area of meeting perceived needs.

Training and preparation for working in spiritual-power-oriented societies

What has been most detrimental to effective mission work in regards to spiritual power is the lack of a sense of the necessity to learn about where the non-believers are in their spiritual journey. Since behaviour reflects perceived needs, it is important to investigate the meaning and function in the observance of pre-Christian ritual. This investigation makes it possible to define the perceived needs for spiritual power to be met and dealt with in the framework of Christianity. It is always helpful for a Christian to be able to look at life through others' lens in order to better understand their needs and behaviour.

Four universals of worldview help in the collecting and organising of data: (1) classification, (2) the person-group relation, (3) causality and (4) the perception of time and space. Classification of spiritual powers is the way people categorise them (gods and goddesses, ancestor spirits, malevolent spirits, guardian spirits), how and if they distinguish between supernatural and natural, the arrangement of the spiritual powers (hierarchical, geographical) and the interrelationship of each group with human beings.

The way in which spiritual power relates to the person or group varies from society to society. In Thailand, skilled artisans and performers, such as bronze casters and boxers, express their respect before a performance to their teachers and to the spirit masters of their professions, who are seen as the "owners" of the art and the giver or withholder of successes in it. Respect and a consciousness of knowing one's place in society are observed in language and behaviour. For the Kamwe, a hierarchical arrangement of spiritual powers exist, with the ancestors closest to the family. The older members of the family are closest to becoming ancestors, so they must be respected. Therefore, it is very serious and even dangerous to disagree with an elder, because he or she may place a curse on a person that could cause barrenness, death of children, illness or death.

Causality deals with the forces that are at work in the universe. Many societies see sickness and misfortune as caused by offending a spirit or an ancestor spirit, being cursed by an elder, failing to show respect, or a bad interpersonal relationship. Often the good things that happen to a person are seen as due to help from the spirit world, too.

How time and space are perceived affects working with the spiritual. The appropriate time and place for meeting the spiritual, the arrangement of people to interact most effectively with spiritual powers, the flow of spirit power and the use of objects with spiritual power are all part of the basic assumptions of a society and affect the behaviour of the people. If the time for dealing with the spiritual powers is after sundown, it may be best to have Christian worship at that time. If spiritual activity and gatherings are centred in the home, church could more effectively centre in the home and for the extended family group.

To understand the process of contextualisation, the cross-cultural worker needs to distinguish between cultural forms and their meanings. *Forms* are the customs and structures, both visible and invisible, that make up a culture; *meanings* are the personal interpretations of the people within the culture. Meanings, since they are in the people who use the forms, can be changed by these people. In contextualisation we are assisting Christians in attaching new meanings to their cultural forms by using them for new purposes. For the Kamwe in Nigeria, some of their local music with drum accompaniment was usable for praising God; other local music was not. The decision for what was usable was in the hands of the local believers. Dancing these songs of praise when the moon was full proved to be a natural way of communicating the gospel to new areas as the dance attracted outsiders and non-Christians. Using the dance at this time and place and in this way was suggested by the local believers.

The tendency in the past has been to refuse certain cultural forms that may have been used in interacting with the spirit world, and the result has been a form of Christianity that looks and feels foreign. As a result, those not interested in abandoning their traditional ways are not interested in following Christ. The challenge we face today is to capture local cultural forms and empower them for God's purposes. However, if these forms have been empowered for evil, that power will need to be broken before the forms can be used for God. Again, the local Christians best know the meaning and whether it has spiritual significance or not.

Besides being able to approach another society as a learner with an open mind, the missionary must learn as much about the spirit world as possible before entering the new environment. A careful study of spiritual power, both God's and Satan's, in Scripture is essential. There are also many books available today to enrich one's understanding and challenge one's faith in a God of power. Courses on spiritual warfare are available at some Christian universities and seminaries. Seminars on spiritual warfare sponsored by churches and mission organisations are available in many parts of the world. But the most valuable training of all is to experience doing spiritual warfare by arranging to work alongside a Christian with such a specialised ministry or be on a team focusing on ministry to those who are oppressed by evil spirits. This experience will increase the Christian's understanding of the power of the Holy Spirit in believers and the activity of the Evil One in the world today.

Conclusion

The shortest and most effective bridge for reaching those in spiritual-power-oriented societies is simply moving from a pagan power source to the true God as power source. This involves little or no conversion from spiritual power to secular power. The cultural results of this change of power source are likely to be forms of Christianity that look very similar to their non-Christian predecessors but with God as the power source. Places of meeting God and the rituals conducted as well as the practitioners would reflect the previous ways but would also be limited to being appropriate to biblical Christianity and using only the power of the true God.

I have shown how many of the practical, everyday problems in the world today involve spiritual powers. The church must develop a reputation for dealing with both the physical and spiritual dimensions of these problems, always seeking a Christian solution. The past has shown us the dangers involved in "transplanting the church" from one society to another. The theological abstractions of the West often have very little relevance to life as people in other societies experience it. It is far better to define carefully the church and what it means to accept Christ from a scriptural base, and then let believers develop and grow as a church through God's Word and Spirit. They will find answers to their needs from the Bible, and in this way their spiritual power needs will be met.

Notes

[1] Lesslie Newbigin, *Honest Religion of Secular Man* (Philadelphia: Westminster Press, 1966), 18.

[2] Charles H. Kraft, *Christianity with Power: Your Worldview and Your Experience of the Supernatural* (Ann Arbor, Mich.: Servant Books, 1989), 31–32.

[3] Gary Witherspoon, *Language and Art in the Navajo Universe* (Ann Arbor, Mich.: University of Michigan Press, 1977), 24.

[4] See, for example, Homer G. Barnett, *Innovation: The Basis of Cultural Change* (New York: McGraw-Hill, 1953); Abraham H. Maslow, *Motivation and Personality* (New York: Harper & Row, 1970), 53; Melville S. Herskovits, *Man and His Works* (New York: Alfred A. Knopf, 1951); Ralph Linton, "Universal Ethical Principles: An Anthropological View," in *Moral Principles of Action: Man's Ethical Imperative,* ed. Ruth Nanda Anshen (New York: Harper & Brothers, 1952), 646.

[5] Diedrich Westermann, *Africa and Christianity* (London: Oxford University Press, 1937), 84.

[6] Marguerite G. Kraft, *Understanding Spiritual Power: A Forgotten Dimension of Cross-Cultural Mission and Ministry* (Maryknoll, N.Y.: Orbis Books, 1995).

[7] Alan R. Tippett, *Solomon Islands Christianity* (London: Lutterworth Press, 1967), 5.

[8] Charles H. Kraft and Marguerite G. Kraft, "The Power of God for Christians Who Ride Two Horses," in *The Kingdom and the Power,* ed. Gary Greig and Kevin Springer (Ventura, Calif.: Regal Books, 1985).

[9] Wayne T. Dye, "Toward a Theology of Power for Melanesia: Part 2," *Catalyst* 14:2 (1984).

[10] Alan R. Tippett, *Introduction to Missiology* (Pasadena, Calif.: William Carey Library, 1987), 186.

[11] Alan R. Tippett, *Verdict Theology in Missionary Theory* (Pasadena. Calif.: William Carey Library, 1973), 89–90.

[12] Rosalind J. Hackett, "Sacred Paradoxes: Women and Religious Plurality in Nigeria," in *Women, Religion, and Social Change,* ed. Yvonne Yazbeck Haddad and Ellison Banks Findley (Albany, N.Y.: State University of New York Press, 1985), 263.

[13] Ibid., 265.

21

Contextualisation
and spiritual power

CHARLES H. KRAFT

Most of the world is heavily involved in enslavement to and manipulation of spiritual powers. In addition, a large percentage of the world's Christians participate in what I have called "dual allegiance," since they seldom find within Christianity the spiritual power they crave for healing, blessing, guidance and deliverance from demons. They may attend church faithfully but continue their pre-Christian practice of going to shamans, temples or shrines for spiritual power, since they know there's no healing in the church and the hospital is too slow and expensive.

This being so, it seems strange that we find virtually no discussion of spiritual power in publications concerning contextualisation. Missionaries, development workers and others from the West who seek to help cross-culturally have largely ignored this facet of biblical teaching and social concern. We have neither assisted converts to deal effectively with spirit world problems in ways that are both biblically and culturally appropriate nor dealt with spiritual power in our theorising about contextualisation.

Where are the discussions concerning biblically legitimate and culturally appropriate approaches to such areas of Christian experience as warfare prayer, deliverance from demons, healing, blessing and cursing, dedications, visions, dreams, concepts of the territoriality of spirits, angels, demons and the like? Shouldn't we be discussing the contextualising of spiritual warfare? What are the scriptural principles applicable to every cultural situation and what are the cultural variables in this important area? Something this important to non-Western and, increasingly, to Western Christians needs to be discussed and dealt with.

The biblical validity of dealing with spiritual power

Though the concept has been questioned by ivory tower theoreticians, spiritual warfare is an important biblical reality and, for those of us who are practitioners, a continual existential reality. Jesus treated Satan and demonic forces as real foes, frequently casting out demons and thus setting free people he called "captives" and "oppressed" (Luke 4:18). Such language is warfare language. Furthermore, Jesus calls Satan "the ruler of this world" (John 14:30). In a similar vein, Paul refers to Satan as "the evil god of this world" who blinds people to God's Good News (2 Cor. 4:4), and John says that "the whole world is under the rule of the Evil One" (1 John 5:19).

Like most of the world today, biblical peoples saw the world as populated by enemy spirits that could cause trouble if they were not properly dealt with. Unfortunately, through most of its history the people of Israel chose to deal with these spirits as the animistic peoples around them did rather than as God commanded them to. So God is constantly warning his people against worshipping the gods of the nations around them and punishing them when they disobey.

Note, as one of many examples, what God said to Solomon in 1 Kings 11 (especially vv. 9–13) concerning the penalty Solomon would have to pay for disobeying God by turning to other gods. God was angry with Solomon and took the kingdom away from his son because of his idolatry. In Acts 5, then, Peter asks Ananias why he "let Satan take control" of him (v. 3) that he should lie to the Holy Spirit about the price of the property he had sold. And in 1 Corinthians 10:20–21 we are warned against eating what has been offered to demons. This warning is given even more sternly in Revelation 2:14 and 20.

But Jesus came "to destroy what the Devil had done" (1 John 3:8) and gives his followers "power and authority to drive out all demons . . . to heal the sick" (Luke 9:1, 2) and to do the works that he himself did while on earth (John 14:12). We can't be either biblical or relevant without a solid approach to spiritual power.

A personal failure

What can we do about evil spirits? This was a burning question for the Nigerian leaders I was attempting to guide. But I, their missionary, knew virtually nothing about the subject. My three-volume semi-nary theology textbook had only two references to Satan and none to demons. And that's about all I had learned about the enemy king-dom and its activities, in spite of the prominence of that subject in Scripture. So my Nigerian friends were on their own. I couldn't help them.

But now, forty years later, God has led me into regular and fre-quent open conflict with demonic "rats" with the aim of setting cap-tives free. I deeply regret that I didn't know in the late 1950s what I know now. In that setting I contributed to the growth of a dual-alle-giance church. That memory and my present experience have led me to commit myself to raise this issue wherever possible in missiological circles in hopes that coming generations will be better able to deal with spiritual power than I was.

The danger of overcontextualisation

I use the term *overcontextualisation* to signify situations in which people have come to practise at least parts of their Christianity, and in this case techniques relating to spiritual power, in ways that fit in with the surrounding culture but fail to measure up to biblical stan-dards. Appropriate Christianity balances cultural appropriateness with scriptural appropriateness. An overcontextualised Christianity loses that appropriateness at the scriptural end, though it may serve well the culturally inculcated desires of any given society.

Though it is of great importance to see the use of spiritual power contextualised, it is also of great importance not to overdo it. By this I mean that there are several ways in which people have got into spiritual power and carried their emphasis too far. One of the per-versions that is widespread in America is the so-called "Name it, claim it" or "Word faith" heresy. Advocates of this approach teach that if we generate enough faith and with it claim anything we might happen to want, we can manipulate God into doing our will. We can thus gain material things, healing or whatever strikes our fancy. God wants us to be prosperous, they say, so all we have to do is to pro-duce the faith and God will grant us our desires. This is overcontextualisation because it makes God captive to the Ameri-can ideal of prosperity for everyone.

Another perversion is the one that holds that since God can heal without the use of medicine, we should not use medicine. There are, unfortunately, several deaths every year in the United States as a result of people denying themselves or their children medical assistance on this premise. They fail to see that it is God who heals through medicine and doctors as well as apart from them.

The opposite is also an overcontextualisation. Many Christians have so secularised their understandings of healing that they place all their faith in medicine and doctors and little or none in God. If someone is ill or experiencing emotional problems, their only thought is to get the person medical or psychological help, perhaps with a perfunctory prayer that God will lead the secular professional. If they pray at all in earnest concerning healing, it is only after all secular means have failed.

In many societies Christian healers use the methods of shamans rather uncritically. In Korea, for example, an unfortunately large number of pastors who seek to bring about physical healing and deliverance do so by using violence, loudness and other very un-Christlike dramatic techniques in their ministries. Both in Korea and in Africa I have heard of people being beaten in attempts to free them from demons. Certain American healers are also given to displays that make good drama but are quite unlikely to be methods Jesus would endorse.

Three crucial dimensions

On balance, however, spiritual power in Scripture is never an end in and of itself. There are other, often more important concerns. When Jesus' followers came back from a power-filled excursion into the towns and villages of Galilee reporting with excitement that "even the demons obeyed us when we gave them a command in your name" (Luke 10:17), Jesus cautioned them and pointed them to their relationship with the God who provides the power. This relationship, resulting in our names being written in heaven (Luke 10:20), should be an even greater cause of rejoicing than our power over demons.

So, as crucial as the power issue is both scripturally and contextually, we dare not diminish the traditional evangelical emphasis on a commitment to Christ. It is our relationship with Jesus that results in salvation, freedom, love and the other fruits of the Spirit that enrich our lives for time and eternity.

Nor dare we neglect the issue of truth. Yet, in keeping with the implications of the Greek word for truth, this is to be an experienced truth, not simply intellectual truth. Jesus spent most of his time teaching, demonstrating and leading his followers into experiencing truth. Thus, John 8:32 should read, "you will *experience* the truth, and the truth will set you free." That continual experiencing of the truth leads to ever-deepening understanding both of the truth dimension of Christianity and also of the power and relationship dimensions.

So, our Christian experience and our efforts at contextualisation are to be concerned with three crucial dimensions. The most important of these is our relationship to Christ, with all the love and obedience that entails. Built on this, then, are the understanding that comes from continually experiencing his truth and the spiritual power Jesus gives us to use as he used it to express his love to others. Any approach to Christianity that neglects or ignores any of these three dimensions is an incomplete and unbalanced Christianity.

Evangelical Christianity has usually been deficient in that it has ignored the power dimension. It has, however, been strong on conceptual truth and focused on allegiance and relationship, though this has in practice often been treated largely as a byproduct of truth and knowledge. Pentecostal and charismatic Christianity have often been more relevant to the peoples of the non-Western world through their emphasis on spiritual power, but they have often compromised their strength through overemphasis on tongues and emotion and/ or a negative attitude towards the cultures of the receptor peoples.

When we look at these three dimensions in relation to Western evangelical missionary work, we come up with a chart such as the following:

	Allegiance	Truth	Power
Traditional Religion	Wrong allegiance	Counterfeit truth	Satanic power
Western Christianity	True allegiance	God's truth	/////////////
Biblical Christianity	True allegiance	God's truth	God's power

Where the power dimension has not been dealt with by the advocates of (Western) Christianity, the people continue to go to their traditional sources of power, even though they have pledged allegiance to Christ and are learning biblical truth. Any attempt to rectify this situation must apply biblical emphasis and guidelines to the missing dimension.

Secularisation or a bridge from power to power?

Having largely ignored spiritual power issues, Western witness has tended unwittingly to recommend secular answers to traditional peoples to solve problems they would ordinarily consider spiritual.

Western secular medicine and hospitals, for example, are offered as the answer to health problems, secularising schools as the right way to deal with what Westerners perceive as ignorance, secular agricultural techniques, even secular approaches to church management and leadership, not to mention insights into culture and communication that largely leave out the activity of the Holy Spirit. Without intending it, then, our strategy has been to secularise in order to christianise.

What this approach has produced is secular churches (like most of those in North America and Europe), able only to avail themselves of the power of secular techniques and structures to replace traditional methods of blessing, healing, teaching and organising. There is, of course, a certain amount of power in these techniques. But they are stronger on human and/or naturalistic power than on spiritual power. For most of the traditional peoples of the world, however, healing was and is a spiritual matter, not a secular one. So are agriculture and human and animal fertility.

Though Doug Pennoyer makes a case for the use of secularisation on the way to Christianity,[1] I'm afraid secularisation has for many peoples clouded rather than assisted much of what a scriptural approach to conversion should engender. It has changed the subject from what ought to have been a change of spiritual power sources to a change from spiritual to secular answers to what traditional peoples have always regarded as spiritual problems.

Simply moving from a pagan power source to the true God as the Source is, I believe, the shortest bridge for power-oriented people, since it involves little or no conversion from spiritual power to secular power. The conversion is, rather, from one power to another Power, as it was for Abraham. The cultural results of an approach that focuses on such change of power source are likely to be forms of Christianity that look very similar to their pagan predecessors but with a different source of power. The Christian practitioners would look very like native shamans and other healers, but would work only in ways appropriate to biblical Christianity and only under the power of the true God. The places of worship and the ways in which worship and other rituals are conducted would look as much like their pagan predecessors as the places and rituals Abraham captured for the true God looked like their predecessors.

As with Israel, the practices and personnel would undoubtedly change over time to be less like their pagan models, especially where the models involved prohibited practices such as divination. But they would have started at points familiar to the people rather than with foreign practices that give the impression that God's whole system has to be imported. And when a substitution is made for unbiblical practices in the spiritual power area, let it be a spiritual power substitution, not a secular one.

I will speak below more specifically about such substitutions.

Animism versus God-given authority

Most of the world, including most of the adherents of "world religions," practice what missiologists call animism. This is the belief and the practices that go with it that the world is full of spirits that can hurt us unless we are careful to appease them. Animists may or may not believe in a high god. When they do, this god is usually seen as benign and thus in little if any need of attention. All animists agree, however, that the spirits need to be watched and kept happy, lest the spirits hurt them. In addition, most animists believe that evil spirits can inhabit material objects and places such as certain mountains (for example, Old Testament high places), trees, statues (for example, idols), rocks (for example, the Ka'aba in Mecca), rivers (for example, the Ganges), territories, fetishes, charms and any other thing or place that is dedicated to the spirits. Animists also believe in magic and the ability of at least certain people to convey power through curses, blessings, spells and the like.

In areas such as healing, dedicating and blessing, for example, we and animists do essentially the same things but the source of their power is Satan; our source is God. We learn both from Scripture and from practical experience that many, if not all of the rules that apply to God's interactions with humans also apply to the ways the enemy interacts with us.[2] For example, obedience to God in prayer, worship, sacrifice and service enables God to carry out his purposes in the world. On the other side, when people obey Satan in these same ways, he is enabled to accomplish his purposes. The importance of obedience and the fact that this is a warfare issue are thus underlined.

For example, animists believe that objects such as idols or implements used in religious rituals may be dedicated to gods or spirits and thus contain spiritual power. The Bible shows that objects can be dedicated to our God and thus convey God's power (for example, Paul's handkerchiefs, the Ark of the Covenant). On the surface, containing and conveying power look the same, especially since what animists believe to be power *contained* in objects is in reality satanic power *conveyed* by them.

Our authority as Christians versus the authority Satan can give his followers is an important issue at this point. But when we exercise the power and authority Jesus gives us to do things animists do, such as healing, casting out demons, blessing people and objects, dedicating buildings, praying for rain or against floods, it is not, as some contend, because we are animists. We are simply exercising the authority Jesus gave his disciples (Luke 9:1) and told them to teach to their followers (Matt. 28:19).

We may summarise some of the major issues in this discussion by means of the following table (see Table 21-1) designed to show many of the contrasts between animism and God-given authority. Note again that the primary expressions of each of these areas will look very similar at the surface level. It is in the underlying power and motivations that they differ.

Satan has a lot at stake in protecting himself from the power of God, which he knows is infinitely greater than his own and, in addition, has been passed on to us. Satan's primary strategy, therefore, is to keep us ignorant and deceived so that we cannot use God's power against him.

Thus a very important first step in contextualising spiritual power is to help God's people to know who they are scripturally and how this is to be expressed culturally. Scripturally, we are the children of God, made in God's image, redeemed by Jesus Christ to be heirs of God and joint heirs with him (Rom. 8:17). This gives us all the power and authority Jesus gave his followers to cast out demons and cure diseases (Luke 9:1), to do the works Jesus himself did (John 14:12), to be in the world what Jesus was (John 20:21) and to crush the enemy under our feet (Rom. 16:20). Scripturally, then, we need to follow Jesus' example, always using his power to show his love.

Christians in other societies, like we in the West, will be accountable to God to adopt scripturally and culturally appropriate models of spiritual power. But appropriate ways of exercising power in other cultural contexts may look quite different from the appropriate expressions in Western societies, and certainly different from the perversions we often see in Western lands.

Satan the contextualiser

Satan is an excellent contextualiser. He does an expert job at meeting people at the point of their perceived needs in culturally appropriate ways. The fact that he often does so through deceit is not usually recognised. I am told that there's a Japanese volcano

Table 21-1: Animism vs. God-given authority

	Animism	God-given authority
POWER	Believed to be contained in people and objects	God *conveys* his power through people and objects
NEED (in order to utilise spiritual power)	Need to learn how to manipulate spirit power through magic or authority over spirits	We are to submit to God and learn to work with him in the exercise of power and authority from him
ONTOLOGY (what is really going on)	Power from Satan; he is the one who manipulates	Power from God; he empowers and uses us
GOD	God is good but distant, therefore ignore him	God is good, therefore relate to him. He is close and involved with us
SPIRITS	Fearful and can hurt us, therefore appease them	They are defeated, therefore assert God's authority over them
PEOPLE	Victims of capricious spirits who never escape being victims	They are captives, but we can assert Jesus' authority to free them
COST	Those who receive power from Satan suffer great tragedy later	Those who work with God experience love and power throughout life
HOPE	No hope	Assurance of hope in God's victory

where people have erected signs imploring the spirits not to allow it to erupt again. There are also shrines and a temple there at which visitors can add their petitions to those of decades' worth of earlier visitors. Satan's ability to deceive in Japan in contextually appropriate ways is enhanced by the fact that the language shows no adequate distinction between spirits of whatever level and a high god. All are called *kami* and generally considered to be of the same nature and capriciousness. Attempting to appease the *kami* of the volcanic mountain is, therefore, not seen as essentially different from what Christians do on Sundays, except by the handful of Christians who have gone deeply enough into biblical Christianity to understand the difference.

In addition, our enemy has duped a large percentage of the world's population into believing that ancestors continue to participate in human affairs. All he needs to do now to be culturally relevant is to assign demons to impersonate those who have died. With regard to reincarnation, likewise, he has long since convinced people of the logic of the recycling of persons. All he has to do in this matter is to assign demons to recount for people the details of the lives of real people who lived in the past, as if these lives were their former lives. Very convincing, and very contextualised. And, since people have such a need for spiritual power, how better to gain control of them than by giving certain of them (for example, shamans) that power?

In addition to these larger areas of satanic contextualisation, demonic beings are quite skilled at providing for "smaller" needs for things such as money, position, fame, control, revenge, even security and wantedness. But all with an eventual price tag attached.

And doctrinally, Satan has produced counterfeit systems of faith that are disturbingly similar to what God has revealed in Judaeo-Christianity. Advocating righteousness, truth, peace, gentleness and other admirable virtues seems so much like what Jesus taught. How can those systems be wrong merely because they leave out the need for a relationship with Jesus? Just about every Christian doctrine and ritual has its parallels in the religions of the world, contextualised to make sense and to imitate the truth. And animistic systems are amazingly similar worldwide, leading us to suspect that there is a single mind behind them.

Indeed, in looking at Satan's activities cross-culturally, we find many quite predictable things. And these predictabilities will be in terms of the ways of thinking and behaving of the receptor society, whether or not they fit our logic. That is, Satan contextualises his deceit. In Western societies, for example, where people are quite unaware of spiritual reality, Satan likes to capture people through apparently innocent games such as Dungeons and Dragons, through membership in apparently constructive organisations such as Freemasonry, through philosophical or psychological ideas that appear erudite and innocent. In non-Western, family-oriented societies, what could be more logical than the satanic lie that one's ancestors are still alive and participating in the lives of their descendants? Or that it would be better to be with my ancestors when I die, even if they are in hell, than to go to heaven? Or that people reincarnate after they die?

Cross-cultural constants

Beyond the differences in cultural understandings and expression there are basic things that are the same cross-culturally. In working for God there are basics, such as obedience to him, preceded by listening to him and following his lead, whether in life in general or in bringing freedom to captives. With regard to Satan's kingdom, there are basics relating to how Satan attracts people, how he influences and/or enters them, and the kind of strategies he uses to keep them under his influence. In addition to these basics concerning God and Satan, there are certain basics of "human-beingness" relating to such things as how we use our wills, our capability for relating to the spirit world and our vulnerability to temptation and deceit.

That both God and Satan work in partnership with people in terms of their culture is a constant we can expect to find in every cultural context. Underlying this is the fact that both God and Satan have plans for any given people and their culture, and they work with human will to seek to accomplish those plans. Though it is apparent that Satan is having great influence on the human scene, we learn from Scripture, especially the events surrounding Jesus' life, death and resurrection, that God is working out his own purposes in the background and that Satan's ultimate defeat is certain. We, therefore, can expect to find both Satan and God working with their human partners in every cultural context. According to Romans 1:16–2:16, God is working in conscience and culture so that, whatever excuses those who choose Satan's way may give, they are accountable to God for their disobedience.

PERSON AND CULTURE

In dealing with culture, it is always important to distinguish cultural structure from the persons who operate those structures. Contextualisation studies usually focus on the structuring, leaving implicit the fact that it is *people* who produce and operate the structures. Culture does not run itself. Culture is like the script of a play, memorised but regularly altered by the actors for a variety of reasons, some good, some bad, some conscious, many unconscious.

In dealing with spiritual reality we must recognise that both human persons and spirit beings are involved in the way cultural structuring is used. Most cultural structuring is capable of being used either for good or for evil. Such things as status and prestige, for example, provided by a society on the basis of birth and/or achieve-ment, can be used by those who have them either to help others or to hurt them. The fact that given people have status and the power that goes with it is not in and of itself a bad thing. Satan, however, entices people to use their status to hurt others, while God gently prods his people to use their status and the authority and power that goes with it to assist the powerless.

But in each case, the spiritual being (God or Satan) works *with* people in terms of the cultural structuring in which the people are involved. In dealing with spiritual warfare, as with all studies of contextualisation, then, our primary focus needs to be on *people* within culture, not simply on culture itself.

The important place of human habit must, however, be recognised. Any power that culture seems to have is really the power of human habit. Thus, any attempts to change culture are really attempts to change habits. The structuring is a function of the script produced by and followed fairly closely by the actors out of habit (once they have memorised it). When we find enemy influence contextualised within socio-cultural patterns and habitually followed, it is to *people* we appeal for changes in their habits. We cannot appeal to an im-personal thing like a cultural structure or pattern.

FORMS, MEANINGS AND EMPOWERMENT

As mentioned earlier, a major problem in contextualisation is the problem of changing the meanings of familiar forms. In seeking to assist people to accept and practise Christianity in terms of their own cultural forms, we are assisting them to use those forms for new purposes and with new or modified meanings. John the Baptist was reinterpreting a form (baptism) that was well known as a way of initiating Gentile converts into Judaism. When the church decided to use it to signify initiation into the church, it was largely following John's lead. When the church used baptism in Gentile territory, then, the meaning was more like its use in the initiation of Gentiles into Judaism and of converts to Greek religions into those religions. In either case the meaning was in part the same as that of previous practice and in part a modification of that meaning.

But cultural forms can also be empowered. God regularly flows his power through words such as "in Jesus' name" and the com-mands we give to demons. When such words are conveying God's power, we may call them "empowered language forms." James rec-ommends that we use anointing oil to bring healing to the sick (James

5:14). If the oil is to be effective, it needs to be dedicated in the name of Jesus and thus empowered. The elements used in the Lord's Supper can also be dedicated for specific purposes such as blessing and healing and thus empowered.

In many non-Christian societies, it is the usual thing for at least certain people to dedicate the things they make to spirits or gods, especially if those things are to be used for religious purposes or in dangerous pursuits. In the South Pacific, those who made the large canoes used for fishing and/or for warfare regularly dedicated them to their gods. When such things are dedicated to satanic spirits, they are empowered by those spirits. Many a missionary and traveller who has brought such dedicated things home has experienced difficulties because he or she has unwittingly invited enemy spirits into the home.

Nevertheless, breaking the power of such objects is usually not difficult. Since we have infinitely more power in Jesus Christ than such objects can contain, we simply have to claim Jesus' power to break the enemy's power in the object.

In contextualising the power of Christ, it is important to disempower whatever has been empowered with satanic power before attempting to use it. Satanic power can be broken over rituals, buildings, carvings, songs and any other custom or artifact a people wants to capture for God's use. In this way we can capture for Christ cultural forms traditionally used by the enemy. But we shouldn't try to use the forms until the power is broken.

Even after the power is broken, there may still be a meaning problem, since people may for centuries have associated rituals and other cultural forms with their allegiance to satanic spirits. Considerable pressure must be exerted by the Christian community, often for several generations, to capture and completely transform the meanings of once pagan customs. The difficulties encountered in such a process are, however, infinitely preferable to the syncretism that results from the simple importation of foreign customs in hopes that if the power dimension is ignored, it will go away.

Often, under missionary tutelage, the first converts attempted to replace with foreign customs as many as possible of their customs that reminded them of their old involvement with shamans, rituals and evil spirits. This is unfortunate for at least two reasons: (1) it gives the impression that Christianity is intended to be foreign and, usually, secular; and (2) the new system does not adequately meet the converts' need for spiritual power. The people, therefore, continue to go to shamans for blessing, healing and other spiritual power needs since the foreign Jesus they have been presented with has no power. One meaning that missionary Christianity usually carries, then, is "powerless."

Ground-level warfare

Spiritual warfare has to be waged on at least two levels: ground level and cosmic level. Ground-level warfare involves dealing with the spirits (demons) that inhabit persons.[3] As already mentioned, our enemy contextualises his approach to the problems and concerns most prominent in any given society. In Asian societies, for example, where the relationship between mother-in-law and daughter-in-law is a difficult one, demons will often be active in pushing mothers-in-law to be oppressive and daughters-in-law to hate them. In African societies, where fear of the unknown is endemic, demons push all the buttons they can to increase the fear and the practice of going to diviners (where demonic influence is increased) for relief. In Latin America, Asia and Europe, where male domination of women and children is culturally inculcated, the enemy kingdom is very active in increasing the abuse and the pain felt by women and children. And we can speak of satanic enhancement of racism and social-class oppression in many parts of the world.

With regard to techniques people use for dealing with demons, then, the enemy is also active in seeing to it that culturally appropriate excesses are regular occurrences. In Korea and Africa, for example, it is common to hear of deliverance sessions that involve the same kind of abusive beating that frequently occurs between husbands and wives, fathers and children, not to mention in pagan attempts to deal with demonisation. Contextualised attempts at deliverance may thus be orchestrated by Satan himself. It is not unknown for people to be killed when such methods are used, thus fulfilling a demon's intent to destroy those it inhabits.

The appropriate and proper approach to getting people free from demons in any society seems, however, to always be the same: deal with the spiritual and emotional garbage to weaken the demons, then kick them out. Fighting physically with them is never a good idea. And even when it is necessary to physically restrain a demonised person, it is God's power wielded through words, not that wielded through physical force, that gets the demons out.

In many societies children are routinely dedicated to gods/spirits at birth. It is customary for non-Christian and even many Christian families in Chinese, Japanese and Korean societies to write the exact date and time of a child's birth and to register it at a temple. Such dedications both empower the inherited family spirits and add spirits.

Additional spirits are usually also present, having gained entrance through occult involvement or negative emotional reactions such as anger, hatred, unforgiveness, fear and the like. I recently worked to free a Chinese woman missionary from family demons. These had been strengthened at times when her parents dedicated her at birth and when they took her to a temple for healing. She was also carrying demons who entered when she was involved in practising Chinese martial arts under a master who, without her awareness, dedicated all he did to demonic spirits. But she had no idea that these things that had happened long ago could be responsible for the daily (and nightly) torment she experienced. She believed in demons but had not known that demons could live in Christians.

Cosmic-level warfare

Above the "ground level" are at least five kinds of higher-level spirits that live "in the air" (Eph. 2:2). Dealing with them is ordinarily known as cosmic-level warfare.

Cosmic-level spirits are apparently in charge of ground-level spirits, assigning them to people and supervising them as they carry out their assignments in people or do their tempting and harassing of people from outside of them.

Cosmic-level spirits

Most of the peoples of the world recognise that there are specific spirits attached to nations, regions, mountains, rivers and other geographical features. When people enter the territory of a given god, they need to show respect to that god. In the Old Testament we continually find Israel honouring the Baals and other gods when they were in territory they believed to belong to these gods. In Hosea 2:8 we see Israel attributing its prosperity to the Baal gods. Solomon, in order to cement relationships and keep peace with the surrounding countries, married wives from Ammon, Moab and Edom and erected altars to their gods to show honour to their countries (1 Kings 11:1–10).

Though Westerners may consider these gods to be imaginary, the Bible shows God and his people taking them seriously. We are, however, warned against giving them honour or fearing them.

Cosmic-Level Spirits

Territorial spirits, such as those over nations mentioned in Daniel 10:13 and 21 (called "Prince of Persia" and "Prince of Greece"), spirits over regions and spirits over cities

Institutional spirits, such as those assigned to churches, governments, educational institutions, occult organisations (e.g., Scientology, Freemasonry, Mormonism), non-Christian religions (e.g., the gods of Hinduism, Buddhism, animism), temples, shrines

Vice spirits, such as those assigned to oversee and encourage special functions, including vices such as prostitution, abortion, homosexuality, gambling, pornography, war, music, cults and the like

Nature, household and cultural item spirits, such as those residing in trees, rivers, homes and cultural items such as dedicated work implements, music, rituals, artifacts used in religious worship and the like

Ancestor spirits, believed by many peoples to be their physically dead ancestors who still participate in the activities of the living community

---

People who have been under the sway of territorial spirits for generations have a great deal of understanding of what territory the spirits have influence over and what results from this influence. Any approach to Christianity in such areas, therefore, needs to recognise the reality of the spirits over the area and to gain understanding of their assignments. We will then have to deal with them by taking away their rights as we work with the true God to retake territory that is rightfully his.

Discussions of the contextualisation of biblical understandings of the spirit world and spiritual warfare need to take into account these levels of spirits and what to do about them. Following are several specific topics

GODS, IDOLS AND DIVINATION

Our efforts to contextualise spiritual power must recognise that God is uncompromising with regard to other gods, idols and the ways in which their power is engaged. The Bible is clear that worship of any god but the true God is not permitted. We are to "worship no god but me [Yahweh]" (Exod. 20:3). There are, then, to be no idols made or worshipped because "I am the Lord your God and I tolerate no rivals" (Exod. 20:5). And among the warnings in the

New Testament is the command at the end of 1 John: "My children, keep yourselves safe from false gods!" (1 John 5:21).

Perhaps the clearest indication of what God feels about his people having relationships with other gods is found in the story of the people of Israel at Peor in Numbers 25. God became very angry at the Israelite leaders who attended feasts with Moabite women "where the god of Moab was worshipped" and where "the Israelites ate the food and worshipped the god Baal of Peor" (vv. 2–3). God was so angry at them that he commanded that those who had participated in that worship should be killed publicly (v. 4). Contextualisation of idolatry, then, is impossible for Christians.

Several other practices are also forbidden to God's people and cited as the reasons why God gave his people the right to drive out the inhabitants of Palestine. In Deuteronomy 18:9–13 God condemns sacrificing children, divination, looking for omens, using spells or charms and consulting spirits of the dead. "God hates people who do these disgusting things, and that is why he is driving those nations out of the land as you advance" (v. 12).

God doesn't tolerate appeasing pagan gods or spirits or seeking information, health, wealth or blessing from them. God's answer is to relate to him and allow him to take care of the opposing spirits and to provide the blessings we need.

It is frightening to think what such total condemnation says to those Christians who continue to seek spiritual power from traditional shamans, priests and shrines. Though pagan worship is condemned, in at least one case God's prophet (Elisha) indicated that God would be understanding if the king's servant (Naaman) continued to accompany his master to a pagan temple (2 Kings 5).

In attempting to see biblical Christianity contextualised, then, we recognise that God allows no rivals. Though God allowed Israel's belief in many gods to continue for some time, he insisted that there be no compromise with regard to allegiance. Places of worship and even rituals and transition rites such as circumcision and baptism, used by pagans in pre-Christian observances can, however, be captured, purified and used to honour the true God.

ANCESTORS

One of Satan's cleverest deceptions is to convince people that their loved ones continue to participate actively in human life. Since demons already know everything about those who have died, they can do an excellent job of impersonation and, in the process, exert a great amount of control over people. Posing as ancestors, demons give and take away, binding people to false beliefs and the rituals that go with them.

Academics argue about whether it is really the ancestors who appear to their living family members. Some point to the passage concerning King Saul's excursion to the "witch of Endor" (1 Sam. 28:3–19). But I maintain that this account and the fact that at the Transfiguration Moses and Elijah appeared to Jesus (Luke 9:28–31) have nothing to do with the possibility that ancestors are conscious of and interacting with human life.

So, we are left scripturally with no encouragement to believe that the dead interact with the living. And, in fact, we are warned sternly not to attempt to contact the dead (Lev. 19:31; Deut. 18:11). The practice of diviners seeking information about this life, and especially about the future, from the deceased is widely known, both in Scripture and in contemporary societies. We learn from Deuteronomy 18:12 that "The Lord your God hates people who do these disgusting things."

To free people spiritually from satanic deception in ancestral matters, we have to deal with the family demons that ancestral practices invite in. These need to be banished. So do the spirits inhabiting the ancestral tablets and any other paraphernalia associated with the reverence and/or worship accorded them.

REINCARNATION

Reincarnation is another area of demonic deception. Since demons know people's lives in detail, it is easy for them to tell people someone else's life as if it was their own past life.

Scripture is clear that "everyone must die once, and after that be judged by God" (Heb. 9:27). There is no scriptural allowance for anyone to be reborn into another earthly existence. God has created each of us unique and eternal. This belief, therefore, like idolatry and divination, cannot be contextualised. Dealing with the demons of reincarnation may, however, be the first step toward freeing people from this lie.

SHRINES AND DEDICATED PLACES

Satan has the ability to heal and bless those who come to places dedicated to him. But his power can be broken and such places captured for Christ, as were high places, altars and rituals in the Old Testament. Or Christian power centres could be constructed after patterns familiar to recently converted people. In Japan, for example, where it is the custom for people to go to power places whenever they feel the need, Christian shrines could be constructed that look like Shinto shrines but function under the authority and power of Jesus Christ.

Such shrines would, of course, differ in several respects from normal Shinto shrines. And those who minister could be young people, thus providing for youth a kind of ministry for which they would usually have to wait several years.

Conclusion

We have surveyed some of the aspects of spiritual power that need to be carefully but effectively dealt with in any consideration of appropriate Christianity. It is unfortunate that in most situations missionised from the West these issues have not been taken seriously. People have, therefore, moved into an allegiance to Christ without fully giving up their previous allegiances to traditional spirits and gods. This and many other problems that have arisen because of the lack of attention to the contextualisation of spiritual power desperately need to be faced and worked through to discover answers that are both scripturally and culturally appropriate.

Notes

[1] F. Douglas Pennoyer, "In Dark Dungeons of Collective Captivity," in *Wrestling with Dark Angels*, ed. C. Peter Wagner and F. Douglas Pennoyer (Ventura, Calif.: Regal Books, 1990).

[2] See Charles H. Kraft and David M. DeBord, *The Rules of Engagement* (Colorado Springs, Colo.: Wagner Publications, 2000).

[3] See "Categories of Spirits," page 189, in Chapter 14 herein.

Appendix

Statement on spiritual warfare

A Working Group Report

The Intercession Working Group (IWG) of the Lausanne Committee for World Evangelization met at Fairmile Court in London July 10–14, 1993. We discussed for one full day the subject of spiritual warfare. It had been noted at our IWG Prayer Leaders' Retreat at The Cove in North Carolina, USA, the previous November, that spiritual warfare was a subject of some concern in the evangelical world. The IWG asked its members to write papers reflecting on this emphasis in each of their regions and these papers formed the basis of our discussion.

We affirmed again statement 12 on "Spiritual Conflict" in The Lausanne Covenant:

We believe that we are engaged in constant spiritual warfare with the principalities and powers of evil who are seeking to overthrow the church and frustrate its task of evangelization.
We know our need to equip ourselves with God's armor and to fight this battle with the spiritual weapons of truth and prayer. For we detect the activity of our enemy, not only in false ideologies outside the church, but also inside it in false gospels which twist Scripture and put man in the place of God.
We need both watchfulness and discernment to safeguard the biblical gospel. We acknowledge that we ourselves are not immune to worldliness of thought and actions, that is, to surrender to secularism. . . .

We agreed that evangelization is to bring people from darkness to light and from the power of Satan to God (Acts 26:17). This involves an inescapable element of spiritual warfare.

We asked ourselves why there had been almost an explosion of interest in this subject in the last 10 years. We noted that the Western church and the missionary movement from the West had seen the remarkable expansion of the church in other areas of the world without special emphasis being given to the subject of spiritual warfare.

Our members from Africa and Asia reminded us that in their context, the powers of darkness are very real and spiritual warfare is where they live all the time. Their families are still only one or two generations removed from a spiritist, animist or occult heritage.

This led to a discussion of the effects of one generation on another. We noted that in the context of idolatry, the Bible speaks of the sins of the fathers being visited upon their descendants to the third and fourth generation.

Likewise, the blessing of God's love is shown to successive generations of those who love him and keep his laws. We wondered if the time we have had the gospel in the West has made us less conscious of the powers of darkness in recent centuries.

We noted, also that the influence of the enlightenment in our education, which traces everything to natural causes, has further dulled our consciousness of the powers of darkness.

In recent times, however, several things have changed:

Change in Initiatives: The initiative in evangelization is passing to churches in the developing world, and as people from the same background evangelize their own people, dealing with the powers of darkness has become a natural way of thinking and working. This is especially true of the rapidly growing Pentecostal churches. This has begun to influence all missiological thinking.

Increased Interest in Eastern Religions: The spiritual bankruptcy of the West has opened up great interest in Eastern religions and drug cultures and brought a resurgence of the occult in the West.

Influx of Non-Christian Worldview: The massive migrations of peoples from the Third World to the West has brought a torrent of non-Christian worldviews and practices into our midst. Increasing mobility has also exposed developing countries to new fringe groups, cults and freemasonry.

Sensationalization of the Occult: The secular media has sensationalized and spread interest in these occult ideas and practices. This was marked by the screening of the film "The Exorcist." In the

Christian world the books by Frank Perretti and the spate of "How to . . ." books on power evangelism and spiritual warfare have reflected a similar trend.

Lausanne's Involvement in the Process: We in Lausanne have been part of the process, especially in the track on spiritual warfare at Lausanne II in Manila and in the continuing life of that track under the aegis of the AD2000 and Beyond movement.

We recognize that this emphasis will be with us for the foreseeable future. Our concerns are:

To help our Lausanne constituency to stay firmly within the balanced biblical teaching on prayer.

To provide clarity, reassurance and encouragement to those whom the emphasis is causing confusion and anxiety.

To harness what is biblical, Christ-exalting and culturally relevant in the new emphasis to the work of evangelization so that it yields lasting fruit.

We noted the following dangers and their antidotes:

Reverting to Pagan Worldviews: There is a danger that we revert to think and operate on pagan worldviews or on an undiscerning application of Old Testament analogies that were, in fact, superseded in Jesus Christ. The antidote to this is the rigorous study of the whole of Scripture, always interpreting the Old Testament in the light of the New.

A Preoccupation with the Demonic: This can lead to avoiding personal responsibility for our actions. This is countered by equal emphasis on "the world" and "the flesh" and the strong ethical teachings of the Bible.

A Preoccupation with the Powers of Darkness: This can exalt Satan and diminish Jesus in the focus of his people. This is cured by encouraging a Christ-centered and not an experience-centered spirituality or methodology.

The Tendency to Shift the Emphasis to "Power" and Away from "Truth": This tendency forgets that error, ignorance and deception can only be countered by biblical truth clearly and consistently taught. This is equally, if not more important, than tackling bondage and possession by "power encounters."

It is also the truth that sets us free, so the Word and the Spirit need to be kept in balance.

Emphasis on Technique and Methodology: We observed the tendency to emphasize technique and methodology in the practice of spiritual warfare and fear that when this is dominant it can become a substitute for the pursuit of holiness and even of evangelism itself.

To combat this there is no substitute for a continuous, strong, balanced and Spirit-guided teaching ministry in each church.

Growing Disillusionment: We had reports of growing disillusionment with the results of spiritual warfare in unrealized expectations, unmet predictions and the sense of being marginalized if the language and practice of spiritual warfare is not adopted and just general discomfort with too much triumphalist talk. The antidote to all of this is a return to the whole teaching of Jesus on prayer, especially what he says about praying in secret that avoids ostentation.

Encountering the Powers of Darkness by the Peoples Themselves: While recognizing that someone initially has to go to a people to introduce the gospel, we felt it was necessary always for the encounter with the powers of darkness to be undertaken by Christian people within the culture and in a way that is sensitive in applying biblical truth to their context.

Caution Regarding Territorial Spirits Concept: We are cautious about the way in which the concept of territorial spirits is being used and look to our biblical scholars to shed more light on this recent development.

Warfare Language Can Lead to Adversarial Attitudes: We heard with concern of situations where warfare language was pushing Christians into adversarial attitudes with people and where people of other faiths were interpreting this as the language of violence and political involvement.

We saw that the language of peace, penitence and reconciliation must be as prominent in our speech and practice as any talk of warfare.

We are concerned that the subject and practice of spiritual warfare is proving divisive to evangelical Christians and pray that these thoughts of ours will help to combat this tendency. It is our deep prayer that the force for evangelization should not be fragmented and that our love should be strong enough to overcome these incipient divisions among us.

In his cross and resurrection, Jesus triumphed over all the powers of darkness; believers share in that triumph. We would like to see evidence of this in our unity in prayer.

Bibliography

Adeyemo, Tokunboh. *Salvation in African Traditional Religion.* Nairobi: Evangel Publishing House, 1979.

Alexander, William M. *Demonic Possession in the New Testament.* Grand Rapids, Mich.: Baker Book House, 1980.

Allender, Dan, and Tremper Longman. *Bold Love.* Colorado Springs, Colo.: NavPress, 1992.

Allison, Norman E. "Make Sure You're Getting Through." *Evangelical Missions Quarterly* 20 (1984): 165-70.

Althaus, Paul. *The Theology of Martin Luther.* Philadelphia: Fortress, 1966.

Amstutz, Wendell. *Exposing and Confronting Satan and Associates.* 5th ed. Rochester, Minn.: National Counseling Resource Center, 1991.

Anderson, Neil. *The Bondage Breaker.* Eugene, Ore: Harvest House Publishers, 1990.

———. *Living Free in Christ.* Ventura, Calif.: Regal Books, 1993.

———. *Released from Bondage.* San Bernardino, Calif.: Here's Life Publishers, 1991.

———. *Resolving Personal Conflicts.* La Habra, Calif.: Freedom in Christ Ministries, 1992.

———. *Spiritual Conflicts and Counseling.* La Habra, Calif.: Freedom in Christ Ministries, 1992.

———. *Steps to Freedom in Christ.* La Habra, Calif.: Freedom in Christ Ministries, 1993.

———. *Victory over the Darkness: Realizing the Power of Your Identity in Christ.* Ventura, Calif.: Regal Books, 1990.

———. *Walking Through the Darkness.* San Bernardino, Calif.: Here's Life Publishers, 1991.

Anderson, Neil, and Charles Mylander. *Setting Your Church Free.* Ventura, Calif.: Regal Books, 1994.

Anderson, Neil, and Steve Russo. *The Seduction of Our Children.* Eugene, Ore: Harvest House Publishers, 1991.

Andres, Friedrich. *Die Engellehre der griechischen Apologeten des zweiten Jahrhunderts und ihr Verhältnis zur griechisch-römischen Dämonologie.* Paderborn: F. Schöningh, 1914.

The Apostolic Fathers with an English Translation. Vol. 1. Translated by Kirsopp Lake. Cambridge, Mass.: Harvard University Press, 1975.

Aren, Gustav. *Evangelical Pioneers in Ethiopia.* Studia Missionalia 32. Stockholm: EFS Forlaget, 1978.

313

Arnold, Clinton E. *Ephesians: Power and Magic: The Concept of Power in Ephesians in Light of Its Historical Setting.* Society for New Testament Studies Monograph 63. Cambridge: Cambridge University Press, 1989.

————. *Powers of Darkness: Principalities and Powers in Paul's Letters.* Downers Grove, Ill.: InterVarsity Press, 1992.

————. *Three Crucial Questions About Spiritual Warfare.* Grand Rapids, Mich.: Baker Book House, 1997.

————. "What About Territorial Spirits?" *Discipleship Journal* (May/June 1994): 81.

Augsburger, David W. *Conflict Mediation Across Cultures.* Philadelphia: Westminster Press, 1992.

————. *Pastoral Counseling Across Cultures.* Philadelphia: Westminster Press, 1986.

Aulen, Gustaf. *Christus Victor: An Historical Study of the Three Main Types of the Idea of the Atonement.* London: SPCK, 1970.

Ayisi, E. O. *An Introduction to the Study of African Culture.* London: Heinemann Education Books, 1979.

Baasland, Ernst, and Reidar Hvalvik. *De apostoliske fedre.* Oslo: Luther, 1984.

Bailey, Alice A. *The Reappearance of the Christ.* New York: Lucis Publishing Company, 1984.

Barclay, William. *The Gospel of John.* 2d ed. Philadelphia: Westminster Press, 1956.

Barker, Peter. *Peoples, Languages and Religion in Northern Ghana: A Preliminary Report.* Accra, Ghana: GEC, 1986.

Barnett, Homer G. *Innovation: The Basis of Cultural Change.* New York: McGraw-Hill, 1953.

Bartels, Lambert. *Oromo Religion: Myths and Rites of the Western Oromo of Ethiopia.* Berlin: D. Reimer, 1990.

Bawa, Yamba C. "Cosmologies in Turmoil: Witchfinding and AIDS in Chiawa, Zambia." *Africa* 67 (1997): 200-223.

Beattie, John, and John Middleton, eds. *Spirit Mediumship and Society in Africa.* London: Routledge & Kegan Paul, 1969.

Bediako, Kwame. *Christianity in Africa; the Renewal of a Non-Western Religion.* Edinburgh: Edinburgh University, 1995.

————. *Theology and Identity: The Impact of Culture upon Christian Thought in the Second Century and Modern Africa.* Oxford: Regnum, 1992.

————. "Understanding African Theology in the Twentieth Century." *Bulletin for Contextual Theology in Southern Africa and Africa* 3:2 (June 1994): 1-11.

Bernal, Dick. *Storming Hell's Brazen Gates, Isaiah 45:2: Through Militant, Violent, Prevailing Prayer!* San Jose, Calif.: Jubilee Christian Center, 1988.

Blue, Ken. *Authority to Heal.* Downers Grove, Ill.: InterVarsity Press, 1987.

Blumhardt, Johann Christof. *Blumhardt's Battle: A Conflict with Satan.* Translated by Frank S. Boshold. New York: T. E. Lowe, 1970.

Bond, George C. "Ancestors and Protestants: Religious Coexistence in the Social Field of a Zambian Community." *American Ethnologist* 14 (February 1987): 55-72.

Bosch, David J. *Transforming Mission: Paradigm Shifts in Theology of Mission.* Maryknoll, N.Y.: Orbis Books, 1991.

Boyd, Gregory. *God at War.* Downers Grove: InterVarsity Press, 1997.

Brant, Howard. "Power Encounter: Toward an SIM Position." *International Journal of Frontier Missions* 10:4 (October 1993): 185-92.

Bridge, Donald. *Signs and Wonders Today.* Downers Grove, Ill.: InterVarsity Press, 1985.

Brøgger, Jan. *Belief and Experience Among the Sidamo: A Case Study Towards an Anthropology of Knowledge.* Oslo: Norwegian University Press, 1986.

Brown, Colin, ed. *The New International Dictionary of New Testament Theology.* Exeter: Paternoster, 1975. S.v. "Flesh," by H. Seebass.

———. *That You May Believe: Miracles and Faith Then and Now.* Grand Rapids, Mich.: Eerdmans, 1985.

Brunner, Frederick Dale. *A Theology of the Holy Spirit: The Pentecostal Experience and New Testament Witness.* Grand Rapids, Mich.: Eerdmans, 1970.

Bubeck, Mark I. *The Adversary: The Christian Versus Demon Activity.* Chicago: Moody Press, 1975.

———. *Overcoming the Adversary.* Chicago: Moody Press, 1984.

———. *The Satanic Revival.* San Bernardino, Calif.: Here's Life Publishers, 1991.

Bufford, Rodger K. *Counseling and the Demonic.* Dallas, Tex.: Word Books, 1988.

Buhrmann, M. V., "Religion and Healing: The African Experience." In *Afro-Christian Religion and Healing in South Africa*, edited by G. Oosthuizen, 25-34. Lewiston, N.Y.: Edwin Mellon Press, 1989.

Bull, Dennis L., Joan W. Ellason, and Colin A. Ross. "Exorcism Revisited: Positive Outcomes with Dissociative Identity Disorder." *Journal of Psychology and Theology* 26:2 (1998): 188-96.

Burnett, David G. *Clash of Worlds.* Eastbourne, England: MARC Europe, 1990.

———. *Unearthly Powers: A Christian Perspective on Primal and Folk Religions.* Eastbourne, England: MARC Publications, 1988.

———. *World of the Spirits.* Tunbridge Wells: Monarch, 2000.

Busia, K. A. "Ancestor Worship." *Practical Anthropology* 6 (1959): 23-28.

Caballeros, Harold. "Defeating the Enemy with the Help of Spiritual Mapping." In *Breaking Strongholds in Your City*, edited by C. Peter Wagner, 123-46. Ventura, Calif.: Regal Books, 1993.

Caird, G. B. *Paul's Letters from Prison – Ephesians, Philippians, Colossians, Philemon.* Oxford: Oxford University Press, 1976.

———. *Principalities and Powers: A Study in Pauline Theology.* Oxford: Oxford University Press, 1956.

Caplan, Lionel. "The Popular Culture of Evil in Urban South India." In *The Anthropology of Evil,* edited by David Parkin, 110-27. New York: Blackwell, 1985.

Carr, Wesley. *Angels and Principalities: The Background, Meaning and Development of the Pauline Phrase* hai archai kai hai exousiai. Cambridge: Cambridge University Press, 1981.

Catechism of the Catholic Church. Mahwah, N.J.: Paulist Press, 1994.

"'Celebration Ephesus' in Historic Turkish Ruins." 1999. Charisma News Service: Maranatha Christian Journal. Online.

Chadwick, Henry, translator. *Origen: Contra Celsum.* Cambridge: Cambridge University Press, 1965.

Chiundiza, Richmond. "High Level Powers in Zimbabwe." In *Engaging the Enemy: How to Fight and Defeat Territorial Spirits,* edited by C. Peter Wagner, 121-28. Ventura, Calif.: Regal Books, 1991.

Cho, Paul Yonggi, "City Taking in Korea." In *Engaging the Enemy: How to Fight and Defeat Territorial Spirits,* edited by C. Peter Wagner, 117-20. Ventura, Calif.: Regal Books, 1991.

Christenson, Evelyn. *Battling the Prince of Darkness: Rescuing Captives from Satan's Kingdom.* Wheaton, Ill.: Victor Books, 1990.

Cohen, Eric. "Christianity and Buddhism in Thailand: The 'Battle of the Axes' and the 'Contest of Power.'" *Social Compass* 38:2 (1991): 115-40.

———. "The Missionary as Stranger: A Phenomenological Analysis of Christian Missionaries' Encounter with Fold Religions," *Review of Religious Research* 31:4 (June 1990): 337-50.

Cole, Victor B. "The Christian and African Traditional Religion and Culture: Some Basic Principles of Understanding and Approach." Unpublished (1989).

Comaroff, J. J. *Of Revelation and Revolution: Christianity, Colonialism and Consciousness in South Africa.* Chicago: Chicago University Press, 1991.

Crapanzano, Vincent. *Case Studies in Spirit Possession.* New York: Wiley, 1977.

Crossman, Eileen. *Mountain Rain: A Biography of James O. Fraser.* London: OMF, 1982.

Danfulani, Umar H. D. "Exorcising Witchcraft: The Return of the Gods in New Religious Movements on the Jos Plateau and the Benue Regions of Nigeria." *African Affairs* 98 (1999): 167-93.

Dassmann, Ernst. *Reallexikon für Antike und Christentum.* Stuttgart: Hiersemann, 1969. S.v. "Exorcismus" by K. Thraede.

Dawson, John. *Taking Our Cities for God: How to Break Spiritual Strongholds.* Lake Mary, Fla.: Creation House, 1989.

———. "Seventh Time Around: Breaking Through a City's Invisible Barriers to the Gospel." In *Engaging the Enemy: How to Fight and Defeat*

Territorial Spirits, edited by C. Peter Wagner, 135-42. Ventura, Calif.: Regal Books, 1991.

Dickason, C. Fred. *Angels: Elect and Evil.* Chicago: Moody Press, 1975.

————. *Demon Possession and the Christian.* Chicago: Moody, 1987.

Dickson, Kwesi A., and Paul Ellingworth. *Biblical Revelation and African Beliefs.* London: Lutterworth, 1969.

Dix, Gregory, ed. *The Treatise on the Apostolic Tradition of St. Hippolytus of Rome.* London: Curzon Press, 1986.

Douglas, Mary. "Sorcery Accusations Unleashed: The Lele Revisited, 1987." *Africa* 69 (1999): 177-93.

Dubois, Abbe J. A. *Hindu Manners, Customs and Ceremonies.* 3d ed. Oxford: Clarendon Press, 1906.

Dundes, Alan. "Wet and Dry: The Evil Eye," in *The Evil Eye: A Casebook,* edited by Alan Dundes. London: Garland, 1981.

Dye, Wayne. "Toward a Theology of Power for Melanesia. Part 1." *Catalyst* 14:1 (1984): 57-75.

————. "Toward a Theology of Power for Melanesia: Part 2." *Catalyst* 14:2 (1984): 158-80.

Earhart, Byron H. *Religions of Japan: Many Traditions Within One Sacred Way.* New York: HarperCollins, 1984.

Edwards, Adrian C. "On the Non-existence of an Ancestor Cult Among the Tiv." *Anthropos: International Review of Ethnology and Linguistics* 79:1-3 (1984): 77-112.

Eitel, Keith E. *Transforming Culture: Developing a Biblical Ethic in an African Context.* Nairobi: Evangel Publishing House, 1986.

Engelsviken, Tormod. *Besettelse og åndsutdrivelse i Bibelen, historien og vår egen tid.* Oslo: Lund, 1978.

————. "Exorcism and Healing in the Evangelical Churches of Ethiopia." *Journal of Mission Theology* 1:1 (1991): 80-92.

Ensign, Greyson, and Edward Howe. *Bothered? Bewildered? Bewitched?: Your Guide to Practical Supernatural Healing.* Cincinnati: Recovery Publications, 1984.

Evans, Mary J. "'A Plague on Both Your Houses': Cursing and Blessing Reviewed." *Vox Evangelica* 24 (1994): 77-90.

Evans-Pritchard, E. E. *Witchcraft, Oracles and Magic Among the Azande.* Oxford: Clarendon Press, 1976.

Ferguson, Sinclair B. and David F. Wright, eds. *New Dictionary of Theology,* Leicester: Inter-Varsity Press, 1988. S.v. "Myth" by I. Howard Marshall.

Fisher, G. Richard, Paul R. Blizard, and M. Kurt Goedelman. *Drugs, Demons and Delusions.* St. Louis: Personal Freedom Outreach, 1991.

Frangipane, Francis. *The Three Battlegrounds.* By the Author, 1989.

Fraser, George A. "Exorcism Rituals: Effects on Multiple Personality Disorder Patients." *Dissociation: Progress in the Dissociative Disorders Special Issue: Possession* 6:4 (1993): 239-44.

———. "Satanic Ritual Abuse: A Cause of Multiple Personality Disorder." *Journal of Child and Youth Care* (Special Issue 1990), 55-65.

Friesen, James G. *Uncovering the Mystery of MPD*. San Bernardino, Calif.: Here's Life Publishers, 1991.

Garrett, Susan R. *The Demise of the Devil*. Philadelphia: Fortress Press, 1989.

Gehman, Richard J. *African Traditional Religion in Biblical Perspective*. Nairobi, Kenya: East African Educational Publishers, 1989.

Gibbs, Nancy. "Angels Among Us." *Time* (December 27, 1993), 56-65.

Gilkey, Langdon. *Maker of Heaven and Earth: The Christian Doctrine of Creation in the Light of Modern Knowledge*. Lanham, Md.: University Press of America, 1959.

Goodman, Felicitas. *How About Demons?* Bloomington, Ind.: Indiana University Press, 1988.

Graham, Billy. *Angels: God's Secret Agents*. Garden City, N.Y.: Doubleday, 1981.

———. *Storm Warning*. Dallas, Tex.: Word Books, 1992.

Grant, Robert M., ed. *Theophilus of Antioch. Ad Autolycum*. Oxford: Oxford University Press, 1970.

Green, Michael. *I Believe in Satan's Downfall*. Grand Rapids, Mich.: Eerdmans, 1981.

Greenlee, David. "Territorial Spirits Reconsidered." *Missiology* 22 (1994): 507-14.

Grieg, Gary, and Kevin Springer, eds. *The Kingdom and the Power*. Ventura, Calif.: Regal Books, 1993.

Hackett, Rosalind J. "Sacred Paradoxes: Women and Religious Plurality in Nigeria." In *Women, Religion, and Social Change*, edited by Yvonne Yazbeck Haddad and Ellison Banks Findley, 247-71. Albany, N.Y.: State University of New York Press, 1985.

Hammond, Frank, and Ida Mae Hammond. *Pigs in the Parlor*. Kirkwood, Mo.: Impact Books, 1973.

Hammond-Tooke, W. D. "The Aetiology of Spirit in Southern Africa." In *Afro-Christian Religion and Healing in South Africa*, edited by G. Oosthuizen, 43-65. Lewiston, N.Y.: Edward Mellon Press, 1989.

Hanegraaff, Hank. *Counterfeit Revival: Looking for God in the Wrong Places*. Dallas, Tex.: Word Books, 1977.

Hanegraaff, Woulter J. *New Age Religion and Western Culture: Esotericism in the Mirror of Secular Thought*. New York: Brill Academic Publishers, 1996.

Hansen, Andr. *Ungdomsskrifter af Athanasius den Store*. Vidnesbyrd af Kirkefædrene XVII. Oslo: Christiania, 1891.

Harper, Michael. *Spiritual Warfare*. Ann Arbor, Mich.: Servant Books, 1984.

Harris, Grace. "Possession 'Hysteria' in a Kenya Tribe." *American Anthropologist* 59 (1957): 1046-66.

Harris, Olivia. "The Dead and the Devils Among the Bolivian Laymi." In *Death and the Regeneration of Life*, edited by Maurice Bloch and

Jonathan Parry, 45-73. New York: Cambridge University Press, 1982.

Hayes, Stephen. "Christian Responses to Witchcraft and Sorcery," *Missionalia* 23 (1995): 339-54.

Hayford, Jack. *Moments with Majesty.* Portland: Multnomah Press, 1990.

Heissig, Walther. "Banishing of Illnesses into Effigies in Mongolia." *Asian Folklore Studies* 45:1 (1986): 33-43.

Henry, Rodney L. *Filipino Spirit World.* Manila: OMF, 1986.

Herskovits, Melville S. *Man and His Works.* New York: Alfred A. Knopf, 1951.

Hezel, Francis X. "Spirit Possession in Chuuk: A Socio-cultural Interpretation." *The Micronesian Counsellor Occasional Papers,* no. 11 (July 1993).

Hiebert, Paul G. *Anthropological Insights for Missionaries.* Grand Rapids, Mich.: Baker Book House, 1985.

————. *Anthropological Reflections on Missiological Issues.* Grand Rapids, Mich.: Baker Book House, 1994.

————. "The Flaw of the Excluded Middle." *Missiology: An International Review* 10 (January 1982): 35-48.

————. "Spiritual Warfare: Biblical Perspectives." *Mission Focus* 20:3 (September 1992): 41-46.

————. "Spiritual Warfare and Worldview." Online.

Hiebert, Paul Daniel Shaw, and Tite Tienou. *Understanding Folk Religion.* Grand Rapids, Mich.: Baker Book House, 1999.

Hill, Harriet. "Witchcraft and the Gospel: Insights from Africa," *Missiology* 24 (1996): 323-44.

Hoole, Charles R. A. "Territorial Spirits: An Indian Perspective." *Dharma Deepika* (December 1998), 45-51.

Hopson, Jay. "Confronting the Queen of Heaven: A Missions Trip Report." 1999. End Time Prophetic Vision. Online.

Hung, Daniel M. "Mission Blockade: Ancestor Worship." *Evangelical Missions Quarterly* 19:1 (January 1983): 32-40.

Hunt, Dave. *The Seduction of Christianity.* Eugene, Ore: Harvest House Publishers, 1985.

Ice, Thomas, and Robert Dean. *A Holy Rebellion: Strategies for Spiritual Warfare.* Eugene, Ore: Harvest House Publishers, 1990.

Idowu, E. Bolaji. *African Traditional Religion: A Definition.* London: SCM, 1973.

————. *Olodumare: God in Yoruba Belief.* London: Longman, 1962.

————. *Towards an Indigenous Church.* London: Oxford University, 1965.

Ikenga-Metuh, E. *God and Man in African Religion: A Case Study of the Igbo of Nigeria.* London: Geoffrey Chapman, 1981.

————. "Towards An African Theology of Man." Unpublished (1981).

Irvine, Doreen. *From Witchcraft to Christ.* Eastbourne: Kingsway, 1994.

Itioka, Neuza. *The Gods of Umbanda.* São Paulo: ABUB, 1988.

————. *God Wants Your City.* São Paulo: Sepal Editora, 1999.

Jacobs, Cindy. *Possessing the Gates of the Enemy.* Grand Rapids, Mich.: Chosen Books, 1991.

Jacobsen, J. C. *Djævlebesværgelse. Træk af Exorcismens Historie.* Forlag: Gad, 1972.

Johnson, Harmon A. "Authority over the Spirits." M.A. thesis, Fuller Theological Seminary School of World Mission, 1969.

Johnstone, Patrick. *Operation World: A Day-to-Day Guide to Praying for the World.* Grand Rapids, Mich.: Zondervan Publishing House, 1993.

Jones, Brad. "Celebration Ephesus: A Follow-Up Report." 1999. Atoka, Okla.: Church Renewal, Inc. Online.

Jones Violet R., and L. Bevan Jones. *Women in Islam.* Lucknow, India: Lucknow Publishing House, 1941.

Kallas, James. *Jesus and the Power of Satan.* Philadelphia: Westminster, 1966.

———. *The Real Satan from Biblical Times to the Present.* Minneapolis, Minn.: Augsburg Publishing House, 1975.

———. *The Satanward View.* Philadelphia: Westminster, 1966.

———. *The Significance of the Synoptic Miracles.* London: SPCK, 1961.

Kato, Byang H. *African Cultural Revolution and the Christian Faith.* Jos, Nigeria: Challenge, 1975.

———. *Theological Pitfalls in Africa.* Nairobi: Evangel Publishing House, 1975.

Katz, Paul. "Demons or Deities?: The Wangye of Taiwan." *Asian Folklore Studies* 46:2 (1987): 197-215.

Kawakami, Mitsuyo. "The View of Spirits as Seen in the Bon Observances of the Shima Region." *Japanese Journal of Religious Studies* 15 (June-September 1988): 121-30.

Kelsey, Morton T. *God, Dreams and Revelation: A Christian Interpretation of Dreams.* Minneapolis, Minn.: Augsburg Publishing House, 1968.

———. *Psychology, Medicine and Christian Healing.* New York: Harper, 1988.

Kinnaman, Gary D. *Overcoming the Dominion of Darkness.* Ventura, Calif.: Revell, 1990.

Knott, Michael. "Spiritual Warfare Series (2): Spiritual Warfare in Relation to Possessing the Land." Cyberpastor. Online.

Koch, Kurt. *Christian Counseling and Occultism.* Grand Rapids, Mich.: Kregel, 1972.

———. *Demonology Past and Present.* Grand Rapids, Mich.: Kregel, 1973.

———. *Occult ABC.* Grand Rapids, Mich.: Kregel, 1978.

———. *Occult Bondage and Deliverance.* Grand Rapids, Mich.: Kregel, 1971.

———. *The Revival in Indonesia.* Grand Rapids, Mich.: Kregel, 1971.

Kole, Andre, and Al Janssen. *Miracles or Magic.* Eugene, Ore: Harvest House Publishers, 1984.

Korem, Dan. *Powers: Testing the Psychis and Supernatural.* Downers Grove, Ill.: InterVarsity Press, 1988.

Korem, Dan, and Paul Meier. *The Fakers: Exploding the Myths of the Supernatural.* Rev. ed. Grand Rapids, Mich.: Baker Book House, 1981.

Kraft, Charles H. *Anthropology for Christian Witness*. Maryknoll, N.Y.: Orbis Books, 1996.

———, ed. *Behind Enemy Lines*. Ann Arbor, Mich.: Servant Books, 1994.

———. *Christianity with Power: Your Worldview and Your Experience of the Supernatural*. Ann Arbor, Mich.: Servant Books, 1989.

———. *Deep Wounds, Deep Healing*. Ann Arbor, Mich.: Servant Books, 1994.

———. *Defeating Dark Angels*. Ann Arbor, Mich.: Servant Books, 1992.

———. *I Give You Authority*. Grand Rapids, Mich.: Chosen/Baker Book House, 1997.

———. "What Kind of Encounters Do We Need in Our Christian Witness?" *Evangelical Missions Quarterly* 27:3 (July 1991): 258-65.

Kraft, Charles H., and David M. DeBord. *The Rules of Engagement*. Colorado Springs, Colo.: Wagner Publications, 2000.

Kraft, Charles H., and Marguerite G. Kraft. "The Power of God for Christians Who Ride Two Horses." In *The Kingdom and the Power*, edited by Gary Greig and Kevin Springer, 345-56. Ventura, Calif.: Regal Books, 1985.

Kraft, Marguerite G. *Understanding Spiritual Power: A Forgotten Dimension of Cross-Cultural Mission and Ministry*. Maryknoll, N.Y.: Orbis Books, 1995.

Kyeyune, David, "Dialogue Between Christianity and African Religion in Uganda: Relation Between the Spirits and the Living Relatives." In *Dialogue with the African Religions A Selective Report of the Meeting Organised by the Secretariat for Non-Christians that Took Place at the Pastoral Institute of Eastern Africa, Gaba, 5-7 August 1974*, edited by A Shorter et al., 41-43. Kampala, Uganda: Gaba Publications, 1975.

Ladd, George. *Jesus and the Kingdom*. New York: Harper, 1964.

Lambert, Tony. *China's Christian Millions: The Costly Revival*. London: Monarch, 1999.

Lampman, Jane. "Targeting Cities with 'Spiritual Mapping,' Prayer." *Christian Science Monitor* (September 23, 1999). Available online.

Lan, David. *Guns and Rain: Guerrillas and Spirit Mediums in Zimbabwe*. London: James Curry, 1987.

Lane, Anthony N. S., ed. *The Unseen World*. Grand Rapids, Mich.: Baker Book House, 1996.

Lea, Larry. *The Weapons of Your Warfare: Equipping Yourself to Defeat the Enemy*. Altamonte Springs, Fla.: Creation House, 1989.

———. "Binding the Strongman." In *Engaging the Enemy: How to Fight and Defeat Territorial Spirits*, edited by C. Peter Wagner, 83-96. Ventura, Calif.: Regal Books, 1991.

Leadership Ministries Worldwide. *What the Bible Says to the Minister*. Chattanooga, Tenn.: Leadership Ministries Worldwide, 1991.

Lee, Jung Young. *Ancestor Worship and Christianity in Korea*. Studies in Asian Thought and Religion, vol. 8. Lewiston, N.Y.: Edwin Mellen Press, 1988.

Lewis, C. S. *The Screwtape Letters.* New York: Macmillan, 1961.

Lewis, Herbert S. "Spirit Possession in Ethiopia: An Essay in Interpretation." In *Proceedings of the Seventh International Conference of Ethiopian Studies. University of Lund, 26-29 April 1982,* edited by Sven Rubenson. Uppsala: SIAS, 1984.

Lim, Guek Eng. "Christianity Encounters Ancestor Worship in Taiwan." *Review of Theology* 8:2 (October 1984): 225-35.

Lindsell, Harold. *The World, the Flesh, and the Devil.* Minneapolis, Minn.: World Wide Publications, 1973.

Lingenfelter, Sherwood. *Transforming Culture: A Challenge for Christian Mission.* Grand Rapids, Mich.: Baker Book House, 1992.

Linn, Dennis, and Matthew Linn. *Healing Life's Hurts.* New York: Paulist, 1978.

——. *Deliverance Prayer.* New York: Paulist, 1981.

——. *Healing of Memories.* New York: Paulist, 1974.

Linton, Ralph. "Universal Ethical Principles: An Anthropological View." In *Moral Principles of Action: Man's Ethical Imperative,* edited by Ruth Nanda Anshen. New York: Harper & Brothers, 1952.

Lowe, Chuck. *Territorial Spirits and World Evangelization?* Sevenoaks, Kent: Mentor/OMF, 1998.

——. "Do Demons Have Zip Codes?" *Christianity Today* (July 13, 1998), 57. Available online.

MacArthur, John. *How to Meet the Enemy: Arming Yourself for Spiritual Battle.* Wheaton, Ill.: Victor Books, 1992.

MacMullen, Ramsey. *Christianizing the Roman Empire.* New Haven, Conn.: Yale University Press, 1984.

MacNutt, Francis. *Healing.* Notre Dame, Ind.: Ave Maria Press, 1988; revised and expanded 1999.

——. *The Power to Heal.* Notre Dame, Ind.: Ave Maria Press, 1997.

Maharaj, Rabindranath R. *Death of a Guru.* London: Hodder, 1974.

Mallone, George. *Arming for Spiritual Warfare: How Christians Can Prepare to Fight the Enemy.* Downers Grove, Ill.: InterVarsity Press, 1991.

Marocco, James. *You Can Be a Winner in the Invisible War: The Power of Binding and Loosing.* Kahului, Hawaii: Bartimaeus Publishing, 1992.

Mangalwadi Vishal, Vijay and Desai Martis, and Maganbhai Bhagwanji. *Burnt Alive,* rev. ed. Mumbai, India: GLS Publishing, 1999.

Martin, Malachi. *Hostage to the Devil.* New York: Perennial Library, 1976.

Maslow, Abraham H. *Motivation and Personality.* New York: Harper & Row, 1970.

Mbiti, John S. *African Religions and Philosophy.* London: Heinemann Educational Books, 1969.

——. *Concepts of God in Africa.* London: SPCK, 1970.

McAlpine, Thomas H. *Facing the Powers: What Are the Options?* Monrovia, Calif.: MARC, 1991.

McGregor, Peter. *Jesus of Spirits.* New York: Stein and Day, 1966.

McMahon, T. A. "The New Spiritual Warfare Strategies–Part 1." *The Berean Call* [Bend, Oregon], May 1997. Online.

Melton, J. Gordon, and Isotta Poggi. *Magic, Witchcraft and Paganism in America: A Bibliography*. New York: Garland Publishing, 1992.

Meyer, Birgit. *Translating the Devil: Religion and Modernity Among the Ewe in Ghana*. Edinburgh: EUP, 1999.

Middleton, John, and E. H. Winter, eds. *Witchcraft and Sorcery in East Africa*. London: Routledge & Kegan Paul, 1963.

Milango, Emmanuel. *The World in Between: Christian Healing and the Struggle for Spiritual Survival*. Maryknoll, N.Y.: Orbis Books, 1984.

Millett, Kate. *The Politics of Cruelty*. New York: Norton & Company, 1994.

Millikan, Rob. "Celebration Ephesus." Atoka, Okla.: Church Renewal, Inc., 1999. Online.

Mitchell, Roger E. "Patron Saints and Pagan Ghosts: The Pairing of Opposites." *Asian Folklore Studies* 45:1 (1986): 101-23.

Montgomery, John Warwick, ed. *Demon Possession*. Minneapolis, Minn.: Bethany Fellowship, 1976.

———. *Principalities and Powers: The World of the Occult*, rev. ed. (Minneapolis, Minn.: Bethany Fellowship, 1981).

Moore, Art. "Spiritual Mapping Gains Credibility Among Leaders." *Christianity Today* (January 12, 1998). Available online.

Moreau, A. Scott. *Essentials of Spiritual Warfare: Equipped to Win the Battle*. Wheaton, Ill.: Harold Shaw Publishers, 1997.

———. *The World of the Spirits: A Biblical Study in the African Context*. Nairobi, Kenya: Evangel Publishing House, 1990.

———. "Broadening the Issues: Historiography, Advocacy, and Hermeneutics." In *The Holy Spirit and Mission Dynamics*, edited by C. Douglas McConnell, 123-35. Pasadena, Calif.: William Carey Library, 1997.

———. "Religious Borrowing as a Two-Way Street: An Introduction to Animistic Tendencies in the Euro-North American Context." In *Christianity and the Religions: A Biblical Theology of World Religions*, edited by Edward Rommen and Harold Netland, 166-82. Pasadena, Calif.: William Carey Library, 1995.

Morioka, Kiyomi. "Ancestor Worship in Contemporary Japan: Continuity and Change." In *Religion and the Family in East Asia*, edited by George De Vos and Takao Sofue, 201-13. Berkeley and Los Angeles: University of California Press, 1986.

Morris, Leon. *The Book of Revelation*. Tyndale New Testament Commentaries. Leicester, England: Inter-Varsity Press, 1987.

Mungadze, Jerry. "Is It Dissociation or Demonization? Sorting Out Spiritual and Clinical Issues in the Treatment of Dissociative Disorders." *Journal of Psychology and Christianity* 19:2 (2000): 139-43.

———. "Multiple Personality Disorder; No Longer a Rare Diagnosis." *Treatment Centers Magazine* 9 (1992).

————. "Treating Dissociative Identity Disorder an Update." *Treatment Centers Magazine* 9:2 (1997).

Murphy, Ed. *The Handbook for Spiritual Warfare*. Nashville, Tenn.: Thomas Nelson, 1992.

Musk, Bill. *The Unseen Face of Islam*. Eastbourne: Monarch 1992.

Myers, Ruth. *Thirty-one Days of Praise*. Singapore: The Navigators, 1992.

Nasir, Mumtaz. "*Baithak*: Exorcism in Peshawar (Pakistan)." *Asian Folklore Studies* 46:2 (1987): 159-78.

Nauman, St. Elmo, ed. *Exorcism Through the Ages*. Philosophical Library, 1974.

Nee, Watchman. *Sit, Walk and Stand*. London: Victory Press, 1957.

Nelson, H. G. "Ancestor Worship and Burial Practices." In *Religion and Ritual in Chinese Society*, edited by Arthur P. Wolf, 251-77. Stanford, Calif.: Stanford University Press, 1974.

Nicoll, Robertson W., ed. *The Expositor's Greek Testament*. Grand Rapids, Mich.: Eerdmans, 1980.

Newbigin, Lesslie. *Foolishness to the Greeks: The Gospel and Western Culture*. Grand Rapids, Mich.: Eerdmans, 1986.

————. *Honest Religion of Secular Man*. Philadelphia: Westminster Press, 1966.

New Catholic Encyclopedia. New York: Catholic University of America, 1967. S.v., "Exorcism" by E. J. Gratsch; "Diabolical Possession (in the Bible)" by J. Jensen; and "Diabolical Possession (Theology of)" by L. J. Elmer.

Noll, Richard. "Exorcism and Possession: The Clash of Worldviews and the Hubris of Psychiatry." *Dissociation: Progress in the Dissociative Disorders Special Issue: Possession* 6:4 (1993): 250-53.

North, Gary. *Unholy Spirits: Occultism and New Age Humanism*. Ft. Worth, Tex.: Dominion Press, 1986.

Nyamiti, C. *African Tradition and the Christian God*. Eldoret, Kenya: Gaba Publications, 1989.

Nyirongo, L. *The Gods of Africa or The God of the Bible? The Snares of African Traditional Religion in Biblical Perspective*. Potchefstroom, South Africa: Potchefstroom University for Christian Higher Education, Institute for Reformational Studies, 1997.

Oberman, Heiko A. *Luther: Man Between God and the Devil*. New York: Doubleday, 1992.

O'Brien, Peter. "Principalities and Powers: Opponents of the Church." In *Biblical Interpretation and the Church: Text and Context*, edited by D. A. Carson, 110-50. Exeter, England: Paternoster Press, 1984.

Oji, E. D. "*Ikpu Alu* (Atonement) in Igbo Traditional Religion." B.A. thesis. Jos, Nigeria, ECWA Theological Seminary, 1988.

Oosthuizen, Gerhardus C. "Interpretation of Demonic Powers in Southern African Independent Churches." *Missiology: An International Review* 16 (1988): 3-22.

————. "The Interpretation of and Reaction to Demonic Powers in Indigenous Churches." In *Like a Roaring Lion*, edited by P. De Villiers, 63-89. Pretoria: C. B. Powell Bible Centre, University of South Africa, 1987.

Orr, J. Edwin. *Are Demons for Real?* Wheaton, Ill.: Scripture Press, 1970.

Otis, George. *The Last of the Giants: Lifting the Veil on Islam and the End Times.* Grand Rapids, Mich.: Baker Book House, 1991.

————. *The Twilight Labyrinth: Why Does Spiritual Darkness Linger Where It Does?* Grand Rapids, Mich.: Chosen Books, 1997.

————. "An Overview of Spiritual Mapping." In *Breaking Strongholds in Your City: How to Use Spiritual Mapping to Make Your Prayers More Strategic, Effective and Targeted*, edited by C. Peter Wagner, 29-47. Ventura, Calif.: Regal Books, 1993.

Overmyer, Daniel L. *Religions of China.* New York: HarperCollins, 1986.

Packer, J. I. "What Did the Cross Achieve? The Logic of Penal Substitution." *Tyndale Bulletin* 25 (1974): 1-45.

Page, Sydney H. T. *Powers of Evil: A Biblical Study of Satan and Demons.* Grand Rapids, Mich.: Baker Book House, 1995.

Parrinder, G. *African Traditional Religion.* London: SPCK, 1962.

Passantino, Bob, and Gretchen Passantino. "Sad Facts About Satanic Ritual Abuse." *Christian Research Journal Winter* 1992, 21-23; 32-34.

————. "Satanic Ritual Abuse in Popular Christian Literature: Why Christians Fall for a Lie Searching for the Truth." *Journal of Psychology and Theology* 20:3 (Fall 1992): 299-305.

————. "Satan's Sideshow: The True Lauren Stratford Story." *Cornerstone* 18 (1990): 24-28.

Payne, Leanne. *Restoring the Christian Soul Through Healing Prayer.* Westchester, Ill.: Crossway Books, 1991.

Peck, M. Scott. *People of the Lie: The Hope for Healing Human Evil.* New York: Simon & Schuster, 1983.

Penn-Lewis, Jesse. *War on the Saints.* New York: Thomas E. Lowe, 1912.

Pennoyer, F. Douglas. "In Dark Dungeons of Collective Captivity." In *Wrestling with Dark Angels*, edited by C. Peter Wagner and F. Douglas Pennoyer, 250-70. Ventura, Calif.: Regal. 1990.

Peretti, Frank E. *The Oath.* Nashville, Tenn.: Word Books, 1995.

————. *Piercing the Darkness.* Westchester, Ill.: Crossway Books, 1989.

————. *The Prophet.* Westchester, Ill.: Crossway Books, 1992.

————. *This Present Darkness.* Westchester, Ill.: Crossway Books, 1986.

————. *The Visitation.* Nashville, Tenn.: Word Books, 1995.

Peterson, Dean A. "Spirit Possession Among the Maasai in Tanzania." *Africa Theological Journal* 14:3 (1985): 174-78.

Philpott, Kent. *The Deliverance Book: A Handbook for Ministers and Those about to Have Deliverance.* Van Nuys, Calif.: Bible Voice, 1977.

————. *A Manual of Demonology and the Occult.* Grand Rapids, Mich.: Zondervan, 1973.

Piper, John. "Angels and Prayer: Daniel's Experience and Ours." January 12, 1992. Bethlehem Baptist Church. Online.

Pobee, J. *Toward an African Theology.* Nashville, Tenn.: Abingdon, 1979.

Polkinghorne, John. *Science and Theology: An Introduction.* London: SPCK, 1998.

Powlison, David. *Power Encounters: Reclaiming Spiritual Warfare.* Grand Rapids, Mich.: Baker Book House, 1995.

Priest, Robert J., Thomas Campbell, and Bradford A. Mullen. "Missiological Syncretism: The New Animistic Paradigm." In *Spiritual Power and Missions: Raising the Issues,* edited by Edward Rommen, 9-87. Pasadena, Calif.: William Carey Library, 1995.

Prince, Derek. *Blessing or Curse: You Can Choose!* Milton Keynes: Word Books, 1990.

Prince, Raymond. "Indigenous Yoruba Psychiatry." In *Magic, Faith and Healing,* edited by Ari Kiev, 84-120. New York: Free Press, 1974.

Ray, B. C. *African Religions: Symbol, Ritual and Community.* Englewood Cliffs, N.J.: Prentice-Hall, 1976.

Reddin, Opal, ed. *Power Encounter: A Pentecostal Perspective.* Springfield, Mo.: Central Bible College Press, 1989.

Redfield, Robert. *The Little Tradition.* Chicago: Chicago University Press, 1955.

————. *Peasant Society and Culture.* Chicago: University of Chicago Press, 1956.

Reid, David. "Japanese Christians and the Ancestors." *Japanese Journal of Religious Studies* 16 (1989): 259-83.

Reimer, Reginald E. "Religious Dimension of the Vietnamese Cult of the Ancestors." *Missiology: An International Review* 3 (1975): 155-68.

Reminick, Ronald A. "Evil Eye Belief Among the Amhara." In *Evil Eye,* edited by Clarence Maloney, 85-101. New York: Columbia University Press, 1976.

Richards, John. *But Deliver Us from Evil: An Introduction to the Demonic Dimension in Pastoral Care.* London: Darton, Longman, and Todd, 1974.

Richards, Larry. *The Screwloose Lectures.* Dallas, Tex.: Word Books, 1980.

Ro, Young-chan. "Ancestor Worship: From the Perspective of Korean Tradition." In *Ancestor Worship and Christianity in Korea,* edited by Jung Young Lee, 7-20. Lewiston, N.Y.: Edwin Mellen Press, 1988.

Roberts, Alexander, and James Donaldson, eds. *The Ante-Nicene Fathers.* Grand Rapids, Mich.: Eerdmans, 1986.

Rockstad, Ernest. *Demon Activity and the Christian.* Andover, Kans.: Faith and Life. 1976.

————. *Triumph in the Demonic Crisis.* Cassette series. Andover, Kans.: Faith and Life, 1976.

Rogers, Don. "Territorial Spirits." *Strateia* (April 1999). Available online.

Rogers, Everett. *Diffusion of Innovations.* 4th ed. New York: Free Press, 1995.

Rogers, Martha L. "A Call for Discernment – Natural and Spiritual: In Introductory Editorial to a Special Issue on SRA." *Journal of Psychology and Theology* 20:3 (Fall 1992): 175-86.

Rommen, Edward, ed. *Spiritual Power and Missions: Raising the Issues.* Pasadena, Calif.: William Carey Library, 1995.

Rommen, Edward, and Harold Netland, eds. *Christianity and the Religions: A Biblical Theology of World Religions.* Pasadena, Calif.: William Carey Library, 1995.

Roness, Atle. *Demonbesettelse: Psykiatriske og teologiske synspunkter.* Oslo: Luther, 1981.

Rosik, Christopher H. "Some Effects of World View on the Theory and Treatment of Dissociative Identity Disorder." *Journal of Psychology and Christianity Special Issue: Dissociative Identity Disorder* 19:2 (2000): 166-80.

Ross, Colin A. *Satanic Ritual Abuse: Principles of Treatment.* Toronto: University of Toronto Press, 1995.

———. "Response: Critical Issues Committee Report: Exorcism in the Treatment of Patients with MPD." *ISSMP-D News,* 11:2 (1993): 4.

———. "Twelve Cognitive Errors about Multiple Personality Disorder." *American Journal of Psychotherapy* 44:3 (July 1990): 348-56.

Ryder, Daniel. *Breaking the Circle of Satanic Ritual Abuse: Recognizing and Recovering from the Hidden Trauma.* Minneapolis, Minn.: CompCare Publishers, 1992.

Ryle J. C. *Ryle's Expository Thoughts on the Gospels,* Vol. 3. Grand Rapids, Mich.: Baker Book House, 1977.

Sæverås, Olav. *On Church – Mission Relations in Ethiopia 1944-1969: With Special Reference to the Evangelical Church Mekane Yesus and the Lutheran Missions.* Studia Missionalia Upsaliensia XXVII. Drammen: Tangen-Trykk, 1974.

Sanders, J. Oswald. *Satan Is No Myth.* Chicago: Moody Press, 1975.

Sandford, John, and Mark Sandford. *A Comprehensive Guide to Deliverance and Inner Healing.* Grand Rapids, Mich.: Chosen/Baker Book House, 1992.

Sandford, John, and Paula Sandford. *Healing the Wounded Spirit.* Tulsa, Okla.: Victory House, 1985.

———. *Transformation of the Inner Man.* Tulsa, Okla.: Victory House, 1982.

Scanlan, Michael, and Randall J. Cirner. *Deliverance from Evil Spirits.* Ann Arbor, Mich.: Servant Books, 1980.

Schlier, Heinrich. *Principalities and Powers in the New Testament.* New York: Herder and Herder, 1961.

Schartz, Ted, and Duane Empey. *Satanism: Is Your Family Safe?* Grand Rapids, Mich.: Zondervan Publishing House, 1988.

Seamands, David. *Healing for Damaged Emotions.* Wheaton, Ill.: Victor Books, 1981.

————. *Healing of Memories*. Wheaton, Ill.: Victor Books, 1985.

Shaw, Rosalind. "The Invention of African Traditional Religion," *Religion* 20 (1990): 339-53.

————. "The Politician and the Diviner: Divination and the Consumption of Power in Sierra Leone." *Journal of Religion in Africa* 26 (1996): 30-55.

Shea, William H. "Wrestling with the Prince of Persia: A Study on Daniel 10." *Andrews University Seminary Studies* 21:2 (1983): 225-50.

Sherman, Dean. *Spiritual Warfare for Every Christian*. Seattle, Wash.: YWAM, 1990.

Silvoso, Edgardo. *That None Should Perish*. Ventura, Calif.: Regal Books, 1994.

Singleton, Michael. "Ancestors, Adolescents and the Absolute: An Exercise in Contextualization." *Pro Mundi Vita* 68 (1977): 1-35.

————. "Spirits and 'Spiritual Direction': The Pastoral Counseling of the Possessed." In *Christianity in Independent Africa*, edited by Edward Fashole-Luke, Richard Gray, Adrian Hastings, and Godwin Tasie, 471-78. Bloomington, Ind.: Indiana University Press, 1978.

Skarsaune, Oskar. "Misjonstenkningen i oldtiden og middelalderen." In *Missiologi i dag*, edited by by Jan-Martin Berentsen, Tormod Engelsviken and Knud Jørgensen, 89-109. Oslo: Universitetsforlaget, 1994.

————. "Myte og realitet i kristendomshistorien." *Religion og Livssyn*, 2 (1998): 25-29.

Skjerbæk Madsen, Ole. "The Maitreya – Theosophy of Asger Lorentsen and the Shan-Movement." In *New Religions and New Religiosity*, edited by Eileen Barker and Margit Warburg, 191-203. Aarhus, Denmark: Aarhus University Press, 1998.

Smedes, Lewis B. *Ministry and the Miraculous*. Dallas, Tex.: Word Books, 1987.

Smith, Ed M. *Beyond Tolerable Recovery*. Rev. ed. Campbellsville, Ky.: Theophostic Ministries, 2000.

Smith, Henry N. "Ancestor Practices in Contemporary Hong Kong: Religious Ritual or Social Custom?" *Asia Journal of Theology* 3 (April 1989): 31-45.

————. "Christianity and Ancestor Practices in Hong Kong: Toward a Contextual Strategy." *Missiology: An International Review* 17 (January 1989): 27-38.

————. "A Typology of Christian Responses to Chinese Ancestor Worship." *Journal of Ecumenical Studies* 26 (Fall 1989): 628-47.

Spurgeon, Charles. *Spiritual Warfare in a Believer's Life*. Compiled and edited by Robert Hall. Lynnwood, Wash.: Emerald Books, 1993.

Sterk, Vernon J. "Territorial Spirits and Evangelization in Hostile Environments." In *Engaging the Enemy: How to Fight and Defeat Territorial Spirits*, edited by C. Peter Wagner, 145-63. Ventura, Calif.: Regal Books, 1991.

Steyne, Philip M. *Gods of Power: A Study of the Beliefs and Practices of Animists.* Houston, Tex.: Touch Publications, 1989.

Sturlason, Snorre. *Norges kongesagaer.* Oslo: Gyldendal, 1988.

Sumrall, Lester. *The Reality of Angels.* Nashville, Tenn.: Thomas Nelson, 1982.

Tappert, Theodore G., ed., *The Book of Concord: The Confessions of the Evangelical Lutheran Church* Philadelphia: Fortress Press, 1959.

Taylor, J. V. *Primal Vision.* London: SCM, 1963.

Tienou, Tite. *The Theological Task of the Church in Africa.* Achimota, Ghana: Africa Christian Press, 1990.

———. "Indigenous African Christian Theologies: The Uphill Road." *International Bulletin of Missionary Research* 14:2 (April 1990): 73-77.

Timmons, Tim. *Chains of the Spirit: A Manual for Liberation.* Washington, D.C.: Canon Press, 1973.

Tippett, Alan R. *Introduction to Missiology.* Pasadena, Calif.: William Carey Library, 1987.

———. *People Movements in Southern Polynesia.* Chicago: Moody, 1971.

———. *Solomon Islands Christianity.* London: Lutterworth Press, 1967.

———. *Verdict Theology in Missionary Theory.* Pasadena, Calif.: William Carey Library, 1973.

Torrey, E. Fuller. "The Zar Cult in Ethiopia." In *Proceedings of the Third International Conference of Ethiopian Studies, Addis Ababa 1966.* Addis Ababa: Institute of Ethiopian Studies, 1969.

Torrey, Reuben A. *Baptism with the Holy Spirit.* New York: Fleming H. Revell, 1897.

———. *What the Bible Teaches.* New York: Fleming H. Revell, 1898.

Tozer, A. W. *Gems from Tozer: Extracts from the Writings of A. W. Tozer (1897-1963).* Harrisburg, Pa.: Christian Publications, 1979.

Trimingham, J. Spencer. *The Christian Church and Mission in Ethiopia.* London: Founder's Lodge, 1950.

Trimble, Derrick. "Celebration Ephesus: 5,000 Christians Express God's Love for Turkey." *Joel News International* 294 (October 19, 1999). Available online.

Trinidad, Bill. "Spiritual Mapping and Warfare Prayer as Catalysts for Church Growth." *The Alliance Page* (n.d.). Available online.

Trott, Jon, and Mike Hertenstein. *Selling Satan: Mike Warnke and His Ministry of Deception.* Chicago: Cornerstone Library, 1993.

Turaki. Yusufu. *Tribal Gods of Africa: Ethnicity, Racism, Tribalism and the Gospel of Christ.* Jos, Nigeria: Cross Roads Communications, 1997.

———. "Christian Worldview Foundations: A Methodological Approach." *Orientation* 67-70 (January-December 1993): 81-100.

———. "Understanding Folk Elements in Christian Expressions of African Religion: A Methodological Approach." Unpublished.

Unger, Merrill. *Biblical Demonology: A Study of the Spiritual Forces behind the Present Unrest.* Wheaton, Ill.: Scripture Press, 1952.

————. Demons in the World Today: A Study of Occultism in the Light of God's Word. Wheaton, Ill.: Tyndale, 1971.

————. What Demons Can Do to Saints. Chicago: Moody, 1977.

Van Benschoten, Susan C. "Multiple Personality Disorder and Satanic Ritual Abuse: The Issue of Credibility." Dissociation Progress in the Dissociative Disorders 3:1 (March 1990): 22-30.

van Dam, Willem Cornelis. Dämonen und Besessene. Aschaffenburg, Norway: Paul Pattoch, 1970.

Van der Kolk, Bessel A. "The Body Keeps the Score: Memory and the Evolving Psychobiology of Posttraumatic Stress." In Essential Papers on Posttraumatic Stress Disorder, edited by Mardi J. Horowitz, et al., 301-26. New York: New York University Press, 1999.

————. "The Psychological and Biological Processing of Traumatic Memories." Seattle, Wash., 1995. TMs [photocopy].

Van der Kolk, Bessell A., Jennifer A. Burbridge, and Joji Suzuki. "The Psychobiology of Traumatic Memory." In Psychobiology of Posttraumatic Stress Disorder, edited by Rachael Yehuda and Alexander C. McFarlane, 99-113. New York: New York Academy of Sciences, 1997.

Van Der Walt, B. J. A Christian Worldview and Christian Higher Education for Africa. Potchefstroom, South Africa: Potchefstroom University for Christian Higher Education, Institute for Reformational Studies, 1991.

————. The Liberating Message: A Christian Worldview for Africa. Potchefstroom, South Africa: Potchefstroom University for Christian Higher Education, Institute for Reformational Studies, 1994.

Van Rheenen, Gailyn. Communicating Christ in Animistic Contexts. Grand Rapids, Mich.: Baker Book House, 1991.

Villanueva, Eric. "Territorial Spirits and Spiritual Warfare: A Biblical Perspective." Christian Research Institute Journal (June 30, 1994). Available online.

von Harnack, Adolf."Det Kampf gegen die Herrschaft der Dämonen." In Die Mission und Ausbreitung des Christentums in den ersten drei Jahrhunderten, 4th ed., edited by F. Andres, 151-70. Leipzig: J. C. Hinrichs, 1924.

Wagner, C. Peter. Confronting the Powers: How the New Testament Church Experienced the Power of Strategic-level Spiritual Warfare. Ventura, Calif.: Regal Books, 1996.

————. Confronting the Queen of Heaven. Colorado Springs, Colo.: Wagner Institute for Practical Ministry, 1998.

————. How to Have a Healing Ministry in Any Church. Ventura, Calif.: Regal Books, 1988.

————. The Third Wave of the Holy Spirit: Encountering the Power of Signs and Wonders Today. Ann Arbor, Mich.: Vine Books, 1988.

————. Warfare Prayer: How to Seek God's Power and Protection in the Battle to Build His Kingdom. Ventura, Calif.: Regal Books, 1992.

Wagner, C. Peter, ed. *Breaking Strongholds in Your City: How to Use Spiritual Mapping to Make Your Prayers More Strategic, Effective, and Targeted.* Ventura, Calif.: Regal Books, 1993.

——. *Engaging the Enemy: How to Fight and Defeat Territorial Spirits.* Ventura, Calif.: Regal Books, 1991.

——. "The Key to Victory Is Binding the 'Strong Man.'" *Ministries Today* (November-December 1986), 84.

——. "Position Statement on the Philosophy of Prayer for World Evangelization." AD2000 United Prayer Track (n.d.). Available online.

——. "Summary: Mapping Your Community." In *Breaking Strongholds in Your City,* edited by C. Peter Wagner, 223-32. Ventura, Calif.: Regal Books, 1993.

——. "Territorial Spirits." In *Engaging the Enemy: How to Fight and Defeat Territorial Spirits,* edited by C. Peter Wagner, 43-50. Ventura, Calif.: Regal Books, 1991.

——. "Territorial Spirits and World Missions." *Evangelical Missions Quarterly* 27:3 (July 1989): 278-88.

Wagner, C. Peter, and F. Douglas Pennoyer, eds. *Wrestling with Dark Angels: Toward a Deeper Understanding of the Supernatural Forces in Spiritual Warfare.* Ventura, Calif.: Regal Books, 1990.

Wagner, Doris. *How to Cast Out Demons.* Ventura, Calif.: Regal Books, 2000.

Walker, Andrew. *Enemy Territory: The Christian Struggle for the Modern Mind.* Grand Rapids, Mich.: Zondervan, 1987.

Walker, Sheila S. *Ceremonial Spirit Possession in Africa and Afro-America: Forms, Meanings, and Functional Significance for Individuals and Social Groups.* Leiden, Netherlands: E. J. Brill, 1972.

Walsch, Neale Donald. *Conversations with God: An Uncommon Dialogue.* New York: Hampton Roads Publishing Company, 1995.

Walsh, Brian J., and J. Richard Middleton. *The Transforming Vision: Shaping a Christian World View.* Downers Grove, Ill.: InterVarsity Press, 1994.

Warner, Timothy. *Spiritual Warfare: Victory over the Powers of This Dark World.* Westchester, Ill.: Crossway Books, 1991.

——. "Dealing with Territorial Demons." In *Engaging the Enemy: How to Fight and Defeat Territorial Spirits,* edited by C. Peter Wagner, 51-54. Ventura, Calif.: Regal Books, 1991.

Warnke, Mike. *The Satan Seller.* Plainfield, N.J.: Logos International, 1972.

Weinberg, Steven. "A Unified Physics by 2050?" *Scientific American* 281:6 (December 1999): 36-43.

Wells, David F. *God the Evangelist.* Grand Rapids, Mich.: Eerdmans, 1987.

West, Martin. "The Shades Come to Town: Ancestors and Urban Independent Churches." In *Religion and Social Change in Southern Africa: Anthropological Essays in Honour of Monica Wilson,* ed, by Monica Wilson, Michael Whisson, and Martin West, 185-206. Cape Town, Republic of South Africa: D. Phillip, 1975.

Westermann, Diedrich. *Africa and Christianity.* London: Oxford University Press, 1937.

Westermarck, Edward. *Pagan Survivals in Mohammedan Civilization*. London: MacMillan, 1933.

Wey, Heinrich. *Die Funktionen der bösen Geister bei den griechischen Apologeten des zweiten Jahrhunderts nach Christus*. Winterthur: Keller, 1975.

"What Is a Prayer Journey?" 1998. Colorado Springs, Colo.: Christian Information Network, Global Harvest Ministries. Online.

White, John. *Daring to Draw Near: People in Prayer*. Downers Grove: InterVarsity Press, 1977.

———. *The Fight: A Practical Handbook for Christian Living*. Downers Grove, Ill.: InterVarsity Press, 1976.

———. *When the Spirit Comes with Power: Signs and Wonders Among God's People*. Downers Grove, Ill.: InterVarsity Press, 1988.

White, Thomas. *The Believer's Guide to Spiritual Warfare*. Ann Arbor, Mich.: Vine Books, 1990.

———. *Breaking Strongholds: How Spiritual Warfare Sets Captives Free*. Ann Arbor, Mich.: Vine Books, 1993.

Whiteman, Darrell. *Melanesians and Missionaries*. Pasadena, Calif.: William Carey Library, 1983.

Wiersbe, Warren. *The Strategy of Satan: How to Detect and Defeat Him*. Wheaton, Ill.: Tyndale House Publishers, 1979.

Williams, Daniel Day. *The Demonic and the Divine*. Philadelphia: Fortress Press, 1990.

Williams, Don. *Signs, Wonders and the Kingdom of God*. Ann Arbor, Mich.: Servant Publications, 1989.

Wimber, John, and Kevin Springer. *Power Evangelism*. London: Hodder and Stoughton, 1986.

———. *Power Healing*. London: Hodder and Stoughton, 1986.

Wink, Walter. *Engaging the Powers: Discernment and Resistance in a World of Dominion*. Philadelphia: Fortress Press, 1992.

———. *Naming the Powers: The Language of Power in the New Testament*. Philadelphia: Fortress Press, 1984.

———. *The Powers that Be: Theology for a New Millennium*. New York: Doubleday, 1998.

———. *Unmasking the Powers: The Invisible Forces that Determine Human Existence*. Philadelphia: Fortress Press, 1986.

———. *When the Powers Fall: Reconciliation in the Healing of Nations*. Philadelphia: Fortress Press, 1998.

Witherspoon, Gary. *Language and Art in the Navajo Universe*. Ann Arbor, Mich.: University of Michigan Press, 1977.

Wolf, Arthur P. "Gods, Ghosts and Ancestors." In *Religion and Ritual in Chinese Society*, edited by Arthur P. Wolf, 131-82. Stanford, Calif.: Stanford University Press, 1974.

Wright, Nigel. *The Satan Syndrome: Putting the Power of Darkness in Its Place*. Grand Rapids, Mich.: Zondervan, 1990.

Young, Richard Fox. "Magic and Morality in Modern Japanese Exorcistic Technologies: A Study of Mahikari." *Japanese Journal of Religious Studies* 17 (March 1990): 29-49.

Yu, Carver T. *Being and Relation: A Theological Critique of Western Dualism and Individualism.* Edinburgh: Scottish Academic Press, 1987.

Zimbabwe Catholic Bishops' Conference. "Communion Between the Living and the Dead: Christian Response to Spirit Possession." *AFER: African Ecclesial Review* 29 (October 1987): 309-14.

Zvarevashe, Ignatius M. "The Problem of Ancestors and Inculturation." *AFER: African Ecclesial Review* 29 (August 1987): 242-51.

World Vision

From the Lausaunne Committee ...

100 pp. ⬥MARC
2001
L-031
$7.95

SPIRITUAL CONFLICT IN TODAY'S MISSION
Tormod Engelsviken and
A. Scott Moreau, editors
Commissioned by the
Lausanne Committee for
World Evangelization

This companion book to *Deliver Us from Evil* is an excerpt anthology of current evangelical thought on the issue of spiritual conflict and Christianity. Topics include: an extensive examination of the three causes of affliction (God, the Devil and nature), a survey of the church's dealings with and perspective on the demonic, an iteration of the Western church's stance on hell, Satan and spiritual warfare, stories from around the world of evangelism efforts that encounter the demonic, a definition of the syncretic practices of combining major world religions with traditional religion, and more. The Lausaunne Committee closes with a brief caution against adopting dualism in Christianity.

1168 pp.
2000
R-031
$59.95

EVANGELICAL DICTIONARY OF WORLD MISSIONS
A. Scott Moreau, General editor
Harold Netland and Charles Van Engen, Associate editors

This invaluable resource provides more than 1,400 articles on mission theory and practice, theology and history. Contributions from more than 300 missionaries, theologians and educators provide a broad survey of the history of world mission as well as current trends and research.

72 pp. ⬥MARC
L-027
1996
$4.95

MODERN, POSTMODERN AND CHRISTIAN
John Reid, Lesslie Newbigin & David Pullinger, editors

The authors explain the basis tenets of modernity and postmodernity and help you effectively communicate the gospel in a postmodern world. Ideal for group study.

94 pp. ⬥MARC
1996
L-028
$6.50

MINISTRY IN ISLAMIC CONTEXTS
Various authors

This booklet concisely sets the scene for accomplishing effective Christian ministry in Islamic contexts in a culturally sensitive manner.